VOLUME I

THE PROCESS OF ADMISSION
TO ORDAINED MINISTRY

The meaning of episcopal and presbyteral ministry and the structuring of the Church which is revealed in the procedures of installation or ordination to the episcopacy (bishop, superintendent, ecclesiastical inspector, etc.) and to the presbyterate (priest, pastor, etc.) in the Roman Catholic Church and certain Lutheran, Reformed, Anglican and Methodist Churches in Western Europe and in the United States.

James F. Puglisi, s.a.

Ju

VOLUME I

THE PROCESS OF ADMISSION
TO ORDAINED MINISTRY

Epistemological Principles
and
Roman Catholic Rites

A Comparative Study

Translated from the French by

Michael S. Driscoll and Mary Misrahi

Preface by Hervé Legrand, O.P.

A PUEBLO BOOK

The Liturgical Press   Collegeville, Minnesota

BV664.5
.P8413
1996
vol. 1

A Pueblo Book published by the The Liturgical Press

Design by Frank Kacmarcik

© 1996 by The Order of St. Benedict, Inc., Collegeville, Minnesota. All rights reserved. No part of this book may be reproduced in any form or by any means, electronic or mechanical, including photocopying, recording, taping, or any retrieval system, without the written permission of The Liturgical Press, Collegeville, Minnesota 56321. Printed in the United States of America.

Library of Congress Cataloging-in-Publication Data

Puglisi, J. F.
    [Etude comparative sur les processus d'accès au ministère ordonné. English]
    The process of admission to ordained ministry : a comparative study / James F. Puglisi ; translated by Michael S. Driscoll and Mary Misrahi.
        p. cm.
    "A Pueblo book."
    Based on the author's thesis (doctoral)—Université de Paris (Sorbonne).
    Includes bibliographical references and index.
    Contents: v. 1. Epistemological principles and the Roman Catholic rites.
    ISBN 0-8146-6128-9
    1. Ordination—History of doctrines.   2. Ordination (Liturgy)—History.
I. Title.
BV664.5.P8413   1996
262'.1—dc20   96-14468
                                                                        CIP

APR 07

DOCN AOA- 7338

To my parents and sister and brother

Contents

Note to the Reader

Two kinds of footnote numeration are used in this study: the numbers refer to footnotes; the numbers preceded by an asterisk (*) refer to the liturgical texts that are reproduced in a separate volume.

On October 3, 1990, the two Germanies were reunified. This event brought about a revision of the ecclesiastical structures of the Churches of Germany. In September 1990, the parallel organizations of RDA and RFA (East and West Germany) decided to fuse. In this study I have maintained the distinction between East and West in the third volume of the analytical study and the fourth volume of liturgical texts, because these texts were created by the individual Churches and denote a historical and often theological stage in the evolution of the liturgy in the Churches involved.

Concerning the Catholic Church, I have designated the Western part, the only one taken into consideration in my work, as Latin Catholic, especially when it deals with the Churches of the Latin rite which have produced the Gallican, Frankish, or Romano-German rites. I have reserved the adjective Roman for the rituals of the Church of this city, all the while being conscious of their progressive reception in the Latin Church. Concerning the conjunction of the adjectives Catholic and Roman, see the enlightening research of Y. CONGAR, "Romanité et catholicité. Histoire de la conjonction changeante de deux dimensions de l'Eglise," *RSPT* 71, 2 (1987) 161–190.

A final aid for the reader not familiar with certain technical terms is a small glossary found at the end of the third volume. It is accompanied by a list of some Churches with their equivalent in English.

Preface

It is not often that one is asked to introduce such an original and useful work as *The Process of Admission to Ordained Ministry: A Comparative Study*. A member of the Francisan Friars of the Atonement, a Congregation whose vocation is essentially ecumenical, the author was able to devote six or seven years of dedicated and methodical investigation to this study, which was accepted as a "grande thèse" by the theological faculty of the Institut catholique de Paris, and which simultaneously earned him the title of "docteur en science des religions" at the Sorbonne (Paris IV). It is a work which is original in its method and precious in its documentation; it will produce great fruits in ecumenical dialogue.

AN ORIGINAL AND FRUITFUL METHOD

The theology of ministry until now has too often been elaborated from statements either from the Fathers of the Church, or from Council formulations or confessional writings, which have only rarely been successfully detached from the contexts of their genesis. These contexts have often been polemic. James Puglisi, with a simple but fundamental intuition, has situated his work beyond these enunciations and given himself a wider base in proposing the ecclesiological and liturgical structures of the ordination rites as the key to the understanding of ministry.

Such a methodological principle, the foundations of which were put in place by the great Belgian liturgical scholar B. Botte,[1] or by the eminent German Lutheran canonist H. Dombois,[2] allows us to recover

---

[1]See for example, Dom B. BOTTE, "Caractère collégial du presbytérat et de l'épiscopat" in *Etudes sur le sacrement de l'ordre*, Lex Orandi 22 (Paris: Cerf, 1957) 118–124.

[2]H. DOMBOIS, *Das Recht der Gnade. Ökumenisches Kirchenrecht*, I, 2nd ed. (Witten: Luther Verlag, 1969) 35–37 and passim.

an understanding of ministry from the processes of its genesis and development in the Church assembled in prayer. Such a method is more fruitful than the systematic articulation of particularized, historically conditioned and heterogeneous statements that lack the original structural setting in which they need to be understood. More fruitful too, as the reader will see, than a general reflection on the concept of ministry in relation to the concept of the Church. The Church is not a *civitas platonica* which exists as a transpersonal subject other than in and through our representation. What exists in reality are persons, placed through grace in noncontingent relationships with each other, relationships of which they themselves are not the progenitors. Among these relationships are ministers who become such in the Church at the end of a canonical and liturgical process which needs to be interpreted because the relations fashioned in the liturgical celebration are the matrix of the position ministers occupy in and vis-à-vis the Church, matrix being understood in the sense of origin or model of action in the Church.

The method adopted is thus inductive: it starts from the particular character of each ritual with its particular orientation. Although the adage *lex orandi, lex credendi* has been in vogue for a long time,[3] James Puglisi is the first to engage in a systematic research of this kind.[4]

The harvest is very rich in that which concerns the relation between Church and ministry. One sees immediately that the split between ministry and concrete Church, such as is seen in the practice of absolute ordinations or in the celebration of private Masses, is an historical and doctrinal deviation which merits correction. Even more importantly, the devolving role of the assembly in the ordination processus considerably illuminates the theology of vocation to ordained ministry as an objective call of the Church to an apt person, even if the latter does not wish to be ordained. It also provides the

---

[3]On the adage, see P. DE CLERCK, "'Lex orandi, lex credendi': The Original Sense and Historical Avatars of an Equivocal Adage," *Studia Liturgica* 24, 2 (1994) 178–200.

[4]A first attempt, undertaken on the same methodological bases, may be read in H.-J. SCHULZ, "Das liturgisch—sakramental übertragene Hirtenamt in seiner eucharistischen Selbstverwirklichung nach dem Zeugnis der liturgischen Überlieferung," in P. BLÄSER, S. FRANK, P. MANNS, et al. *Amt und Eucharistie* (Paderborn: Verlag Bonifatius-Druckerei, 1973) 208–255.

criteria of reception of the ordained by the community, if not the participation of the community in the choice of its ministers. These last two points are of an evident actuality in Europe and North America at the present time, in which an alarming decrease in the number of "candidates" for ordained ministry goes hand in hand with a renewal of interest by local Churches in the amelioration of the processes by which their bishops are chosen.

An ecclesiology elaborated from its liturgical base also renews in a convincing manner the classical debates such as the articulation between Christology and pneumatology, between order and jurisdiction, confession of faith and succession in the apostolic ministry.

In addition, the importance of the eschatological dimension of ministry is highlighted. The systematic analysis of the biblical readings allows many discoveries. This last point brings us to the richness of the documentation.

AN EXCEPTIONAL DOCUMENTATION

Not only is the bibliography very ample and quasi exhaustive, but its publication in its present state will be a mine of information for enlarging the research. Not only are the rituals made available and the biblical readings detailed, but a large number of comparative tables already indicate numerous possible lines of research (see volume IV).

Despite this, the whole field of Christian liturgies could not be covered. The author restricted his research to the Church in the West: he lacked the historical and linguistical knowledge to study the Eastern liturgical families. This restriction is not a lacuna but wisdom on his part. On the other hand, we may regret that there is no systematic treatment of the diaconate. The diaconate has been considerably developed after Vatican II, and the tripartite division of ministry remains a disputed question in the ecumenical debate. Perhaps James Puglisi has at least elaborated the necessary methodology for such a study, a study which is clearly needed.

AN IMPORTANT CONTRIBUTION TO THE ECUMENICAL DIALOGUE

Until the present, the classical methodology in this domain has been to start from what divides us in order to try to find solutions to controversial questions: the priestly dimension of ordained ministry, apostolic succession and the "invalidity" which its absence entails.

James Puglisi proceeds in a different manner. He rightly prefers to begin by the inventory of what is incontestably held in common, and from there, to situate the differences which remain. Thus the evaluation of differences is placed on its proper horizon. The work reveals considerable ecumenical agreement: the existence of a considerable and incontestable homology in the practice of different Churches in the process of access to the ordained ministries, despite the differences of dogmatic expression. This convergence is revealed as being much deeper than we usually admit or realize in the ecumenical dialogue. It would certainly be unwarranted to oppose orthopraxis and orthodoxy: however, James Puglisi places us on the best road towards a mutual recognition of ministries, for he founds his reflections on the effective structuration and auto-definition of the Churches. He is right to suggest that it is not on the validity of the ministry alone that the ecclesiality of a Church should be judged, but that it is on the basis of the ecclesiality of a Church that the value of its ministry should be discerned. In this he makes Hans Dombois' remark his own: "If the ancient Churches knew what they were doing, and if they were limiting themselves to doing only that, and if the Churches of the Reformation were doing what they assert, then we should be very close to the unity of Christians."[5]

James Puglisi's work opens the way for future study and reveals the justice of a remark made by one of his fellow American colleagues: "Were there to be essential agreement on the nature of Christian ministry, there would inevitably be that kind of common understanding of worship and church membership and ecclesiastical structure which would in effect indicate the basic reunion of Christians into one community."[6]

This work does not treat all the questions concerning ordination vis-à-vis an ecumenical theology; for example, the question of the ordination of Christian women is not treated, simply because this question was never asked in the way it is being asked at the present time, before the second half of the twentieth century. We may also observe

[5]H. DOMBOIS, *Das Recht der Gnade* . . . , 195.
[6]B. COOKE, *Ministry of Word and Sacraments* (Philadelphia: Fortress Press, 1976) 1.

that the author is more interested in structures and their mutations than in their genesis. Yet in spite of these inevitable limits, James Puglisi's study constitutes a reference that will quickly become a classic, because he has given us the documentary and epistemological bases which allow us to study the questions which remain. He offers us innumerable lines of research. "Puglisi"—for I am sure his work will rapidly become known as such—has its place in every serious theological library, and should not be absent from any ecumenical or liturgical library.

Hervé Legrand, O.P.
Professor, Institut catholique de Paris
Director of Doctoral Studies

Introduction

The process of ecumenical dialogues (bilateral and multilateral) has until the present sought such consensus as common reflection upon the essential truths of the faith has been able to ascertain. These dialogues have sometimes led to thoroughly studied mutual declarations on points of faith, such as the Gospel, grace, justification, the sacraments, etc. In a number of cases, however, ecumenical agreement remains on the level of theological discussion without entering into the concrete ecclesiastical practices of the Churches concerned. An entire dimension of reality therefore remains unexplored, with the risk of creating a chasm between theological discourse and ecclesiastical practice, between orthodoxy and orthopraxis.

The present study attempts to fill this void by studying the steps leading to and the process of admission to the ordained ministries or the ministries of direction in the Churches (Catholic and Protestant) such as they are found in the rituals of ordination and/or installation. Is it not in these rituals, in fact, that the structure of each Church and the process of building up the local communion of Christians are most clearly revealed?

We will not concentrate therefore on the convergences and the agreements already achieved theoretically and theologically, which are studied elsewhere.[1] This work will study the liturgical and canonical

[1] See, for example the studies of the following authors: G. F. MOEDE, "Amt und Ordination in der Ökumenische Diskussion," in *Der priesterliche Dienst. V. Amt und Ordination in ökumensicher Sicht*, ed. H. Vorgrimler (Freiburg/Basel/Vienna: Herder, 1973) 9–71; H. SCHÜTTE, *Amt, Ordination und Sukzession im Verständnis evangelischer und katholischer Exegeten und Dogmatiker der Gegenwart sowie in Dokumenten ökumenischer Gespräche* (Dusseldorf: Patmos-Verlag, 1974) esp. 359–410; N. EHRENSTRÖM and G. GASSMANN, *Confessions in Dialogue. A Survey of Bilateral Conversations among World Confessional Families 1959–1974* (Geneva: W.C.C., 1975) esp. 180–195; W. MARRAVEE, "Emerging Ecumenical Consensus on the Ordained Ministry. A Survey of Bilateral and Multilateral

institutions which give admittance to the ministry of direction. The analysis will follow an interdisciplinary method which is historical, liturgical and ecumenical, but principally ecclesiological.[2] Nevertheless, more emphasis will be given to structures than to their origins, in order to discern first and foremost the concepts which underlie them, the doctrinal meaning of ordained ministry, and the

Consensus Statements," *Eglise et théologie* 11, 3 (1980) 195–222; ibid., part II, 11, 4 (1980) 399–419; A. JOOS, "Specificità relazionale e unità personalizzata dei ministeri ecclesiali. Una prospettiva promettente di approfondimento ecumenico attuale sulla distinzione tra 'sacerdozio comune' e 'ministero ordinato,'" *Lateranum* NS 47, 1 (1981) 287–332; G. H. VISCHER, *Apostolischer Dienst: Fünfzig Jahre Diskussion über das kirchliche Amt in Glauben und Kirchenverfassung* (Frankfurt am Main: Verlag Otto Lembeck, 1982); L. SARTORI, "I ministeri nei testi di 'consenso' ecumenico," *Dialoghi ecumenici ufficiali. Bilanci e prospettive*, ed. D. Valentini (Rome: LAS, 1983) 71–100; the proceedings of the colloquium on the Lima document published in *Il ministero ordinato nel dialogo ecumenico. Riflessioni di teologi cattolici sul documento di Lima 1982. Atti del VII convegno di teologia sacramentaria 22–24 Novembre 1984*, G. FARNEDI and Ph. ROUILLARD (eds.) (Scritti in onore di Gerardo J. Békés) (Rome: Pontificio Ateneo S. Anselmo, 1985); A. BIRMELE, *Le salut en Jésus Christ dans les dialogues œcuméniques* (Paris/Geneva: Cerf/ Labor et Fides, 1986) esp. 159–253, 333–339, 372–375, 394–396, 461–468; R. MAGNANI, *La successione apostolica nella tradizione della Chiesa. Ricerca nel BEM e nei documenti del dialogo teologico bilaterale a livello internazionale* (Bologna: Edizioni Dehoniane, 1990).

[2]The necessity of a knowledge of history for ecclesiological study is strongly emphasized by B.F.J. Lonergan, and again by J. A. Komonchak: see B.F.J. LONERGAN, *Method in Theology*, reprint of 2nd ed. (1st ed. 1971) (Toronto: University of Toronto Press, 1991) 175–234 and J. A. KOMONCHAK, "*History and Social Theory in Ecclesiology*," *Lonergan Workshop II*, ed. F. Lawrence (Chico, CA: Scholars Press, 1981) 1–53. Lastly, the liturgico-canonical or institutional and ecumenical dimensions are treated by the Lutheran H. Dombois and have found an echo in the thought of certain Catholics, for example, J. Hoffmann and H.-M. Legrand. See the major work of H. DOMBOIS entitled *Das Recht der Gnade. Ökumenisches Kirchenrecht*, I, 2nd ed. (Witten: Luther Verlag, 1969); a commentary by J. HOFFMANN, "Grâce et institution selon Hans Dombois: une nouvelle approche du mystère de l'Eglise," *RSPT* 52, 4 (1968) 645–676; ibid., 53, 1 (1969) 41–69 and id., "L'horizon œcuménique de la réforme du droit canonique. A propos de deux ouvrages de Hans Dombois," *RSPT* 57, 2 (1973) 228–250, as well as the application to an institutional and ecclesiological reflection by H.-M. LEGRAND, "Grâce et institution dans l'Eglise: les fondements théologiques du droit canonique," in *L'Eglise: institution et foi*, J.-L. MONNERON, M. SAUDREAU, G. DEFOIS, et al. (Brussels: Facultés universitaires Saint-Louis, 1979) 139–172.

structuring of the Church which is implicit. Therefore, the study of the morphology of these institutions will occupy an important place in the analysis.

The theological task will consist chiefly in uncovering the theology implicit in the articulation of the ritual elements and procedures, and in discussing the balance of the whole. The prayer of ordination or of installation will be studied within this context, as will the imposition of hands.

The importance of the ordination ritual[3] resides in the fact that it is a process that represents in a demonstrative way the structuring of each Church, because in all the Churches the process is at the same time an ecclesial act as well as confessional, epicletical and juridical, as we shall see in the first part of this work. One would not want to impose the meaning of the ministry upon the structures, but rather let these structures speak for themselves through the texts which elucidate them and the theology which underlies them. Nonetheless, we shall seek the underlying unity in the multiple forms of expression in the concrete life of each Church.

In our research we will begin with the tradition of the early Church, because it presents a vision close to the time of the New Testament and the original way of balancing ecclesiologically the different elements of the process of admission to ordained ministry. Here the various ministries are found in the context of the ministry of

[3]Concerning the dyad "myth–rite," which is highly important in religious studies, see the following studies: J. CAZENEUVE, *Sociologie du rite. (Tabou, magie, sacré)* (Paris: Presses universitaires de France, 1971) esp. 9–38 and 217–321; M. DOUGLAS, *Natural Symbols, Explorations in Cosmology* (New York/London: Pantheon Books/Barrie and Jenkins, 1970); several studies by M. ELIADE, *Patterns in Comparative Religion,* trans. from French *[Traité de l'histoire des religions]* by R. Sheed, reprinted (1st ed., 1958), (NY/Cleveland: World Publishing Co., 1971) esp. chs. X–XIII; id., *Aspects du mythe* (Paris: Gallimard, 1969); A. VERGOTE, *Interprétation du langage religieux* (Paris: Seuil, 1974) 73–93; id., *Religion, foi, incroyance. Etude psychologique* (Brussels: P. Mardaga, 1983) esp. ch. III: "L'expérience religieuse," 111–187 and ch. V: "Les trois pratiques expressives et performatives: la prière, le rite et l'éthique," 257–315; M. MESLIN, *Pour une science des religions* (Paris: Seuil, 1973) esp. 139–262; id., *L'expérience humaine du divin. Fondements d'une anthropologie religieuse* (Paris: Cerf, 1988) 135–234; G. VAN DER LEEUW, *La religion dans son essence et ses manifestations. Phénoménologie de la religion,* French edition updated by author with the collaboration of the translator J. Marty (Paris: Payot, 1970) esp. third part, 332–524; V. TURNER, *The Ritual Process. Structure and Anti-Structure* (Chicago: Aldine Publishing, 1969).

the Church. The first part, therefore, will be devoted to exploring the consolidation of the tradition from the very first ritual, namely, the *Apostolic Tradition*. This ritual, which influenced the East, underwent some changes and successive theological adjustments in the West which account for the changes in the meaning of the ordained ministry (Chapters 1 and 2).

The second volume of this study will examine the meaning of the ministry of direction and the structuring of the Church, applying the same method to several ordination or installation liturgies from the Reformation (Lutheran traditions in Chapter 1 and the Reformed traditions in Chapter 2), from Anglicanism (Chapter 3), and from Methodism (Chapter 4). A theological reflection (Chapter 5) closes this part with an examination of some of the most frequent biblical images, the functions of the ordained ministries, and the theological and ecclesiological foundation of the ministry and the structuring of the Church, all within the framework of ordination.

In the third volume, a certain number of rituals currently used in the Latin Catholic Church, the Anglican Communion, and the Protestant Churches will be analyzed according to the ecclesiological model proposed, with the same end in view: to discern the meaning of the pastoral ministry of direction and the structuring of the Church according to the concrete process of ordination followed by the Churches (Chapter 1: the Catholic Church; Chapter 2: the Lutheran Churches; Chapter 3: the Reformed Churches; Chapter 4: the Anglican Churches; and Chapter 5: the Methodist Churches). In the last chapter (6), we will show the convergences which exist in the reality of the practice of the Churches in regard to admittance to the ministry of direction, as well as the ecclesial structuring. It will also be possible to identify those areas in which the different ecclesial traditions diverge and the ecclesiological imbalances which may have resulted. This plan of study will end with the epistemological and methodological concerns that have arisen during the research, as well as some reflections of an ecumenical nature.

In order to facilitate our research into the evolution of the rituals, three charts will compare the structure of ordinations, the ordination prayers, and the scrutinies or examinations of the elect at the time of ordination or installation. A fourth chart gives the correspondence of biblical readings used during ordination in each Church. Due to the method adopted, it was important to present these ordination rituals in their totality and not to look at the ordination prayers alone. The reader will find in the fourth volume the complete texts of the rituals in English translation, with notes identifying their sources. This is the first time that such a collection of ordination texts has been presented.

It is necessary to explain certain options chosen during this work. It is limited to the Churches of the West due to the complexity of the Eastern traditions, and for want of the linguistic competence indispensable for working with liturgical texts of the Eastern rites. One would hope that other scholars would take up this task with the same purpose and the same ecclesiological methodology.

Secondly, it was necessary to restrict the choice of examples to the Churches of western Europe and the United States for the sake of the accessibility of the texts, even though one may find some very interesting adaptations in areas of Asia, Latin America and Africa. In many cases, these texts from the principal ecclesial traditions of Europe and America constitute the basic texts in these geographical areas.

Thirdly, the rituals which will be presented for the Anglican and Protestant Churches come from the Churches which belong to ecclesial organizations such as the Lutheran World Federation (LWF), the World Alliance of Reformed Churches (WARC), the Lambeth Conference, and the World Methodist Council (WMC). This selection makes it possibile to study some Churches which differ greatly within the same confessional family. The breadth of the field of investigation will guarantee the validity of such a study.

To help the reader unfamiliar with certain technical terms there is a brief glossary at the end of the fourth volume of this work. It is accompanied by a list of Churches with their equivalent in English.

**The Meaning of the Episcopal and Presbyteral
Ministry According to the Ordination Rituals
of the Western Church to the Eighth Century
and the Structuring of the Church Which Is
Revealed Therein**

Chapter 1

Study Documents

A complete ordination ritual of the early Church is not found before the time of the *Apostolic Tradition* at the beginning of the third century. Assuredly, several documents of the early Church speak of various aspects of the responsibilities of the bishop or the presbyter, but none give a coherent and complete text of an ordination ritual for the episcopacy and the presbyterate.[1]

[1]Several authors have studied the literature of the New Testament and the early Church concerning the question of the ministry and the ministries. For example, see the following: P. BONY, E. COTHENET, J. DELORME, et al., *Le ministère et les ministères selon le Nouveau Testament. Dossier exégétique et réflexion théologique* (Paris: Seuil, 1974); Y. CONGAR and B.-D. DUPUY (eds.), *L'épiscopat et l'Eglise universelle* (Paris: Cerf, 1962); K. KIRK (ed.), *The Apostolic Ministry. Essays on the History and the Doctrine of Episcopacy* (London: Hodder & Stoughton, 1946); T. OSAWA, *Das Bischofseinsetzungsverfahren bei Cyprian. Historische Untersuchungen zu den Begriffen iudicium, suffragium, testimonium, consensus* (Frankfurt am Main/Berne: P. Lang, 1983); L. MORTARI, *Consacrazione episcopale e collegialità. La testimonianza della Chiesa antica* (Florence: Vallecchi, 1969); J. D. LAURANCE, *"Priest" as Type of Christ. The Leader of the Eucharist in Salvation History according to Cyprian of Carthage* (N.Y./Berne/Frankfurt am Main/Nancy: P. Lang, 1984); A. JILEK, *Initiationsfeier und Amt. Ein Beitrag zur Struktur und Theologie der Ämter und des Taufgottesdienstes in der frühen Kirche (Traditio Apostolica, Tertullian, Cyprian)* (Frankfurt am Main/Berne/Cirencester: P. Lang, 1979); G. KRETSCHMAR, "Die Ordination im frühen Christentum," *Freiburger Zeitschrift für Philosophie und Theologie* 22, 1–2 (1975) 35–69; J. COLSON, *L'évêque dans les communautés primitives* (Paris: Cerf, 1951); id., *Ministre de Jésus-Christ ou le sacerdoce de l'Evangile* (Paris: Beauchesne, 1966); O. BÂRLEA, *Die Weihe der Bischöfe, Presbyter und Diakone in vornicänischer Zeit* (Munich: Rumänische akademische Gesellschaft, 1969); A. LEMAIRE, *Les ministères dans l'Eglise* (Paris: Centurion, 1974); E. J. KILMARTIN, "Ministry and Ordination in Early Christianity against a Jewish Background," *Studia Liturgica* 13, 2–4 (1979) 42–69 (= *Ordination Rites. Papers Read at the 1979 Congress of Societas Liturgica*, eds. W. Vos & G. Wainwright [Rotterdam: Liturgical Ecumenical Center Trust, 1980]), to read with the article by L. A. HOFFMAN, "Jewish Ordination on the Eve of Christianity," *Studia Liturgica* 13, 2–4 (1979) 11–41 (= *Ordination Rites . . .* , eds. W. Vos & G. Wainwright); lastly, P. F. BRAD-

After the *Apostolic Tradition*, we must wait several more centuries for further witnesses for the Western Church. The process of admission to ordained ministry established in the ritual of the *Apostolic Tradition* will be recast again and again down through the centuries; certain elements will assume more importance, while others will leave only vestigial traces. New elements, furthermore, will be added, and a new balance will establish itself in the rituals of the Western Church.

A. THE *APOSTOLIC TRADITION* OF HIPPOLYTUS OF ROME
(beginning of the third century)

This document, attributed to Hippolytus, contains precious information about the life of the Church and its organization in the third and fourth centuries. Its importance is obvious, as it gives the first complete ritual for the process of admission to ordained ministry, certain elements of which may predate the third century. The history of the transmission of the text of the *Apostolic Tradition* is very complex and presents some difficulties.[2] Most liturgists agree that it is a

---

SHAW, *Ordination Rites of the Ancient Churches of East and West* (N.Y.: Pueblo Publishing Company, 1990).

[2]For this history the books of Botte and Dix have important bibliographies: B. BOTTE, *La Tradition apostolique de saint Hippolyte. Essai de reconstitution*, 5th ed. improved by A. Gerhards and S. Felbecker (Münster: Aschendorff, 1989); G. DIX, *Apostolikē Paradosis. The Treatise on the Apostolic Tradition of St. Hippolytus of Rome, Bishop and Martyr*, 2nd revised ed., preface and bibliography by H. Chadwick (London: SPCK, 1968) (hereafter: *Treatise*). The text established by Botte is also published in id., *La Tradition Apostolique d'après les anciennes versions*, 2nd ed. (Paris: Cerf, 1968). [The English translation of quotations from the *Apostolic Tradition* is taken from: William A. Jurgens, *The Faith of the Early Fathers* (Collegeville, Minn.: The Liturgical Press, 1970), vol. I; note that the chapter, or section, numbers do not always correspond to those in the French version—ed.] For a discussion of other difficulties and hypotheses see J.-M. HANSSENS, *La liturgie d'Hippolyte. Ses documents—Son titulaire—Ses origines et son caractère*, 2nd ed. corrected and augmented (Rome: Pont. Institutum Orientalium Studiorum, 1965); A. SANTANTONI, *L'ordinazione episcopale. Storia e teologia dei riti dell'ordinazione nelle antiche liturgie dell'Occidente* (Rome: Anselmiana, 1976) 27f.; P. F. BRADSHAW, *Ordination Rites . . .*, 3–5, 20–103 and note 3 on page 252 for some complementary bibliography. Concerning the problem of authorship of Hippolytus of Rome, see M. METZGER, "Nouvelles perspectives pour la prétendue *Tradition apostolique*," *Ecclesia orans* 5, 3 (1988) 241–259; J. MAGNE, "En finir avec la 'Tradition' d'Hippolyte," *BLE* 89, 1 (1988) 5–22, and the articles by A.-G. MARTIMORT, "La Tradition apostolique d'Hippolyte," *L'Année canonique* 23 (1979) 159–173; id., "Nouvel examen de la

had a very clear conception of the episcopal ministry as distinct from, but related to, that of the presbyters. It is precisely in his anti-Gnostic treatise that one finds his ideas concerning *episkopē*.

The threat of Gnosticism was already felt in the first Christian communities, some of whose members were already suspect.[7] The author of the Pastoral Epistles gives a response to the disciples whom he had installed as leaders of the communities founded by him: they should teach "that which is consistent with sound doctrine" (Titus 2: 1); *episkopē* "must have a firm grasp of the word that is trustworthy in accordance with the teaching"(Titus 1:9); and Timothy was exhorted with the following: "continue in what you have learned and firmly believed, knowing from whom you learned it" (2 Tim 3:14).

St. Irenaeus shows how the Gnostic threat became a question of life or death for the Christian communities, and at the same time he explains the basis of this heresy:

"But, again, when we refer them to that tradition which originates from the apostles, [and] which is preserved by means of the successions of presbyters in the Churches, they object to tradition, saying that they themselves are wiser not merely than the presbyters, but even than the apostles, because they have discovered the unadulterated truth. For [they maintain] that the apostles intermingled the things of the law with the words of the Saviour; and that not the apostles alone, but even the Lord Himself, spoke as, at one time from the Demiurge, at another

Behind (New York: Paulist, 1984). See also A. Faivre, *Ordonner la fraternité . . .*, 56–72 and J.M.R. TILLARD, *L'Eglise locale. Ecclésiologie de communion et catholicité* (Paris: Cerf, 1995) 166–219. In addition, the authority of presbyters in Irenaeus has been emphasized by W. C. VAN UNNIK, "The Authority of the Presbyters in Irenaeus' Works," in J. JERVELL and W. A. MEEKS (eds.), *God's Christ and His People: Studies in Honour of Nils Alstrup Dahl* (Oslo: Universitetsforlaget, 1977) 248–260. In spite of the confusion of terminology in Irenaeus, we are on the way to the establishment of a clear distinction between presbyterate and episcopacy; see, for example, the historical study presented in chapter VI of R. ZOLLITSCH, *Amt und Funktion des Priesters. Eine Untersuchung zum Ursprung und zur Gestalt des Presbyterats in den ersten zwei Jahrhunderten* (Freiburg/Basel/Vienna: Herder, 1974).

[7]For example, cf. 1 Tim 6:4-5, 20; Titus 3:9; and 2 Tim 4:3. R. E. Brown has even suggested that a branch of the Johannine community ended up in the Gnostic camp, carrying with them the fourth Gospel. This fact would explain (for Brown) the epilogue of the fourth Gospel; see R. E. BROWN, *The Community of the Beloved Disciple* (New York: Paulist, 1979) and also id., *The Churches . . .*, 37–39, 121–123.

from the intermediate place, and yet again from the Pleroma, but that they themselves, indubitably, unsulliedly, and purely, have knowledge of the hidden mystery: this is, indeed, to blaspheme their Creator after a most impudent manner! It comes to this, therefore, that these men do now consent neither to Scripture nor to tradition."[8]

As we can see, Irenaeus' response was the same as that of the author of the Pastoral Epistles: fidelity to apostolic tradition. It is precisely because of the struggle against Gnosticism that St. Irenaeus emphasizes the importance of continuity with the teaching of the apostles in the Churches. This teaching transmitted by the apostles contains the faith or "the rule of truth" given through baptism (*Adv. Haer.* I, 9, 4, and *Proof of the Apostolic Preaching*, 6–7). It is baptismal faith (or the "chapters of the seal") that St. Irenaeus refers to when he recalls the tradition or the teaching. The bath of regeneration and faith confer the Holy Spirit, the Spirit of Jesus in whose name one believes and is baptized (*Adv. Haer.* V, 11, 2: III, 17, 2, and *Proof of the Apostolic Preaching*, 7). The Gnostics tried to deny the Spirit to the apostles and to the Church, but Irenaeus refuted this affirmation because the Holy Spirit is found only in the Church, which consists of the apostles and their disciples, since one receives the Spirit only by participating in Christ, that is to say, only in the Church (*Adv. Haer.* III, 24, 1). Further, Irenaeus shows that it is the apostles (and after them, their disciples), not only through their preaching but also through baptism in water and the Spirit, who "dispensing and administering to the faithful the Holy Spirit . . . established the churches" (*Proof of the Apostolic Preaching*, 41 and 3). The power given by Christ to the apostles or to their disciples to engender others as children of God is "the Spirit for which David had asked (Ps 51:10: *pneuma hēgemonikon*), bringing distant tribes to unity" (*Adv. Haer.* III, 17, 2). We see clearly that the comments of Irenaeus are framed in the context of baptismal faith. We shall see that the *episkopoi* will take the place of the apostles in the apostolic functions of preaching, conferring baptism, and celebrating the Eucharist (cf. *Proof of the Apostolic Preaching*, 41; 100, and *Adv. Haer.* IV, 18, 5; 26, 2).

The Gnostics invoked a secret tradition transmitted through a hidden succession of teachers.[9] Irenaeus replies that the tradition is

[8] *Adv. Haer.* III, 2, 2.
[9] Ibid., III, 4, 3.

clearly enunciated in the four Gospels and that it is maintained through an unbroken succession of *episkopoi* in the Churches.[10] These *episkopoi* are found in every local Church.[11]

How can one explain the fact that the titles of *presbyteroi* and *episkopoi* were sometimes interchangeable? The mission of transmitting the apostolic kerygma inserted the *episkopos* in the lineage of the elders *(presbyteroi)* who knew the apostles and had received from them the tradition; it is this which bestows upon the bishop the title of *presbyteros*. The two passages which follow show how Irenaeus uses the title of presbyter for both the disciples of the apostles and the *episkopoi* : a) ". . . Also the elders who were disciples of the apostles . . . ," and b) "But, again, when we refer them to that tradition which originates from the apostles, [and] which is preserved by means of the successions of presbyters in the Churches . . ."[12] In order to elucidate this idea it will suffice to compare this last passage with the one which contains the celebrated expression *charisma veritatis certum* : "Wherefore it is incumbent to obey the presbyters who are in the Church—those who, as I have shown, possess the succession from the apostles; those who, together with the succession of the episcopate, have received the certain gift of truth *(charisma veritatis certum)*, according to the good pleasure of the Father."[13]

In this text we note that the *episkopoi* have received the "sure charism of truth" which guarantees the authenticity of the teaching of the Word of God. To combat the Gnostics one had to be able to establish the uninterrupted succession of teaching from apostle to disciple. Perhaps one of the symbols of this succession was expressed

---

[10]Cf. ibid., III, 2, 1 and III, 3, 1f.

[11]Ibid., IV, 33, 8 and also III, 3, 1 with III, 4, 3–5, 1.

[12]Ibid., V, 5, 1 and III, 2, 2. Cf. also III, 3, 1.

[13]Ibid., IV, 26, 2. Here is the text in Latin: quapropter eis qui in ecclesia sunt presbyteris obaudire oportet, his qui successionem habent ab apostolis, sicut ostendimus, qui cum episcopatus successione charisma veritatis certum secundum placitum Patris acceperunt . . . Nevertheless, Y. Congar has noted that the meaning of the expression *"charisma veritatis certum"* is open to discussion. For the different interpretations and a selective bibliography, see Y. CONGAR, *I Believe in the Holy Spirit*, vol. 2, *Lord and Giver of Life*, trans. from French *[Je crois en l'Esprit Saint*, vol. 2, *"Il est Seigneur et Il donne la vie"* by B. Smith (N.Y./London: Seabury Press/Geoffrey Chapman, 1983) 44 note 18. Cf. A FAIVRE, *Ordonner la fraternité . . .* , 315–329 and J.M.R. TILLARD, *L'Église locale . . .* , 179–183.

through the imposition of hands (1 Tim 4:14; 2 Tim 1:6), a sign of a received charism. In this sense one can also adduce St. Irenaeus, *Adv. Haer.* IV, 26, 2.[14] In any case, it was in the context of the succession of teaching that the lists of episcopal successions were drawn up, flowing from the mission given by the apostles to certain men installed in the Churches for their supervision and for the transmission of *"charisma veritatis certum."*

J. D. Zizioulas notes that these lists were not intended to erect a unique and universal apostolic succession. They are, rather, according to the words of Hegesippus, **"successions"** (in the plural)—links with the apostles through the local communities ("in each city"; see Eusebius, *Hist. Eccl.*, I, 22, 3, 5)."[15] The *episkopos*, for Irenaeus, is a teacher. He teaches not only through his word, but also through his conduct, which must be absolutely perfect and above reproach, as is already indicated in 1 Tim 3:2 (cf. *Adv. Haer.* III, 3, 1). One must avoid at all costs false presbyters (cf. *Adv. Haer.* IV, 26, 3). It is important to be in a succession of teaching in relationship to the apostles (which ensures fidelity to the Gospel). However, the simple facts of personal integrity and doctrinal authenticity are not sufficient. There is a necessary interaction between doctrinal succession and successions that are identifiable thanks to legitimate election.[16]

These lists can, however, be seen in different ways, because we may suspect that even in their earliest composition the principle of

---

[14]L. LIGIER, "Le *Charisma veritatis certum* des évêques: ses attaches liturgiques, patristiques et bibliques," in *L'homme devant Dieu. Mélanges offerts au Père Henri de Lubac*, vol. 1, *Exégèse et patristique* (Paris: Aubier, 1963) 247–268, esp. 250–262, and J. D. QUINN, "'Charisma veritatis certum': Irenaeus, *Adversus haereses* 4, 26, 2," *Theological Studies* 39, 3 (1978) 520–525. Apostolic succession which is "transmitted" through consecration and the imposition of hands is not *explicitly* attested by Irenaeus; however, is there not an allusion to ordination in this passage of Book IV? The liturgical evidence given by Ligier seems to offer an affirmative response. A confirmation is found in the *AT* (cf. *AT* 2) and in the writings of Pope Cornelius (Cornelius to Fabian, quoted in EUSEBIUS OF CAESAREA, *Hist. Eccl.* VI, 43, 10).

[15]J. D. ZIZIOULAS, "Episkopē and Episkopos . . . ," 34.

[16]Cf. *Adv. Haer.* III, 3, 1. Tertullian, a contemporary of St. Irenaeus, uses the same argument against the Gnostics: cf. *De praescriptione haereticorum*, 32, 1. To be established in the episcopacy means to be elected and ordained (cf. TERTULLIAN, ibid., 32, 2 and CYPRIAN, *Ep.* 33, 1).

one bishop per diocese was perhaps neither universal nor established from the beginning. This can be deduced from the disorder in the succession lists in Rome.[17] Moreover, the Ignatian corpus does not name the bishop of Rome, the only Church so omitted. Lastly, it seems that there may have been some elders in Corinth, according to the letter of Clement (1 Clement 44), a letter which was not even signed by him.[18]

Similarly, looking closely at the list of the *episkopoi* for the Church of Rome, we note that this list does not begin with the Apostles Peter and Paul but with those upon whom the office of *episkopē* had been conferred *(katastasis)*. For Irenaeus, therefore, the apostles are unique: no one could succeed them. Theologically, the *episkopoi* succeed only to the ministers appointed by the apostles. The raison d'être of the *episkopē* is to ensure fidelity to the preaching of the Gospel and to the teaching of the apostles. According to Michele Maccarrone, this is shown by the *topos* according to which the episcopacy is always "in the Church" and "from the apostles."[19] Being a "successor of the

---

[17]IRENAEUS, *Adv. Haer.* III, 3, 3 offers a different order from that of Hegesippus (EUSEBIUS OF CAESAREA, *Hist. Eccl.* IV, 22, 3).

[18]Concerning the question of more than one bishop, cf. J. FUELLENBACH, *Ecclesiastical Office and the Primacy of Rome. An Evaluation of Recent Theological Discussion of First Clement* (Washington, D.C.: Catholic University of America Press, 1980) 24; G. KONIDARIS, "De la prétendue divergence des formes dans le régime du christianisme primitif: ministres et ministères du temps des Apôtres à la mort de saint Polycarpe," *Istina* 10, 1 (1964) 68; A. LEMAIRE, *Les ministères aux origines de l'Eglise. Naissance de la triple hiérarchie: évêques, presbytres, diacres* (Paris: Cerf, 1971) 150ff.

[19]Cf. *Adv. Haer.* III, 3, 3. For the discussion of *topos* see M. MACCARRONE, "Lo sviluppo dell'idea dell'episcopato nel II secolo e la formazione del simbolo della cattedra episcopale," in G. G. MEERSSEMAN et al., *Problemi di storia . . . ,* 164–166. C. Vogel affirms that "originally the idea of *successio* implies less a succession of persons from the apostles on, in an uninterrrupted chain, than a succession in the ministry of each predecessor. Symbolized by the *cathedra*, the uninterrupted *successio apostolica* constitutes less a proof of the validity of the ordination than a guarantee of the orthodoxy of the doctrine. In this way the pre-Constantine equation of *diadochē (successio)* and *paradosis (traditio)* will only become with Eusebius the modern equation *diadochē (successio)* equals *katalogos (series episcoporum)*. The idea that the bishops succeed to the apostles *ordinatione vicaria* has been, as far as we know, expressed clearly for the first time by Firmilian of Caesarea (ca. 268) and expressly extended to all bishops in a *votum* of an African dignitary in the time of St. Cyprian (*Ep.* 75, 16)": C. VOGEL, "Unité

apostles," the *episkopos* has the responsibility to see that the apostles remain the foundation on which the Church is built.

In these lists the *episkopos* represents a link to the apostles, and therefore to their preaching. Continuity in the apostolic succession serves as a sign and a guarantee of uninterrupted continuity in the apostolic faith. It is interesting to note that Irenaeus does not construe succession from the imposition of hands, but from the throne or the seat, i.e., from the local Eucharistic assembly over which the *episkopos* presides.[20] This shows again that succession derives from a function which is the *episkopē* of the local Churches, and from the *charisma veritas certum* [21] conferred by the apostles on certain persons: it is a succession of office.

This notion that the continuity of teaching resides specifically in a place shows also that, for Irenaeus, the connection between the *episkopos* and his Church is very important, as is the continuity of the *episkopoi* upon the same seat. Apostolic succession for him means not only an uninterrupted succession of persons, but an uninterrupted continuity of communities.[22] Since apostolic succession is inherent in the entire local Church and not in the sole person of the *episkopos,* we see that succession is not something that the bishop possesses personally outside of the local Eucharistic community where he presides.

To conclude this rapid study of St. Irenaeus, it seems timely to quote some remarks of J. D. Zizioulas concerning the balance between history and eschatology in the thought of Irenaeus. In a chapter entitled "Apostolic Continuity and Succession," he discusses two possible approaches to the question of the continuity of the Church with the apostles: one is called "historical," the other, "eschatological." The first is basically linear. It is rooted in the concept of apostleship which defines the apostles as men charged with a mission to

---

de l'Eglise et pluralité des formes historiques d'organisation ecclésiastique du IIIe au Ve siècle," in Y. CONGAR and B.-D. DUPUY (eds.), *L'épiscopat et l'Eglise universelle* (Paris: Cerf, 1962) 598f.

[20] *Adv. Haer*. III, 3, 1–IV, 1.

[21] *Adv. Haer*. III, 3, 3; IV, 26, 2.

[22] See E. MOLLAND, "Le développement de l'idée de succession apostolique," *RHPR* 34, 1 (1954) 21–23; A. EHRHARDT, *The Apostolic Succession in the First Two Centuries of the Church* (London: Lutterworth, 1953) 107–131.

accomplish. They are sent with a message, and invested with an authority and a charism to proclaim this message. A schema of this continuity can be expressed thus: "God sends Christ—Christ sends the apostles—the apostles transmit the message of Christ by establishing Churches and ministers."[23]

The second approach is "eschatological." It is founded on the eschatological function of apostleship. The apostles are not seen as envoys, but rather as a *college*. Zizioulas explains the difference between the two approaches: "(the difference) is considerable and corresponds to that between mission and eschatology. Mission requires *sending* to the ends of the earth, whereas *eschata* imply the *convocation* of the dispersed people of God from the ends of the earth to one place (*Didachē* 9, 4; 10, 5. Cf. Matt 25:32; John 11:52)."[24] The image which can best express this approach is that of Christ surrounded by the apostles who become "the *foundations* of the Church in a presence of the Kingdom here and now (Rev 21:14)."[25] One should not oversimplify these two approaches, however, given the complexity of the concept of apostleship in the New Testament.

Concerning Irenaeus, Zizioulas notes the subsequent danger of eliminating the eschatological dimension at the expense of the historical perspective; a danger which is

". . . overcome in Irenaeus' theology thanks to two factors which survive so strongly in his theology: Pneumatology and the centrality of the eucharist. The Church is to be found only where the Spirit is (*Adv. Haer.* III, 24, 1) and the apostolic tradition comes to the Church not just through history but as a *charism* (*Adv. Haer.* IV, 26, 2). At the same time, true and orthodox doctrine is to be synthesized with the eucharist: 'our doctrine agrees with the eucharist and our eucharist with our doctrine,' (*Adv. Haer.* IV, 18, 5). This synthesis safeguarded the apostolic kerygma from objectification in its transmission through history."[26]

---

[23]J. D. ZIZIOULAS, "Apostolic Continuity and Succession," id., *Being as Communion. Studies in Personhood and the Church* (Crestwood, NY: St. Vladimir's Seminary Press, 1985) 173.

[24]Ibid., 174.

[25]Ibid., 175.

[26]Ibid., 190ff. In another article, the author explores the ramifications of these two types of pneumatology for the structural organization of the Church. See id., "Implications ecclésiologiques de deux types de pneumatologie," in B. BOBRIN-

Commenting upon the Gnostic crisis and the response of Irenaeus, Zizioulas confirms that the fact that the Churches "had access to apostolic teaching, not through theologians and doctors or lists of presbyters, whose principle function was, in fact, to teach, but through the bishops, that is to say, the heads of the Eucharistic assemblies (whose function was not primarily to teach), [this fact] shows that once again the ministry of the *episkopē* was closely related to the ecclesiology of the local Church and to its Eucharistic character."[27]

A few conclusions on the meaning of the ordained ministry in the writings of Irenaeus will conclude this brief study:

1) The terms *episkopos* and *presbyteros* are interchangeable, but the term *episkopos* is applied to the person who is established in every Church by the apostles and their successors (III, 3, 1; V, 20, 1).

2) The function of these *episkopoi* is to maintain continuity with apostolic teaching, transmitting faithfully what they have received (III, 3, 1), which is baptismal faith: "the chapters of the seal" (*Proof. . . . ,* 6–7, 41, 100).

3) The bishop deserves the title "presbyter" because he has received the mission of passing on the teaching of the apostles and in so doing he continues in the lineage of the elders who knew the apostles or their successors (III, 2, 2; V, 5, 1).

4) The presbyters appear as a collegial entity whose function is teaching (IV, 26, 2; IV, 27–32).

5) The *episkopoi* have received the *charisma veritatis certum*, a gift necessary for them to maintain the authenticity of apostolic teaching (IV, 26, 2) and to fulfill their proper office.

6) The connection to the apostles in faith is the very foundation of episcopal authority. Theologically, the *episkopoi* succeed to the ministers whom the apostles established, and not to the apostles themselves (the apostles are unique and no one can succeed them). For there can be no complete identification of the *episkopoi* with the apostles, the latter being distinct from the *episkopoi* in the theology of

---

SKOY, C. BRIDEL, B. BÜRKI, et al., *Communio sanctorum. Mélanges offerts à Jean-Jacques von Allmen* (Geneva: Labor et Fides, 1982) 141–154.

[27]J. D. ZIZIOULAS, "Episkopē and Episkopos . . . ," 34; id., "The Bishop in the Theological Doctrine of the Orthodox Church," *Kanon* 7 (1985) 23–35, where the author notes that there existed only one episcopal Eucharist in each city until the fourth century (p. 23).

Irenaeus (note that in the episcopal lists no apostle was called *episkopos*);[28] rather, one should speak of a relationship between the *episkopoi* and the apostles. But the bishops succeed to the seat *(cathedra)* in a local community. They are also the head of the Eucharistic gatherings (III, 3, 1–4, 1) of this community.

7) Irenaeus often insists on the fact that episcopal succession takes place *in the Church* (III, 2, 2; 3, 3; IV, 26, 2; 32, 1; etc.). This apostolicity and this continuity are therefore characteristics of the local community and do not exist apart from the Eucharistic community.

8) Henceforth, from around the year 150, the *episkopē* is exercised by a single person in each Church, in continuity with other men such as Timothy, Titus, Polycarp, and others, who have received the responsibility to ensure sound doctrine. Nonetheless, others in the community share this function with the bishop (the presbyters). In all this it is implicit that the *episkopē* serves the unity of the kerygma and of the community in truth. Since this structure is found in "all the Churches," the *episkopē* has served as the basis for a greater unity between the Churches in the communion of apostolic faith. The presbyters have shared responsibility for this function, by teaching and by interpreting the faith (cf. IV, 27–32). The ministry of the *episkopos*, however, is very distinct from that of the presbyters, even though they are linked.

b. *Cyprian of Carthage* († 258)

Cyprian was born at the beginning of the third century. After having received his intellectual formation in Carthage, he became a Christian toward the year 246. A few years after his baptism he entered the presbyterate and became bishop of Carthage around 249. At that time Carthage was the largest and most important of the Churches of Africa. During his ministry Cyprian had to deal with several crises: the persecutions under Decius (250); the elections of rival episcopal candidates in Carthage and in Rome; the problem of the *lapsi*, Christians who apostatized; and, lastly, the persecution under Valerian (257) aimed at the heads of the Church.[29] Through the

[28]On the other hand, we will see, infra, in Cyprian that the apostles themselves are the first bishops: cf. A, 1, b, 24 ff.; CYPRIAN, *Ep.* 66, 5.

[29]Cf. P. MONCEAUX, *Histoire littéraire de l'Afrique chrétienne depuis les origines jusqu'à l'invasion arabe*, vol. 2: *Saint Cyprien et son temps*, reprinted [1 ed., 1902] (Brussels: Culture et Civilisation, 1966).

letters and other writings of St. Cyprian one has a clear enough picture of the structures and procedures in his Church. We note in particular the importance that St. Cyprian attaches to the *electio* of the ministers of the Church. For him the people play an important role in the elections,[30] but they do not act alone, since the collaboration of the neighboring bishops and the presence of the clergy of the local Church are also required. The local Church is a *fraternitas* over which God presides.[31] The entire process of *ordinatio* is a highly significant moment in which the ecclesial communion of the Church finds expression, in its unity and its diversity, through the proper testimony of the clergy, the vote of the people, and the consensus of the neighboring bishops.[32] For St. Cyprian these elements are constitutive of the unity of the Church. All these elements, comprising each a part of the judgment of God, cannot be separated; otherwise the unity of the Church would be destroyed. In the thought of Cyprian, it is the bishops who, before any others, express the *"iudicium Dei,"* but they do so in concert with the clergy and the people of the local Church.[33] The clearest text depicting the role of the different members of the Church is found in letter 55, where he speaks of the election of Cornelius, the Bishop of Rome: "Cornelius was made bishop by the judgment *(iudicio)* of God and of His Christ, by the testimony *(testimonio)* of almost all of the clergy, by the vote *(suffragio)* of the people who were then present, by the college of venerable bishops and good men, when no one had been made before him, when the place of Fabian, that is, when the place of Peter and the position of the episcopal chair were vacant."[34]

---

[30]*Ep.* 38 (for the choice of clerics); *Ep.* 43, 1; 55, 8; 59, 5–6; 67, 4–5; 68, 2 (for the election of bishops). See also the study on the procedure and the vocabulary in Cyprian: T. OSAWA, *Das Bischofseinsetzungsverfahren* . . . , 79–85; J. GAUDEMET, *Les élections dans l'Eglise latine des origines au XVIe siècle* (Paris: F. Lanore, 1979) 14f.

[31]*De dominica oratione*, 8. See also *Ep.* 60, 1; 66, 5.

[32]*Ep.* 55, 8; 59, 5; 67, 5. Concerning the designation of the entire action under the name of *ordinatio* see *Ep.* 1, 1; 38, 2; 66, 1; 67, 4. When it is a question of the designation of other members of the clergy, the participation of the bishops of other Churches is lacking: cf. *Ep.* 29, 38.

[33]*Ep.* 43, 1; 59, 5; 67, 4–5; 68, 2. For the continuity in the development of these ideas see L. MORTARI, *Consacrazione episcopale* . . . , 13–19; T. OSAWA, *Das Bischofseinsetzungsverfahren* . . . , 67–78, 103–106.

[34]*Ep.* 55, 8.

All the prescriptions necessary for the ordination to be just and regular (*Ep.* 67, 4) are mentioned here. P. Grossi has shown in his study of the concept of ecclesiastical consensus how much their sense of responsibility regarding the Church moved all the members of the community, and how the idea of unanimity was linked to that of the unity of the faith.[35] Two other prescriptions should be noted: the election should have the approval of the faithful and be carried out with the participation of the college of bishops; and, the episcopal see must be vacant. In the first prescription we see clearly that the Churches were conscious of being partners in witnessing to the faith, as they were in receiving the election of the elect as a judgment of God; in the second, it is the principle insisted upon from the time of Ignatius of Antioch, that there be just one bishop per given locality, which is evident.[36]

These texts of Cyprian clearly show that the local Church was involved both in the choice of its bishop and in that of other ministers. Even though Cyprian used the hyphenated name *clerus-plebs*, there was no division between these two realities, since the Church, as we have already said, is a *fraternitas* which draws its principle and origins from the very life of the Trinity.[37] The central focus of this unity is found in the bishop surrounded by his presbyterium in the midst of his people. In fact, St. Cyprian expresses this reality in this manner: ". . . the bishop is in the Church and the Church is in the bishop" and ". . . the Church which is one, Catholic, is not divided nor rent, but is certainly united and joined, in turn, by the solder of the bishops adhering to one another."[38] In this way the bishop personifies

[35]P. GROSSI, "Unanimitas. Alle origini del concetto di persona giuridica nel diritto canonico," *Annali di storia del diritto* 2 (1958) 228–331.

[36]For the references to a single bishop in one place, see Cyprian, *Ep.* 49, 2; 55, 8; 59, 6; *De Catholicae Ecclesiae Unitate*, 8. As for the theological meaning of the episcopal elections in the early Church, see H.-M. LEGRAND, "Theology and the Election of Bishop in the Early Church," *Concilium* 7, 8 (1972) 31–42; id., "La réalisation de l'Eglise en un lieu," in B. LAURET and F. REFOULE (eds.), *Initiation à la pratique de la théologie*, vol. 3, *Dogmatique*, 2 [2nd. ed. corrected] (Paris: Cerf, 1986) 194–201.

[37]*De Catholicae Ecclesiae Unitate*, 6; *Ep.* 51; cf. *De dominica oratione*, 30. Cf. Y. CONGAR, "La collégialité de l'épiscopat et la primauté de l'évêque de Rome," in id., *Ministères et communion ecclésiale* (Paris: Cerf, 1971) 96f.

[38]*Ep.* 66, 8. Cf. also *Ep.* 55, 24; *De Catholicae Ecclesiae Unitate*, 5. See also the work of J. COLSON, *L'évêque, lien d'unité et de charité chez saint Cyprien de Carthage*

and represents his Church. Elsewhere Cyprian insists that the elect be examined in the presence of the people.[39] All of these prescriptions show that the responsibility for the faith of the local Church is shared by the entire Church, as P. Grossi has suggested in another context (cf. supra p. 23 and note 35).

The ministers of the Church are received by the local Church as given by God, through his judgment, of which the neighboring bishops who are present are the instrument. We cannot help wondering what can be the significance of these neighboring bishops. Cyprian has emphasized the primacy of each bishop in his Church (*episcopum in ecclesia esse et ecclesiam in episcopo*). Later, in the same letter (66), he shows how the bishop personifies and represents his Church. But in his exegesis of Mt 16:18 he writes that the episcopacy is the guarantee of the unity of the Church, the foundation upon which Christ built his Church: the bishop is its visible rock (*ecclesia supra episcopos constituatur*).[40] In this case, the presence of the bishops witnesses to the

---

(Paris: S.O.S., 1961) esp. 45–47; D.-T. STROTMANN, "L'évêque dans la Tradition orientale," in Y. CONGAR and B.-D. DUPUY (eds.), *L'épiscopat . . .* , 322.

[39]*Ep.* 38, 1. Cf. A. VILELA, *La condition collégiale des prêtres au IIIe siècle* (Paris: Beauchesne, 1971) 269–270. The expression "the bishop is in the Church and the Church is in the bishop" (*Ep.* 66, 8) can also demonstrate the necessity of the acceptance of the person of the bishop by the local Church.

[40]*Ep.* 33, 1. Here is a good example of the expression of Cyprian: *episcopus, id est apostolus*. J. D. Zizioulas sees in this formula the retreat of the episcopacy from its Christological connotations (presiding at the Eucharist, administering the gifts of the Spirit through ordination, etc.) and the accentuation of the apostolic connotations (governing, teaching and judging). The author writes: ". . . it is clear that the image [Cyprian] holds of episcopacy is no longer Christ-centered as was the case with Ignatius, the Syriac *Didascalia*, Hippolytus, etc., and becomes Peter-centered. When in later centuries the centrality and catholicity of the local Church will be lost, this will lead to an episcopacy conceivable in iteself, as a ministry *above* the local community and a succession of the 'apostolic college,'" J. D. ZIZIOULAS, "Episkopē and Episkopos . . . ," 35–36. See also id., *L'Eucharistie, l'Évêque et l'Église durant les trois premiers siècles* (Paris: Desclée de Brouwer, 1994) 138–173.

Furthermore, Cyprian does not maintain the distinction between apostles and bishops held by Irenaeus and Tertullian. We have already noted this fact for Irenaeus (see *supra*) and, in the same line of thought, Tertullian speaks of the first (after the apostles) in the list of succession as being the first bishop and, when he does this, he does not give this title to any of the apostles (cf. note 16).

identity in the faith and in the apostolic ministry of this local Church which is celebrating the election/ordination along with the apostolic Church across time and space. Each bishop is considered as the foundation and the unity of the Church in two ways: 1) There is one Church, one altar, one priesthood, one see; all these realities are in strict relationship with the bishop;[41] 2) In solidarity with the other bishops, the new bishop is the rock upon which the unity of the universal Church is built.[42] As was said above, the presence and the actions of these neighboring bishops are seen as bearing unimpeachable and personal witness to the apostolic faith, and as the expression of God's judgment: the decision of the Church is communicated (in this sense the neighboring bishops pass on the apostolic ministry to the elect) and received in the communion of the local Churches (the bishops receive the new bishop as representing his Church in relationship to the other Churches) and of the Christian people of the local community with its ministers.

For Cyprian, the quasi-identification of the bishops with the apostles, regarded as the first bishops, is evident (i.e., the bishops have the same position in relationship to the Church as the apostles[43]). The bishops function, therefore, as witnesses to the faith of their Church in the same way as the apostles. When the bishops gather for the ordination of a colleague, they acknowledge the faith of this Church by receiving its head into the episcopacy, which is one throughout the whole Church (cf. *De Catholicae Ecclesiae Unitate*, 5 and *Ep.* 66, 8). They receive, therefore, a decision, God's judgment. It should be noted, moreover, that no local Church sits above any other.

[41]*Ep.* 43, 5 and also 55, 8; 68, 2. Without the bishop there would be no Eucharist, no baptism, no forgiveness of sins, no reconciliation of sinners: cf. *Ep.* 34, 3; 72, 2; 73, 7.

[42]*Ep.* 66, 8: already quoted infra, p. 23 ("the Church which is one . . .") and which specifies: *"cohaerentium sibi invicem sacerdotium glutino copulata."* Cf. also *De Catholicae Ecclesiae Unitate*, 5, and H. von CAMPENHAUSEN, *Ecclesiastical Authority and Spiritual Power in the Church of the First Three Centuries*, trans. from German *[Kirchliches Amt und geistliche Vollmacht]* by J. A. Baker (London: Adam & Charles Black, 1969) 275f., who gives also the following references: *Ep.* 55, 1; 59, 14; 60, 1; 68, 3; 73, 26.

[43]*Ep.* 3, 3 *(apostolos, id est episcopos et praepositos Dominus elegit)*; 66, 4. Even the Twelve are known by the name of bishop: cf. *Ep.* 67, 4 *(de ordinando in loco Judae episcopo)*. See also the remarks of J. D. Zizioulas already quoted, supra, note 40.

It remains for us to consider the concept of the presbyterate in the writings of Cyprian. Due to the quasi-identification of the bishop with his Church, on the one hand, and with the apostles, on the other, it seems as if there is little room for the presbyters. But it is quite the contrary: in his letters, Cyprian calls the presbyters his *conpresbyteri* (co-presbyters). These latter belong to a college of which the bishop is the head, and they act collegially, especially when they sit together and make decisions concerning the government of the Church.[44] Cyprian tells us that these co-presbyters share in his priesthood.[45] For in his absence they preside at the Eucharist, they are responsible for the care of the Church, they reconcile the *lapsi*, and they instruct the catechumens.[46]

In conclusion, let us emphasize the salient points concerning the structuring of the Church and the process of admission to ordained ministry according to Cyprian:

1) *Ordinatio* means a process of admission to ordained ministry which includes the selection *(electio, iudicium, suffragium, testimonium,* and *consensus)*[47] and the imposition of hands.[48]

2) The local Church *(clerus et plebs)* is active in the selection of its ministers.

3) The examination of the elect is done before the people (*Ep.* 38, 1).

4) The local Church bears the responsibility for the apostolic faith.

5) The local Church cannot designate its new head by itself; it needs the consensus of the neighboring bishops, which is seen as the decision of God *(iudicium Dei)*.

6) These elements are constitutive of the unity of the Church. The cooperation of the heads of the local Churches demonstrates also that

---

[44]*Ep.* 14, 1, 4; 19, 2 and also 1, 1; 71, 1.

[45]*Ep.* 61, 3. Cf. J. A. MOHLER, *The Origin* . . . , 61f.; M. BENEVOT, "'Sacerdos' as Understood by Cyprian," *JTS* NS 30, 2 (1979) 417–421. See also the study of J. D. LAURANCE, *'Priest' as Type* . . . , esp. 198ff.

[46]*Ep.* 5, 2; 12, 1; 18, 1; 19, 2; cf. also H.-M. LEGRAND, "The Presidency of the Eucharist According to the Ancient Tradition," *Worship* 53, 5 (1979) 424ff.; on the "priest doctors," A. VILELA, *La condition collégiale* . . . , 310–314.

[47]*Ep.* 38; 55, 8; 61, 3; 66, 1; 67, 4; 68, 2; cf. also T. OSAWA, *Das Bischofseinsetzungsverfahren* . . . , 67–99 for all the references to the letters of Cyprian.

[48]*Ep.* 49, 1; 67, 5.

ecclesial communion requires catholicity. And, lastly, the apostolicity of the local Church, and that of the whole Church, as well as that of the ministry, are integral elements of the *koinōnia* of the Church.

7) The new ministers are received by the local Church as given by God, from the judgment of God.

8) The neighboring bishops as heads of the apostolic Churches bear witness to the apostolic faith of this Church, in that they receive the one elected as head of his Church.

9) In becoming a bishop of an apostolic Church, the new bishop is the link between his Church and the other apostolic Churches. His reception as a colleague in the one and same episcopacy by the other bishops is an expression of the *koinōnia* among the Churches.

10) The Church is seen as a *fraternitas*. The bishop dwells, therefore, in his Church as a brother, but at the same time as its head.

11) The bishop is surrounded by his co-presbyters.

12) These presbyters form a college.

13) The presbyters help the bishop govern the Church, taking his place in the Eucharistic celebration, imposing hands during the reconciliation of penitents (always along with their bishop, but in his absence they may act alone), and instructing the catechumens.

14) The co-presbyters "are never qualified sacerdotally independently of the bishop. They are so qualified together with him."[49]

2. STRUCTURE OF ORDINATIONS IN THE *APOSTOLIC TRADITION*

In order to describe the specific nature of the ordained ministry and to discern the concepts which underlie the liturgical institution of ordinations, we will examine their structures rather than their genesis. Moreover, the study of the morphology of ordinations will reveal the structuring of the Church, because the examination of each element of the process of admission to a particular ministry in the Church seeks to determine "who does what," and allows us to allocate the various roles among the different actors in the entire process and to determine the relationships which are extablished in the actions of this liturgical institution.[50]

[49]H.-M. LEGRAND, "The Presidency . . . ," 424ff.

[50]This general methodological principle is articulated by H. DOMBOIS: "Die Frage nach dem Kirchenrecht kann nicht durch die allgemeine Erörterung der

a. *Bishop*

In the *Apostolic Tradition,* ordination is understood as a liturgical continuum consisting of several steps: election, laying on of hands and prayer, kiss of peace, and the Eucharist.

α) *Election.* The *Apostolic Tradition* offers a description of the process through which one became a bishop at the beginning of the third century: "Let the bishop be ordained after he has been chosen by all the people. When someone pleasing to all has been named, let the people assemble on the Lord's Day with the presbyters and with such bishops as may be present. All giving assent, the bishops shall impose hands on him, and the presbytery shall stand by in silence. Indeed, all shall remain silent, praying in their hearts for the descent of the Spirit. Then one of the bishops present shall, at the request of all, impose his hand on the one who is being ordained bishop, and shall pray thus, saying: . . ."[51] (the ordination prayer follows).

Begriffe Kirche und Recht beantwortet werden, sondern nur durch eine Interpretation der hier zu verfassenden Bezüge. Es geht darum, wie hier Gott dem Menschen, der Mensch Gott begegnet, um die Relationen, die sich im gottesdienstlichen Handeln, und damit auch im Umgang der Glieder am Leibe Christi miteinander ausbilden." ("The question about ecclesiastical law cannot simply be answered by a general discussion of the terms 'Church' and 'law.' An encompassing interpretation of the *dynamics of the relation* [italics ours] between the two realities has to be provided. We are looking at how God encounters humanity and how humanity encounters God, in order to form relations within our acts of worship and the dealings with the Body of Christ as members of the congregation") in *Das Recht der Gnade . . . ,* I:37. For an introduction to the work of Dombois see J. HOFFMANN, "Grâce et institution . . . , 645–676 and 53, 1 (1969) 41–69. This methodological principle makes us conscious of the fact that we have reflected very little on the ways of admission to the ministries that are the rites of ordination. In them we may better observe the structure of the Church, because the process is at the same time *an ecclesial act* (we will see that the whole Church is active in the process) which reveals the relationship existing between the ordained ministry, the other ministries, and the responsibility of all Christians; at the same time, it is *a liturgical act* which is celebrated within the Eucharist, where normally all the members of the Church are present and which includes a symbolic system (some of the liturgical gestures, such as the imposition of hands) and the epiclesis; lastly, this process is also *a juridical act,* because a concrete charge is conferred on a member of the community by God and received by the entire Church. Here we see clearly how God encounters humanity and how humanity encounters God.

[51]B. BOTTE, *La Tradition apostolique . . . ,* 5–7.

This text supposes that the election was done "by all the people," including the clergy, that is to say, by the entire local community. That the election was the work of the local community is affirmed already by other documents anterior to the *Apostolic Tradition,* but without details regarding the procedure.[52] Still, it is clear that the selection

[52]For example, the *Didachē* (15, 1), the *First Letter of Clement* (44, 2–3), St. Irenaeus, *Adv. Haer.* (III, 12, 10; IV, 15, 1). The same fact is verified by Cyprian who is later than the *Apostolic Tradition: Ep.* 55, 8; 67, 3–5; see also A. JILEK, *Initiationsfeier* . . . , 58–62 and E. J. KILMARTIN, "Ministry and Ordination . . . ," 54–59 for some other examples. Concerning the letters of Cyprian, see the commentary of T. OSAWA, *Das Bischofseinsetzungsverfahren* . . . , 46–47, 79–81 and 206. The following articles are also useful: W. RORDORF, "L'ordination de l'évêque selon la Tradition Apostolique d'Hippolyte de Rome," *QL* 55, 2–3 (1974) 138 reprinted in id., *Liturgie, foi et vie des premiers chrétiens,* (Paris: Beauchesne, 1986) 124 (hereafter, *Liturgie*); K. RICHTER, "Zum Ritus der Bischofsordination in der 'Apostolischen Überlieferung' Hippolyts von Rom und davon abhängigen Schriften," *ALW* 17/18 (1975/1976) 12–14. A. Santantoni believes he knows how the election took place:
"Ci pare naturale pensare, come il testo sembra suggerire, che l'elezione da parte di tutto il popolo seguisse normalmente a una indicazione—*cum nominatus fuerit*—: una specie di designazione da parte di alcuni membri della comunità, che il popolo poi veniva chiamato ad approvare e a confermare—*et placuerit omnibus*—. Così si arrivava all'unanimità e il nuovo vescovo era veramente l'*electus ab omni populo*" ("It seems to me logical to think, as the text seems to suggest, that the election on the part of the entire people follows normally an indication—*cum nominatus fuerit*—: a kind of designation on the part of certain members of the community that the people later were called to approve and to confirm—*et placuerit omnibus*—. Thus they arrived at unanimity and the new bishop was truly the *electus ab omni populo*"): A. SANTANTONI, *L'ordinazione episcopale* . . . , 28.
It seems that T. Osawa (at least for Cyprian) is in agreement with Santantoni in believing that the people in the writings of Cyprian did not have the right of initiative in the election of their leader. See, for example, his conclusions on page 206. Along the same line, cf. H. von CAMPENHAUSEN, *Ecclesiastical Authority* . . . , 273f. The interpretation of Osawa seems to correct the opinions of certain theologians as, for example, P. GRANFIELD, "The *Sensus Fidelium* in Episcopal Selection," *Concilium* 137 (1980) 33–38, especially the authors whom he quotes in note 9, p. 37; and E. J. KILMARTIN, "Episcopal Election: The Right of the Laity," *Concilium* 137 (1980) 39–43. Lastly, we find pertinent the observation of a Protestant theologian who has studied the *Apostolic Tradition;* he observes, "It would be a grave misunderstanding, however, to suppose that the election of the bishop in this form were due to such concepts as sovereign popular right or majority rule. Rather, the People of God are here viewed as corporate instruments

of a bishop was the business of the local Church and that his ordination could take place only with the consent of all.

The text of the *Apostolic Tradition* adds: the elect must be above reproach. This recommendation helps us understand the role of the entire local community in this process, because only the people and the clergy of the local Church can know if the elect is truly above reproach. We see here the connection with 1 Tim 3:2-5 and the qualities required of the *episkopos*: that he be "above reproach, married only once, temperate, sensible, respectable, hospitable, an apt teacher, not a drunkard, not violent but gentle, not quarrelsome, and not a lover of money. He must manage his own household well, keeping his children submissive and respectful in every way . . ." This text from the First Letter to Timothy must be read in conjuction with what follows in verse 7, which says "he must be well thought of by outsiders" because "the Church must always be one Church for society."[53]

Again, one notes the unity of the Church in the act of the nomination of a chosen one and in the approval given jointly by the people and the presbyterium *(conveniet populum una cum praesbyterio)*, who are therefore truly co-responsible actors in the choice of their leaders.

Another circumstance casts light on this "unity in action" of the community. According to the tradition already established,[54] the ordination must take place on a Sunday: the first day of the week, the day of the resurrection, of Pentecost, and lastly, the day of the Eucharistic assembly, the feast of the real communion of this people.[55] This

---

of his will through his loving Spirit": J. E. STAM, *Episcopacy in the Apostolic Tradition of Hippolytus* (Basel: Friedrich Reinhardt, 1969) 18.

[53]H.-M. LEGRAND, "La réalisation de l'Eglise . . . ," 196f.

[54]Cf. T. MICHELS, *Beitrage zur Geschichte des Bischofsweihetages im christlichen Altertum und im Mittelalter* (Münster: Aschendorff, 1927) 7–15, 48–52; W. RORDORF, "L'ordination de l'évêque . . . ," 142f., reprinted in *Liturgie*, 128f.

[55]On the meaning of Sunday for the early Church see W. RORDORF, *Sabbat et dimanche dans l'Eglise ancienne* (Neuchâtel: Delachaux et Niestlé) 1972; id., "Origine et signification de la célébration du dimanche dans le christianisme primitif," *LMD* 148 (1981) 103–122 reprinted in *Liturgie*, 29–48; id., *Sunday—The History of the Day of Rest and Worship in the Earliest Centuries of the Christian Church* (Philadelphia/ Westminster/London: SCM, 1968, especially 177–237 for the link between the Eucharistic celebration and the eschatological meaning of Sunday; to read with H. CAZELLES, "Bible et temps liturgique: eschatologie et anamnèse," *LMD* 147 (1981) 11–28.

Eucharistic context should be emphasized, because it is very important for understanding the meaning of ordination, notably its eschatological dimension. Zizioulas has shown that two ways of understanding the continuity of the Church existed from the time of the New Testament: the historical, and the eschatological.[56] He sees in Hippolytus a synthesis of these two approaches in which the charismatic event of ordination takes place in an eschatological context:

"It is not enough to think of ordination as a historical transmission of apostolicity. Ordination must also be a movement coming from the side of the eschatological finality, from the convoked and not just from the dispersed people of God. Hence all ordinations would have to take place in an epicletic context and, more than that, in the context of the community of the Church gathered *epi to auto,* with the apostles not as individual originators of ministry but as a presiding college. It is for this reason that not only all charismatic manifestations in the primitive Pauline Churches took place during the eucharistic gatherings (see 1 Cor 14), but also, as is implied in the *Didachē* (ch. 15 [on ordination] is joined with 14 [on the Sunday eucharist] with the word "therefore") and clearly evidenced by Hippolytus' *Apostolic Tradition* (*AT* 2), ordination to the ministry in the early Church took place in the same context."[57]

β) *Imposition of Hands.* It is within the Eucharistic/eschatological framework that the ordination of an elect will take place (cf. *AT* 4). One can now describe what takes place in this manner: on the normal day of assembly of the local Church, the bishops of the neighboring Churches gather with the presbyterium and the faithful of this local community; the bishops and the presbyterium surround the elect. The *AT*, in repeating the prescription of consent by all, later indicates that the bishops impose hands on the elect, while the presbyterium stands without any action. And then, while *all* (bishops, presbyters, and faithful) keep silent, *all* pray in their hearts for the descent of the Spirit *(in corde propter discensionem spiritus).* The epiclesis is effected by all the community present. Here we have a truly moving and meaningful picture.

The Eucharistic framework, a gathering in time and space with other human participants, is the place where one encounters the

---

[56]J. D. ZIZIOULAS, *Being as Communion* . . . , 171–181.
[57]Ibid., 192f.

eschaton, as on Pentecost when the apostles gathered with others to await the Holy Spirit.

We must stop for a moment at this point to discern better the respective roles of each person, in order to ascertain the meaning of the act of ordination. Above all, we note that the local community is present in all its components. It lacks only the bishop who is the head of it. Until now the presbyterium and the faithful have played the principal role. They have been active in the entire procedure of the election of their leader, witnessing to his virtues as a person, but above all, to his faith. But although they are active in the selection of the elect, they do not have the capacity to ordain him by themselves.[58] They need the participation of the heads of the neighboring Churches.

[58]Even if all the constituents of the local Church are active in the election of a bishop, a priest, or a deacon, the ordination does not coincide with the choice of the elect because he is not the delegate of the community. Nevertheless, in the words of St. Jerome (*Ep.* 146), the Church of Alexandria would have carried out these episcopal ordinations *alone,* without the participation of other heads of neighboring Churches. According to his letter, this praxis continued until the time of bishop Denys (247–264). This claim does not enjoy support: cf. C. VOGEL, "Chirotonie et Chirothésie. Importance et relativité du geste de l'imposition des mains dans la collation des ordres," *Irénikon* 45, 1 (1972) 16–18 reprinted in id., *Ordinations inconsistantes et caractère inamissible* (Turin: Bottega d'Erasmo, 1978) [78]–[80]; id., "L'imposition des mains dans les rites d'ordination en Orient et en Occident," *LMD* 102 (1970) 69f. reprinted in *Ordinations . . . ,* [129]f; J. LECUYER, "Le problème des consécrations épiscopales dans l'Eglise d'Alexandrie," *BLE* 65, 4 (1964) 241–257; id., "La succession des évêques d'Alexandrie aux premiers siècles," *BLE* 70, 2 (1969) 81–99 (with a complete bibliography). Lécuyer questions several interpretations of Vogel: cf. J. LECUYER, *Le sacrement de l'ordination. Recherche historique et théologique* (Paris: Beauchesne, 1983) 152–164. The question is not yet definitively settled, as is shown in the article by K. MC DONNELL, "Ways of Validating Ministry," *Journal of Ecumenical Studies* 7, 2 (1970) 209–265, esp. 231–234, but it seems that the author may not have been aware of the work either of Vogel or of Lécuyer. A. Vilela sees in the phrase *praesbyterium adest quiescens* (*AT* 2) a negative rubric. He asks: "Might this not reflect in some manner the memory of an earlier time when the presbyterium played a decisive role in the ordination of its presiding presbyter?," A. VILELA, *La condition collégiale . . . ,* 345. We should compare this passage with pp. 173–179. In this vein, cf. P. F. BRADSHAW, "The Participation of Other Bishops in the Ordination of a Bishop in the *Apostolic Tradition of Hippolytus,*" in E. A. LIVINGSTONE (ed.), *Studia Patristica,* XVIII, 2. Papers of the 1983 Oxford Patristics Conference. Critica, Classica, Ascetica, Liturgica (Kalamazoo, Mich./Louvain: Cistercian Publications/Peeters Press, 1989) 335–338.

Even though the local community does not impose hands, it joins with the bishops present in participating in the epiclesis, the central prayer; the Latin (L) and the Sahidic, Arabic, and Ethiopian versions (SAE) of the *AT* all indicate that *all* remain silent, praying in their hearts for the descent of the Spirit.[59] This fact is not without significance: in the first place, it means that the act of ordination is the work of all; but just as in the Eucharist all celebrate while only one presides, so it is in the celebration of ordination.[60] Secondly, the imposition of hands accompanied by an epiclesis of the liturgical assembly signifies that the bishops are the ministers of the Spirit in the communion of the Church. Thirdly, each bishop witnesses to the apostolic faith of the Church in which the ordination takes place; by his participation in the ordination, he also receives the new bishop as a guarantor of apostolic faith; as H.-M. Legrand states: "In this circumstance, the Churches are partners in witnessing to the apostolic faith in which their communion is expressed."[61]

AT 2 ends with a second imposition of hands: "Then one of the bishops present shall, at the request of all, impose his hand on the one who is being ordained bishop, and shall pray thus, saying: . . ." Assuredly, the gesture of imposing hands in itself has many meanings, whether in the Old Testament or in the New Testament.

In the Old Testament, the imposition of hands signified either a

[59]Here is the text of the *AT* 2: L: Omnes autem silentium habeant orantes in corde propter discensionem spiritus; SAE: Presbyteri stabunt et illi omnes silebunt et orabunt in corde suo ut descendat spiritus sanctus super eum.

[60]Cf. H.-M. LEGRAND, "La réalisation de l'Eglise . . . ," 199. Several times he points to this fact: for example, id., "Le développement d'églises-sujets: une requête de Vatican II—fondements théologiques et réflexions institutionnelles," in G. ALBERIGO (ed.), *Les églises après Vatican II: dynamisme et prospective* (Paris: Beauchesne, 1981) 159–169. Concerning the Eucharistic and sacramental dynamic: "all celebrate, but only one presides" in the tradition of the early Church, see LEGRAND., "The Presidency . . . ," 432–438.

[61]H.-M. LEGRAND, "La réalisation de l'Eglise . . ." See also the conclusions of J. Lécuyer concerning the relationship between "order" and "apostolicity of the mission of the Church": "1) the episcopal body is therefore always a body of witnesses . . . and 2) he (the bishop) receives the deposit of the New Law in a special way which distinguishes him from the simple confirmed: he is its witness, the official representative . . . ," J. LECUYER, "Mystère de la Pentecôte et apostolicité de la mission de l'Eglise," in B. BOTTE, A. GELIN, J. SCHMITT, et al., *Etudes sur le sacrement de l'Ordre* (Paris: Cerf, 1957) 201–208.

private or a liturgical blessing, or the consecration of victims or levites, or yet again investiture to carry out a determined function.

In the New Testament we find that this gesture exhibits a continuity of meaning with the Old Testament: Jesus blessed, healed, and freed through the imposition of hands (e.g., Mk 8:23, 25; 10:16; Mt 19:13; Lk 4:40; 13:13; etc.). We also see the disciples of Jesus using the same gesture (Acts 5:12; 9:12; Mk 16:18; 1 Tim 4:14; etc.).[62] In the New Testament, outside of the Gospels, the use of the gesture of the imposition of hands is related to service in the community or the designation of ministers. The following observations can be made: 1) It is difficult to conclude from the New Testament texts alone (Acts 6:6; 13:3; 1 Tim 4:14; 5:22; 2 Tim 1:6)[63] that this was a fixed and stable rite;

[62]Among the works which study this gesture and its usage, consult the following: J. COPPENS, *L'imposition des mains et les rites connexes dans le Nouveau Testament et dans l'Eglise ancienne. Etude de théologie positive* (Paris: J. Gabalda, 1925); id., "L'imposition des mains dans les Actes des Apôtres," in J. KREMER (ed.), *Les Actes des Apôtres: traditions, rédaction, théologie* (Gembloux: J. Duculot, 1979) 405–438; F. CABROL, "Impositions des mains," *DACL* 7:1 (1926) cols. 391–413; P. GALTIER, "Imposition des mains," in *Dictionnaire de théologie catholique* (Paris: Letouzey et Ané, 1927) 7:2, cols. 1302–1425; the articles of J.-T. Maertens have great interest for the anthropological and sociological interpretation of the gesture: J.-T. MAERTENS, "Un rite de pouvoir: l'imposition des mains," *Sciences religieuses/Studies in Religion* 6, 6 (1976–1977) 637–649 and 7, 1 (1978) 25–39. Concerning the use of the gesture for ordinations, read J. COPPENS, *L'imposition . . .* ; E. FERGUSON, "Jewish and Christian Ordination: Some Observations," *Harvard Theological Review* 56, 1 (1963) 13–19; id., "Laying on of Hands: Its Significance in Ordination," *JTS* NS 26, 1 (1975) 1–12; G. KRETSCHMAR, "Die Ordination . . . ," 35–69; L. A. HOFFMAN, "Jewish Ordination . . ."; E. J. KILMARTIN, "Ministry and Ordination . . ."; L. LIGIER, "La prière et l'imposition des mains: autour du nouveau Rituel romain de la Confirmation," *Gregorianum* 53, 3 (1972) 407–484, in particular 419–427; M. PATERNOSTER, *L'imposizione delle mani nella Chiesa primitiva* (Rome: Ed. liturgiche, 1977); C. H. TURNER, "*Cheirotonia, cheirothesia, 'epithesis cheirôn* (and the Accompanying Verbs)," *JTS* 24, 96 (1923) 496–504; C. VOGEL, *Ordinations . . .* , [69]–[132]; [149]–[162]; [197]–[225]; E. LOHSE, *Die Ordination im Spätjudentum und im Neuen Testament* (Göttingen: Vandenhoeck und Ruprecht, 1951; O. BÂRLEA, *Die Weihe . . .* ; P. F. BRADSHAW, *Ordination Rites . . .* , passim; J. K. COYLE, "The Laying on of Hands as Conferral of the Spirit: Some Problems and a Possible Solution," in E. A. LIVINGSTONE (ed.), *Studia Patristica*, XVIII: 2, 339–353.

[63]This is the opinion of most of the exegetes. See the following articles which give the opinions of the exegetes: M. MIGUENS, *Church Ministries in New Testament Times* (Arlington, Va.: Christian Culture Press, 1976) 104–108; J. COPPENS,

2) The meaning of this gesture varies: a) Acts 6:6—entrance into community service; b) Acts 13:3—sending on a mission; c) the Pastoral Letters—the necessity of a service to maintain the teaching established by the apostles in all its purity; 3) In all the texts (except 1 Tim 5) there is a link between the gesture meaning the Spirit and the gesture when it signifies the gift of God *(charisma tou theou)*; 4) When it refers to the gift, this latter is never conferred for the sole benefit of the person, but in view of service towards others;[64] and 5) This gesture is always performed in a context of prayer.

Returning now to the context of *AT* 2, it seems that there may have been two impositions of hands (not simultaneous, but successive), and not just one: the first one was performed by all of the bishops present, while the second was performed by one bishop chosen by all. During this last imposition, it was this bishop who recited the prayer.

Several attempts have been made to explain the meaning of this double imposition of hands. Here are the basic different explanations: 1) Some see in the imposition of hands a sign of approval, a consent, a kind of preparation for ordination;[65] 2) For others, this is the most solemn moment, when the gift of the Holy Spirit is given to the ordinand.[66] A third solution has been proposed by W. Rordorf based

---

"L'imposition des mains . . . ," 415–423; R. E. BROWN, *Priest and Bishop;* id., *The Churches* . . . , 31–46, 61–74; and E. J. KILMARTIN, "Ministry and Ordination . . . ," 47–51.

[64]See the commentaries in the exegetical work of P. BONY, E. COTHENET, J. DELORME, et al., *Le ministère* . . . , for example, 104–105, 221, 335–342.

[65]J.-M. HANSSENS, *La liturgie d'Hippolyte* . . . , 114–116; J. COPPENS, *L'imposition des mains* . . . , 145–156; P. de PUNIET, "Consécration épiscopale," *DACL* (1914) 3^2: 2588–2594; CHANOINES REGULIERS DE MONDAYE, "L'évêque, d'après les prières d'ordination," in Y. CONGAR and B.-D. DUPUY (eds.), *L'épiscopat* . . . , 753; M. PATERNOSTER, *L'imposizione* . . . , 6; O. BÂRLEA, *Die Weihe* . . . , 166f. Bârlea, according to Rordorf, has overly schematized the gesture of the imposition of hands, even seeing a tradition of the South joined to a tradition of the North in the text of the *AT*. See the commentaries of A. SANTANTONI, *L'ordinazione episcopale* . . . , 30f; V. RAFFA, "Partecipazione collettiva dei vescovi alla consacrazione episcopale," *EL* 78, 2 (1964) 105–113 and especially note 14, and that of W. RORDORF, "L'ordination de l'évêque . . . ," 145, reprinted in id., *Liturgie*, 131.

[66]W. H. FRERE, "Early Ordination Services," *JTS* 16, 63 (1914/1915) 323ff.; id., "Early Forms of Ordination," in H. B. SWETE (ed.), *Essays on the Early History of the Church and the Ministry* (London: Macmillan, 1918) 275, 278–279; G. DIX,

upon the late Syriac version of the prayer of the *AT* found in the text of the *Testament of Our Lord Jesus Christ*, 21 (fifth century) and in the Arabic collection of the *Canons of Hippolytus*, 2 (second half of the fourth century). Rordorf considers that the phrase which follows the first imposition of hands ("all shall remain silent . . .") is an introduction to the second. For Rordorf, the first imposition of hands occurs in a chain of succession (a collegial action), and the second is an act of consecration (God gives his Spirit).

Rordorf seems here to be too analytical in the face of an ecclesial vision which does not separate one action from another, but which sees the action as one continuous whole. It has already been noted above that the *AT*, and with it the early Church, saw in the election by the people and in the ordination by qualified ministers two aspects of the same liturgical act.[67] This act should be considered in its totality and in its aspect as an act of reception and of tradition in the unity of the Spirit. It is an act of reception because these bishops, witnesses to the faith of their own Churches, receive the elect as a witness to the apostolic faith of his Church and to tradition, the gift of the Spirit being given to the elect by the ministry of the other bishops, while the local Church receives its leader. Cyprian understood this well, and saw in this the judgment of God. This entire dynamic takes place in an epicletic context, that is to say, in the communion of the Holy Spirit.

The imposition of hands is joined to the great prayer of ordination which will be studied later (cf. infra, 3). Suffice it to note here that this prayer invokes the Holy Spirit, praying that he confer a charism on the newly ordained. This is reminiscent of the New Testament, where the imposition of hands is accompanied "by prayers and prophesies" (cf. 1 Tim 4:14; Acts 6:1-6; 13, 1-3).

γ) *Kiss of Peace and the Eucharist.* The rite of ordination is completed with the kiss of peace and the celebration of the Eucharist: "And when he has been made bishop let all salute him with the kiss of peace, because of his having been made worthy. The deacons shall

---

Treatise . . . , 3. For a discussion of these opinions, see J. E. STAM, *Episcopacy* . . . , 19–22; K. RICHTER, "Zum Ritus . . . ," 16–18; A. SANTANTONI, *L'ordinazione episcopale* . . . , 29–31; L. MORTARI, *Consacrazione episcopale* . . . , 28–30.

[67]Cf. supra A, 1, b, conclusions, pp. 26f.; L. MORTARI, *Consacrazione episcopale* . . . , 33–50 and H.-M. LEGRAND, "Theology and the Election . . ."

then bring the offering to him; and he, imposing his hand on it, along with all the presbytery, shall give thanks saying: 'The Lord be with you.' And all shall respond: 'And with your spirit'" *(meta tou pneumatos sou)* *(AT* 4).

Two comments are in order: 1) This kiss of peace (given by *all*) is a sign of the real communion of all the participants: the one being ordained, and his Church (deacons, presbyters and faithful); 2) Just as the act of ordination reveals the faith of the Church, this faith and this *koinōnia* will now be signified in their full import in the Eucharistic celebration, presided over by the one who is the head of this Church. The new bishop, surrounded by the presbyterium and assisted by the deacons, fulfills the first act of his episcopal ministry by presiding at the Eucharist. The words spoken at the beginning of the Eucharistic dialogue are significant and reveal the reality which has just taken place: "The Lord be with you . . . and with your spirit *(kai meta tou pneumatos sou)*." The *ekklesia*, greeted by the new bishop, responds back to him that he has, due to his ordination, a "spirit," that is, a special charism.[68]

Conclusions. From this analysis of the ritual elements a certain vision of the faith of the Church emerges. As L.-M. Chauvet says: "The ritual gestures of the Church are *not simple appendages* that accompany the faith: they constitute *formative elements* of faith." [69]

This vision is sustained by certain concepts which serve also to give structure to the Church. Let us try to identify them:

1) The ordination of a bishop in the *AT* is presented as a liturgical continuum composed of three steps, namely, the *election* (by the people, including the clergy), the *ordination* (by the imposition of hands performed by the bishops), and the *taking of office* (at the moment when it is clearly said that he has become the head of the local community), symbolized by the new bishop's presidency at the Eucharist at the end of the ordination.

[68]Cf. B. BOTTE, "L'Esprit Saint et l'Eglise dans la 'Tradition apostolique' de saint Hippolyte," *Didaskalia* 2, 2 (1972) 221–233; W. C. VAN UNNIK, "*Dominus vobiscum*: The Background of a Liturgical Formula," in A.J.B. HIGGINS (ed.), *New Testament Essays. Studies in Memory of Thomas Walter Manson (1893–1958)* (Manchester: Manchester University Press, 1959) 270–305.

[69]L.-M. CHAUVET, *Du symbolique au symbole. Essai sur les sacrements* (Paris: Cerf, 1979) 85.

2) The context of this entire continuum is that of a Eucharistic celebration (the day of the ordination is the normal day of the Eucharistic gathering); the ordination is completed by the celebration of the first Eucharist of the newly ordained; there the *communio* is visibly realized.

3) In addition, we should note the eschatological aspect proper to the Eucharistic context: there the Church perceives itself as a convocation, emphasizing the eschatological character of the people of God who are convened. The Eucharist is celebrated on Sunday, as we have seen, a day full of eschatological significance. It is also the day when the apostolic kerygma is proclaimed in the midst of the saints convened for the feast of the Lamb. Here we have the synthesis of the historical and eschatological dimensions, the attestation of what is not yet accomplished, but one day will be.

4) The local community (clergy and faithful) is actively engaged in the choice of its leader, and, by this act, the Christians of the locality are witnesses to the faith of the elect and also to his conduct, which must be above reproach. The community is also active at the moment of the epiclesis when "*all* . . . pray in their hearts for the descent of the Spirit." All this demonstrates that faith is the responsibility of the entire local Church.

5) Even though the Christians of the locality are active in the entire ordination process of their leader, they themselves cannot ordain. They need the participation of the other bishops, because the bishop is not alone in the episcopal responsibility which is vested in him. The meaning of the presence of the neighboring bishops is twofold: they receive the elect among them as a colleague chosen to represent the faith of this local Church in their vicinity, and they are the ministers of the gift of the Spirit bestowed by the imposition of their hands. It is not they who make the chosen one a bishop, but the Spirit: the bishops are witnesses to the activity of the Spirit in this Church, and above all they are the ministers of the charism received by the new bishop.

6) The new bishop is received by the local Church as a gift of God given to God's people; this point will become clearer as we examine the ordination prayer.

7) The kiss of peace exchanged by all expresses the way in which the *koinōnia* among the Churches is built up: the bishop being the link

between his community and the others, he is witness not only to the faith of his community, but also to the charity of the community. He represents this reality as well among the other local Churches.

8) The Eucharistic celebration shows clearly the position of the new bishop: he finds himself both *in relationship to* and at the same time *among* his co-Christians. The physical aspects of the celebration indicate this clearly: at the head of his people, the bishop presides, while all celebrate the Eucharist.

9) The new bishop is in a position of reception; he receives the gift of God, which is both charism and vocation. Again, we note the activity of the Spirit in the process, choosing the elect and equipping him for his ministry.

10) In conclusion, we note that this entire process is truly ecclesial through its *communal* dimension, because the whole Church is involved; it is *liturgical,* because it is composed of the symbolic linking with the past of the imposition of hands accompanied by an epiclesis; and lastly, it is *juridical,* because the new bishop takes office concretely through this process: an office which concerns the local and the universal (catholic) Church.

b. *Presbyter*

In comparing the ordination of presbyters to that of the bishop in the *AT*, one notes immediately the simplicity and soberness of the former: "When a presbyter is to be ordained, the bishop shall impose his hand upon his head, while the presbyters likewise touch him and let it be done as indicated before in the ordination of a bishop, praying and saying: . . ." (followed by the ordination prayer) (*AT* 7).

α) *Election.* The *AT* does not give instructions concerning the election of presbyters. In section 8, we note that a deacon is chosen *(eligatur* or *qui electus est)* "after the fashion of those things said above." It is not very clear how the bishop and the deacon are elected, and the author of the *AT* does not provide any clearer explanations concerning the election of presbyters. As we saw with Cyprian, it seems that the participation of the people in their selection may have lasted for a long time (cf. supra, pp. 21ff.).[70]

---

[70]Cyprian is not alone in mentioning the role of the people: already in the early Church one can see traces of this element in the directives given by Paul for the choice of presbyters (1 Tim 3:2; Titus 1:6f.). Here he speaks of "a good

β) *Imposition of Hands.*[5] In the ordination of a presbyter, the principal actors are four: the local bishop, the presbyterium, the chosen one, and the Holy Spirit.

It is the bishop who imposes hands upon the elect, because he is the minister of the gift of God (see above, the prayer of episcopal ordination). Nevertheless, he does not perform this gesture alone: the presbyterium does it with him.

In order to understand the meaning of this collective gesture, we must read what is said regarding the ordination of a deacon:

"In the ordaining of a deacon, this is the reason why the bishop alone is to impose his hands upon him: he is not ordained to the priesthood, but to serve the bishop and to fulfill the bishop's command. He has no part in the council of the clergy, but is to attend to his own duties and is to acquaint the bishop with such matters as are needful. He does not receive that Spirit which the presbytery possesses and in which the presbyters share. He receives only what is entrusted to him under the authority of the bishop. For this reason the bishop alone shall ordain a deacon. On a presbyter, however, let the presbyters impose their hands because of the common and like Spirit of the clergy. Even so, the presbyter has only the power to receive, and has not the power to give. That is why a presbyter does not ordain the clergy; for at the ordaining of a presbyter, he but seals while the bishop ordains" (followed by the ordination prayer) (*AT* 8).

It is clear that the other presbyters impose their hands because they possess in common the same Spirit, and they share the same ministerial charism. The presbyters are members of the "council of the clergy" *(consilii in clero* or *consiliarius [symboulos] totius cleri [klēros])*. Here we encounter a collegial reality. But the *AT* is also clear about the limits of power of the presbyters, namely, that the presbyter has only the power to receive, not the power to give: it is the bishop alone who ordains both presbyters and deacons. This reinforces what has already been said concerning the bishop as the minister of the

---

witness," which seems to indicate the consultation of the community. The *Didachē* 15, 1 knows of election by the assembly, and *1 Clement* 44, 3 attests to the approval of the Church before the installation of presbyters. Cf. J. DELORME, "Diversité et unité des ministères d'après le Nouveau Testament," in P. BONY, E. COTHENET, J. DELORME, et al., *Le ministère . . .* , 340–341. See also A. JILEK, *Initiationsfeier . . .* , 40.

gift of God. This will become more evident in our examination of the ordination prayer.

In comparing the two texts (*AT* 7 and 8) with another text dealing with the institution of widows (*AT* 10), a clear distinction appears in the terminology. In section 10 we read:

"When a widow is appointed (*instituitur/kathistasthai*), she is not ordained (*non ordinatur/cheirotonein*), but is chosen by name (*eligitur*) . . . A widow shall be appointed by word only (*instituatur/kathistasthai*), and shall join the rest. But hands shall not be laid on her (*non autem imponetur manus*), because she does not offer the offering (*non offert oblationem/prosphora*), nor has she a liturgical duty (*liturgiam/leitourgia*). Ordination (*cheirotonia*) is for the clergy (*clero/klēros*), on account of their liturgical duties (*propter liturgiam/leitourgia*); but a widow is appointed (*instuitur/kathistasthai*) for prayer which belongs to all."

There is therefore a clear distinction between ordination and installation. The difference resides in the fact that the clerics (bishop, presbyter and deacon) receive a charism, a special grace for a function which is not common to all. This function for the bishop and the presbyter is the pastoral ministry, which includes the building up and the presidency of the community. As for the deacon, his function is the service of the bishop, of the community, and of the altar. The ordination prayers confer the content of the special charism. We note that neither widows (*AT* 10), lectors (*AT* 11), virgins (*AT* 12), nor subdeacons (*AT* 13) receive the imposition of hands (*cheirotonia*); they are merely installed (*kathistasthai*). They do not receive, therefore, a special gift of the Spirit.[71]

According to *AT* 7, the presbyters form a *consilium* or a senate of which one becomes a member through the imposition of hands and

---

[71]On the question of technical terminology found here and there in the oriental documents, see C. VOGEL, "Chirotonie . . . ," 7–21, 207–238, reprinted in id., *Ordinations . . . ,* [69]–[116]; id., "L'imposition des mains . . . ," 57–72, reprinted in *Ordinations . . . ,* [117]–[132]; L. MORTARI, *Consacrazione episcopale . . . ,* 33–55. E. Schillebeeckx presents the same material but with a more ecclesiological than factual interpretation, see E. SCHILLEBEECKX, *Ministry: Leadership in the Community of Jesus Christ*, trans. from Dutch [*Kerkelijk ambt: Voorgangers in de gemeente van Jezus Christus*] by John Bowden (New York: Crossroads, 1981) 46–48; id., *The Church with a Human Face*, trans. from Dutch [*Pleidooi voor Mensen in de Kerk*] by John Bowden (New York: Crossroads, 1985) 138–140.

the epiclesis conferring the Holy Spirit common to the presbyterium. This explains why the other presbyters impose hands with the bishop.

These presbyters (as distinct from the deacons) share a specific ministry which is described in priestly terms. The texts clearly say (*AT* 10, 8) that the presbyters "offer an oblation" (for which reason they have received the imposition of hands) and that they are ordained for the priesthood (which is why the other presbyters also impose their hands).[72] The difference between bishop and presbyter is clarified in the *AT* when it explains that the presbyter "has only the power to receive and has not the power to give" (*AT* 8). B. Botte explains that this text is speaking of the differing ecclesiastical responsibilities, that is, that the presbyter can receive the Spirit, but not confer it.[73]

The role of the bishop in all this is clear: he is the head of the local Church, the minister of the gift of the Spirit, bound closely to the presbyterium, and he presides at the distribution of ministries within the community. It is he alone who ordains the presbyters and the deacons.

The role of the presbyters is to sit in council around the bishop (*AT* 4, 7, 8) and to offer oblation in liturgical service with the bishop who presides over the presbyterium, and to share in the sacerdotal ministry of the bishop.

The relationships between bishop, presbyter and community merit examination. The bishop and the presbyter, because of the gift they have received, occupy a special place at the heart of the community. They find themselves now facing the people at the same time that they serve them as their brothers and sisters: all the liturgical celebrations show this clearly (cf. *AT* 2–4, 7, 21–22, 26). It is through the gift of God which they have received that they find themselves at the head of the people, without ever having been separated from them. Through receiving this gift they receive a new status within the community.[74] According to the text, inasmuch as the presbyterium exists

[72]Cf. B. BOTTE, "L'ordre d'après les prières d'ordination," in B.BOTTE, A. GELIN, J. SCHMITT, et al., *Etudes sur le sacrement* . . . , 15f.

[73]B. BOTTE, *La Tradition Apostolique* . . . , 25, n. 7.

[74]L.-M. Chauvet speaks of this status in terms of "a recognition of a new relationship of rank between the bishop, the ordinand and the community which is becoming established, a relationship which itself is founded on the recognition of the *original* dependence of all people on God": L.-M. CHAUVET, *Du symbolique* . . . , 138.

for the service of the community through its role in the council with the bishop, there is not separation but rather collaboration between the different elements of the community. (No division exists between them such as is later expressed in the distinction between clergy and laity.) This unity between the ministers and the community is a fundamental truth in the Church. The link between the presbyter and the bishop to the concrete community is clearly shown.[75]

γ) *Admission of Confessors to the Ordained Ministry* (*AT* 9). The formal link between the ministers and the community is also present when it is a question of the reception of a confessor as a minister in the *Apostolic Tradition* (*AT* 9).[76]

---

[75]This balanced vision will not be able to maintain itself. The Church later will need to make pronouncements on the necessity of the link of the presbyter and of the deacon to a concrete community; this will be formalized especially in canon 6 of the Council of Chalcedon (451) from which comes the adage "There is no presbyter without service in an urban church, cemetery, or monastic church." Cf. infra, II and the article of C. VOGEL, "Titre d'ordination et lien du presbytre à la communauté locale dans l'Eglise ancienne," *LMD* 115 (1973) 70–85, reprinted in id., *Ordinations . . .* , [133]–[148]. As for the bishop, see Cyprian, *Ep.* 66, 8 ("the bishop is in the Church and the Church in the bishop") and canon 18 of the Council of Ancyra (314) which stipulates that a bishop who is not accepted must be content to remain in the ranks of presbyter.

[76]For the text of subsequent canonical prescription (Coptic [can. 34], Arabic [can. 24] and Ethiopian [can. 24]), see C. VOGEL, "Le ministre charismatique de l'Eucharistie. Approche rituelle," in P. GRELOT, J. DUPONT, P.-R. TRAGAN, et al., *Ministères et célébration de l'Eucharistie* (Rome: Ed. Anselmiana, 1973) 191–195, reprinted in C. VOGEL, *Ordinations . . .* , [207]–[211].

The texts derived from the *AT* present some modifications. Thus the *Canons of Hippolytus* (336–340, Arabic) add a precise detail in canon 6: "If someone's slave has endured punishment because of Christ, he is thus a presbyter of the flock: even though he has not received the mark of the priesthood, he has nevertheless received the Spirit of priesthood. The bishop will therefore omit the part of the prayer which refers to the Holy Spirit.". Here the distinction between martyr/freeman and martyr/slave is at stake. We see the same type of distinction in the *Testament of Our Lord* (450–500); this time the distinction is made between the confessor and the martyr: "In view of the diaconate and even the presbyterate, hands shall not be imposed on one who proves or declares to have been in chains, imprisoned or tortured because of the name of the Lord. In fact, he already has the dignity of the clergy, having been protected by the hand of God in his confession. . . . If it is a matter of a confessor who has not been dragged before the authorities and not been in chains, but simply confessed his faith, he will be made worthy (of the presbyterate) by the imposition of hands

"If a confessor has been in chains for the name of the Lord, hands are not imposed on him for the diaconate or presbyterate; for he has the honor of the presbyterate by the fact of his confession. But if he is to be ordained a bishop *(instituitur/ kathistasthai)*, hands are to be imposed upon him *(imponetur ei manus)*. If, however, he is a confessor who was not summoned before the authorities and was not punished in chains and was not imprisoned, but was offered private and passing indignity for the name of the Lord, even though he confessed, hands are to be imposed upon him *(imponatur manus super eum)* for every office of which he is worthy."

In the three other versions, the author established a distinction between a "martyr," who truly suffered, and a "confessor," who was only subjected to annoyances. But the fact that hands may not be imposed upon him in view of the presbyteral or diaconal ministry is the most salient point. Vogel has already noted the importance of the confessor in the paleochristian conception. He saw a connection between the imposition of hands and the possession of the Holy Spirit: "the martyr . . . is the perfect imitator of Christ; . . . he is filled with

---

and the prayer of ordination. Moreover, the bishop will not recite the whole prayer when he prays over him; as the bishop continues the prayer, the confessor receives the full effect of ordination" (canon 39).

Lastly, in the *Apostolic Constitutions* (ca. 380) a different tradition is presented:

"A confessor is not ordained; for he is so by choice and patience, and is worthy of great honor *[timē]*, as having confessed the name of God, and of His Christ, before nations and kings [Acts 9:15}. But if there be occasion, he is to be ordained *[cheirotonein]* either a bishop, priest, or deacon. But if any one of the confessors who is not ordained snatches to himself any such dignity upon account of his confession, let the same person be deprived and rejected" (VIII, 23, 2–4). These texts are reproduced and commented upon by C. VOGEL, "Le ministre charismatique . . . ," 195–198, reprinted in id., *Ordinations . . . ,* [211]–[214].

One will note the power of the bishops in the regulation of their entrance into the ministry; one can attribute this to the difficulties encountered in the communities at this time. Nevertheless, in this collection of texts we note that in the early Church the "charismatic" ministry had existed for a long time; this tradition goes back to the New Testament. [On this subject, see M. LODS, *Confesseurs et martyrs, successeurs des prophètes dans l'Eglise des trois premiers siècles* (Neuchâtel/Paris: Delachaux et Niestlé, 1958) which shows the line of development; cf. also E. COTHENET, "Prophétisme et ministère d'après le Nouveau Testament," *LMD* 107 (1971) 29–50].

the Spirit. A bestowal did not take place since the martyr was already in possession of the Holy Spirit."[77]

The ecclesial reception is decisive here. In this case, the imposition of hands as the means of ecclesial mediation is relativized: we know that the confessors could be called to sit in the presbyterium without any imposition of hands;[78] this demonstrates that the ministerial charge is linked to a concrete community, who had the right to receive the charism possessed by the confessor, and this outside the "uninterrupted chain of the imposition of hands."[79]

[77]C. VOGEL, Le ministre charismatique . . . , 194f. (=[210]f.). It is also interesting to note the application of the concept of "martyr" to the ministry of the Word as seen in B. COOKE, *Ministry to Word and Sacraments. History and Theology* (Philadelphia: Fortress Press, 1976) 60, 64, 235 and 544.

[78]Cf. E. SCHILLEBEECKX, *Ministry* . . . , 45–56, who shares the opinion of C. Vogel concerning the question of the necessity of the acceptance of the Church in ministerial matters. Opposing Schillebeeckx and Vogel, Lécuyer, basing himself on the commentary of B. Botte, believes that a true ministerial charge is not implied in the case of the confessors (*AT* 9). See the argumentation of J. LECUYER in *Le sacrement de l'ordination* . . . , 41–43. It seems to us that H.-M. Legrand goes farther in his analysis of the case of confessors. It is worthwhile to mention his argumentation:

"The implications of this text [he is referring to canon 6 of the *Canons of Hippolytus*] seem clear, for [1] in antiquity, a slave was never ordained; [2] it is not a matter of bestowing on him an honory position in the assembly, for it is expressly stated that he is "presbyter for the flock"; [3] he could thus be led to preside at the Eucharist without having received the imposition of hands (parallel canons), for in certain regions, the presbyter could be brought to preside at the Eucharist apart from the bishop (Africa, Asia, Rome) a presbyter could be led to preside at the Eucharist apart from the bishop. Although we have little proof of the effective force of these canonical dispositions, their spirit is not at all surprising, for confessors and martyrs are, very precisely, the successors of the prophets and teachers, whom we have already seen preside at the Eucharist (Acts 13: 1–2; *Didachē*). Note, finally, that this Christian is not an ordinary Christian: his presbyteral ministry is accepted as such, even if he has not acceded to it through ordination." Cf. H.-M. LEGRAND, "The Presidency . . . ," 426f.

[79]H.-M. Legrand has noted that in the case of *AT* 9, there is no opposition between ordained ministry and charism. We read there rather "the conviction that the ordained ministries of priest and deacon belong to the charismatic order and that it is sufficient, in this particular case, that they be accepted by the *ecclesia* (an acceptance whose basis is itself also pneumatological)." Some biblical evidence, notably 1 Cor 12:28 (the ministries of government are among the charisms) and 2 Tim 1:6 (ordination bestows a gift of the Spirit) demonstrates the absence of any

Conclusions. Before going on to a more detailed analysis of the ordination prayers, let us attempt to draw some conclusions from our study of the structure of the process of admission to the presbyterate in the *Apostolic Tradition.*

1) The most striking fact is the collegial aspect of the presbyterium. The presbyter is never seen alone. He is always *in* the presbyterium (*AT* 7 and 8).

2) Even though the presbyters together impose hands on the ordinand, this imposition of hands is not considered identical to that conferred by the neighboring bishops during episcopal ordination, because the presbyters can receive the "common spirit" but they cannot give it (*AT* 8). On the other hand, this demonstrates clearly that the bishops are the ministers of the gift of the Spirit. This is seen above all in episcopal ordination (the college of bishops is enlarged because the ordinand has received the Spirit who is common to them), and later in the fact that the bishop alone can ordain other ministers *(cheirotonia)* in his own community (*AT* 8).

3) The newly ordained enters into his pastoral office from the moment that he enters into the presbyterium (through the imposition of hands and prayer). This presbyterium functions as senate or council.

4) The presbyter is ordained to the priesthood in order to help the bishop accomplish his pastoral office (cf. *AT* 8, 3), to offer the oblation, and in view of liturgical service (*AT* 10).

5) As in the case of the bishop, we note that this procedure is truly *ecclesial* in its communal dimension; it is *liturgical,* because the ordination takes place during the liturgical assembly; and it is at the same time *juridical,* because the newly ordained assumes his concrete responsibility from the moment that he enters into the presbyterium.

EXCURSUS: DEACON

In the early Church, deacons collaborated directly with the bishops. They had a specific ministry and their own role. The present study envisages only the essential and fundamental functions of the episcopal and presbyteral ministries, that is, the *episkopē.* This minis-

---

opposition between charism and function. See H.-M. LEGRAND, "La réalisation de l'Eglise . . . ," 213–214 [the quotation is taken from p. 214].

try is a function of responsibility within the communion and in the life of the local Churches. In short, it is the overseeing of the growth of each community in truth and in faithfulness to apostolic teaching. Nonetheless, one cannot relegate the diaconate to the shadows, because for the *Apostolic Tradition* the three ordained ministries form a whole in the service of the community. Moreover, we can better grasp the specific character of the ordained ministry as a charism and as an office by studying the specific dimension of the diaconate.

1. ELECTION*7

In the rubric of the *AT* 8 we read: "When a deacon is to be ordained he is chosen after the fashion of those things said above, the bishop alone in like manner imposing his hands upon him as we have prescribed." The election of the deacon is therefore similar to that of the bishop, excluding the intervention of the neighboring bishops.[80] This only confirms that Christians of the local Church had the right to select their ministers. Nonetheless, as we have already seen, election does not mean ordination, which requires the participation of many wills, the will of the Christians of the locality, and the will of those who are already in the ministry. This fact demonstrates the solidarity of Christians in their responsibility for the life of faith in the Church, as well as the multiplicity of services in the Church springing from the diversity of the gifts of the Spirit.

Even though the text does not say explicitly that the ordination of deacons took place during the Eucharistic celebration, we should presume a Eucharistic context, following what we have seen in the case of episcopal ordination, because ordination implies that the ordinand is ordained in the liturgical context in which his ministry will be exercised (see infra, pp. 78ff.).

2. IMPOSITION OF HANDS*7

"In the ordaining of a deacon, this is the reason why the bishop alone is to impose his hands upon him: he is not ordained to the priesthood, but to serve the bishop and to fulfill the bishop's command."

Again we note the role of the presidential ministry of the bishop. The bishop is clearly the head of the community. In the context of

[80]*AT* 2: "Let him be ordained bishop who has been chosen by all the people": Cf. A. JILEK, *Initiationsfeier . . .* , 58–62.

presbyteral ordination, we have already studied the meaning of this imposition of hands. The text says that the deacon does not belong to the council of the clergy, and that he is not ordained to the priesthood. The *Apostolic Tradition* underscores the place of service which belongs to the deacon: "he is ordained to serve the bishop . . ." This text reveals the direct relationship between the bishop and the deacon which challenges our overly hierarchical conception today— bishop, priest and deacon—the deacon seen as an assistant to the priest.

Furthermore, the ministerial unity between the episcopacy and the presbyterate is affirmed: one can "consider the presbyterate as being a prolongation of the episcopacy, of which it shares at its own level the function . . . of presiding."[81] The diaconate in turn is seen in the light of a different rationale, that of the building up of the Church through service. This can be clearly seen as we examine the prayer which accompanies the imposition of hands (infra 3, c).

The *Apostolic Tradition* speaks of the liturgical functions of each ordained ministry. The bishop and the presbyter offer oblation, and the deacon has a liturgical task which consists of carrying to the altar the bread and the wine (*AT* 4, 8, 21), breaking the Eucharistic bread (*AT* 22), and administering communion by the chalice (*AT* 21, 22). Elsewhere we note that the deacon's ministry in daily life corresponds to his role in liturgical service (cf. *AT* 24, 25, 28, 34 and 39), but always under the authority of the bishop. It is in serving his brethren that he is the minister of Christ, and it is in this light that the Church, in the time of Hippolytus, understood diaconal ministry as a charism for serving the community as a sign of Christ who was sent to serve in obedience the will of God and to show us the divine plan of salvation.

Conclusions. The analysis of the elements of the process of admission to the diaconate sheds light on a number of points important for our

---

[81]H.-M. LEGRAND, "La réalisation de l'Eglise . . . ," 202. In this passage the author is not interested directly in *AT* 8 but rather in the distinctions and similarities between the presbyterate and the episcopacy. See also the remarks of A. JILEK, *Initiationsfeier* . . . , 66–72, and id., "Bischof und Presbyterium. Zur Beziehung zwischen Episkopat und Presbyterat im Lichte der Traditio Apostolica Hippolyts," *ZKT* 106, 4 (1984) 394f.

understanding of the structure of the Church at the time of the *Apostolic Tradition*. Let us try to identify them:

1) As for the episcopacy and the presbyterate, the liturgy of ordination of a deacon is conceived of as a continuum composed of three stages: the election, the ordination (through the imposition of hands conferred by the bishop alone, and the epiclesis) and *the taking of office*.

2) The concurrence of several persons is required for the ordination of a deacon: that of the local Church (seen in the election of the deacon), and that of the bishop, who imposes hands upon him. This fact reinforces a point we have already noted: election does not signify ordination, and this participation of many wills in the context of the gathering of local Christians brings out the important role played by the Holy Spirit, a role that we see in the choice of the ordinand and in the epiclesis in which one prays that the Holy Spirit may give the Church this minister for the building up of the Body of Christ.

3) The ministry of the deacon is in relation to the bishop, for the service of the local Church. The diaconate is not conceived of in terms of presbyteral ministry; in effect he does not belong to the senate of clergy, but he is directly responsible to the bishop. The rubric is quite clear concerning the relationship between bishop and deacon: the deacon receives the imposition of hands from the bishop *alone* ". . . to fulfill the bishop's command" (*AT* 8). In the same rubric we see that the deacons and the presbyters are both in an immediate relationship to the bishop, because the deacon does not belong to the presbyterium; he does not receive the common spirit, the bishop alone ordains the deacon, and the deacon tells the bishop what is needed; the presbyters are ordained by the bishop but the other presbyters also impose hands (*AT* 8), and the ministry of the bishop and of the presbyter is qualified as priestly. The meaning, therefore, of this rubric reserving to the bishop the imposition of hands and forbidding it to the priests is that the deacon is in the direct service of the bishop. This means that the deacon, while being of a lower rank than the priests, is not their auxiliary.

4) Throughout this entire document the principal category of diaconal ministry is *service*, whether in the liturgy or in daily ecclesial life. The specific nature of this ministry resides in the fact that the diaconate joins the service of the brethren to that of the altar; this

articulation expresses one extremely important meaning of the Eucharistic reality.

3. ORDINATION PRAYERS

As we have already noted above, the entire procedure of election, imposition of hands and assumption of office constitutes a liturgical continuum, and these three stages should not be opposed one to the other. It is only in order to facilitate our analysis that we have separated the ordination prayer from its proper place in the entirety of the liturgical action. In the thought of the author of the *Apostolic Tradition*, this prayer and the imposition of hands constitute a whole in both episcopal and presbyteral ordinations.

Because the *Apostolic Tradition* has had such a great influence on the other prayers of epiclesis in the Churches of both East and West (especially in the prayer of episcopal ordination), this latter will be discussed in particular detail.

a. *Bishop*[*2-*3]

The prayer is divided into several parts according to the tense of the verbs used: the present, and the past (that is, verbs and participles in the aorist tense in Greek).[82] These different parts, separated in the beginning, come together in the middle of the prayer. The following is a detailed examination:

The first part is in the present tense, the "eternal present" of the "God and Father of Our Lord Jesus Christ" who sees and knows all things, because he is at the beginning of all.

Next follows, at the beginning of the second section, a series of verbs in the aorist tense whose function is one of anamnesis, linked to the wisdom of God which is revealed in the history of salvation, past, present, and future. What is the activity in history of this God who lives "in the highest heavens"? He intervenes through "the word of his grace" (*dia logou charitos sou*—cf. Acts 20:32) to establish

---

[82]Without accepting all of his interpretations, we borrow this excerpt of the ordination prayer found in the *AT* from C. J. PINTO DE OLIVEIRA, "Signification sacerdotale du ministère de l'évêque dans la Tradition Apostolique d'Hippolyte de Rome," *Freiburger Zeitschrift für Philosophie und Theologie*, 25, 3 (1978) 398–427. See also the studies of the CHANOINES REGULIERS DE MONDAYE, "L'évêque, d'après . . . ," 742–744 and 768; A. JILEK, *Initiationsfeier* . . . , 7–37; id., "Bischof . . . ," 376–391.

the boundaries *(horous)* of his Church (those who are called—*ek kaleō*),[83] to predestine "the race of the just of Abraham," to establish "leaders and priests" *(archontas . . . hiereis katastēsas)*; God's faithfulness to his promises is thus made manifest because he never leaves his sanctuary without service *(aleitourgēton)*. All of this is centered on God who is glorified in all his work. In this section we find a clear anamnesis of the election of the people of God and the care that God takes of them. We must also note that the whole movement of this passage tends, on the one hand, to make what has gone out from God return to God in glory, and, on the other hand, to bring out the eschatological aspect of the prayer with movement from eternity to eternity. With the intervention of God in history, a true irruption of the eschaton is made manifest in time. We note that the verb "to establish" *(kathistēmi/ constituere)* emphasizes the act of God giving the people ministers (cf. Heb 5:1; the apostles also appoint ministers: Acts 6:3 and Titus 1:5). And with this the second part ends.

The third part of the prayer begins with the abrupt phrase, "and now," which does not refer to the present tense of the first section (the "eternal" present) nor to the past tense of the second section. It is clear that we are in the present *(kai nyn)*; we have here a prayer of petition. The intervention of God in history which is happening now ("now let your power which comes from you extend . . .") is not exactly the same as we saw before (in "through the word of your grace . . ."), yet it is not something totally different either (it is the extension of the action of God through time). The request for the power

---

[83]Cf. G. KRETSCHMAR, "Die Ordination . . . ," 44. The author distances himself from B. Botte on the interpretation of the term *horos*. Botte thought that the *horoi* were the rules of the Church (cf. *AT* 3). Kretschmar believes that "these 'horoi' were not simply rules, but the lines of demarcation between the different levels of ordination, corresponding to the charisms of the Old Testament, and between the particular communities (cf. Apostolic Canons, 36)." The interpretation of C. J. PINTO DE OLIVEIRA, "Signification sacerdotale . . . ," 407 approaches the same view. Moreover, the expression *dia logou charitos sou* seems to have been borrowed from Acts 20:32, where "his message (of God) is able to build up" [the Church]. This phrase takes on new meaning in the context of the ordination prayer where the bishop receives the grace necessary for a pastor/leader—"a message that is able to build you up and to give you the inheritance among all who are sanctified" (Acts 20:32). Cf. also A. JILEK, *Initiationsfeier . . . ,* 16; id., "Bischof . . . ," 379.

which comes from God, the sovereign Spirit *(tou hēgemonikou pneumatos)* does not mean explicitly here that the Spirit is sent down upon the one to be ordained. It is for this reason that a question mark is placed on the chart (see Chart II. 1, vol. IV). We recall that, according to *AT* 2, one of the bishops imposes hands on the head of the ordinand while reciting this prayer. After this phrase a series of verbs in the past tense appears again: God gave the Spirit to Jesus Christ who gave it to the apostles, who have established the Church in every place. In any case, the schema here is clearly from the New Testament. First of all, the power of the Spirit is given to the Son for his messianic and prophetic mission (one is reminded of the episodes of the baptism in the Jordan, the temptation of Jesus and the beginning of his ministry in Galilee [Luke 4:14—*kai hypestrepsen ho Iēsous en tē dynamei tou pneumatos eis tēn Galilaian*—then Jesus, *filled with the power of the Spirit*, returns to Galilee]). Secondly, this power is transmitted by Christ to the apostles for their evangelical mission (the scene of Pentecost itself and its foretelling by Christ in Acts 1:8—*alla lēmpsesthe dynamin epelthontos tou hagiou pneumatos eph' hymas, kai esesthe mou martyres*—but you will receive *power when my Holy Spirit* has come upon you; and you will be my witnesses).

What is this Church, and for what purpose was it founded? It is the Church in every place *(kata topon, per singula loca)*, the true sanctuary of God; it is founded for the glory and the praise of God's name. It is here that we rejoin the structure of the first part of the prayer, in which the word is the means which God uses to intervene with his people and to establish them. In the second part we have a different intervention, this time the power of God, that is, the Spirit, intervening but still for the sake of the people of God who, as in the first case, are destined to glorify God. Here it is not directly a question of service in the sanctuary, but rather the establishment of the Church as the place of the glorification of God (doxology). Within the Church the new bishop will serve the people and help them give glory to God. So this intervention is centered on God, as in the first case. This action of the Spirit in the Church makes of the *ecclesia* the temple of the Holy Spirit.

This power is specified with a second request,[*3] for the sovereign Spirit, the directing principle.[84] It is this Spirit who is invoked for the

[84]Thus B. BOTTE, "L'ordre d'après . . . ," 14f.; similarly, cf. J. LECUYER,

one who is be ordained bishop, because he must tend the flock, exercise the high priesthood, and above all build up the Church, in which God is praised and glorified.

In the passage which follows, once more all the verbs are in the present tense. Here we do not have a request to send the Spirit, but an appeal to the Father himself, that he might grant pastoral qualities to the one he has chosen for the episcopacy. In this way, within his Church, God appoints someone to watch over it *(episkopeō)*, always in view of the service of God. The choice is always in the context of a judgment that God has made for his people, in keeping with the wisdom and providence he showed at the time of the replacement of Judas (cf. Acts 1:24ff. where the Church calls upon the judgment of God who "knows the hearts of all" and where Matthias is called to the apostolic college by the choice of God).

The functions of the new bishop are listed in two categories: firstly, those which show the purpose of God for his people within the continuity of the history of salvation: for example, tending the flock, exercising the sovereign priesthood by serving God, making propitious the face of God, and offering the gifts of God's people (the Church); secondly, the functions which enter into history as new events stemming precisely from a second intervention of God, namely, that of the Spirit and of Jesus Christ ("in virtue of the Spirit of the sovereign priesthood"). These last functions are even more determinative in the context of the New Testament, whether in the commandment, ordination, or the power given by God to the apostles.

As we consider the terms "sovereign priesthood" *(archierateuein)* and "service" *(leitourgounta)*, it is important to note a certain parallelism with the first anamnesis. In the first instance, God appointed the leaders and the priests *(archontas* and *hiereis)*, not allowing his sanctuary to be without service *(aleitourgēton)*. In the second case, we pray to the Father for the bishop (head and priest of the new covenant in the Church), that he might exercise the sovereign priesthood *(archierateuein,* active present tense) in serving *(leitourgounta)* God through the fulfillment of certain tasks corresponding to his office. This is expressed explicitly within this same passage, where the term "sovereign priesthood" appears for a second time, but this time

"Episcopat et presbytérat dans les écrits d'Hippolyte de Rome," *RechSR* 41, 1 (1953) 30–50; A. JILEK, *Initiationsfeier . . .* , 18–22.

it is the "Spirit of the sovereign priesthood" upon whom the three decisive functions depend, namely, the forgiveness of sins, the distribution of ministries, and the power to undo all bonds; it is not a power *(exousia)* which belongs to the person of the bishop, but rather one which is subordinated to the Spirit. This priesthood is therefore a charism given to the new bishop, an explicit charism for the accomplishment of his responsibilites, without reproach.[85]

Lastly, we see a present and timely intervention of God in history, which returns to God. Indeed, the new bishop is at the head of this Church precisely to please God "by offering up a pleasant perfume" through Jesus Christ, through whom all glory and praise rise up to God, with the Holy Spirit, in the Church. The first service[*4] of this new bishop is therefore to give thanks *(eucharistein)*, surrounded by the presbyterium and at the head of his people, in complete union with the representatives (the neighboring bishops) of the other Churches.

After this summary overview of the prayer of episcopal ordination, it is possible to analyze it in greater detail, paying closer attention to the biblical images utilized, to the qualities required of the ordinand and to the gifts which he receives. These three points will permit us to determine more clearly the specific nature of the episcopate and its substance in the eyes of the author of the *Apostolic Tradition*.

α) *Biblical Images Employed.* In this prayer, the principal biblical images referring to the bishop are those of shepherd (leader) and high priest. A connection exists between the heads of the Churches and the priests of the Old Testament, and between the description of the bishop as head and as high priest. This connection is established in the two appeals addressed to the Spirit. In the first, it is asked that the ordinand might tend the holy flock of God and exercise the sovereign priesthood without reproach.

The expression *pneuma hēgemonikon* is a borrowing from Psalm 51:10, where we find the idea of a spiritual principle of divine origin operating in humans to teach them the way of the Lord. Several authors believe that here Hippolytus is thinking of the baptism of Jesus, and of the scene of Pentecost for the apostles.[86] This biblical image

[85]Cf. C. J. PINTO DE OLIVEIRA, "Signification sacerdotale . . . ," 412f.

[86]J. LECUYER, "Episcopat et presbytérat . . . ," 34–39, where we find references to the Fathers and to some secular authors of the period. See also K. RICHTER, "Zum Ritus . . . ," 25–28; A. JILEK, *Initiationsfeier . . .* , 21f.

acquires a prophetic meaning, because it signifies at the same time the task of feeding the flock spiritually with the Word and the teaching of Christ. The responsibility of being the leader is thus expressed in the form of a pastoral/prophetic image. Even the word "to graze" *(poimainein)* has been translated into Latin sometimes by *pascere* (cf. Jn 21:15 [v.16 in Greek] and 1 Pet 5:2), sometimes by *regere* (Mt 2:6; Acts 20:28; cf. Rev. 2:27; 7:17). To be the head in this sense means to govern, to gather, and to feed—in short, to be the pastor of the flock.

The *Apostolic Tradition* in turn links the term "priests" of the phrase "leaders and priests" of the Old Testament with the term "sovereign priesthood" of the phrase "that he may feed . . . and that he may exercise the sovereign priesthood . . ." The parallelism between this first passage and the second continues. Indeed, the leaders and the priests are appointed for the continual service of the temple, just as the new bishop is appointed pastor and high priest to serve God night and day (cf. Heb 7:25). It must be emphasized that we have here aspects of the same function, and not two separate functions. The Church has taken the place of the sanctuary, and at the head of this Church we find the bishop, who, as pastor and high priest, makes propitious the face of God and offers the gifts *(prospherein soi ta dōra)* of the Church. This brings us to the second appeal to the holy Spirit, for the sovereign priesthood.

Here we have an invocation referring to the prophetic and pastoral office of the bishop in terms of sovereign priesthood. Pinto de Oliveira agrees with scholarly opinion in saying that, with Hippolytus, we reach the end of a process which qualified with Old Testament priesthood the ministry of the bishop, which the New Testament avoided doing.[87] The three powers *(exousia)*—forgiving

---

[87]C. J. PINTO DE OLIVEIRA, "Signification sacerdotale . . . ," 414–423. Cf. also P.-M. GY, "Remarques sur le vocabulaire antique du sacerdoce chrétien," in B. BOTTE, A. GELIN, J. SCHMITT, et al., *Etudes sur le sacrement . . .* , 125–145; id., "La théologie des prières anciennes pour l'ordination des évêques et des prêtres," *RSPT* 58, 4 (1974) 599–617 (especially on the Greek vocabulary); id., "Ancient Ordination Prayers," *Studia Liturgica* 13, 2–4 (1979) 86–89 (= *Ordination Rites . . .* , eds. W. Vos & G. Wainwright) (here, the author has reprinted his earlier articles but with some supplementary details). H.-J. SCHULZ has shown the close connection between the pastoral ministry of the bishop and his presidency at the Eucharist in "Das liturgisch-sakramental übertragene Hirtenamt in seiner eucharistischen Selbstverwirklichung nach dem Zeugnis der liturgischen

sins (an allusion to baptism and the responsibility of the bishop in Christian initiation—cf. *AT* 15ff.), distributing the different offices, and loosing all bonds (cf. Jn 20:23; Acts 1:26; Mt 18:18)—depend upon the Spirit of the sovereign priesthood. Furthermore, the Spirit of the sovereign priesthood corresponds (in the epiclesis) to the sovereign Spirit given to the apostles who founded the Church throughout the world. The power of the Father, which is the Spirit, conferred as the spirit of government and of pastoral authority, is also the power which is the Spirit of the sovereign priesthood. The bishop is pastor and high priest in virtue of the same Spirit. In the epiclesis it is the apostles who build up the Church. In the intercession, the bishop does so "by the power . . . given to the apostles." There are three apostolic functions (the apostles have in fact built up the Church by exercising the power to forgive—cf. Jn 20:23; Acts 1:26; Mt 18:18) connected to a ministry, described as priestly, which the author brings into continuity with the pastors of the Old Testament, with Christ, and with the apostles.

Finally, we should note that we are not speaking of two different spirits, but one alone, the Spirit of Christ given first to the apostles *(spiritus principalis)* and then to the bishop who exercises, by virtue of the same Spirit *(spiritus primatus sacerdotii)*, a pastoral ministry (as head) and a sacerdotal ministry (as high priest) in the Church: "Under the new economy, one alone is both leader and priest: Christ is king and priest; the apostles, and the bishops after them, receiving from him the unique *pneuma* who was given to him by the Father, are also kings, leaders of the people *(archontes)* and priests *(hiereis)* by the power of the one and only *pneuma* who is both *hēgemonikon* and *archieratikon*."[88]

β) *Qualities Requested for the Ordinand.* First and foremost the community prays that the bishop be able to fulfill without reproach his role as pastor/head and as high priest; secondly, he must lead a "blame-

---

Überlieferung," in P. BLÄSER, S. FRANK, P. MANNS et al., *Amt und Eucharistie* (Paderborn: Bonifatius-Druckerei, 1973) 208–255. H.-M. Legrand in studying the category of "ministry of presidency" of the Eucharist confirms the sacerdotal qualification attributed to the ministry of presidency: see H.-M. LEGRAND, "The Presidency . . . ," 421–428.

[88]Thus the CHANOINES REGULIERS DE MONDAYE, "L'évêque d'après . . . ," 759. Cf. also the remarks of A. SANTANTONI, *L'ordinazione episcopale . . .* , 35–40.

less," "gentle," "pure," and "humble" life. These are the qualities that are already required in the Pastoral Epistles (cf. 1 Tim 3:1-7; 2 Tim 2:25; Titus 1:6-9). All these qualities have as their aim to allow the bishop to fulfill faithfully his functions and to offer to God a "sweet perfume." This expression is very close to the way in which St. Paul uses sacrificial vocabulary, of the charity of Christ offering himself for all (cf. Eph 5:2): through the exercise of the apostolic ministry, the ministerial life of charity becomes a liturgical act of thanksgiving to God (cf. 2 Cor 2:14-16). "The expressions of worship of the prayer of episcopal ordination . . . become the perfect description of the bishop in the Church of God. He is, also, a Christian among his brothers and sisters, who in himself and in his relation with others must be pleasing to God as an acceptable gift in gentleness, purity of heart and the exercise of supreme God-centered charity, loving God for himself, loving his neighbor for the love of God, which expresses itself in the fact of his being the pastor and the guide of his brethren on the path to eternal salvation."[89]

γ) *Gifts Received by the Ordinand.* With the imposition of hands, the elect receives a special charism, the sovereign Spirit of the leaders and the high priests.[90] One should note that he does not receive the

---

[89]G. FERRARO, *Le preghiere di ordinazione al diaconato, al presbiterato e all'episcopato* (Naples: Dehoniane, 1977) 250–256: the quotation is taken from page 256. Cf. also G. DELLING, "Osmē," in *TDNT* (Grand Rapids, Mich.: Wm. B. Eerdmans, 1967) 5, 493–495.

[90]Cf. B. BOTTE, *La Tradition Apostolique* . . . , 9, n. 4; J. LECUYER, *Le sacrement de l'ordination* . . . , 40f., 210–212; CHANOINES REGULIERS DE MONDAYE, "L'évêque d'après . . . ," 753; K. RICHTER, "Zum Ritus . . . ," 27–32. The same thing among Protestant authors such as G. WAINWRIGHT, "Some Theological Aspects of Ordination," *Studia Liturgica* 13, 2–4 (1979) 135 (". . . all Christian ministry is and remains dependent on the Spirit's empowerment") (= *Ordination Rites.* . . , eds. W. Vos & G. Wainwright) and G. KRETSCHMAR, "Die Ordination . . . ," 40–42, 65–67 ("Er [der Bischof] hat das *pneuma hēgemonikon* empfangen, die Fülle des, nur durch ihn—im Regelfall—kommt deshalb der Geist in Stufen und mit bestimmten Aufgabenstellungen in die in Ortsgemeinden gegliederte Christenheit . . .") ["He (the bishop) has received the *pneuma hēgemonikon*, the plenitude of the Spirit, and so it is only through him normally that the Spirit descends in degrees upon the Christian community divided into local communities, with specific tasks . . ."] (p. 40). We are in agreement with the author that the bishop receives the fullness of the Spirit, but not when he explains the way in which the Spirit descends, because the *AT* does not

priesthood, but rather a priestly ministry, because it is through the service of the bishop that the saving action of Christ is made present sacramentally. The epiclesis (". . . now pour out . . .") joins the two references to the history of salvation (the history before Christ, and that accomplished with Christ) in continuity with this same work of Christ in the pastoral and sacerdotal ministry. The Christological functions of the ministry of the bishop (to feed, to exercise the sovereign priesthood, etc.) are therefore integrated into the apostolic functions (the three powers) by the pneumatological action (". . . that by the power of the Spirit of the sovereign priesthood . . ."). Here we see the theological function of the epiclesis, that is, the prolongation of the work of Christ until the present, but also the preservation of the place of Christ as the author of salvation and as the only high priest. Pastoral ministry is qualified as priestly: according to the *Apostolic Tradition,* this reality belongs to the domain of the gifts of God—it is a charism.

Conclusions. From this analysis what conclusions can be drawn? Let us start with general conclusions concerning the prayer and the structure; then conclusions more specifically related to the precise aim of this study will be drawn.

A. GENERAL CONCLUSIONS: 1) The structure of the prayer is clearly Trinitarian, from the first words to the Amen. We see how God in his wisdom is the origin of all things, and how, in his providence, he grants all that is necessary to the people he has chosen. Christ is the mediator of the salvation which comes from the Father and of all that is returning to the Father. The Holy Spirit actualizes the command given by Christ, and he is the power which comes from God through Christ *(dia tou . . . christou)* for the edification of the Church, in which he gives the power to accomplish certain functions in order that the Church may remain forever the place of the glorification (doxology) of the name of God. Is the Trinitarian structure of the ordination prayer a personal contribution of its author, or is it the norm already established by the Church of Rome? This must remain an open question.[91]

---

speak of *Stufen* in the sense of the author: Cf. *AT* 3. For a discussion of the difficulty of interpreting the word *horous* (besides the quotations from Botte and Lécuyer), see G. FERRARO, *Le preghiere . . .* , 180–183; A. JILEK, *Initiationsfeier . . .* , 16; id., "Bischof . . . ," 379f.

[91]P.-M. Gy has suggested that Hippolytus influenced the rules of the prayer

2) This text manifests a concern for good order, for stability, both in the organization of the prayer and in its content.

3) There is a certain parallelism between a first mention of the history of salvation of the old covenant and a second mention of the history accomplished in Christ. We note that the Church substitutes herself for the old covenant. There is no rupture, because continuity with the past is ensured by the intervention of the Spirit, at work that the Church be built up everywhere as a sanctuary for the glory and continual praise of God. The work begun in the ancient Temple continues in the Church. Just as there was continuity with the old dispensation, so too there will be continuity in the new, with the prolongation of the saving activity of Christ, thanks to his Spirit, through the ministry of the bishop.

B. SPECIFIC CONCLUSIONS: 1) According to the prayer of ordination, the bishop has received a personal charism *(pneuma hēgemonikon)* which at the same time is a function *(pneuma tō archieratikō;* cf. also 2 Tim 1:6). This grace is the same as Jesus Christ received for his mission and which he gave to the apostles for theirs *(AT 3)*. This grace was conferred on the chosen one to help him continue the pastoral task which consists in overseeing the building up of the sanctuary in continuity with all the leaders chosen by God. The new bishop is, indeed, chosen by God to continue this service *(leitourgia)* night and day, and, at the head of his people, to give thanks to the triune God.

2) According to the biblical images used, the new bishop is shepherd (head) and high priest for his people. His ministry, which consists in guiding, ruling, and feeding, is essentially pastoral. Seen in its continuity with the old covenant and with the personages present there, this ministry of the bishop can be qualified as "royal" and "prophetic." "Royal," because this ministry is the continuation of the function of the leaders and the pastors from all time; and "prophetic," because of nuances in the context of the use of *"pneuma hēgemonikon."* In addition, the bishop receives the power of the Spirit which was received by Christ (scene of his baptism/royal-messianic sense) and by the apostles (scene of Pentecost/prophetic-evangelical sense).

---

but "it is not easy to know, from the ordination prayer of the *Apostolic Tradition*, what an ordination prayer may have been before," P.-M. GY, "Ancient Ordination . . . ," 81.

3) The pastoral ministry of the bishop is qualified as priestly. The second appeal to the Spirit *(pneumati tō archieratikō)* grounds the service of the *episkopē* of the Church in the Spirit of the sovereign priesthood of Christ. Only Christ fully has the right to be called high priest. Nevertheless, the new bishop manifests in the midst of his community the unique priesthood of Christ. First, the epiclesis of the Spirit over the bishop links the pastoral function to the service of God *(leitourgounta).* Secondly, the function of presiding at the Eucharist and the other sacraments is part of the pastoral ministry bestowed by the gift (grace) of God.

4) The powers of the bishop are rooted also in the action of the Spirit (of the sovereign priesthood) and are seen as a continuation of the saving action of God through the pastoral ministry which is bestowed upon him. These powers are threefold: to forgive sins, to distribute the pastoral offices, and to bind and to loose. From the position occupied by the apostles in the second anamnesis (they build up the Church in the place of the Temple), from the fact that the bishop has received the same Spirit as they, and from the two allusions to the replacement of Matthias *("kardiognōsta pantōn"* and *"didonai klēros"*—cf. Acts 1:24 and 26), we conclude that the *AT* sees the bishop as the successor of the apostles considered collegially. In addition, we note that the prayer does not say anywhere that the Spirit was bestowed upon each one of the apostles, but upon the apostles as a group. It is, then, the apostles as a collegial reality who possess the sovereign Spirit. One can conclude (with R. Béraudy) that "the new bishop cannot be the successor of the apostles and share in the gift of the Spirit except as he is included in the college which succeeded to the apostolic college."[92]

5) Lastly, the community prays that the life of the ordinand remain without fault so that he may faithfully fulfill his responsibilities and offer to God a sweet perfume (cf. 2 Cor 2:14-16 and Eph 5:2).

b. *Presbyter*[*6]

The prayer of ordination of presbyters[*6] compared with that of the bishop is striking in its simplicity and brevity.[93] The concern of the

[92]R. BERAUDY, "Le sacrement de l'Ordre d'après la Tradition Apostolique d'Hippolyte," *BCE* 38–39 (1962) 344.

[93]These qualities may indicate that the text of the prayer for presbyteral ordination is very ancient and prior to Hippolytus. For P.-M. GY "in the body of the

author of the *Apostolic Tradition* to maintain continuity in these prayers is noteworthy. There is a connection—a kind of thread—between the gaze that God rested in the past on his people (the typology of Moses and the elders) and his present intervention. The prayer begins immediately with the epiclesis: "Look upon this your servant and grant him the Spirit of grace and the counsel of presbyter, so that he may support and govern your people with a pure heart." It is clear, in this text, that the presbyter is ordained for the people and not primarily to assist the bishop. The parallel Moses = bishop/elder = priest has not yet been made. This will appear only in a development posterior to the *Apostolic Tradition*.[94]

D. N. Power emphasizes that this identification is not found in Hippolytus, in the face of certain commentators who place the origins

---

prayer the personal influence of Hippolytus does not appear either, and no mention is made of specifically Christian tasks of presbyters, that is why one could suspect some rabbinic background, especially in connection with the typology of the seventy elders and Moses . . . ," "Ancient Ordination . . . ," 82. A. VILELA, *La condition collegiale* . . . , 354–357, even speaks of the composition of this prayer in a Christian community which came from Judaism; D. N. POWER echos some other exegetes who suggest a community governed still by a presbyteral college, without an individual bishop at its head, as the place of origin of this prayer: *Ministers of Christ and His Church. The Theology of the Priesthood* (London: Geoffrey Chapman, 1969) 36. But one should avoid seeing too quickly in this prayer a reflection of the Jewish praxis in the first centuries of the Christian era. See the article of the American rabbi L. A. HOFFMAN, "Jewish Ordination . . . ," and of the Lutheran G. KRETSCHMAR, "Die Ordination . . . ," esp. 46–55.

To explain the difference between the prayers of episcopal and presbyteral ordination, there was a discussion among the Anglicans Frere, Dix, and Turner. Frere believed that the ordination prayer for the bishop was used for presbyteral ordination: W. H. FRERE, "Early Ordination Services . . . ," and Dix and Turner thought the presbyteral prayer, although older, should be completed by the addition of the introduction of the prayer for the ordination of a bishop: G. DIX, *Treatise* . . . , and C. H. TURNER, "Cheirotonia, . . ." Botte maintained that the addition of the first part of the prayer for episcopal consecration to the prayer for presbyteral ordination seems very unlikely because of the typology developed in that of presbyteral ordination: cf. B. BOTTE, *La Tradition Apostolique d'après* . . . , 21. For a discussion of the theses proposed by the authors quoted, see B. KLEIN-HEYER, *Die Priesterweihe im römischen Ritus: eine liturgiehistorische Studie* (Trier: Paulinus-Verlag, 1962) 18–25. On the problems in the reconstruction of this prayer, see R. BERAUDY, "Le sacrement de l'Ordre . . . ," 345–346.

[94]Cf. Ve 954 (ed. Mohlberg, 121–122); Ge 145 (ed. Mohlberg, 25); Gr 29a (ed. Deshusses, 95).

of the Spirit of the presbyterium in the Spirit possessed by the bishop. According to these opinions, the presbyteral office would be derived from that of the bishop.[95] This does not mean that the presbyters act independently from the presbyterium and from the bishop, but rather that the common spirit is bestowed upon the presbyters *for* the governing of the people, as was the case for the seventy elders of Israel (as a group collectively). Along this same line, B.-D. Dupuy follows this typology and extends it to include the very action of Christ regarding the Twelve and the Seventy. Emphasizing the relationship between two parallel situations, he concludes: ". . . as the Twelve represent the tribes of Israel, so the Seventy recall the elders who, by God's order, were to assist Moses.

"Just as the elders of Jerusalem were appointed to serve the people with Moses and to prophesy, so too the Seventy were appointed by Christ to help him in his work. The apostolic ministry does not, then, stem simply from the college of the Twelve, as if it were an extension and an amplification of it."[96]

The episcopacy was not seen, therefore, as the source of the presbyteral ministry. Furthermore, there is no mention of the bishop in this prayer.

After a brief anamnesis in the past tense, a second request is made on behalf of the elect: "And now, O Lord, grant that there may ever be preserved among us the Spirit of your grace, and make us worthy that, in faith, we may give praise to you and minister to you in simplicity of heart." The "us" used in this second prayer is spoken by

---

[95]D. N. POWER, *Ministers of Christ* . . . , 35–36. These opinions do not rest directly upon the *AT*. Power gives references on page 35, nn. 21ff. The argument of Power seems to be confirmed by A. JILEK, *Initiationsfeier* . . . , 42–46; and id., "Bischof . . . ," 393–396.

[96]B.-D. DUPUY, "Teologia dei ministeri ecclesiastici," in J. FEINER and M. LÖHRER (eds.), *Mysterium Salutis. Nuovo corso di dogmatica come teologia della storia della salvezza*, vol. 8, *L'evento salvifico nella comunità di Gesù Cristo*, 2nd ed., trans. from German [*Das Heilsgeschehen in der Gemeinde: Gottes Gnadenhandeln* (Mysterium Salutis. Grundriss heilsgeschichtlicher Dogmatik, 4: 2)] by D. Pezzetta (Brescia: Queriniana, 1977) 613. P.-M. GY, "La théologie des prières . . . ," 609, emphasizing that the prayer of presbyteral ordination gives "the impression of a prayer of rabbinic ordination barely Christianized," refers to a more specialized study of the typology of Moses and the seventy elders found in the work of E. LOHSE, *Die Ordination* . . . .

the bishop surrounded by his presbyters who also impose hands on the head of the ordinand (cf. *AT* 7). The bishop as head of the presbyterium admits him to it (the liturgical gesture expresses this theological reality). According to the prayer, all the members of the presbyterium have the same Spirit *(et nunc . . . presta indeficienter conservari in nobis spiritum gratiae tuae . . .).* The governance of this community was essentially collegial.[97] One finds evidence for this in the concelebrations of the Eucharist (*AT* 4), of baptism (*AT* 21), and of presbyteral ordinations (*AT* 7, 8).

Does the new presbyter participate in the priesthood? The text, here, does not employ priestly vocabulary. One must look for the answer elsewhere. In *AT* 8 regarding the ordination of deacons, it is clear that the deacon "does not receive that Spirit which the presbytery possesses and in which the presbyters share," and, he "is not ordained to the priesthood, but to serve the bishop . . ." P.-M. Gy notes, on the other hand, that Hippolytus in his commentary on Daniel "speaks of the *taxis* of bishops, *'hiereis* and levites.'" There is therefore a discrepancy here between the text of the prayer and the thought of Hippolytus.[98] The ministry of the presbyters being clearly differentiated from that of deacons, the prayer qualifies the ministry as priestly, therefore indirectly (without using this vocabulary) as a result of the participation of the presbyters in the pastoral ministry of the bishop already described as sacerdotal.

After this overview of the prayer of presbyteral ordination, it remains for us to study the biblical images employed, the qualities requested for the ordinand, and the gifts which he receives.

α) *Biblical Images Employed.* Among the biblical images used in this prayer the typology of Moses and the elders (cf. Num 11:17-25) stands out.

In the typology of the Old Testament, the episode described in the prayer "[Look upon this your servant] as also you looked upon your

---

[97]Cf. G. H. LUTTENBERGER, "The Priest as a Member of a Ministerial College. The Development of the Church's Ministerial Structure from 96 to c. 300 A.D.," *RTAM* 43 (1976) 39–42; in the same vein, A. VILELA, *La condition collégiale . . . ,* 355–357; A. JILEK, "Bischof . . . ," 396–401.

[98]P.-M. GY, "Ancient Ordination . . . ," 87. See also the remarks of H.-M. LEGRAND concerning the theological balance of the prayers of the *AT*: "La réalisation de l'Eglise . . . ," 206.

chosen people and commanded Moses to choose presbyters [*praes-byteros*], whom you filled with your Spirit, which you gave to your servant" clarifies the nature of the office of the presbyters within the community: a collegial participation in the governing of the people (in common with the head), and the exercise of the gift of prophesy. The individual enters into his office through his association with the collegial body of the elders, receiving with them the Spirit given by God. The typology presented in the prayer shows that it is God who has filled with the Spirit the elders chosen by Moses. The allusion to the episode of Numbers 11:16-25 implies that the Spirit has been transmitted to the presbyters for a specific task: that of governing the people and of helping Moses by serving him in the council. These elders were effectively the collaborators of Moses in his ministry.

β) *Qualities Requested for the Ordinand.* The petition begs for two qualities for the new presbyter: that he have "a pure heart" (*in corde mundo*) and be "made worthy" (*dignus*). The first request applies to the newly ordained and to the manner in which he must fulfill his ministry.

The second, however, refers to a group of persons (". . . make *us* worthy") who possess the *pneuma* common to the entire presbyterium. One prays that the charges bestowed by the Spirit be fulfilled with the required worthiness. J. Lécuyer comments on the passage: ". . . the bishop who ordains asks, on behalf of himself and, at the same time, of the newly ordained and the other presbyters who assist him, for the grace to preserve intact the *pneuma* common to the entire presbyterium; the passage in the first person plural emphasizes this communal possession of one same grace, which obligates all the servants of one same Master."[99]

γ) *Gifts Received by the Ordinand.* Two other biblical allusions help us to understand better the ministerial context of the presbyterate. The first allusion is found in the phrase "the Spirit of grace and of counsel" (*spiritum gratiae et consilii/pneuma charitos kai symboulias*), and the second in the words "that he support and govern" (*ut adiubet* [sic!] *et gubernet* or *ut sustineat et gubernet* [for the Ethiopian version]/ *antilēmpsis* and *kybernēsis*). These two expressions come from St. Paul.

---

[99]J. LECUYER, "Episcopat et presbytérat . . . ," 44f.

In the first case, the spirit of grace and of counsel of the presbyterium is conferred. D. N. Power again notes that possibly the *pneuma charitos* in the prayer of the *AT* does not refer directly to the Holy Spirit. This expression has several affinities with the New Testament usage of the word *charis*, which often indicates a gift of the Spirit which is linked to the ministry of the Church.[100]

A second reference is made to this Spirit of grace ("grant . . . the Spirit of your grace and make us worthy. . ."*6). Here, as we have already noted, the invocation is made for a group of persons among whom the ordinand is found. It is clear that the grace requested for the ordinand is already present in the other members of this group.

The second part of the epiclesis explains the reason for calling upon the Spirit ("that he may support and govern your people"), and it specifies that the grace received must help the ordinand to accomplish his ministry, which consists of advising the bishop and governing the people of God. These two tasks are already found in St. Paul's list of charisms (1 Cor 12:28) received for the building up of the Body. The newly ordained sees himself, therefore, as receiving a charism of counsel, of wisdom, and of assistance which should be exercised collegially (cf. *AT* 8) for the good, the edification, and the growth of the people.

Conclusions. As with the prayer of episcopal ordination, we can draw from our study some general and some specific conclusions.

A. GENERAL CONCLUSIONS: 1) The structure of the prayer does not contain the personal mark of the author. It is neither clearly Trinitarian nor truly Christological in its composition. From this fact, certain authors affirm the ancient character of this prayer and even its possible Jewish origins, because the prayer does not mention the specifically Christian functions vested in the presbyters.

2) One is struck by the simplicity of the prayer which, in itself, may be another proof of the great age of its composition.

---

[100]Cf. for example its use in the following passages which speak either of the foundation of the ministry of God's grace *(charis)* or of the ministry of Paul bestowed through the grace of God: Rom 15:15-16; 1:4-5; 12:3, 6; 1 Cor 3:10; 15:10; 2 Cor 12:9; Gal 2:9; Eph 3:7; Phil 1:7; Heb 10:29 and 1 Cor 12, where the gifts have their origin in the common source of the one Spirit: see D. N. POWER, *Ministers of Christ . . .*, 32.

3) Again one finds a certain parallelism between the new and the old dispensations. The use of an Old Testament typology which has its own image for the ministry of presbyters demonstrates this well.

B. SPECIFIC CONCLUSIONS: 1) The presbyter receives a special charism (*spiritus gratiae et consilii praesbyterii*) to assume the task of helping and governing the people of God. This charism is conferred by the imposition of hands.

2) The grace of this ministry is shared by all the members of the college, as is shown in the second part of the prayer.

3) Each member is established in his office by his entrance into the presbyterium.

4) The bishop himself is also a member of the presbyterium.

5) Lastly, priestly vocabulary is not specifically used in the prayer itself to describe the presbyteral ministry, which is, however, described as sacerdotal in the rubric concerning the ordination of deacons. The association of the ministry of presbyters to the pastoral ministry of the bishop explicates this priestly qualification.

EXCURSUS: DEACON[*8]

The deacon, as we have already seen in the rubric which governs his ordination, is ordained by the bishop to fulfill the tasks which are entrusted to him. The prayer[*8] of diaconal ordination[101] draws together the service of the deacon and that of Christ who, sent by the Father to serve his will in obedience, makes known his plan. This parallelism attests to the Christological foundation of the diaconal ministry (cf. Rom 15:8; Lk 22:27; Phil 2:7). Thus one aspect of the presence of Christ is actualized in the world, for the diaconal ministry in the Church reflects and makes present the very ministry of Christ. Christ revealed the love and the plan of God by his service (*diakonia*) to the poor, the sick, and the weak; and the deacon represents Christ (who came to serve and not to be served) specifically through the exercise of his particular ministry.[102]

[101] For a discussion of some difficulties in the reconstruction of the Latin text of this prayer, see R. BERAUDY, "Le sacrement de l'Ordre . . . ," 350–351.

[102] In the writings of the Fathers before Hippolytus, we see the identification of the service of the deacon with the *diakonia* of Jesus Christ: one should "revere the deacons as Jesus Christ," cf. IGNATIUS OF ANTIOCH, *Trall.* 2:1–3; 3:1. For other references to the AnteNicene Fathers, see L. OTT, *Le sacrement de l'Ordre* (Paris: Cerf, 1971) 31–40.

We note that the prayer is addressed to God in the same way as the prayers of episcopal and presbyteral ordinations:

"O God, who have created all things and have set them in order through your Word;[103] Father of our Lord Jesus Christ, whom you sent to minister to your will and to make clear to us your desires, grant the Holy Spirit of grace and care and diligence to this your servant, whom you have chosen to serve the Church and to offer in your holy places the gifts which are offered to you by your chosen high priest, so that he may serve with a pure heart and without blame [1 Tim 3:13], and that, ever giving praise to you, he may be accounted by your good will as worthy of this high office: through your Son Jesus Christ, through whom be glory and honor to you, to the Father and the Son with the Holy Spirit, in your holy church both now and through the ages of ages. Amen" (AT 8).

First of all, we should note that the text of this prayer is very difficult to reconstruct, because the Latin manuscript is full of lacunae. In fact, B. Botte followed the Ethiopian version of the AT for the prayer of diaconal ordination. We encounter a problem in the use of the quotation from 1 Timothy 3:13, because the prayer does not quote the exact words of the Epistle itself, where we read: "For those who serve well as deacons *gain a good standing (bathmon heautois kalon peripoiountai/gradum bonum sibi acquirent)* . . ." For the French translation, Botte chose the Ethiopian version (E) where the text is rendered in Latin as *"gradum **maioris ordinis** assequatur."* It would seem that the Pauline text was modified or interpreted by the Ethiopian version. The other version, that of the *Testament of Our Lord* (T), is closer to the scriptural text *("dignus sit gradu hoc magno et excelso").* It is this version that G. Dix translated: ". . . in order that he (the deacon) may be recognized worthy of this great and exalted office . . ." It is believed that the text of the T version corresponds to the original of the AT.

Diaconal ordination bestows a gift of the Spirit linked to the imposition of hands by the bishop, as in any ordination. Here, specifically, the deacon receives the "Spirit of grace and of zeal."[104] Since every

---

[103]See the note concerning the choice of the term given by Botte in the French translation: A. JILEK, *Initiationsfeier* . . . , 54 and 12.

[104]The Latin version of this text is the following: *spiritum sanctum gratiae et solicitudinis et industriae*; the Ethiopian version reads: *spiritum gratiae tuum* . . . .

ordination is linked to a specific office, this gift confers the task of serving the Church *(ministrare ecclesiae)* and of presenting in the sanctuary the gifts for the Eucharist (cf. *AT* 4, 21, 22). In what way does the deacon provide service in the Church? In the *AT*, it is clear that the deacon is the right arm of the bishop *(AT* 8), especially in taking care of the sick *(AT* 24, 34) and in teaching the Word along with the presbyters *(AT* 39). All these activities are performed under the authority of the bishop. All this is included in the phrase *ministrare ecclesiae* (to serve the Church). We see in this that the deacon, too, is concerned with the building up of the Body of Christ. The deacon's service of the Church in the daily life of its members is seen also in his role at the altar and in the liturgy (cf. *AT* 4, 21, 22). His service *(diakonia)* is always accomplished for the glory of the name of God and to ensure that the deacon, after having served God through service without blame in a pure life, "may obtain a superior rank" (E), or "may be worthy of this great and exalted office" (T) (cf. 1 Tim 3:13),[105] and "ever give praise to you (God)." Like all the prayers of the *AT*, this one concludes with a Trinitarian doxology which glorifies God through Jesus Christ and the Holy Spirit. There is lacking, however, any reference to the Church (a reference which is found in the prayers of episcopal and presbyteral ordination and in the Eucharistic prayer). This may be explained by the fact that the final phrase of the ordination prayer is lacking in the Latin palimpsest, which obliges us to refer to later versions of this text to complete it.

1. BIBLICAL IMAGES EMPLOYED

In this prayer, the principal biblical image concerning the deacon is that of Christ the servant (cf. Lk 22:27; Rom 15:8; Phil 2:7). We note that the image of the first part of the prayer is precisely that of God who sent his Son, who is faithful and obedient, and who reveals the

---

Botte thought that what we have here is a "translation doublet," since the meaning of the Latin version is close to that of *sollicitudo:* cf. B. BOTTE, *La Tradition apostolique . . .* , 27.

[105]It is B. Botte who gives the reference 1 Tim 3:13 in the text *(AT* 8). For a discussion of the interpretation of this quotation, see our commentary in the text (pp. 67f.) and the brief remarks of J. M. BARNETT, *The Diaconate: A Full and Equal Order. A Comprehensive and Critical Study of the Origin, Development, and Decline of the Diaconate in the Context of the Church's Total Ministry and a Proposal for Renewal* (N.Y.: Seabury, 1979) 61–65.

plan of God (of eternal salvation). In the rubric we read that the deacon is ordained to do what the bishop indicates for him. We see, therefore, that the image is intended to identify the deacon with Christ, an identification that one finds in certain early Fathers, as, for example, Ignatius of Antioch. The image that he uses in his letter to the Magnesians is the following: The bishop presides in the place of God, the presbyters in the place of the council of the apostles; to the deacons is entrusted the service of Jesus Christ.[106] It seems that this image was repeated in the prayers of the *AT* and applied to the ordained ministers. All three (bishop–presbyter–deacon) are called "servants," but, in the case of the deacon, the prayer makes explicit the double service: that of the Church (in daily life), and that of the altar. One thinks of Christ, who came in all humility and who washed the feet of his disciples, demonstrating the fraternal service of the new commandment of love (cf. Jn 13).

If we compare this biblical image referring to the deacon with his different functions, described by the author in detail, we get a clear picture of the specific nature of this ordained ministry. We have seen that the deacon should see to the needs of the sick (two places: *AT* 24 and 34); that he plays a role in the instruction of the community during the prayer meetings (cf. *AT* 39), and that he has specific duties at the altar, especially during the Eucharistic celebration (cf. *AT* 4, 21, 22). This shows us that the deacon assumes at once a service *(diakonia)* of charity, of the Word, and of the liturgy, in order to be the sign of Christ the servant of the community.

2. QUALITIES REQUESTED FOR THE ORDINAND

As in the case of the bishop and the presbyter, we ask God that the deacon might exercise a ministry "without blame," and that he live a life of purity without blemish. Here again we hear the echo of the prescriptions of the Pastoral Epistles (1 Tim 3:8-13). The author prays that the deacon may lead an honorable life: he must be worthy, keep his word, not drink too much wine, nor seek dishonest gain (1 Tim 3:8); in short, he must act like a serious and honest person. Our author supposes that the deacon (like the presbyters and bishops) is married and the father of a family; that he knows how to raise his children and manage his own household (1 Tim 3:12): these are

---

[106]IGNATIUS OF ANTIOCH, *Magn.* 6, 1; cf. also *Trall.* 2, 3.

indispensable qualities in someone called to collaborate in the organization and the direction of the Church communities, viewed in a domestic context. Omitted from this list are the testimony of the people and the fact that the future deacon cannot be a neophyte, and the prescription that he should possess personal qualities enabling him to welcome and to teach. Might not this discrepancy indicate that certain tasks were not entrusted to the deacons in these communities, notably, service at the Eucharistic celebration, teaching, and the welcoming of strangers? The text sums up all the required qualities in one phrase full of meaning: ". . . that he may serve with a pure heart and without blame."

3. GIFTS RECEIVED BY THE ORDINAND

The deacon receives a specific charism linked to the imposition of hands by the bishop. The bishop asks God to bestow the Spirit of grace and of zeal upon the servant whom he has chosen to serve the Church. We observe that the candidates's personal qualities (due to nature and to grace) are not sufficient for admission to the diaconal ministry; in addition, the deacon must receive a specific gift of the Spirit which confers at the same time a ministerial office ("to serve the Church"). Upon receiving this gift of ministry, the deacon acquires all that is necessary for the exercise of this office. The epiclesis bears on the ministry of Christ the servant through all time and everywhere.

Conclusions:

A. GENERAL CONCLUSIONS: 1) We remark the Trinitarian structure of this prayer in which the three Persons are active in the plan of salvation and in the life of the Church. In respect to salvation, it is God who is the source of all: he creates and disposes; Christ is the means through whom the Father accomplishes his plan, and the Spirit is the force who actualizes all divine activity. On the ecclesial level, it is God who gives a minister to the Church; it is the *diakonia* of Christ which serves as the model for the deacon and which is prolonged through space and time; lastly, it is the Spirit who qualifies the person chosen for service and who enriches this community by his gifts.

2) As Christ followed the will of God and revealed his plan, the deacon is to serve the Church (doing what the bishop instructs him to do) and present in the sanctuary the gifts offered by him who is

established as the high priest (in this the actions of the deacon reveal the way in which his service of the brethren becomes *"eucharistia"* in his ministry to the altar).

3) In the process of diaconal election we see again that, just as in the case of the other ordained ministers, the deacon's vocation is mediated by the will of the Christian people of the locality. The expression of this will is confirmed and recognized as being the decision of God himself in the prayer of epiclesis ("the servant whom *you* have chosen").

4) The specific nature of the diaconate resides in the fact that the deacon's service of the brethen (cf. *AT* 24, 25, 28, 34, 39) and his *diakonia* at the Eucharistic celebration are linked (cf. *AT* 8, 21, 22).

B. SPECIFIC CONCLUSIONS: 1) A specific charism of the Spirit is conferred upon the deacon for a well-defined office in and for the Church.

2) The Holy Spirit thus gives to the Church a minister. "The Church" here, of course, means a local community.

3) We can reconstruct the general context of the ordained ministries by comparing the three rituals of admission to the ordained ministry in the Church of the *AT*. We find wide collaboration between the members of this community in discerning the will of God (the choice of each minister); there is a multiplicity of services corresponding to the diversity of the charisms given by the Spirit in and for the Church (the prayers of epiclesis); the powers necessary to carry out each ministry are bestowed during the admission of each to his specific office (episcopal, presbyteral and diaconal): each office fulfills specific functions in the Church.[107]

4) Lastly, we consider the very meaning of ordination. The process of ordination, in fact, consists in a *confessional* and *liturgical* act in which the bishop, in the name of the entire community, beseeches the grace of God for the chosen one; this act is an *ecclesial* procedure involving the entire community, and, at the same time, it is a *juridical* act because the deacon is installed in a concrete office in and for the Church.

---

[107]In his study, J. D. LAURANCE showed the same tendency in Cyprian. See his conclusions in *'Priest' as Type* . . . , 223–230, esp. 227f.

4. RELATIONSHIP BETWEEN THE EPISCOPACY AND THE PRESBYTERATE

Since we are discussing the *AT* alone, we should recall certain facts already noted. Before all else, the structural elements identical in the ordination of a bishop and in that of a presbyter are the imposition of hands and the prayer.

The bishop and the presbyter are ordained in the same way to enter into their ministry. We must nonetheless emphasize that, for the bishop, the imposition of hands by the neighboring bishops is required, whereas for the presbyter it is simply a matter for the bishop of the place and his presbyterium; in both cases, the presence of the people of the locality is required. This fact points up the special position that the bishop occupies both in the community and outside of it: he is the head of this local community, a witness to the faith of his brothers and sisters before the other Churches, and a witness as well to the faith of the whole Church within his own Church, which is not the case for the presbyters. In the prayer of episcopal ordination, the bishop is associated both to Christ and to the apostles: he receives the gift of the sovereign Spirit whom Christ received, which was given to the apostles, who founded the Church throughout the world.

For the ordination of a bishop, the presbyters cannot ordain because they have only the power to receive (*AT* 8). It is therefore necessary that they be ordained by the bishop, but with the other members of the presbyterium who "also impose hands." These facts demonstrate what these two ministries have in common, but they also reveal the specific nature of each.

The prayer of presbyteral ordination makes it clear that the bishop is also a member of the presbyterate, while being its head. The bishop and the presbyterate collaborate, therefore, very closely in the exercise of the pastoral ministry. In comparing this prayer with that of episcopal ordination, we see that the bishop occupies the first place in the direction and the pastoral service of the Church. But in fact there exists a time lag between the dates of these two prayers in the collection of texts of the *AT*: the prayer of presbyteral ordination represents very probably an earlier stage than that of episcopal ordination. However, put together, these prayers may indicate the absence of a clear distinction between bishop and presbyter, as seen in

the New Testament and even in the earliest Christian writers.[108] If
this is the case, we should note that the *AT* is positioned between its
two contemporaries (Irenaeus and Cyprian) discussed at the beginning of this study.

In Irenaeus we saw a clarification of the role of bishops and that of
of presbyters, a clarification which is maintained until Cyprian.[109] We
can then situate the *AT* at the mid-point of this movement (not only
chronologically, but also theologically). In the *AT*, the fundamental
substance of office is that of pastoral ministry, which includes governing the local Church, overseeing its edification through teaching
(feeding the flock) and celebrating the Eucharist. In the New
Testament, this ministry is designated by the term *episkopē*, and we
find both *episkopoi* and *presbyteroi* who fulfill this ministry.[110] The distinction between the two became clear around the year 150: according to the *AT*, the presbyters participate in the responsibilities of the
episkopē, which is a collegial entity in which the bishop has a distinct
role (meaning that one of the presbyters is at the head of the presbyterium). The two roles are distinguished liturgically, yet we see the
bishop and the presbyters imposing hands together over the gifts for
the Eucharist (*AT* 4), they govern together (*AT* 7, 8), and they concelebrate baptism (*AT* 21).

[108]The literature which explores this question is vast and we must limit our-
selves to giving only a few references: for the New Testament see P. BONY,
E. COTHENET, J. DELORME et al., *Le ministère et les ministères* . . . ; R. E. BROWN,
Priest and Bishop . . . ; J. H. ELLIOTT, "Ministry and Church Order in the NT: A
Traditio-Historical Analysis (1 Pt 5, 1–5 & plls.)," *Catholic Biblical Quarterly* 32, 3
(1970) 367–391; A. LEMAIRE, *Les ministères aux origines de l'Eglise* . . . ; id., "The
Ministries in the New Testament: Recent Research," *Biblical Theology Bulletin* 3, 2
(1973) 133–166.

[109]Cf. the study of J. D. LAURANCE, '*Priest' as Type* . . . , ch. 4, esp. 195–221.

[110]The word *episkopein* is found in 1 Pet 5:2 and Heb 12:15 (its use here is not
pertinent to our study); *episkopē* Acts 1:20; 1 Tim 3:1 (two other uses which do
not concern the question here are Lk 19:44 and 1 Pet 2:12); *episkopos* Acts 20:28;
Phil 1:1; 1 Tim 3:2; Titus 1:7 and 1 Pet 2:25. The interchangeability of the terms
presbyteros and *episkopos* is verifiable in Titus 1:5, 7; 1 Tim 3:1; 5:17; Acts 20:17, 28;
it is also suggested by 1 Pet 5, 2-3: "tend the flock of God *(poimanate to* . . .
poimnion tou Theou . . .), exercising the oversight *(episkopountes)* . . ." Elsewhere
Peter addresses the presbyters as a co-presbyter (1 Pet 5:1). But R. E. Brown
notes that the second Greek term *(episkopountes)* is lacking in the manuscript
Vaticanus: cf. R. E. BROWN, "A Brief Survey . . . ," here, p. 24.

For D. N. Power, the structure of the Eucharistic celebration shows the way in which the presbyters participate in the ministry of direction in the community: "Here (in the Eucharistic celebration) we have a perfect example of the way in which the entire Christian community is mirrored in the liturgical assembly; each one occupies that place in the assembly which corresponds to his or her place in the Church, (i.e., the Church community)."[111]

In the Eucharistic celebration the bishop and his presbyters are seen as a collegial entity presiding over the liturgical assembly in the same way that they supervise the direction of the community, in a collegial manner. This does not imply that there exists an equality between the bishop and the presbyters, but the fact that the bishop imposes hands over the gifts *cum omni praesbyterio* (*AT* 4) reveals their common exercise of the pastoral ministry. We recall that the presbyters received the grace to act in common, within the presbyterium, under the presidency and the authority of the bishop. Nevertheless, this does not mean that the presbyteral ministry proceeds from that of the bishop. The typology of Moses does not identify the bishop with Moses, as D. N. Power and A. Vilela have noted.[112] In fact, the prayer of presbyteral ordination says, without hesitation, that the presbyteral ministry has as its aim to help and to rule the *people* of God. It is not necessary to read these texts from a later theological position which sometimes claims that the presbyteral ministry is derived from the episcopate.[113]

After having described the characteristics common to both the presbyteral and episcopal ministries, we shall now attempt to delineate what differentiates them.

The bishop occupies a special place in the Church. He is the head: he has received the grace of the sovereign Spirit through which he "feeds the flock"; it is his prophetic mission to announce the Good News, and the spirit of the high priesthood is bestowed upon him. He is the high priest of a priestly people. The presbyters are not qual-

[111]D. N. POWER, *Ministers of Christ . . . ,* 40.

[112]D. N. POWER, ibid., 34–36 and A. VILELA, *La condition collégiale . . . ,* 354–357.

[113]Cf. the remarks of J.-M.-R. TILLARD, "'Ministère' ordonné et 'sacerdoce' du Christ," *Irénikon* 49, 2 (1976) 145–166, esp. 162–166; id., "L'Evêque et les autres ministères," *Irénikon* 48, 2 (1975) 195–200.

ified as sacerdotal except indirectly (reference is made in the rubric in *AT* 9). It is the bishop who presides over both penance and the Eucharist in the Church, who distributes and coordinates the offices (the ministerial services), and who exercises the power of binding and loosing. Once this is said, we should add immediately that too neat a separation between the roles would not do justice to the communal sense that we find in the *AT* and in the writings of Irenaeus and Cyprian (cf. the conclusions supra).

Conclusions: 1) The bishop and the presbyters (the latter in communion with the bishop) are together charged with a pastoral ministry which includes presiding over the building up of the Church.

2) The bishop surrounded by the presbyters evokes the image of Christ surrounded by the Twelve in the midst of the people previously gathered. This allows us to see the eschatological meaning of the ministry of direction (episcopacy and presbyterate) in the Church: the faithful do not assemble in their own name, but they are *gathered* in the name of Christ who assures them of his presence until he returns.

3) The iconographical association of the bishop and the presbyters with the image of Christ and the Twelve helps us to understand certain tasks which the bishop alone can fulfill: to be the minister of the gift of the Spirit (ordination, cf. *AT* 3, 8), to provide the other offices in the Church, to bind and to loose, to preside at the Eucharist and, normally, to announce the "word of grace." The case of admission of a confessor to ordained ministry shows that even though the bishop is the minister of the gift of the Spirit, he does not control the Spirit. Elsewhere it is affirmed that "all have the Spirit of God" *(omnes enim habemus spiritum dei—AT* 16).

4) The presbyters represent the Seventy and their principal function as a presbyterium, with the bishop at their head, is to govern and to counsel the people.

5) Their role at the celebration of the Eucharist allows us to appreciate the harmonious collaboration existing between the bishop and the presbyterium (and the entire community as well). We have seen that the *episkopē* is exercised by the bishop and the presbyters according to the specific charisms bestowed upon them through ordination. For the bishop, it is the "*spiritus principalis*," and for the presbyter, it is the "spirit of governing and of counsel." As in the daily life of the Church, the bishop and his presbyterium exercise the episcopacy

collegially, in the same way that they preside at the Eucharist *collegially*. So the ministry of the presbyters is not to be considered as deriving from the bishop, but as situated in the line of the episcopacy.

6) We should recall that, as the head of the local community, the bishop plays an essential role concerning his community's relationships with the other local Churches, a role that the presbyters do not play. This is why the other bishops must take part in the ordination of a new bishop, whereas the ordination of a new presbyter is a matter for the local Church alone.

7) Lastly, we need to look at the continuum deacon/bishop/presbyter in order to gain an overall view of ordination and of the structure of the Church as it appears in the *AT*. We saw that diaconal ordination includes all the essential elements of episcopal and presbyteral ordination: it belongs, therefore, to the one ordained ministry. We must see the diaconate in this context, aware of the specific nature of its relationship with the episcopacy and the presbyterate. It is clear that the deacon is ordained in view of service ("to fulfill the bishop's command"), and he is ordained "not to the priesthood, but to serve the bishop." This service allows us to see the relationships among deacons/bishop/presbyters. The presbyter and the deacon are both in an immediate relationship with the bishop: the presbyter, who has received "the common spirit of the presbyterate," participates with the bishop in the sacerdotal and pastoral ministry; the deacon, as we have seen, is in an immediate relationship with the bishop through his service ("[the deacon] is to attend to his own duties and to acquaint the bishop with such matters as are needful"), a service which is oriented towards the community. Thus the relationship of presbyters and deacons to the bishop is not symmetrical. Nor should we conceive of it in a linear descending hierarchy that would make the deacons the immediate subordinates of presbyters. It is more correct to see each of these two groups in an immediate relationship with the bishop, while acknowledging the precedence of the presbyters.

5. LATER INFLUENCE OF THE *APOSTOLIC TRADITION*

The influence of the *AT* is profound and well attested concerning the structure of the celebration and the contents of the ordination prayers.

The structure of ordination forms the nucleus of the ordination rituals from the time of the early Church down to the present.[114] These structural elements gain or diminish in importance in the course of time. Other elements were added, but the imposition of hands and the prayer have remained constant.

Concerning the ordination prayers, we see that the influence of the AT is always strongly felt, without being identical throughout. The influence of the prayer of episcopal ordination, for instance, is greater in the West than in the East. On the other hand, the points of contact with the prayer of presbyteral ordination of the AT are less frequent

---

[114]The rite that we find in the AT has served as the model in the Western Church (by way of the Leonine Sacramentary) and in the East (by way of the *Apostolic Constitutions*, VIII, 4–5; 16–17 [ed. SC 336, 140–151, 216–219]). We find especially the ordination prayers and the imposition of hands at the center of the development in the other rituals in the West down to our day (in the Leonine, Gregorian and Old Gelasian Sacramentaries; also in the ritual of *SEA* and in all the sacramentaries and pontificals). Cf. B. BOTTE, "L'Ordre d'après . . ."; P. JOUNEL, "Ordinations," in A.-G. MARTIMORT and collaborators, *The Church at Prayer. An Introduction to the Liturgy*, new edition, vol. 3, R. CABIÉ, et al., *The Sacraments*, translated from the French *[Les sacrements]* by M. J. O'Connell (Collegeville: The Liturgical Press, 1987) 139–179; J. H. CREHAN, "Medieval Ordinations," in C. JONES, G. WAINWRIGHT and E. YARNOLD (eds.), *The Study of Liturgy* (London: SPCK, 1978) 320–331; P. F. BRADSHAW, "Medieval Ordinations," in C. JONES, G. WAINWRIGHT, E. YARNOLD & P. F. BRADSHAW (eds.), *The Study of Liturgy*, revised edition (London/NY: SPCK/Oxford University Press, 1992) 369–379; P. JOUNEL, "Le nouveau rituel d'ordination," *LMD* 98 (1969) 63–72; B. KLEINHEYER, *Die Priesterweihe . . .*; A. HOUSSIAU, "La formation de la liturgie romaine du sacre épiscopal," *Collectanea Mechliniensia* NS 18, 3 (1948) 276–284.

Moreover, the influence of the AT is present in the rites of some Anglican and Protestant Churches—for example, the rites of ordination of the Anglican Church of England: *Alternative Service Book 1980. Services Authorized for Use in the Church of England in Conjunction with the Book of Common Prayer* (London: SPCK, 1980) 337–396; the rites of ordination of the Episcopalian Church (USA): *The Book of Common Prayer and Administration of the Sacraments and Other Rites and Ceremonies of the Church, According to the Use of the Episcopal Church* (N.Y.: The Church Hymnal Corporation and the Seabury Press, 1979) 511–555; one can also find some elements of the rite of ordination of the AT in the rites of ordination of the United Methodist Church (USA): *An Ordinal, The United Methodist Church: Adopted for Official Alternative Use by the 1980 General Conference* (Nashville, Tenn.: The United Methodist Publishing House, 1979) 88–109.

in the ordination prayers which were posterior to it.[115] To get a clear idea of the nuances which exist between the ordination prayers of the *AT* and those which were derived from it, we will need to follow the development of the later rituals. This will be done in the following part of this first section.

6. CONCLUSION: STRUCTURING OF THE CHURCH AND SUBSTANCE OF ORDAINED MINISTRY

As we said at the beginning of this survey, the liturgical-canonical document attributed to Hippolytus of Rome (?) is a document important for its antiquity and its wide diffusion, and especially for its rich theological content. It remains now to describe the structure of the Church and the substance of the ordained ministries of bishop and presbyter which we find in this document.

a. *Structure of the Church*

One element of the structuring of the Church is revealed in the organization of the document itself. B. Botte has written that the work "was not always well ordered; but it is nevertheless not difficult to distinguish in the book three main parts—the makeup of the Church,

---

[115]For a discussion of the points of contact between the prayer of the *AT* and other prayers, see the articles of P.-M. GY, "La théologie des prières . . . ," and "Ancient Ordination . . . ," 72–73. According to B. BOTTE, "L'Ordre d'après . . . ," 22f., 28, 30, the *AT* has influenced ordination prayers in Syria and in Egypt. Among these ordination texts, we place the *Apostolic Constitutions* and the *Euchologion* of Serapion. Through these two rituals, the *AT* could have influenced rites of the Western Syrian type (for example, the Syrian rite of Antioch [Denzinger/ro 2, 90, 97–98]) and the Coptic rite of the patriarchate of Alexandria [Denzinger/ro 2, 12–13, 23–24], especially for episcopal ordination. In addition, see the articles of B. BOTTE, "Les ordinations dans les rites orientaux," *BCE* 36 (1962) 13–18; J.-M. HANSSENS, "Les oraisons sacramentelles des ordinations orientales," *Orientalia Christiana Periodica* 18, 3–4 (1952) 297–318, esp. 304–318, reprinted in id., *La liturgie d'Hippolyte. Documents et études* (Rome: Pontificia Università Gregoriana, 1970) 263–285, esp. 276–285 where the author has placed in parallel columns the texts of the different rituals translated into Latin and where he comments upon the points in common with the ordinations in the *Apostolic Constitutions*; cf. also E. LANNE, "Les ordinations dans le rite copte; leurs relations avec les *Constitutions apostoliques* et la *Tradition* de saint Hippolyte," *L'Orient syrien* 5, 1 (1960) 81–106; P. F. BRADSHAW, *Ordination Rites . . . ,* 46–56.

Christian initiation, and the observances of the Church."[116] At the beginning of the first part, which Botte called "the makeup of the Church," we find the ordinations and the institutions of other services in the Church. That ordination is seen as an organic whole, including both the election as its beginning and the imposition of hands as its end, is an important fact. The three ordinations take place in a Eucharistic context, and just as the bishop immediately celebrates his rank, so do the presbyter and the deacon. The ecclesiological importance of this structure should not escape us. The existential implications which the Eucharist held for the community is evident. The Church is directly experiencing its very essence in this celebration, that is, the gathering together of a dispersed people into the people of God, the Body of Christ and the Temple of the Holy Spirit.[117] In this context, we realize the importance of the episcopal ministry, since it is the bishop who presides over this process of the building up of the Church.

During an ordination, the local Church receives one of its brothers, at the end of process that it considers a judgment of God, to preside at its edification. We have seen that the entire process of admission to the episcopal ministry takes place in this context. From this process we can draw the following conclusions:

1) The choice of the elect is made by the people of the locality, which should guarantee that he is "above reproach" (*AT* 2). This shows, as we have seen (pp. 18f. and passim), that the entire Church is responsible for the apostolic faith, and not only certain of its members. Here again it is necessary to emphasize the ecclesiological significance of the lists of succession produced (for example) by St. Irenaeus. When a member of the community accedes to the presidency of this community, the members of the community itself act as witnesses to the faith, the rectitude, and the qualifications of the elect who will represent them among the other local Churches. The *AT*

---

[116]B. BOTTE, *La Tradition apostolique* . . . , 25 (= SC 11bis). This correspondence in structure between Christian initiation and the ministries which are exercised in it is discussed by A. JILEK, *Initiationsfeier* . . . , 86–123.

[117]Concerning the existential implications of the Eucharist, cf. the entire work of J. D. ZIZIOULAS, *Being as Communion*; concerning the importance of the Trinitarian articulation of the mystery of the Church, cf. H.-M. LEGRAND, "La réalisation de l'Eglise . . . ," 210–231.

agrees with Irenaeus when it describes those who are at the head of the Church as persons who have a true faith, who are capable of teaching and of looking after all these things (*AT* 1).

2) Although the bishop is chosen by the people, he cannot be ordained without the concurrence of the neighboring bishops: it is not a case here of a relationship between electors and their deputies. The bishops act as witnesses to the faith of their Churches. "They receive the decision of the Church of the ordinand and accept the newly elect as their colleague. This reception takes place in the communion of the Holy Spirit."[118] Ecclesiologically speaking, this fact precludes the possibility of the minister being the delegate of this community or the representative of a part of the *ecclesia*. No single Church can consider itself the source of the ministry: the fact that the participation of the neighboring bishops is necessary shows that the election is the human expression of divine choice (or judgment). The ministries are seen as created by God in the community.

3) The imposition of hands and the epiclesis constitute the end of the process. They take place on Sunday, which underscores the meaning of the Church itself, gathered on this day in the name of God to give him glory. It is the day of the new creation, of the work of redemption accomplished through the victory of Christ over death and sin, and it is the day when the new Temple was built by the Holy Spirit. The prayer of episcopal ordination takes up these themes,

---

[118]H.-M. LEGRAND, "La réalisation de l'Eglise . . . ," 199. The role of the neighboring bishops in this period is corroborated by the narrative of the election of Fabian as the bishop of Rome in 236 (see EUSEBIUS OF CAESAREA, *Hist. Eccl.* VI, 29, 24) and the letters of Cyprian (see P. GRANFIELD, "Episcopal Elections in Cyprian: Clerical and Lay Participation," *TS* 37, 1 (1976) 41–52; R. GRYSON, "Les élections ecclésiastiques au IIIe siècle," *RHE* 68, 2 (1973) 353–404; P. STOCKMEIER, "The Election of Bishops by Clergy and People in the Early Church," *Concilium* 137 (1980) 3–9; in contrast, T. OSAWA is more nuanced and critical of the position of Granfield: cf. *Das Bischofseinsetzungsverfahren . . .* , 83, 113–120. The significance of the collaboration of the faithful of the *ecclesia* in this entire process has been studied by P. GRANFIELD, "The *sensus fidelium . . .*" He emphasizes the pneumatic aspect of the *sensus fidelium* from the New Testament on, concluding that "the selection of bishops is linked to the exercise of charisms. The Church is composed of many persons who share a plurality of gifts or ministries. No single group, however, can claim to have a monopoly on the gifts of the Spirit" (the quotation is found on page 35).

showing God's faithfulness to his promises, particularly at the very moment when he gives a new leader to his people and a high priest to the new spiritual Temple which is to bear witness to him. The prayer presents the episcopacy as a gift of the Spirit to the Church, and the bishops as the ministers of this gift.

4) The prayer of ordination and the text of the Eucharistic prayer are seen as a liturgical act of confession. The very structure of the epiclesis pronounced during the imposition of hands is Trinitarian and expresses the dependence of Jesus the Savior and the Holy Spirit in relation to the action of God. Both (the ordination and the Eucharist) express the sense of communion seen above and were elaborated, one might dare to say, from the Trinitarian conceptualization presented in the *Apostolic Tradition*. The Church, therefore, is the new people of God established by Christ. Built upon the apostles, the Church can subsist only by the gift of the Spirit which God accords from generation to generation (cf. *AT* 3).

We have studied only the episcopal, presbyteral and diaconal ministries, but we should add that all the other ministries are conceived of as gifts of the Spirit (cf. *AT* 10–13). As for Cyprian, he saw the Church as a *fraternitas*, a designation of the Church which remained in force for a long time.[119] This designation corresponds as well to the description of the Church in the *AT*. Even though, in the latter, the different ministries vary in their content and their authority, all the ministers are brothers made worthy by the bath of regeneration, filled with the Spirit through the holy oil, and nourished by the Eucharist (cf. *AT* 21).

5) Considered side by side, episcopal and presbyteral ordinations have an element in common which is important for this study: collegiality. The bishop belongs to a college from the moment he is ordained, just as the presbyter is immediately included in the presbyterate by the fact of his ordination. Before all else, we should note the importance of the required participation of the neighboring bishops in the ordination of a new bishop. This collegial and communal character is the expression of unanimity in the faith and of sacramental

---

[119]J. RATZINGER, *Frères dans le Christ*, translated from the German *[Die christliche Brüderlichkeit]* by H.-M. Rochais and J. Evrard (Paris: Cerf, 1962); Y. CONGAR, "La collégialité . . . ," 96–97.

communion, and it translates itself into the exchange of letters, of visits, etc.[120]

For the *AT*, the presbyter is a part of the presbyterium, a collegial organ presided over by the bishop. The bishop is surrounded by his presbyterium and by the people when they celebrate the Eucharist, another image of this collegial reality. Together, bishop and presbyters exercise their pastoral ministry in the Church.

6) One last point on the structuring of the Church remains to be examined before passing on to the substance of the ministry according to the texts studied—the bond between the bishop of a local Church and the other Churches. Zizioulas defined this relationship in terms of the structure of the Eucharistic community:

". . . the head of this community was related to the other eucharistic communities in the world by his very ordination. The fact that in each episcopal ordination at least two or three bishops from the neighboring Churches ought to take part [Hippolytus, *AT,* 2; Council of Arles, c. 20; I Nicaea, c. 4 and 6, etc.] tied the episcopal office and with it the local eucharistic community in which the ordination to it took place with the rest of the eucharistic communities in the world in a fundamental way. This fact not only made it possible for each bishop to allow a visiting fellow-bishop to preside over his eucharistic community but must have been also one of the basic factors in the appearance of episcopal conciliarity."[121]

This dynamic is present in the entire process of admission to episcopal ministry and especially in its conclusion, during the celebration of the Eucharist, where one can say that the Church builds itself up before the eyes of the faithful: the local Church is established by God, who is giving it a new leader. The faith of this community is con-

---

[120]See W. ELERT, *Eucharist and Church Fellowship in the First Four Centuries,* trans. from the German *[Abendmahl und Kirchengemeinschaft in der alten Kirche hauptsächlich des Ostens]* by N. E. Nagel (St. Louis: Concordia Publishing House, 1966); H.-M. LEGRAND, "Communion ecclésiale et eucharistie aux premiers siècles," *L'Année canonique* 25 (1981) 125–148 (bibliography relative to the liturgical and canonical institutions); C. VOGEL, "Unité de l'Eglise . . . ," 591–636; Y. CONGAR, "La collégialité . . . ," 95–122 esp. note 8; the studies of H.-M. LEGRAND, "La réalisation de l'Eglise . . . ," 275–342 (bibliography), of J. D. ZIZIOULAS, *Being as Communion . . . ,* and of A. JILEK, "Bischof . . ."

[121]J. D. ZIZIOULAS, "The Eucharistic Community and the Catholicity of the Church," *One in Christ* 6, 3 (1970) 325, reprinted in id., *Being as Communion . . . ,* 155; and also see n. 100, supra.

firmed by the act of receiving the new bishop into the communion of the heads of other apostolic Churches. The Eucharistic context expresses symbolically the role of the bishop as the unifying element of the Church, elected to serve its unity and its catholicity.

b. *Substance of the Episcopal and Presbyteral Ministries*

The study of the episcopal and presbyteral ministries leads us to examine more closely the fundamental function of the *episkopē*. In the New Testament we saw that there was no clear distinction between *episkopos* and *presbyteros*: these terms were used interchangeably in the description of the exercise of the *episkopē*.[122] Later on, these concepts will be clarified and made more precise. But in the *AT*, the distinction between the ministry of the bishop and that of the presbyter has not yet been elaborated.

At the end of the preceding paragraph it was emphasized that the ministry is a gift of God for the Church. The prayer of episcopal ordination relates this gift to a fundamental task which is pastoral ("to feed your holy flock and to serve without blame as your high priest"). This is how we should interpret *spiritus principalis*. As for the presbyter, he is defined as a member of the presbyterium presided over by the bishop. There is no explanation of the relationship of subordination between him and the bishop. His membership in the presbyterium is to help him in the guidance of the people of God. This is the interpretation of the "spirit of governing and of counsel."

Clearly, the bishop is installed as the minister responsible for the community, for its daily life, for the vitality and purity of its faith, for its edification and its organization. He does not carry out his responsibilities alone, but surrounded by his presbyters who help and counsel him. We have also seen that the bishop shares collegial responsibility with the other bishops of the entire Church. The pastoral ministry of the *episkopē* is exercised, therefore, collegially at all levels.[123]

---

[122]On this point, it is sufficient to consult the works of the exegetes as found in the collected works P. BONY, E. COTHENET, J. DELORME, et al., *Le ministère et les ministères . . .* , and the works of R. E. BROWN cited supra nn. 6, 63 and 110.

[123]Cf. B. BOTTE, "Caractère collégial du presbytérat et de l'épiscopat" in B. BOTTE, A. GELIN, J. SCHMITT, et al., *Etudes sur le sacrement . . .* , 97–124; also the works of A. JILEK, *Initiationsfeier . . .* , and id., "Bischof . . . ," esp. 395–401.

Since the bishop and the presbyters are ordained to a pastoral ministry of the *episkopē,* they have a ministry which is qualified as sacerdotal. H.-M. Legrand has noted a nuance which is often missed in the commentaries on the ordination prayers of Hippolytus: "The bishop is seen as the high priest *(archiereus)* of the Church *(AT 3,* twice; *AT 34)* and not as its priest, while the presbyters—who have been given the task of governing collegially the Church—are not qualified as sacerdotal, at least directly. This results in the schema: bishop *(archiereus)*/ assembly *(hiereus)* in an equation which will not be preserved later on in the schema: bishop *(archiereus)*/priests *(hiereis)*/ assembly."[124] The fact that episcopal ordination is followed immediately by the Eucharistic celebration, the first act of the new bishop, demonstrates that his pastoral ministry includes presiding over the building up of the Church. In this celebration we see the state of equilibrium H.-M. Legrand writes about: the collegiality (between the new bishop and the other bishops, and between the new bishop and his presbyterium) in the ministry of the *episkopē.* Both participate in the pastoral office of presiding, the bishop having the chief responsibility for the community, and the presbyter assisting him and counseling him in the fulfillment of this office.

There are some tasks which remain proper to the episcopacy, such as ordination within his Church, the distribution of responsibilities, the organization of the different ministries in the community, and the presidency over the presbyterium and at the Eucharist (a celebration which is truly an act of the entire community). In the *AT,* the presbyters do nothing separately from the bishop. Nevertheless, we find elsewhere in the same document that the presbyters assume certain other tasks, but always in accord with the bishop who supervises the organization of the entire community (cf. *AT* 21, 28, 39).

A last observation is in order concerning the text of the *AT.* The prayer for episcopal ordination does not mention the doctrinal role of the bishop. The only indication of the fact that the bishops play a doctrinal role is found in the prologue, where the persons in question ("those who are at the head of the Church"/*eos qui ecclesiae praesunt*) are spoken of in relation to their tasks of teaching and of keeping the faith ("in order that they may know how to teach and be vigilant"/*ut cognoscant quomodo oportet tradi et custodiri omnia*). The role of the

[124]H.-M. LEGRAND, "La réalisation de l'Eglise . . . ," 206.

bishops in the transmission of the faith and in ensuring its understanding is evident here.

One last aspect of the substance of the ministry is revealed by the epicletic structure of the entire process: the ministries studied are the work of the Holy Spirit; the function, as well as the grace conferred, is the gift of the Spirit. We have seen, on the one hand, that the ordained ministries entail a charism for the guidance of the community which sets in motion a process which is *ecclesial, confessional and juridical*: one of the members of the community receives a concrete responsibility through a process which binds as much the Church in which and for which this person is ordained as it does the one who is ordained; we have also seen that the ordinations are celebrated in a Eucharistic context, through the imposition of hands by the bishops accompanied by an epiclesis of the entire assembly. Lastly, we have noted that the ordinations confer a real office recognized by the local Church and at the same time by the entire Church. Thus ordination is necessarily a complex process, because it is founded upon the complex structure of the shared responsibility in the progressive discernment of the call of God evinced in a number of human wills. It is here that one sees the meaning of the *fraternitas* of Christians: members of the same dignity, yes, but differentiated according to the various functions assigned in the Body. However, despite these functional and ministerial differences, all share, in solidarity, the overall responsibility for the life of the community.

B. THE *SACRAMENTARIUM VERONENSE*
(second half of the sixth century)

A period of about three centuries separates the *Apostolic Tradition* and the collection of texts for the episcopal, diaconal and presbyteral ordinations of the *libelli* of Verona, whose compilation was known formerly as the "Leonine Sacramentary." Today this series of *libelli* is called the *Sacramentarium Veronense*[125] (= *Codex Veronensis).*

---

[125]For a discussion of the terminology and of the development of the liturgical books and the collection of the *libelli* of Verona in particuliar see C. VOGEL, *Medieval Liturgy: An Introduction to the Sources,* translated and revised from the French *[Introduction aux sources de l'histoire du culte chrétien au moyen âge]* by W. Storey & N. Rasmussen (Washington, D.C.: Pastoral Press, 1986) 38–46 (+ bibliography) and E. PALAZZO, *Le moyen âge. Des origines au XIIIᵉ siècle* (Paris: Beauchesne, 1993) 62–66.

1. DATING OF THE ORDINATION PRAYERS

Although the dating of the compilation of the *libelli* of Verona places them in the sixth century, certain formularies are from an earlier period. Such is the case with the formularies for ordination (Ve, nos. 942–954) which go back probably to the middle of the fifth century and whose Roman origins are acknowledged. St. Leo the Great is most likely the author.[126]

2. SECTION XXVII OF THE *VERONENSIS*:
ITS RELATIONSHIP WITH THE *APOSTOLIC TRADTION,* AND ITS GENERAL SCHEMA

The points of comparison between the *AT* and the wordings of the *Veronensis* are not very numerous. In the *Veronensis*, there are neither rubrics nor other indications concerning the manner in which the election and the ordination took place. From this point on, these elements are found inserted separately in different liturgical books. Furthermore, in the list of offices, the order given is not the same. In the *Veronensis*, they are given in descending order: bishop, deacon and presbyter, while in the *AT*, the place of the presbyters and deacons is inverted. It is possible that the order adopted in the Sacramentary of Verona may have been intended to emphasize the importance given to the deacon at this time in Rome,[127] an importance that the *AT* had already brought out.

---

[126]Cf. L. C. MOHLBERG, L. EIZENHÖFER and P. SIFFRIN (eds.), *Sacramentarium Veronense*, 3rd ed. improved (Rome: Herder, 1978) LXIV–LXXXV; B. KLEINHEYER, *Die Priesterweihe . . .* , 69–71. Nevertheless, no one has yet proved in a convincing way the attribution of these prayers to Pope Leo I: see K. RICHTER, *Die Ordination des Bischofs von Rom. Eine Untersuchung zur Weiheliturgie* (Münster: Aschendorff, 1976) 24; and D. M. HOPE, *The Leonine Sacramentary: A Reassessment of its Nature and Purpose* (London: Oxford University Press, 1971) 110–118.

[127]On the status of the deacons in Rome one can consult the following works which describe the specific place of the deacons in this Church: F. PRAT, "Les prétentions des diacres romains au quatrième siècle," *RechSR* 3, 5 (1912) 463–475; B. DOMAGALSKI, "Römische Diakone im 4. Jahrhundert—Zum Verhältnis von Bischof, Diakon und Presbyter," in J. G. PLÖGER and H. J. WEBER (eds.), *Der Diakon. Wiederentdeckung und Erneuerung seines Dienstes* (Freiburg/Basel/Vienna: Herder, 1981) 44–56. On the *cursus honorum*, see P.-H. LAFONTAINE, *Les conditions positives de l'accession aux Ordres dans la première législation ecclésiastique (300–492)* (Ottawa: University of Ottawa, 1963) 343–356. Very often the deacons

In Rome the presbyterium is still associated with the priestly ministry of the bishop, but the nature of the relationship has been modified, as the typology used in the ordination prayers attests. In these the presbyters are considered as aides very much inferior to the bishop. The bishop is described as the high priest, who plays a role more governmental than pastoral. All these nuances will appear more clearly as we examine the texts. One last element is noteworthy: according to the *AT,* the election and the ordination took place one person at a time. In contrast, the texts of the *Veronensis* show that several persons were ordained at the same time *(consecratio episcoporum, benedictio super diaconos* and *consecratio presbyteri).* We will first study the structure of the ordinations, then the structure of the ordination prayers.

3. STRUCTURE OF THE ORDINATIONS

To have some idea of the way in which the ordinations took place, it is necessary to refer to the type of liturgical books which are called *ordines,* which were a "part of the ceremonial and constitute the indispensable complement to the sacramentary."[128] The first *ordo* of interest is *Ordo 34,* the old Roman ritual of ordinations which can be dated to around 750 (in its manuscript tradition).[129]

In the episcopal ordination celebrated in Rome we must distinguish the ordination *conferred by* the bishop of Rome as the metropolitan from the ordination *of* the bishop of Rome conferred by the suburban bishops. Of all the *ordines* studied, only OR 40 A and 40 B describe the ordination of the pope.

---

of Rome were elected bishops of the capital: cf. L. OTT, *Le sacrement . . . ,* 55–65; M. ANDRIEU, *Les 'Ordines Romani' du haut moyen âge,* vol. 3, *Les textes (suite) (Ordines XIV–XXXIV)* (Louvain: Spicilegium sacrum Lovaniense, 1951) 567–569 (hereafter cited as ANDRIEU OR followed by the number of the volume in Roman numerals); id., "La carrière ecclésiastique des papes et les documents liturgiques du moyen âge," *RevSR* 21, 3–4 (1947) 90–120; and H. B. PORTER, *The Ordination Prayers of the Ancient Western Churches* (London: SPCK, 1967) 12f.

[128]C. VOGEL, *Medieval Liturgy . . . ,* 135–224 for a complete history of their formation, provenance, influence and content; E. PALAZZO, *Le moyen âge. . . ,* 187–196 and A.-G. MARTIMORT, *Les "ordines," les ordinaires et les cérémoniaux* (Turnhout: Brépols, 1991) 15–47.

[129]Even if the manuscript tradition is from the eighth century, the fundamental elements are much older and go back to the seventh century; see A. SANTANTONI, *L'ordinazione episcopale . . . ,* 64, and also the dating given by C. VOGEL, *Medieval Liturgy . . . ,* 174–176.

OR 34 presents the ordinations in an ascending order (deacon [nos. 5–10], presbyter [nos. 11–13] and bishop [nos. 14–45]). This order may indicate a change in the manner of understanding the different ministries in the Church. We are in the presence of the birth of the hierarchy.[130]

After these brief general observations, we shall now move on to an examination of the ritual of OR 34. The presentation will, however, follow the descending order, which we find in the "Leonine" and later in the Gregorian Sacramentary of the Hadrianum type,[131] which are the sacramentaries used with the Roman ritual.

a. *Bishop*—OR 34, 14–45[*14–*19]

The rite described here is that of the ordination conferred by the pope (the "apostolic lord"—*domnus apostolicus*) acting as the metropolitan. The regions under his rule were central Italy, the islands, and some areas of modern-day France and Germany.[132] Here we move from a very simple rite (that of the *AT*) to one much more complex. Nevertheless, we see that the principal actors are the same: the *domnus apostolicus* and his clergy,[133] other bishops, a delegation of the

---

[130]Cf. A. FAIVRE, *Naissance d'une hiérarchie. Les premières étapes du cursus clérical* (Paris: Beauchesne, 1977) 367–370.

[131]*Benedictio episcoporum*, Gr 21–26; *oratio ad ordinandum presbyterum*, Gr 27–29; *orationes ad ordinandum diaconum*, Gr 30–32.

[132]Cf. ANDRIEU OR III, 570, where he refers to the list established in the *Liber censuum*. Very probably these regions were directly dependent upon Rome due to their evangelization, a relationship of Mother Church to Daughter Church.

[133]In OR 34 the major role is certainly that of the bishop of Rome, called here the *domnus apostolicus*. It is nevertheless indicated that he does not act alone in the ordination of a new bishop, because other bishops are present, as is shown in OR 34, 41–42, and perhaps also in OR 34, 39 (*prostrato domno apostolico cum sacerdotibus . . .*). The word *sacerdos* includes that of *episcopus*, without any doubt. Moreover, ms. Wolfenbüttel 4175 gives the same interpretation. In any case, if OR 34 gives no precise details as to the identity of the one who imposes hands, we should note that in n. 40 the verb used for the act of ordination is in the singular: *benedicet*. It seems reasonable to wonder whether this text does not simply reproduce what we found already in the *AT*: "one of the bishops present . . . shall lay his hands on him who is being ordained bishop, and pray . . ." (*AT* 2). Nevertheless, acccording to the tradition of the early Church, a bishop should be ordained by all the bishops of the province. If this is impossible, three bishops at least (this number varies according to the legislation in force) should gather to proceed to the ordination, while those who are absent should give their consent

clergy and of the faithful from the vacant Church, and the elect. Moreover, the canonico-liturgical continuum which takes place on Sunday in the *AT* is hereafter divided into several steps spread out over several days: the election and the preliminaries, the scrutinies, and the ordination.

α) *Election and Preliminaries.*[*14] The first part of the ritual corresponds to the election by the people and the clergy of "the place where the bishop has deceased." After this election, a delegation from the vacant Church goes to Rome with the elect to present him to the pope and to ask for his ordination. On Friday they present to him the decree *(decretum)* and the request *(rogatoriae litterae)*. The archdeacon then questions the elect to assure that there is no impediment according to the *quattuor capitula*,[134] that is, sodomy, an offense against a consecrated virgin, bestiality, and adultery. Thus being assured of the absence of all impediments, the archdeacon makes him swear on the Gospel and on the tomb of St. Peter. This is the end of the first part, and its meaning is quite clear. The practice which was universal in the early Church is again found here: the local Church (clergy and baptized) plays an active role in the choice of the bishop. We have already discussed in detail the implications of this fact. Let us note the testimony of one particular practice of this period. Pope Celestine I (428), citing again canons 18 of the Council of Ancyra (314) and 18 of the Council of Antioch (341), demanded that "one not impose on the

---

in writing; see for example: the Council of Arles (314), canon 20; the Council of Nicaea I (325), canon 4; the Council of Antioch (341), canon 19; the Council of Sardica (343), canon 6; the *Apostolic Constitutions* (towards 380) VIII, 4, 6; the collection called "the Second Council of Arles" (450), canon 5, and the "Statutes of the early Church" (end of the fifth century), preamble. Cf. J. GAUDEMET, *Les élections . . .* , 16–22. Also useful are the references given by L. MORTARI, *Consacrazione episcopale . . .* , passim.

[134]These questions attest to the concern of the Church for the quality of the moral life of her ministers, necessary especially for the bishop who should be a witness to the faith. Previously, the penitential discipline of the Church provided a safeguard: no one whose name appeared on the list of penitents could be ordained to any ministry. Correctly, M. Andrieu notes "that the questionnaire (the *IV capitula*) was only introduced into the ordination ritual after the abandonment of the ancient penitential discipline: this was the new means of stopping, on the threshold of holy orders, the sinners who fell into sins judged to be too infamous," ANDRIEU OR III, 553.

people a bishop whom they do not want."[135] Several times Leo the Great expressed the same principle (". . . Let those who are going to be called to the episcopacy be requested in peace and calm. Let his election require the support of the clergy, the testimony of the notables, the consent of the curia and of the people. Let him who is to be the head of all be elected by all"; and, ". . . no one shall be ordained without having been requested, or against the wishes of the faithful, because it should not be that a people despise or have an aversion to a bishop whom they would not have wanted and that they become less holy than they ought to be because they were not given the one they wanted").[136] These examples show that the Church was concerned that the choice be truly responsible and conscious. All the community members in fact shared and exercised responsibility for their Church. We must not, however, present too idealized a picture of the Church of that time, because such a system is not without its risks, as we will see when we study the scrutinies.[137]

β) *Scrutinies.*[*15] The pope, surrounded by the bishops and presbyters, presides over the meeting on Saturday evening. After being assured of the fact of the election, of its freedom and of the validity of the choice (absence of the four serious sins, nos. 14–16), the apostolic lord asks the delegation a series of questions (nos. 22–28) dealing with the ecclesiastical career of the elect, his conjugal state, and the way in which he conducts his family life; he inquires, lastly, about the possibility of simony. These questions are asked a second time of the elect

---

[135]CELESTINE I, *Ep. IV, Ad episcopos provinciae Viennensis et Narbonensis,* 5 (PL 50, 434–435).

[136]LEO THE GREAT, *Ep. X, Ad episcopos per provinciam Viennensem constitutos,* 6 (PL 54, 634) and *Ep. XIV, Ad Anastasium Thessalonicensem episcopum,* 5 (PL 54, 673). For other references, see the data established by J. GAUDEMET, *Les élections . . . ,* 13–104.

[137]During this same period, a situation developed which in the ninth century would lead to the crisis of the *investitura laica.* Among the works treating of this subject, see the following: A. DUMAS, "Les élections épiscopales" and "La féodalité épiscopale" in A. FLICHE and V. MARTIN (eds.), *Histoire de l'Eglise depuis les origines jusqu'à nos jours,* vol. 7; E. AMANN and A. DUMAS, *L'Eglise au pouvoir des laïques (888–1057)* (Paris: Bloud & Gay, 1948) 190–219; Y. CONGAR, *L'Eglise de saint Augustin à l'époque moderne* (Paris: Cerf, 1970), ch. 2: "Des Pères au moyen âge" and ch. 3: "L'époque carolingienne"; and B. COOKE, *Ministry . . . ,* 75–112.

himself. The meeting is completed by the ratification of the election by the pope, the announcement of the date of the ordination, and the kiss of peace (nos. 29–31). Some observations are in order concerning the content of the scrutinies and their theological meaning.

At the time of OR 34, there did not yet exist an obligatory *cursus* for the clergy whereby one passed successively from one ministry to the next in order. Until the eleventh century, it was possible to be admitted to the episcopacy either from the diaconate or from the presbyterate.[138] So it was possible to be ordained bishop *without* a preliminary presbyteral ordination.[139] In any case, the pope asked the delegates if the elect had exercised either the diaconal or presbyteral ministry, and for how long. Thus the delegation bore witness to the quality of the ministry exercised by the elect. Moreover, if the elect did not belong to the Church for which he had been elected, it was necessary to produce a dismissorial letter from his bishop *(dimissoria)*.

Two questions were then asked: first, if the elect was married, he was asked what dispositions he had taken to support his family after his ordination; next, the delegation was questioned on the way in which he managed his household (four qualities were required: chastity, hospitality, gentleness *[benignitas]*, and concern for being pleasing to God in all things—these are the qualities required in the Pastoral Epistles [cf.1 Tim 3:2-3; Titus 1:5-9]). Familial responsibility

---

[138]See M. ANDRIEU, "La carrière . . . ," 99–102, 106–107. OR 35 B, 2–6 (Rheinland, ca. 1000) presents the new tradition according to which, at the moment when the elect is presented for episcopal consecration, he is already ordained to the priesthood. Nevertheless, the first witnesses to this practice are already present during the ninth century in France: cf. AMALARIUS OF METZ, *Liber Officialis*, II, 14, 2 and HINCMAR OF RHEIMS, *Ep. XXIX, Ad Adventium episcopum Metensem* (869–870) (PL 126, 186–188) quoted by M. ANDRIEU, "Le sacre épiscopal d'après Hincmar de Reims," *RHE* 48, 1–2 (1953) 27–29.

[139]The tendency to require the rank of priesthood before episcopal consecration would be cited by those who later wanted to prove that the episcopacy was not a sacrament. The question is complex, since in the scholastic elaboration of the theology of orders attempts were also made to affirm or deny that the episcopacy was a true order. Among the numerous articles published on this subject, see A. MC DEVITT, "The Episcopate as an Order and Sacrament on the Eve of the High Scholastic Period," *Franciscan Studies* 20, 1–2 (1960) 96–148; L. OTT, *Le sacrement . . .* , 107–188; J. LECUYER, "Orientations présentes de la théologie de l'épiscopat," in Y. CONGAR and B.-D. DUPUY (eds.), *L'épiscopat . . .* , 781–811, esp. 785–787.

was still seen as good preparation for, and as a guarantee of, the good practice of ecclesial responsibility (cf. 1 Tim 3:5).[140]

Secondly, a question was asked concerning the innocence of the elect relative to a promise of simony. The purpose was to verify the moral value and the good conduct of the elect, as well as the regularity of the election. These delegates, therefore, were the guarantors of the good conduct of the elect. The response *(vos videritis)* of the apostolic lord attests implicitly to the responsibility which the different members of the Church share on this occasion. The first part of the scrutiny ends with the reading of the decree of election. This whole part takes place in the absence of the elect, who is then introduced at this moment.

The pope addresses the elect, adding to the questions asked (no. 27) beforehand to the delegation another, concerning the texts of the Scriptures read in the elect's Church and the canons in force. The addition of these questions shows that the elect will be responsible for the understanding of the faith through the proclamation and the teaching of the Word, and the discipline of the Church. These questions, however, were not asked of the members of the delegation, but only of the one who was destined to be their head and their spokesman with the other Churches. It is he who is responsible for the unity of the faith and for the discipline in his Church. The first part of the scrutiny shows that the faithful, too, have a share in this responsibility, especially concerning the accession of one of their own to the episcopal ministry (and even to the other ordained ministries in the Church).

This second part of the scrutiny ends with a brief speech by the pope to the elect relative to the days of ordination (that is to say, the nights of Saturday to Sunday during the fasts of the Ember days).[141] The pope alludes to an *"edictum"* (= *formata* in no. 44) which the new

---

[140]We see, then, that at this time the marriage of clerics was not an impediment to orders in the episcopal, presbyteral or diaconal ministry. Cf. also OR 36, 27 (Roman, ca. 897) and ANDRIEU OR III, 574–575; OR IV, 114, 140–147. At any rate, conjugal relations could not be maintained; from the end of the fourth century, major clerics had to live in continence: see ANDRIEU OR IV, 139–141, and the research of R. GRYSON, *Les origines du célibat ecclésiastique du Ier au VIIe siècles* (Gembloux: J. Duculot, 1970); also A. FAIVRE, *Ordonner la fraternité . . .* , 146–150.

[141]The *AT* prescribes Sunday for the ordination of the bishop, as we have seen above. This is a fairly strict rule, affirmed throughout the history of ordination. See T. MICHELS, *Beiträge zur Geschichte . . .* In 445 LEO THE GREAT confirmed

bishop will receive to guide him in his episcopal ministry. After having ratified the election and announced the preparatory fast for the ordination the next day, the apostolic lord gives the kiss of peace to the elect. Thus the wish of the vacant Church to have a head *(patronus)* is fulfilled, and all prepare themselves to entreat God through fasting and prayer.

γ) *Ordination, Installation and Eucharist.*[*16–*19] In OR 34, following the tradition of the early Church, the ordination takes place on Sunday, a fact whose ecclesiological and eschatological significance we have already seen. The fast gives it even greater power, reinforcing the paschal character of the event. We note that the ceremony is still simple, but solemn (". . . *cum omni decore"*); it takes place in a Eucharistic context. The central elements are the imposition of hands[142] accompanied by the prayers of ordination, represented here by the gesture of blessing (". . . *tunc benedicet eum . . . ,"* no. 40, and

---

this rule but, speaking of presbyters and deacons, he added that the rule seems to be applied for the vigil between Saturday and Sunday. Here is his very beautiful explanation:

"Those to be ordained are never to receive the blessing except on the day of the Lord's Resurrection, to which the evening of the Sabbath is added as a beginning, as is well known. It is a day which has been hallowed by such great mysteries in the divine plan of events that whatever of major importance the Lord decided on was carried out on this honored day. On this day the Apostles received from the Lord the trumpet of the Gospel to be preached to all nations and also received the sacrament of regeneration to be carried to the entire world. On this day, as blessed John the Evangelist testifies, the Apostles being assembled in one place and the doors being shut, when the Lord entered into their midst, He said: 'Receive the Holy Spirit; whose sins you shall forgive, they are forgiven them; and whose sins you shall retain, they are retained.' Finally, on this day came the Holy Spirit promised by the Lord to the Apostles. Thus we know through some divine plan the custom was introduced and became traditional whereby the rites for the laying of hands on priests are to be celebrated on that day on which all the gifts of grace were conferred."

Ep. IX, Ad Dioscorum Alexandrinum episcopum, 1 (PL 54, 626). Nevertheless, Gelasius I, fifty years later, "only admits as such the Saturdays of the seasonal fasts of June, September and December, as well as those of the first and fourth weeks of Lent" (*Ep. IX, Ad episcopos per Lucaniae,* 11 [PL 59, 52]) quoted in ANDRIEU OR III, 555–556.

[142]The imposition of hands is not mentioned here in the text of OR 34, 40. All the parallel documents, however, require it: cf. OR 35, 65; OR 35A, 8; OR 36, 37. It is also the opinion of L. OTT, *Le sacrement . . . ,* 130. C. Vogel has established

"benedictione expleta . . . ," no. 41), which were certainly the nucleus of the ordinations in Rome. After the blessing came the kiss of peace and the installation of the new bishop, followed by the Eucharistic celebration.

Once again the pope is assisted by bishops, presbyters and other ministers. Number 36 mentions the reading of 1 Timothy 3:1-7, which recalls the qualities of a good bishop. After the reading and the gradual, the elect (already vested in the dalmatic, the chasuble, and wearing sandals) is introduced. The proclamation of the election is then made, followed by the invitatory (no. 38): "The clergy and the people of the city, by common agreement, with the adjacent parishes, have elected such a one, deacon or presbyter, to be consecrated bishop *(episcopum consecrari)*. Let us pray, therefore, for this man, that our God and Savior Jesus Christ may give him the episcopal chair to rule his Church and the people all together *(plebem universam)."*

Let us dwell for a moment on this text, for its contents reveal many features that we have seen in the early Church. This text is, above all, a kind of official report of the election which mentions the name of the Church in which the elect will be in charge. It also affirms that the election has taken place and that it was done regularly, that is, by the clergy and the people of the locality, confirmed by the parishes of the countryside, and done in complete freedom (without promise of simony).[143] The second part of this prayer is an invitatory (to all) to pray for the elect. This corresponds to the silent prayer of all in the

---

an impressive collection of liturgical texts and has shown the importance but also the relativity of the gesture of the imposition of hands; see VOGEL, *Ordinations . . . ,* [69]–[148]. In the case of OR 34, 9 (deacon), 12 (presbyter) and 40 (bishop), he believed that Andrieu was wrong when he affirmed: "the description (of the ordination) is so abridged that it does not even mention the imposition of hands. This rite was nonetheless traditional"; see ANDRIEU OR III, 559 and 569. On the contrary, Vogel preferred to read the text literally: "It is difficult to think that if, at the time when the redactor of *Ordo XXXIV* had composed his directory in a decadent Rome, the rite of the imposition of hands had had the slightest importance, he would not have mentioned it": *Ordinations . . . ,* [131]. Vogel wanted to demonstrate the relativity of the gesture even though it is nearly always present.

[143]See the commentary of A. SANTANTONI on the interpretation of the term *electio* in the light of the historical data of the period: *L'ordinazione episcopale . . . ,* 65–66 and 130–131.

ritual of the *AT*. Here, however, we have a pre-formulated prayer, actually, a litany. A last observation—we find a phrase borrowed from the ordination prayer of the Verona Sacramentary, a phrase which explains the purpose of the prayer itself: that the necessary authority (the episcopal chair) may be conferred for the governance of the Church and the people. We will return to this point later when we examine the prayer of ordination.

Once the prayer of blessing is finished, the apostolic lord is the first to welcome the ordinand with the kiss of peace, which the new bishop then gives to the bishops and to the presbyters. Then the pope places him in front of all the bishops. This emphasizes that the presbyterium and the episcopal body are closely bound one to the other. The kiss of peace is exchanged only among the bishops and the presbyters; it is given neither to the deacons nor to the other ministers, nor to the people. Moreover, through his ordination, the new bishop belongs henceforth to an episcopal college, which is the very meaning of his installation.[144]

δ) *Ordination of the Bishop of Rome, OR 40 A (sixth century).*[*20–*21] The ordination ritual of the Roman pontiff follows that of the ordination of bishops of OR 34, with some minor modifications.

The document in question goes back to the sixth century, and it is the first liturgical witness which gives specific indications concerning the ordination of the bishop of Rome.[145] OR 40 A does not give any indication for the election or for the scrutinies, but begins directly with the ordination ceremony which took place after the psalm and the litany.[*20] The ordination of the pope was conferred by three bishops, the bishop of Ostia, assisted by those of Albano and of Porto. Nothing is said about the imposition of hands by these three bishops, except that the bishop of Albano says the first prayer (= *Adesto*, Ve 945), the bishop of Porto the second (= *Propitiare*, Ve 946[*55]) and, lastly, the bishop of Ostia proceeds to the consecration (= Ve 947[*56–*59]).

---

[144]In fact, the early Church considered absolute ordination as without effect: see canon 6 of the Council of Chalcedon. For the collection of texts and their interpretation, see VOGEL, *Ordinations . . .* , [106]–[109] and [133]–[148]; L. MORTARI, *Consacrazione episcopale . . .* , 121–151.

[145]Cf. ANDRIEU OR IV, 289–294; K. RICHTER, *Die Ordination . . .* , 13–31.

At the moment when one expects the imposition of hands we find the deacons opening the evangelistary over the head of the elect. This gesture is absent in the ritual of ordination of the bishops of Rome in the seventh century. Nevertheless, it was not unknown in ecclesiastical tradition, for already at the end of the fourth century in Syria the *Apostolic Constitutions* (VIII, 4, 6) attest to this gesture performed by deacons in all episcopal ordinations.

J. Lécuyer attempted to explain this gesture from two patristic texts attributed to Severian of Gabala: the imposition of the Gospels on the head signifies the descent of the tongues of fire, that is, the descent (or the gift) of the Holy Spirit upon him for whom the Spirit was invoked.[146]

[146]Cf. Severian of Gabala, in his *Pentecost Homily* (PG 125, 533 ab) and *De Legislatore*, 4 (PG 56, 404). This last homily attributed to Chrysostom by Photius has been restored to Severian. These important texts are reproduced here, translated by the editor, from J. LECUYER, "Note sur la liturgie du sacre des évêques," EL 66, 4 (1952) 369–372. The first text is seen as an explanation of the rite of ordination of bishops. The second seeks to explain why the head of the people should have his head covered (reference to Aaron, the high priest of the people). Here are the texts:

"But again, why on the head? Because the apostles were ordained *(echeirotonounto)* as teachers of the whole world; now, an ordination *(cheirotonia)* always must be done only on the head. The presence of tongues on their head is therefore the sign of an ordination. In fact, ordination is done on the head, as custom requires down to our day *(kathōs kai heōs nyn ekratēse to pragma)*. For since the descent of the Holy Spirit is invisible, we impose the Gospel book on the head of whomever is to be ordained high priest *(epitithetai tē kephalē tou mellontos cheirotonesthai archiereōs to Euangelion)*; and when this imposition is done, one should see there nothing other than a tongue of fire which rests upon the head: a tongue, because of the preaching of the Gospel *(kērygma)*; a tongue of fire because of the words: I came to bring fire to the earth." *(Pentecost Homily)*

"It is for this reason, in the Church also, during the ordination of priests *(en tais cheirontoniais tōn hiereōn)*, the Gospel book is placed on the head of the ordinand, in order that he might learn that he has received the true tiara of the Gospel; in order that he might learn also that, although he be the head of all, he is nonetheless subject to these laws; commanding all, he must himself be commanded by the Law; and that he who gives orders to all is himself receiving the order of the laws . . . Consequently, the imposition of the Gospel book upon the priest *pontifex* signifies that he is subject to an authority . . ." *(De Legislatore)*

Several elements here are interesting for our purpose. We see the link between the apostolic ministry which the bishops receive by their ordination and the

This gesture appears also in another text of the end of the fifth century in Gaul: the *Statuta Ecclesiae antiqua (SEA)*, 2. We will have occasion to return to this document when we study the structure of ordinations in Gaul.

Once the ordination prayer is finished, the archdeacon places the pallium on the new pontiff who, after having taken his place at the chair gives the kiss of peace "to all the priests" *(omnes sacerdotes)*, and he continues the Mass with the *Gloria*. Andrieu maintains that we should not see "a sort of enthronement" here, since the new pope "went to this position because it was there, according to normal practice, that the pontiff is to remain standing for the singing of the *Gloria in excelsis*. . . ."[147]

Conclusions. This cursory presentation of the structure of episcopal ordination allows us to observe a development in the consciousness that the Church had of itself and of its presence in the world. I will try to draw some conclusions, keeping in mind that our purpose here is not to provide a complete history of each element of the ritual, but rather to point out the changes (or the permanent elements) in the theology of ordained ministry and in the structuring of the Church symbolized by these elements.

1) The four centuries which separate the very simple ritual of the *AT* and the Roman ritual of OR 34 were a very fruitful period for the Church, which enjoyed its new freedom, but which passed from a culturally and socially marginal existence to a much more central

event of Pentecost. The idea of the building up of the Church is represented by the feast of Pentecost, the occasion on which unity was restored: the confusion of languages which took place at the destruction of the Tower of Babel is remedied by the event of the building up of the Church. Here we are afforded an eschatological perspective when the apostles, after having received the gift of the Holy Spirit, speak in other languages through the gift of the Spirit (cf. Acts 2:4); they could therefore serve as instruments to call into unity all the nations: they are henceforth teachers of the whole world. The bishops are, through their ordination, the continuation either of the teachers or of the high priests. Comparing the second text, we note that the bishop is at the head of his people and is thus their leader, but that he has an authority over him, which is the Word of God. These attributes are given to him through his ordination. For the interpretation of the rites of the imposition of hands and of the imposition of the Gospel book, see the excellent article by J. LECUYER, "Le sens des rites d'ordination d'après les Pères," *L'Orient syrien* 5, 4 (1960) 463–475.

[147]ANDRIEU OR IV, 294. The *Gloria* was reserved for the bishop in the West until the eighth century: cf. ANDRIEU OR II, 83–84.

position in the society of the high Middle Ages. It is therefore expectable that we notice a parallel development between the position of the Church in relation to the world and its liturgical celebrations in general, and especially those which brought the ministers to their office. The first change we notice is therefore the evolution of the structural elements of ordination. The core, however, remained the same: a liturgical continuum is maintained between the *election* (by the clergy and the people of the particular place), the *ordination* (by the imposition [very probably] of hands accompanied by a prayer), and the *entrance into a concrete office* (by the installation among the other bishops, and the Eucharistic celebration).

2) The importance of the communion within the local Church and among the Churches continues to be attested by the celebrations of the vigil of Saturday when the election by the local Church is received by the other Churches (here, the reception by the metropolitan).[148] The delegation of the Church of the elect is there to attest to his qualities (questions on the exercise of his diaconal or presbyteral ministry, his family life, and his dispositions in general) and also to the regularity of his election (the absence of a possible promise of si-

[148]The canons of the Church show the importance of this reception for the very existence of ordination. For example, the Council of Nicaea (325) canon 6, 2nd part, declared: "It is evident that if anyone is made bishop without the consent of the metropolitan, this great synod determines that such a one shall not be a bishop *(mēde einai episkopon),*" translation from N. P. TANNER (ed.), *Decrees of the Ecumenical Councils,* vol. 1, *Nicaea I to Lateran V* (London/Washington, D.C.: Sheed & Ward/Georgetown University Press, 1990) 9. J. LECUYER, *Le sacrement de l'ordination . . . ,* 66–67, gives another interpretation of this canon, but from the fourth canon of Nicaea on, the metropolitan is seen as having the responsibility of confirming what goes on in his province. It is precisely this spirit that is attested in OR 34.

LEO THE GREAT confirmed this tradition in his letter to Rusticus of Narbonne (458/459): "There is no reason for considering as bishops those who have not been elected by the clergy, nor desired by the faithful, nor ordained by the bishops of the province with the assent of the metropolitan. This is why, given that the problem is often encountered of a clerical order unworthily received in similar circumstances *(male acceptus honor),* we answer without any hesitation that it is necessary to refuse them the episcopal rank which in the light of all evidence has not been given to them," *Ep.CLXVII, Ad Rusticum Narbonensem episcopum* (PL 54, 1203). Here it is clear that the elements required for genuine ordination are election, ordination by the bishops of the province, and the assent of the metropolitan.

mony). As in the *AT*, the approval of the other Churches is also necessary—hence the obligatory presence of the metropolitan (the pope in this case) and of several bishops. The elect, who becomes the link between his Church and the others, responds to the same questions (an attestation to his moral value), but he bears witness also to the faith and the discipline of his own Church (nos. 27, 28). Even though OR 34 presents the scrutinies in their ritualized form, lacking some of their actual vitality, one can still recognize the values emphasized. Lastly, the kiss of peace exchanged and received twice (at the conclusion of the scrutinies and at the end of the ordination) represents a seal of charity and of unity. This gesture signifies the acceptance of the election and the ordination and, at the same time, expresses the communion which exists between the representatives of the Churches.

3) The act of ordination itself is seen in an eschatological context, because it takes place during the Eucharistic celebration on Sunday. The paschal/pentecostal aspect[149] is henceforth accentuated by the fact that the community prepares itself for the ordination by fasting and prayer (cf. Leo the Great). In the case of the ordination *of* the bishop of Rome, the imposition of the evangelistary was added, concretizing the link between the building up of the local Church and the edification of the universal Church on the first Pentecost. This last element would give definite importance to the role of the pope, because it is only during his ordination (in Rome) that we find this imposition of the Gospels.

4) The act of reception is again made visible when the new bishop takes his place among the other bishops. Visually, the collegiality of the episcopacy is very evident. We do not know whether the new bishop himself presided at the Eucharist, but it is certain that he concelebrated at it. He has entered into a concrete office (recall the text *clerus et plebs*) marked both by the ritual and by the blessing prayer, which we will examine later. The ordination is not seen as a personal gift, separated from a specific community; in fact, we know that if this context is absent, the actions of the ordinand would have no effect.[150]

---

[149]Cf. the article by J. LECUYER, "Mystère . . . ," 167–213 for a presentation of this aspect of ordination in the Fathers.

[150]Cf. the following studies: C. VOGEL, "Titre d'ordination . . ."; H.E.J. COWDREY, "The Dissemination of St. Augustine's Doctrine of Holy Orders during the Later Patristic Age," *JTS* NS 20, 2 (1969) 448–481. Against Vogel, H. Crouzel

5) The only thing that may leave us perplexed is the absence of any reference to the active participation of at least three bishops, a rule of the early Church since Nicaea (canon 4) which we have already noted in the *AT*. In Rome it is probable that we are hearing of a privilege reserved to the pope. The usual interpretation of this matter is that ordination is the business of the pope alone, and "without doubt it was a traditional practice which goes back very far, which did not succeed in broaching either the canon of Nicaea, nor those of the later conciliar assemblies."[151]

---

sought to harmonize the complex facts in light of the later development of doctrine, while Vogel insisted upon the divergence and on the importance of ecclesial recognition of the ordained ministry during the first millenium; see H. CROUZEL, "La doctrine du caractère sacerdotal est-elle en contradiction avec la tradition occidentale d'avant le XIIe siècle et avec la tradition orientale?," *BLE* 74, 4 (1973) 241–262 reprinted in id., *Mariage et divorce, célibat et caractère sacerdotaux dans l'Eglise ancienne* (Turin: Bottega d'Erasmo, 1982) [285]–[306].

[151]ANDRIEU OR III, 585. This is the opinion which the liturgists in general follow: cf. V. RAFFA, "Partecipazione collettiva . . . ," 105–140. Nevertheless, in response to the question whether the *Breviatio Ferrandi* is sufficient to prove that in Rome the canonical tradition was not accepted, C. VOGEL wrote a letter expressing a different point of view than that of Andrieu. Since his response to Andrieu has never been published, to my knowledge, here it is in its entirety. His letter is dated May 27, 1981:

Dear friend,

I am responding to your letter of May 22, 1981 giving you *my* point of view (which may not be the correct one). Nevertheless, I ask you to reflect upon my way of analyzing the question. I believe that I am right . . .

Here is the situation in Rome:

1. The Apostolic Tradition (*ca. 200*) required the presence of several bishops at the time of an episcopal ordination. Fragment of Verona: "cum . . . tres qui praesentes fuerint episcopi . . . imponant super eum manus." The document is *Roman.*

2. The situation is the same *in 386*. Siricius, *Ep. ad episcopos* 2: "Ne unus episcopus episcopum ordinare praesumat . . ."—*Roman* document.

3. The situation is the same in the sixth century (Ordo XL A) and still at the *end of the eighth century* (Ordo XL B): several bishops are present and participate in the ordination of the pope. *Roman* documents, although they were transcribed in a Frankish country.

4. The situation is the same in the *ninth century* (if not the tenth century) with Ordo XXXIV 20: "Domnus apostolicus . . . vocatis ad se episcopos vel (=et) presbyteros, iubet eos *sibi consedere* . . ."

It would be erroneous to say, in such a document as Ordo XXXIV, that we should distinguish between "praesentia sacramentalis" et "praesentia mere caer-

b. *Presbyter*[*24, *44–*49]

The social environment in which the Church lived was transformed, as we have seen above. With the new enjoyment of legal existence in secular society, the Church grew, and therefore the functioning of the Church's ministerial system had to adapt itself to new demands. In Rome, we see more frequent participation of the presbyters in the ministry of the bishop as the places of worship multiplied. We know, for example, the importance that cemeteries and titular Churches *(tituli)* had for the Church of Rome and its vitality; it was the Church of the martyrs and very proud of its faith, bathed in the blood of the saints.[152] It was natural that these changes should have been reflected in the way in which the Church ordained its presbyters, because the principle of having just one bishop per locality was the rule, and the presbyters became an extension of the ministry of the *episkopē*.

α) *Election.* OR 34 gives no information on this subject. We have to wait until the end of the eighth century to have some idea of the

---

emonialis"!! *This would be an unforgivable anachronism.* The text says that the bishops are at the side of the bishop of Rome and that, by the very fact of their official presence, they participate in the ordination.

5. Concerning the *Breviatio Ferrandi*:

a. Firstly, canons 4 and 5 reflect faithfully the ancient discipline (several bishops).

b. "Excepta ecclesia Romana" is a *lapsus* or *a mistake* of Ferrandus, because he refers in canon 6 to the letter of Siricius which says exactly the opposite.

c. The *Breviatio* should be mentioned *in the critical edition* of the *Corpus Christianorum, Series Latina,* 149, p. 287.

d. The *Breviatio* dates to the years 523/546 and is thus in contradiction with the Roman discipline of the time—cf. my points 1, 2 and 3.

Therefore, *Ferrandus* has made an error of interpretation.

It is clear that according to Roman usage—often invoked for the other churches—*several* bishops should be present.

[152]Cf. ch. 2: "Organisation et société cléricales" and ch. 8: "La mission chrétienne à Rome de Damase à Sixte" in Ch. PIETRI, *Roma Christiana. Recherches sur l'Eglise de Rome, son organisation, sa politique, son idéologie de Miltiade à Sixte III (311–400)* (Paris: Boccard, 1976), and the first part of the article by G. H. LUTTENBERGER, "The Decline of Presbyteral Collegiality and the Growth of the Individualization of the Priesthood (4th–5th Centuries)," *RATM* 48 (1981) 14–58, esp. 14–36.

procedure as it was carried out in Rome. OR 39, which contains some Gallican elements, gives a description of the ceremonies which took place in Rome before the ordination.[153] We learn that the deacons and the presbyters had to take an oath over the relics of the saints that they had not commited any of the serious sins, the list of which is contained in the *IV capitula*. This was done in the presence of the pope himself *(pontifex)*, some notaries, the archdeacon, and the archpriest (OR 39, 1*[44]). At the Mass of the following Wednesday the elect *(electi)*, already dressed in their vestments, stood in the presbyterium, in the presence of the assembly while the list of their names and of the titles for which they were to be ordained was read to see if there were any objections on the part of the faithful to their nomination (OR 39, 2, 4, 5*[44]-*[46]).[154] On Friday, the same ceremony was repeated a second time (OR 39, 8, 10*[47]).

It is clear, according to these texts, that the understanding of ordained ministry in the *AT* and in the early Church still persisted. The ecclesial dimension of the ministry remains constant. Even though the demographic and sociological situation of the Church has changed, the original import of the responsibility of the people in the choice of their clergy remained alive. Christians had, at the very least, to approve the election, or better, the nomination which was made by the bishop and his clergy. The text of the proclamation teaches us that at this time ordination was always carried out for a concrete office in a particular Church.[155] Another source (also Gallicanized) confirms what we have just seen above (OR 36, towards 897).[156] Moreover, we know that there existed a document, the *"brevis advocationis,"* that the pope himself read in the course of the ordination ceremony (OR 36, 9*[24]). The text is close to that cited above, but two things here are

---

[153]For a general description of OR 39 (dating, provenance, etc.), see ANDRIEU OR IV, 271–280.

[154]The text is the following: *In nomine domini nostri Iesu Christi, si igitur est aliquis qui contra hos viros aliquid scit de causa criminis, absque dubitatione exeat et diceat; tanto memento communionis suae* (If anyone has anything against these men, before God and for the sake of God let him come forth with confidence and speak. However, let him be mindful of his communion), OR 39, 5.*[46]

[155]Cf. the dossier summarizing the tradition of the early Church compiled by C. VOGEL, "Titre d'ordination . . ."

[156]For a general description of OR 36, see ANDRIEU OR IV, 113–119.

striking. First, the formulation of the title is very precise: "Such a one is called to such an office" *(ille et ille advocantur in tali vel tali officio)*. Secondly, the manner of addressing the Church recalls what we saw in Cyprian, namely, that the Church is a *fraternitas*. The words are the same: "Let your brotherhood know that . . ." *(Cognoscat fraternitas vestra . . .)*. The responsibility of the entire Church is implied, and we see here that canon 6 of Chalcedon against absolute ordinations remains in force.[157]

β) *Ordination.* OR 34, 11–13*12–*13 gives very few details. We learn only that the ordination will take place during Mass, and that it will begin after a litany (OR 34, 5, 8). OR 34 does not speak of the imposition of hands by the bishop and the other presbyters (OR 34, 12 notes, however, the presence of other presbyters). As we have seen above, this omission is serious, especially in the light of the insistence of the *AT* on this point.[158]

The simplicity of OR 34 is striking in that the elect (already vested) is presented at the pope's chair (the normal place of the ordination in Rome, no. 11) who consecrates him (no. 12), reciting the prayer (Ve 954). The whole rite concludes with the kiss of peace, which is then exchanged with the other bishops and the presbyters present. The author then says that the new presbyter takes his place in the presbyterium *(stat in ordine presbyterii)*, and the Mass continues. He celebrates the Eucharist, then, according to his new rank.

The other witnesses relative to ordination in Rome are somewhat more developed. After the gradual, the ordination begins with the calling, the proclamation of the election, and the presentation of the elect already vested (OR 39, 19*49; OR 36, 16*27); the invitatory and the litany follow (OR 36, 17). The deacons are ordained (OR 34, 10*11; OR 39, 20*49; OR 36, 18*28) before the presbyters (OR 39, 23*51; OR 36, 21*29).

---

[157]The text, slightly modified, is found in the Gelasian Sacramentary (Ge 141) *Auxiliante Domino.* Cf. B. KLEINHEYER, *Die Priesterweihe* . . . , 49–52.

[158]Ibid., 65–67. However, OR 35, 27 (ca. 950) explains that the pope alone ordains (without the other presbyters imposing hands), but when bishops other than the pope ordain, the presbyters (two or three from among them) should also impose hands (OR 35, 27f.). Cf. also OR 36, 18.*28 It seems that Rome may have really abandoned the ancient tradition in favor of a papal privilege. Cf. P. JOUNEL, "L'ordination sacerdotale dans le rite romain," *BCE* 36 (1962) 46–81 esp. 53.

Then the pope gives them the kiss of peace (OR 39, 24) and they go to their place among the presbyters. As for the ritual of episcopal ordination (OR 34, 44*19), OR 39, 25*52 (OR 36, 23*31) speaks of a consecrated gift or oblation received by the ordinands. For forty consecutive days (OR 36—eight days) they are to receive Communion from this Eucharistic bread. The Roman tradition of the *fermentum* given by the bishop of Rome to his clergy as a sign of unity and of peace allows us to ascribe this custom to the same tradition.[159]

γ) *Day of Presbyteral Ordinations.* The papal instruction (OR 34, 28) to the elect places the diaconal and presbyteral ordinations in the first, fourth, seventh and tenth months of the year. The successive *ordines* prescribe the Saturdays of the *quattuor tempora* (OR 36, 4*22; OR 39, 1, 12*44, *48). We saw that Leo the Great wrote several times to revive the ancient tradition according to which one was ordained legitimately only on Sunday, which begins at dusk on Saturday night, and which is associated with a sort of Easter fast.[160]

This custom was maintained until 494, when Gelasius I added the first and fourth weeks of Lent.[161]

---

[159]Cf. ANDRIEU OR III, 587–591. Innocent I speaks of the usage of the *fermentum* in Rome in his letter to Decentius of Gubbio: "Concerning the 'fermentum' which we send on Sunday to the different 'tituli' . . . , the priests who on that day cannot celebrate with us because of the people who are entrusted to them receive from the acolyte the 'fermentum' made by us, in order that they not feel separated from our communion, especially on that day." INNOCENT I, *Ep. XXV, Ad Decentium episcopum Eugubium*, 5 (ed. R. Cabié, 26f.)

[160]"*Non passim, sed die legitimo ordinatio celebretur . . . die sabbati vespere, quod lucescit in prima sabbati, vel ipso Dominico die fuerit ordinatus. Solum enim majores nostri resurrectionis Dominicae diem hoc honore dignum judicaverunt, ut sacerdotes qui sumuntur hoc die potissimum tribuantur,*" LEO THE GREAT, *Ep. X, Ad episcopos . . . ,* 6 (PL 54, 634). See also id., *Ep. VI, Ad Anastasium Thessalonicensem episcopum*, 6 (PL 54, 620); *Ep. IX, Ad Dioscorum . . . ,* 1 (PL 54, 625–626); here he discusses the fast which must be practiced by the celebrant and the elect. Cf. T. MICHELS, *Beiträge zur Geschichte . . . ,* 20–30.

[161]GELASIUS I, *Ep. IX, Ad episcopos . . . ,* 11 (PL 59, 52) quoted by B. KLEIN-HEYER, *Die Priesterweihe . . . ,* 36. See also his commentaries concerning the meaning of the Ember Days (Quattuor tempora), ibid., 37–47. Also useful is the study by J. JANINI, *S. Siricio y las cuarto Témporas. Una investigación sobre las fuentes de la espiritualidad seglar y del Sacramentario Leoniano* (Valencia: Seminario metropolitano de Valencia, 1958).

Conclusions. 1) The history of Church law shows that the people played a role in the choice of their clergy. From the *AT* to the eighth century, this role was modified according to the emerging needs which resulted from the Church's changing position in society. The active role of the faithful in an election declined to nothing more than an act of approbation given to a nomination already made. The importance of the "testimony," however, was maintained. As for the bishop, the testimony deals with the quality of life and of faith of the elect.

2) The Church sees itself as a fraternal communion *(fraternitas)* (OR 36, 9), a fundamental conception that we have seen from the beginning of this survey.

3) The participation of all the members of the Church (bishop, presbyters, deacons, minor ministers, ecclesiastical notaries, and faithful) in the act of reception of the newly-ordained ministers is evident everywhere.

4) The principal gesture (the imposition of hands) presents some difficulty because it is missing from a document of Roman origin, even if its presence is attested in later documents (from a Frankish or Gallican hand). This fact could signify the relativity of this gesture in the conferring of ordained ministry, or perhaps a Roman peculiarity.

5) By contrast, the prayer is attested by every witness. The ordination was carried out in a confessional and liturgical context by the whole Church.

6) Through his presbyteral ordination, the new presbyter enters into a concrete office and into a collegial body (the presbyterium); this is signified by the kiss of peace, the installation of the presbyter in his rank, and the fact that he celebrates the Eucharist at the ordination.

7) A communal relationship exists between the bishop and the presbyters. This is expressed by the kiss of peace which the ordinand exchanges with his bishop and the other bishops present. Further, the *fermentum* also should be understood in this sense.

4. ORDINATION PRAYERS

OR 34 contains no text for ordination itself. This is why one must refer to the "Leonine Sacramentary" (bishop, Ve 947[*56]–[*59]; presbyter, Ve 954[*60]–[*61]). The prayer for the ordination of the bishop is preceded by another prayer whose function is uncertain (Ve 946*55).[162] These same prayers are again found in the Gregorian Sacramentary of the *Hadrianum* type (bishop, Gr 2, 22–23; presbyter, Gr 2, 29) dating to the eighth century. Moreover, this sacramentary gives a variant for the ordination of the pope (*ad pontificem ordinandum*: Gr 226, 1018*65).

a. *Bishop*[*55–*59]

The ordination formulary proper to the Roman sacramentaries remained in usage until 1968. At that time it was replaced by that of the *AT*. Here is the text from the *Veronensis*:

"Be gracious, Lord, to our supplications, and with the honor of priestly grace inclined over these your servants pour out upon them the power of your benediction, through our Lord Jesus Christ. (Ve 946*55)

"God of all honors, God of all the worthy ranks which serve to your glory in hallowed orders; God who in private familiar converse with Moses your servant also made a decree, among the other patterns of heavenly worship, concerning the disposition of priestly vesture; and commanded Aaron your chosen one should wear a mystical robe during the sacred rites, so that the posterity to come might have an understanding of the meaning of the patterns of the former things, lest the knowledge of your teaching be lost in any age; and as among the ancients the very outward sign of these symbols obtained reverence, also among us there might be a knowledge of them more certain than types and shadows. For the adornment of our mind is as the vesture of that earlier priesthood and the dignity of robes no longer commends to us the pontifical glory, but the splendor of spirits, since even those very things, which then pleased fleshly vision, depended rather on these truths which in them were to be understood. And, therefore, to these your servants, whom you have chosen for the ministry of the high-priesthood [*ad summi sacerdotii ministerium deligisti*], we beseech you, O Lord, that you would bestow this grace [*gratiam largiaris*]; that whatsoever it was that those veils signified in

---

[162]P.-M. Gy thinks that this prayer *Propitiare*[*55] is a doublet leading to the principal prayer. It "has a similar position to the one held by the *super oblata* before the eucharistic prayer," see P.-M. GY, "Ancient Ordination . . . ," 79. On the other hand, Kleinheyer sees here the collect which concludes the litany: cf. B. KLEINHEYER, "Supplicatio litanica," in P. JOUNEL, R. KACZYNSKI and G. PASQUALETTI (eds.), *Liturgia opera divina e umana* (Rome: Ed. liturgiche, 1982) 472–478.

radiance of gold, in sparkling of jewels, in variety of diverse work-manship, this may show forth in the conduct and deeds of these men.

"Complete the fullness of your mystery *[mysterii tui]* in your priests and, equipped with all the adornments of glory, hallow them with the dew of heavenly unction. May it flow down, O Lord, richly upon their head; may it run down below the mouth; may it go down to the utter-most parts of the whole body, so that the power of your Spirit *[ut tui Spiritus virtus]* may both fill them within and surround them without. May there abound in them constancy of faith, purity of love, sincerity of peace. Grant to them an episcopal throne to rule your Church *[ad re-gendam ecclesiam tuam]* and entire people. Be their strength; be their might; be their stay. Multiply upon them your blessing and grace, so that fitted by your aid always to obtain your mercy, they may by your grace be devoted to you; through our Lord . . ." (Ve 947*56–*59)

The Trinitarian structure of the collection of prayers found in the *AT* is not maintained in this long prayer of episcopal consecration. The prayer is, first of all, an invocation to God the Father, who is the origin of everything (cf. *AT* 3). But here it is a matter of the honors and dignities of sacred orders. These orders *(ordines)* have for their purpose the glorification of God. As in the *AT*, the glorification of God, effected by the ministry of the bishops, is the principal theme of this prayer of mostly figurative language. The prayer is organized around the vestments of Aaron the high-priest and the anointing that he received. These themes should be interpreted mystically and allegorically.

One can even ask if a true epiclesis is a part of this prayer, because the gifts of the Holy Spirit were not asked for, but rather God was asked to give his grace to his servants chosen by himself for the min-istry of the high priesthood *(ad summi sacerdotii ministerium)* and to fill them with the fullness of his mystery. It is only through an inter-pretation of this typology that we realize that an indirect request for the gifts of the Spirit was made: the heavenly anointing of the bishop should penetrate him *in order that* the power of the Spirit might fill him inwardly like the oil which covers him.[163] However, in the fifth

[163]R. BERAUDY, "Les effets de l'Ordre dans les préfaces d'ordination du Sacramentaire léonien," in R. FOURREY, M. LALLIER, R. BERAUDY et al., *La tradition sacerdotale: études sur le sacerdoce* (Le Puy: Xavier Mappus, 1959) 83–84; P.-M. GY, "La théologie des prières . . . ," 606–607.

century, what was meant was a spiritual, non-material, anointing, a worthy life, and not just episcopal vestments.[164] According to P.-M. Gy, the typology of the anointing of Aaron, normally applied to the anointing of the baptized, was not abandoned here, but was brought to bear upon the role of the bishop in the whole body of the Church: ". . . it appears from a homily of St. Leo and from patristic exegesis in general that the oil which is poured on the head of Aaron and flows all over his body allegorically expressed the benefit of episcopal ordination for the whole body of the Church. . . ."[165] Thus the bishop was not separated from the entire ecclesial body. Moreover, the prayer itself explains how these exterior things should be interpreted: "For the adornment of our mind is as the vesture of that earlier priesthood; and the dignity of robes no longer commends to us the pontifical glory, but the splendor of spirits, since even those very things, which then pleased fleshly vision, depended rather on these truths which in them were to be understood." This figurative anointing, therefore, represents the granting to the bishop of the necessary power *(tui spiritus virtus)* to fulfill the function which has been entrusted to him. It is not a matter therefore of a "personal sanctification" of the ordinand beyond that received at the moment of entry into the Body of Christ through the sacraments of initiation; he receives, rather, the grace and the help of God to carry out the duties of

---

[164]This is in agreement with the letter of Celestine I of 428 declaring that in Rome there was no distinction proper to a bishop (concerning his vesture): CELESTINE I, *Ep. IV, Ad episcopos* . . . , 1 (PL 50, 431).

[165]P.-M. GY, "Ancient Ordination . . . ," 86. Note 93 gives the following patristic references (which contain two typographical errors: read "Tractatus 4" instead of "Serm. 48" and "SC 25bis, 173" instead of "SC 25, 117": LEO THE GREAT, *Tractatus 4 item in natale eiusdem* (from September 29, 444), 1 (CC 138, 17). Cf. HILARY, *Tractatus in Psalmum CXXXII*, 4–5 (CSEL 22, 686–688); AMBROSE, *De mysteriis*, 30 (SC 25bis, 173); AUGUSTINE, *Enarratio in Psalmum CXXXII* (CC 40, 1926–1935). See also a text of Theodore of Mopsuestia which connects the gift of the Spirit received at the time of his ordination to the ministry which the bishop exercises: THEODORE OF MOPSUESTIA, "Commentary on the Sacraments of Baptism and the Eucharist," in A. MINGANA, *Woodbrooke Studies. Christian Documents Edited and Translated with a Critical Apparatus*, vol. VI, *Commentary of Theodore of Mopsuestia on the Lord's Prayer and on the Sacraments of Baptism and the Eucharist* (Cambridge: W. Heffer & Sons Limited, 1933) 120 (English translation of the Syriac ms. Mingana 561, p. 261).

his charge. It is a very delicate balance: the ministry (episcopal) is a function of the ecclesial body for the service of the whole Body, founded on a gift of God (the power of the Spirit).[166]

This grace (of the Spirit) bestowed through ordination produces certain virtues in the ordinands: "May there abound in them constancy of faith, purity of love, sincerity of peace." Then follows a prayer to the Lord asking him to give them the episcopal chair in order that they may preside over the Church and over the entire people who are entrusted to them *(tribuas eis cathedram episcopalem ad regendam ecclesiam tuam et plebem universam)*.[167] The idea of the leader, present in the *AT*, remains continuous in Roman tradition. The bishop, through his ordination, is at the head of his people. His charge is characterized this time by the image of the episcopal chair, which can evoke the images of authority and power: he has all that is necessary to exercise his office. The image of the episcopal chair can also suggest the image of a pastor. R. Béraudy has rightly shown that in this prayer one can barely distinguish the episcopal function from the grace of the order,[168] which was already so in the *AT*.

---

[166]R. BERAUDY, "Les effets . . . ," 85 and 94f.

[167]Two comments on this subject: 1. the verb *regere* corresponds to the Greek verb *poimainein*, which is inspired by Acts 20: 28 *(poimainein tēn ekklēsian tou theou)*. The Vulgate translates this either by *pascere* (cf. Jn 21:16) or by *regere* (cf. Mt 2:6): the idea of pasturing the flock as well as the actions of the leader vis-à-vis his people; 2. *plebem universam* has been corrected: read *plebem sibi commissam* in the Pontifical of the twelfth end thirteen centuries, because this expression *(plebem universam)* was reserved for the ordination of the bishop of Rome in OR 40B (tenth century). Santantoni adduces a text of the *Liber officialis* (II, 14, 7–8) of Amalarius of Metz which confirms the sense of *plebs universa* as meaning all the faithful of a particular Church, and not the universal Church. Based upon this text, he proposes the following interpretation of this phrase as correct: "*ad regendam ecclesiam tuam et universam plebem sibi commissam*": see A. SANTANTONI, *L'ordinazione episcopale* . . . , 59–60. Further, cf. R. BERAUDY, "Les effets . . . ," 95–96 and J. LECUYER, "La prière d'ordination de l'évêque," NRT 89, 6 (1967) 602–603. See also the meaning that the image of the bishop's chair took in early Christianity, especially concerning the authority and the ministry of the bishop, in the article by E. STOMMEL, "Die bischöfliche Kathedra im christlichen Altertum," *Münchener theologische Zeitschrift* 3, 1 (1952) 17–32; also M. MACCARRONE, "Lo sviluppo . . ."

[168]R. BERAUDY, "Les effets . . . ," 92f.

Before moving on to an examination of the biblical images employed, we must pause a moment at the variant reading given in the *Hadrianum* (Gr 226, 1018*65). The prayer of the Leonine Sacramentary is used with an amplification of the phrase beginning with *"et idcirco . . ."* Here is the English translation with the inclusion in bold type: "And therefore, to this your servant **whom you have given as president of the apostolic see and primate of all the priests** *[sacerdotum]* **that are in the world and teacher of the universal Church,** and chosen *[elegisti]* for the ministry of high-priesthood *[ad summi sacerdotii ministerium].* Grant him the **pontifical** see in order to guide your Church and all your people" ["Grant . . . people" tr. of editor] (Gr 226, 1018*65).

This same prayer is found later, towards the tenth century, in OR 40 B, 6. We can see that this inclusion attributed a true primacy to the bishop of Rome: he is "the head of the apostolic see," the "first among the bishops of the earth," and, lastly, "teacher" of the universal Church. Again, as we have seen elsewhere, it is God who accomplishes everything (he has *given* a leader, and he has *chosen*). This time the word *universa* must be taken probably in a broader sense than when used in the ordination of a bishop by the pope. In fact, if the pope is himself ordained for a concrete office, the pontifical see, what is emphasized is the primacy of the bishop of Rome. Moreover, this is a point which has been made clear since the sixth century.[169]

α) *Biblical Images Employed.* The images of this prayer of consecration are borrowed from the Old Testament: the person of Aaron, his vestments, and his oil of anointing. In addition, we also find the symbol of the chair, or *cathedra*, which is granted to the bishop.

A first comment is in order: the use of the Old Testament typology in the consecratory prayer should not be interpreted as a symbolic explanation of the beginnings of Christian institutions. Rather, we should see in it a "prefiguring" of these institutions in the Old Testament, as, for example, the entire description of the institution of

---

[169]This is the meaning indicated by P.-M. Gy who compares a text of Leo the Great (*Tractatus 3 item in natale eiusdem* [from September 29, 443], 4 [CC 138, 13–15], specifically p. 14) with the included clause: see P.-M. GY, "La théologie des prières . . . ," 602 and 614, where he sees in this Roman addition a formulation of primacy. This is also the interpretation of A. SANTANTONI, *L'ordinazione episcopale . . .* , 200–203.

the Old Testament priesthood, which had great outward glory, but whose beauty was, for the author, entirely inward.

So the images of the ancient priesthood (Aaron, his vestments, and his anointing) serve to indicate the great importance which it had for the people of Israel: without being the reality, it indicated symbolically (or prophetically) the realization of the divine plan of salvation in the institution of the new priesthood. The outward glory of the pontiffs indicates a deeper reality, namely, the beauty of their souls. This anamnetic part supplies the reason[*57] why we ask God to give the elect the grace necessary for the ministry of the high priesthood. This request indicates clearly that the act of ordination communicates a gift, that of ministry *(summi sacerdotii ministerium)*. This gift brings about a change in the elect, because the glory seen in the vestments of the high priesthood must now shine in the life and the actions *(in . . . moribus actibusque clariscat)* of the new bishop. The ministerial office, and not simply the vestments, distinguishes the bishop from the faithful.[170] As in the *AT*, we see here a certain continuity between the old and the new dispensations, between the old and the new priesthoods. But in the Verona Sacramentary it is not made explicit that the continuity of the plan of salvation finds its fulfillment and its superiority in the Christ-event. In fact, Christ is not mentioned at all in this prayer. In the *AT*, the continuity of the two dispensations takes place in Christ through the Holy Spirit, a continuity which follows in the ministry of the apostles, even to the ministry of the new bishop. The image of Aaron and his vestments indicates, therefore, a priestly dignity which is prolonged in the institution of the new priesthood.

How is this dignity transmitted to the elect? The prayer answers this question[*59] with the resumption of the Old Testament typology of the consecration of Aaron: his sanctification by anointing with oil (cf. Ex 28:41; 29:7; 30:30-32). The image is borrowed from Psalm 133. The anointing of Aaron sets him apart for the service of the Lord and of his people. But the anointing of the bishop is spiritual: he is filled with the power of the Spirit *(spiritus virtus)*. A. Santantoni correctly notes that, in the prayer of the *AT*, the power of the sovereign Spirit actualizes the saving plan of God in all aspects of the history of Israel, while in the Leonine prayer only the aspect of worship is

[170]Cf. the letter of CELESTINE I, *Ep. IV, Ad episcopos . . .* , 11, already quoted supra, n. 164.

mentioned.[171] Furthermore, we should note the comment of P.-M. Gy according to whom "the oil which is poured on the head of Aaron and flows all over his body allegorically expressed the benefit of episcopal ordination for the whole body of the Church."[172] We should recall that Aaron, dressed as high priest, represented all of Israel before God when he went into the temple (cf. Ex 28:12, 29ff.). Moreover, the ordinand represents the presence of God among his people (Ex 29:43-46), for the prayer of spiritual anointing is followed by the request "May there abound in them constancy of faith, purity of love, sincerity of peace," important powers for whomever is at the head of a people consecrated to God and who must have a life and a comportment which reveal the glory of God prefigured by the ancient vestments and the sanctifying anointing of Aaron.[173]

The last image used is that of the episcopal chair,*[59] a symbol of the pastoral office which the bishop exercises as the head of all the people who are entrusted to him. E. Stommel has shown that the *cathedra* was the symbol of the episcopal office in its totality: it was the seat of authentic preaching and of episcopal primacy at the liturgical assembly (i.e., the pastoral dimension of the episcopal office). Further, it represented the teaching authority of the bishop as the head of the local Church. From the second century, the *cathedra* was the only external sign of episcopal authority.[174] Despite the transformation of this symbol into a "throne" and the connotation of more

---

[171]A. SANTANTONI, *L'ordinazione episcopale* . . . , 57f.; CHANOINES REGULIERS DE MONDAYE, "L'évêque d'après . . . ," 760f. In this article they also note the aspect of plenitude of the priesthood which the prayer of Leo affirms.

[172]Cf. note 165, supra. Section 5 of the *AT* speaks of the offering of the oil which in Hippolytus is used for baptism and the strengthening of the sick. One can even wonder whether the anointing mentioned in the Eucharistic prayer concerning the oil does not anticipate the Leonine image. Further, in section 5 of the *AT* we see the triple *munus* of Christ applied to the ecclesial body in the sense that the baptized receive the anointing of kings, priests and prophets.

[173]This makes one think of the description found in Ex 19:6; 1 Pet 2:5, 9 and Rev 1:6; 5:10.

[174]Cf. E. STOMMEL, "Die bischöfliche . . . ," esp. 166–196; A. G. LUIKS, *Cathedra en mensa. De plaats van preekstoel en avondmaalstafel in het oudchristelijk kerkgebouw volgens de opgravingen in Noord-Afrika* (Franeker: T. Wever, 1955); M. MACCARRONE, "Lo sviluppo . . ."; the articles by P. BATIFFOL, *Cathedra Petri* (Paris: Cerf, 1938) 105–120.

"secular" honors and tasks, according to the liturgical text under study here it is clear that God remains central: God chooses the minister, God is the author of the gift which makes the candidate able to exercise his office, God is the source of authority *(auctoritas)*, of power *(potestas)*, and of constancy *(firmitas)*. In short, God gives the ordinand all that is necessary to accomplish his ministry;[175] and for the Church, the symbol of the office of the bishop which expresses all this was the *cathedra episcopalis*.

β) *Qualities Requested for the Ordinand.* The principal virtues asked for are: constancy in faith, purity of love, and sincerity of peace. These three realities are essentially those found in the Pastoral Epistles. Thus the new bishop's life and actions will shine in the Church, as did formerly the vestments of the high priest. These qualities requested for the ordinand are not for his own sanctification; these are virtues needed for the service of others in the Church. Without a doubt, such is the meaning of the spiritual anointing which covers *the entire body.* The idea that God does all and is at the origin of all reinforces this interpretation; the bishop does nothing in his own name— it is God, through his Spirit, who acts through the ministry of the bishop.

γ) *Gifts Received by the Ordinand.* In the second part of the prayer, God is asked to fill the elect with the fullness of the mystery of God.[*58] This mystical anointing is nothing less than the pouring out of the Spirit. This gift of God changes the status of the elect, for he is filled with the power of the Spirit in order to enter into a ministerial function which is that both of pastor and of head (the double sense of the expression *ad regendam ecclesiam tuam* which is either to pasture [Jn 21:16] or to rule [Mt 2:6]). The episcopal chair, making clear that he is there to preside and to govern the Church, will be the symbol of the charism attached to the office.

The prayer ends by asking for the blessing and the grace of God on the ordinand, that he may obtain divine mercy and abandon himself to God completely.

[175]These three terms have here a broader meaning than that attributed to them today. They imply an influence and a moral authority which convinces, rather than constrains. Constancy *(firmitas)* describes the quality of the acts of an authority as to their stability, efficaciousness and permanence. Cf. D. N. POWER, *Ministers of Christ . . . ,* 71f.

Conclusions. We have seen that the Leonine prayer expresses the reality of episcopal ministry in a style other than that of the *AT*. Despite this fact, the following conclusions are possible:

1) Although it is difficult to distinguish the presence of an epiclesis, a gift of the Spirit is requested, namely, the grace of God for the ministry of the high priesthood. This gift is destined above all for the service of others, through the exercise of the episcopal office in the heart of a concrete Church *(ad regendam ecclesiam tuam)*; secondly, this is a spiritual charism which enriches the elect himself who receives the anointing of the Spirit in view of fulfilling his office.

2) The functions conferred by this grace are those of the high priesthood. This priesthood is of a charismatic and spiritual order, intended for the whole body of the Church; it should not be considered as a personal gift, but as conferred to promote the sanctification and growth of the members of the ecclesial body.[*58] Besides the sacerdotal functions (described in general terms), the function of the leader is symbolized by the episcopal chair. We have seen that this function is described in largely pastoral terms,[*59] which emphasize the governing of the Church, the gathering of the flock under the crook of the good shepherd, and the teaching (cf. Jn 21:16). This last function is perhaps already expressed at the beginning of the prayer: "Thus may posterity *(secutura posteritas)* be inspired by the ancient examples, and may no generation be ignorant of your teaching (= of the Lord)." By his life and his actions, the bishop should in fact be a guide and a model for his flock.

3) The bishop has all that is necessary to fulfil his task: he is given *auctoritas, potestas, firmitas,* which come from God.

4) There is, therefore, agreement between the end of the prayer and its beginning, where God is described as the source of all the dignities and all the honors. As in the prayer of the *Apostolic Tradition,* everything is intended for the glorification of God.

5) Nevertheless, this prayer does not explicitly say that the bishop presides at the Eucharist; this is explained by a new structuring of the Church in which, from this point on, the presbyters were to preside at the Eucharist, because of the growth of the Church and of the multiplication of places of worship.

6) We can nevertheless aver that, in its strongly allegorical language, this prayer describes the ordained ministry of a bishop in

such a way that ordination appears as a *confessional act*, a *juridical act* (the bishop is given a chair and a concrete Church), and *an ecclesial act* (the prayer comes at the end of a whole process which involves the entire Church and the participation of other local Churches).

b. *Presbyter*[*62]–[*64]

Similar to the prayer of episcopal ordination, that of the ordination of presbyters is strongly marked by Old Testament typology. However, the latter prayer illuminates and even clarifies the first in respect to the substance of the episcopal ministry. In the Verona Sacramentary, the prayer of ordination is preceded by two prayers which were probably the invitatory to the litany[*60] and the collect which concludes it.[*61]

The ordination prayer[*62]–[*64] (like that of the *AT*) can be divided into three parts:[176]

"Holy Lord, almighty Father, everlasting God, bestower of all the honors and of all the worthy ranks which do you service, you through whom all things make progress, through whom everything is made strong, by the ever-extended increase to the benefit of rational nature by a succession arranged in due order; whence the priestly ranks and the offices of the Levites arose and were inaugurated with mystical symbols; so that when you set up high-priests to rule over your people, you chose men of a lesser order and secondary dignity to be their companions and to help them in their labor.[*62] Likewise in the desert you did spread out the spirit of Moses through the minds of seventy wise men, so that he, using them as helpers among the people, governed with ease countless multitudes. Likewise also you imparted to Eleazar and Ithamar, the sons of Aaron, the richness of their father's plenty, so that the benefit of priests might be sufficient for the salutary sacrifices and the rites of a more frequent worship. And also by your providence, O Lord, to the apostles of your Son you added teachers of the faith as companions, and they filled the whole world with these secondary preachers.[*63]

---

[176]We follow here the division suggested by D. EISSING, "Ordination und Amt des Presbyters. Zur Interpretation des römischen Priesterweihegebetes," *ZKT* 98, 1 (1976) 35–51, here pp. 36–43.

"Wherefore on our weakness also, we beseech you, O Lord, bestow these assistants, for we who are so much frailer need so many more. Grant, we beseech you, Father, the dignity of the presbyterate to these your servants. Renew in their inward parts the Spirit of holiness. May they obtain and receive from you, O God, the office of second dignity and by the example of their conduct may they commend a strict way of life. May they be virtuous colleagues of our order [ordinis nostri]. May the pattern of all righteousness show forth in them, so that, rendering a good account of the stewardship entrusted to them, they may obtain the rewards of eternal blessedness, *64 through our Lord . . ." (Ve 954 = Gr 2, 29)

The first part describes the order established by God for all things. The second part shows how God has maintained a harmonious order in the Church even to the present, thanks to the institution of the priesthood (bishops and presbyters) and of levites (deacons). In this prayer, we see again the typology of the Seventy, which clearly identifies Moses with the bishop, and the elder with the priest. The triple typology presents the institution of the sons of Aaron as priests, the selection of the elders of Israel to help Moses in governing the people, and the election of the other disciples to help the apostles in the task of evangelization. To all, the Lord has always given all the graces necessary to fulfill their function. In the third part, the ordaining bishop asks God for the necessary help for himself to fulfill his office. The prayer says: "Grant . . . the dignity of the presbyterate to these your servants. Renew in their inward parts the spirit of holiness [innova in visceribus eorum spiritum sanctitatis]. May they obtain and receive from you . . . the office of the second dignity [secundi meriti munus], and by the example of their conduct may they commend a strict way of life." B. Botte has noted the emphasis placed upon the subordination of these presbyters to the bishop. He thought that this was due to a reaction against a tendency "which arose at the end of the fourth century and of which St. Jerome was one of the first to speak: that the bishop would only be *primus inter pares* among the priests."[177] The prayer responds to this tendency by saying that the presbyterate ranks below the episcopacy in dignity, that it is subordi-

---

[177]B. BOTTE, "L'Ordre d'après . . . ," 18; P.-M. GY, "La théologie des prières . . . ," 607. See also D. N. POWER, *Ministers of Christ* . . . , 68–71.

nated to the episcopal office even though it is very close, since the functions exercised are almost the same. This response corresponds to the idea expressed in the *AT* concerning the participation of the presbyters in the essential and fundamental function of the episcopate. Nevertheless, we must resist the temptation of seeing in the presbyterate a participation in the episcopal priesthood, because under the veil of the typology we see the presbyter exercising the same ministry as the bishop, yet under his authority. We will return to this topic when we study the use and the meaning of the triple typology: Moses, Aaron and his sons, the apostles and their assistants. The prayer also distinguishes the presbyters from the deacons, by qualifying as priestly the ministry of the former (we will see this, infra, while exploring the images used).

The formulation of this prayer apparently bears witness to the growth of the Church. The pastoral charge has become so heavy that the bishop is no longer able to carry it alone; this is the reason why he needs helpers as did Moses, Aaron, and the apostles.[178] Is it possible that the collegiality in governing was waning, from its importance in the *AT*, since the presbyters have an office "of secondary dignity"? Is a split developing between the ministries of bishop and presbyter? In the structure represented by the *Apostolic Tradition*, the presbyters were the true collaborators of the bishop, and it was not seen as necessary to relegate the priests to a secondary rank.[179]

α) *Biblical Images Employed.* The ordination prayer for presbyters is constructed around three images borrowed from the Old Testament. We should even add a fourth one which is less obvious: that of the request based on Psalm 51:12-14. The composition of this prayer follows that of episcopal ordination. The ordination prayer of presbyters is even clearer, because it makes obvious the continuity of the plan of God who establishes everything in good order; it is always God who

[178]Cf. the reference concerning the organization of the Church of Rome during the formative period of the ordination prayers, J. GAUDEMET, *L'Eglise dans l'Empire romain (IVe–Ve siècles)*, 1st ed. [1958] revised (Paris: Sirey, 1989): the spread of Christianity, 87–97; the life of the presbyterium, 370; and the development of the places of worship, 655f.; N.-M. DENIS-BOULET, "Titres urbains et communautés dans la Rome chrétienne," *LMD* 36 (1953) 14–32.

[179]B. BOTTE, "*Secundi meriti munus*," *QL* 21, 2 (1936) 84–88, esp. 87; P.-M. GY, "La théologie des prières . . . ," 606.

provides help for the leaders of his people. The diversity of ministries is seen as a gift of the bounty of God, a sign of the concern that God has for his Church. We have already encountered this theme in the prayer of episcopal ordination in the *AT*. Its description in the Leonine text is influenced by the Old Testament typology which shows three degrees: that of the priesthood (the pontiffs or bishops),[180] those who are ordained to a secondary dignity (or presbyters), and those appointed to levitical service (deacons).[*62] The introduction underscores the unity of the priesthood and the plurality of the degrees of priesthood, with God as the unique source of all.[181] The function of the bishop is also delineated here: it is God who establishes high priests to govern the people, and who chooses for them companions as helpers of a subordinate order and of a lesser dignity.[182]

The first image comes from the typology of the seventy elders, the assistants of Moses. This image is not new; it is present in the prayer of the *AT* and in the derivative texts. This comparison between the elders (presbyters) and Moses (the bishop) was already suggested by certain Fathers of the Church.[183] The episode mentioned here is found

[180]Concerning the typology of the levites and the elders (Aaron and Moses) and the relationship between the ministry of the bishop and that of the presbyters, see H.-J. SCHULZ, "Das liturgisch-sakramental . . . ," 236f.

[181]Cf. D. EISSING, "Ordination . . . ," 38–41. The priestly theme is indicated by the vocabulary: cf. P.-M. GY, "Remarques sur le vocabulaire . . ."; B. BOTTE, "Secundi . . ."

[182]For an examination of the meaning of the words *dignitas, honor, gradus,* and *meritum,* cf. D. N. POWER, *Ministers of Christ . . . ,* 62–65.

[183]Cf. *AT* 7; the *Apostolic Constitutions,* VIII, 16, 4; the *Epitome* of Book VIII of the *Constitutions,* VI (F. X. Funk, *Didascalia et Constitutiones Apostolorum,* reprint [1st ed. 1905] (Turin: Bottega d'Erasmo, 1979) 2, 80, and SC 336, 218f.); the *Testamentum Domini,* I, 30; and the *Euchologion of Serapion,* XXVII, 2 (Funk, 2, 190). Concerning the Fathers, one may consult THEODORE OF MOPSUESTIA, *In Epistolam B. Pauli ad 1 Timotheum,* 3, 8 (Swete, vol. 2, 120); THEODORET, *Quaestiones in Numeros,* XVIII (PG 80, 369C–372B); JEROME, *Commentariorum in Epistolam ad Titum, 1, 5* (PL 26, 595D–598A). One can also see a reference made by IGNATIUS OF ANTIOCH, *Magn.* 6, 1; *Trall.* 3, 1 where the presbyters are referred to as the "sanhedrin" of the bishop. For a discussion of the patristic exegesis of this typology, see the article of J. LECUYER, "L'oasis d'Elim et les ministères dans l'Eglise," in G. J. BEKES and G. FARNEDI (eds.), *Lex orandi, lex credendi. Miscellanea in onore di P. Cipriano Vagaggini* (Rome: Anselmiana, 1980) 295–329.

in Numbers 11: 16-17 and 24-25. These texts have already been commented upon above (supra, I, A, 3, b). At the heart of these two texts we find the gift of the Spirit bestowed upon the elders, this Spirit that the Lord gave to Moses, the leader, pastor and prophet of the people of Israel. The Spirit received by the elders makes them capable of participating with Moses in the government of the people (Num 11:17) and in prophesy as well (Num 11:25; cf. 1 Sam 10:10ff.; 19:20ff.). The Spirit bestowed from above established the Seventy in their office (in the presence of the people) at the same time that a gift was given to them for the good of the people. God has done everything: it is not Moses who grants the Spirit and communicates it to them, but it is God who is the source of the Spirit; and it is the Spirit, the gift of God, who actualizes the plan of God by establishing the collective entity of the Seventy and making them participants in the task of Moses, the head, pastor and prophet.[184]

The text of Verona reads along the same lines: God responds to the request of the pontiff ("bestow these assistants . . .") as God answered Moses in the desert.

The principal function of the presbyters is to be collaborators in the order of the bishops[185] in governing the Christian people. The Old Testament typology links the function of the elders to a communication of the Spirit; the use of this typology by the author of the Leonine text does not have a true epiclesis. Here, the community prays for the dignity of the presbyterate, asking that the Spirit of holiness be renewed deeply within the presbyters. As in the case of the prayer of the *AT*, we note here too a distinction relative to the gift received. The gift of the Spirit of holiness is granted to those who must give an example of a Christian and holy life to others. A more exact meaning of the expression *spiritus sanctitatis* will be presented later.

The second image contained in the ordination prayer rests on the typology of the consecration of Aaron and his sons to the priestly function (cf. Ex 29 and Lev 8-9). This reveals a continuity with the

---

[184]OR 34 retains the position of certain patristic commentaries concerning this episode. See for example, CYRIL OF ALEXANDRIA, *In Ioannis Evangelium, Liber Secundus*, III, 34 (PG 73, 279); THEODORET, *Quaestiones . . .* , (PG 80, 372); the commentary of G. FERRARO, *Le preghiere . . .* , 99–100.

[185]Cf. B. BOTTE, "Caractère collégial . . . ," 107–117; D. EISSING, "Ordination . . . ," 43–44.

typology of the prayer of episcopal ordination which sees Aaron as the symbol of the bishop, the high priest of the Church. The biblical sources emphasize the priestly and cultic aspect of the consecration of Aaron and his sons. Their vocation (the choice) is the work of God, but their consecration is performed by Moses; through these rites, they participate in the priestly function of offering sacrifices for themselves and for all the people, of blessing the people, and of participating in the glory of God (cf. Lev 9:22ff.) so that the people of God might perceive the divine presence. Elsewhere, we learn that the priests also teach the Law to the people (Lev 10:11). The allusion made in the ordination prayer serves to define the ministry of the presbyters. According to the prayer, Aaron is the equal of Moses in his office as head of the people. This is not the case in the biblical passage, because Aaron is an assistant to Moses; he therefore has a secondary place. The author of the prayer wanted to make of Aaron the image of the bishop, and of his sons, the image of the priests who help him. According to this typology, the ministry of the priests is described as sacerdotal because they offer the saving sacrifices (*ut ad hostias salutares*—cf. Lev 1-7) and the normal service of the mysteries (*frequentioris officii sacramenta*—cf. Lev 9:22; Num 8: 22-27). Translating the image presented in the ordination prayer in terms of function in the Church, we see that Aaron is the figure of the bishop, and that the presbyters are the sons who help their father and are under his authority. The priestly ministry of sacrifice is the image of the liturgical office seen in the Eucharistic celebration and in other important times in the life of the Christian community.[186]

A third image concludes this second section of the prayer, the fragility of the great personages mentioned: Moses, Aaron and his sons, and, lastly, the apostles themselves. This image is different from the two others in that it is borrowed from the New Testament. It alludes to the doctors of the faith who help the apostles with their preaching. With this image, the prayer tells us that the presbyters have a role to play in the evangelization of the world. Once again the text says that these preachers are of secondary rank. It seems that conflicts between presbyters and bishops are resolved in the descrip-

[186]Cf. P.-M. GY, "La théologie des prières . . . ," 606; D. EISSING, "Ordination . . . ," 44–46.

tion of the presbyterate as an order close to the episcopacy (relative to the functions exercised), but subordinated and secondary.[187]

The three images used depict a triple typology: the companions of Moses help him to govern the people; the sons of Aaron carry out the liturgical functions because services of worship are more frequent; and the assistants of the apostles help them in the transmission of the faith. This triple typology clarifies the theme of the continuity of the plan of God: according to well-established order, God always grants assistants to the leaders established at the head of the people of God.

To these three images we must add a fourth derived from Psalm 51:10, 12 and from the ordination prayer. In the prayer, we find the phrase: ". . . renew deep within them the spirit of holiness . . ." which is inspired by Psalm 51, 10b and 11b ("put a new and right spirit within me" and "do not take your holy spirit from me").[188] The context of the psalm (vv. 12-13: "Create in me a clean heart, O God; put a new and right spirit within me. Do not cast me away from your presence and do not take your holy spirit from me; restore to me the joy of your salvation and sustain in me a willing spirit!") shows that it is the action of God who creates, liberates, and saves, and that it is the Spirit of God who actualizes and sustains all this work in the human heart. The result of this action is the desire to proclaim the goodness of God, so that others might return to God (Ps 51: 13). In the prayer, the invocation of the gift of the Spirit does not aim at the growth in personal sanctity of the ordinand (as if he ascends to a higher rank, above the other baptized), but rather it asks "for the grace" to accomplish his ministry; to help him in his task of assisting the bishop in the presbyterate. Of course, the minister is exhorted to sanctity in the moral sense: "it is proper that the presbyter be holy." According to the psalm (and the ordination prayer as well), the ministers must desire to lead others to awareness of the goodness of God by "commending by the example of their conduct a strict way of life."

β) *Qualities Requested for the Ordinand.* The prayer emphasizes the need for good conduct in the lives of the new presbyters, who must

---

[187]Cf. the discussion of D. N. POWER, *Ministers of Christ* . . . , 53–56, 69f. and the commentary of D. EISSING, "Ordination . . . ," 46–48.

[188]Cf. G. FERRARO, *Le preghiere* . . . , 123–128.

inspire others by their example. It prays also that "all righteousness show forth" in their lives.

The epiclesis asks for the renewal of the spirit of holiness within them *("innova in visceribus eorum spiritum sanctitatis")*. We have just discussed the meaning of this phrase: the Spirit is given to the ordinand in order to create within him the reality of a presbyter (cf. the images used in the three anamneses) and to give him the "office of secondary dignity." This text is essentially exhortatory: it is of a moral order ("it is proper that the priests be holy"); it does not place them in the order of metaphysical causality (in the sense that the ordained would be sanctified in order to become sanctifiers in the plan of salvation). The purpose of this call to sanctity is to ensure that the ministers exercise their ministerial priesthood in the power of the Spirit.

One last quality required of presbyters is the ability to collaborate with the bishop, or rather, with the episcopal order. The bishop appears here clearly as the head of the community. The collegial reality of the presbyterate is no longer evident: this translates a different *Sitz im Leben* from that of the *AT,* where the bishop and his presbyters appear structurally united. In this new context, the presbyters, who are charged with responsibility for whole communities and who have almost the same duties as their bishop are seen independently from the bishop.

γ) *Gifts Received by the Ordinand.* The prayer speaks of the "dignity of the presbyterate" as "of a secondary rank." It is, of course, a gift of the Spirit conferred for the building up of the Christian people. Through the gift of this grace, the presbyter becomes an attentive collaborator with the bishop and shares the responsibilities of this office.

Conclusions. 1) Firstly, we see that the presbyteral ministry is conferred through the gift of the Spirit. The prayer, through allegories, links the conferred function and the grace necessary for the ministry: both are gifts of the Spirit.

2) The functions conferred are those of governing (expressed by the figure of Moses), of priesthood (the exercise of liturgical functions signified by the typology of the sons of Aaron), and of the ministry of the Word (represented by the figure of the companions of the apostles).

3) We can also speak of a "priestly ministry," but for the bishop, it is a spiritual Christian priesthood, including the charism for the governance of the community, the duty of worship, and the mission of

evangelizing (cf. the connection between the invocation of the Spirit over the elect and the triple anamnesis). It is at this point that we can understand that the "Spirit of holiness" is not intended for the sanctification of the person of the minister, but is conferred so that this minister may exercise his ministry in the power of the Spirit: the charism is indissolubly linked to the function.

4) The prayer emphasizes very strongly that the presbyteral ministry supports that of the bishop, and that the presbyter exercises his ministry under the authority of the bishop. It is not said that the presbyters participate in the ministry or the priesthood of the bishop, but that they exercise the same ministry as the bishop under his authority.

5) The continuity of the plan of God is explicit in the prayer, yet not as clearly as in that found in the *AT*. No reference is made to Christ: we hear of the sole good order that was established by God and maintained to the present. The person of the head is central (God, Moses, Aaron, the apostles, the bishop); in fact, the prayer is not very Trinitarian in structure or content.

6) Lastly, this prayer witnesses to the growth of the Church. This context demands a new organization of its ministries. The number of faithful no longer permits the bishop to gather his presbyterium around him like a council. The presbyters are now engaged in the same tasks as the bishop, but in the communities outside the cities or even in the countryside. In the prayer they can no longer appear as a collective reality. They are the assistants, the collaborators, and the supports of the episcopal ministry.

5. RELATIONSHIP BETWEEN THE EPISCOPACY AND THE PRESBYTERATE

It is in the prayers of presbyteral ordination that we can best grasp the relationship between the episcopacy and the presbyterate. We read that the presbyters participate in the threefold *munus* of the direction of the community: they help in the governing of the Church, in the priestly function, and in the ministry of preaching. At the summit of this ministry we find the person of the bishop, who is always described as the high priest, and whose ministry is that of the high priesthood. The ministry of the bishop is seen as the first rank of sacred orders, while the presbyters hold the second rank. The presbyterate is thus an order subordinate to the episcopacy. The prayer of presbyteral ordination repeats four times that the presbyters support the bishop in his ministry.

The development of the prayers of presbyteral ordination is clear in relationship to the *AT*. The essential nature of the presbyteral ministry is henceforth made explicit. At what price? The price is the obliteration of the concept of the collegiality of the presbyterate. We no longer see the presbyterate as a senate in the Leonine formulae. Conversely, the specific nature of the presbyteral ministry is clarified by reference to the triple *munus*.

Briefly, the bishop is seen clearly as the head, the priest, the pastor, and the teacher of the community. But it would be incorrect to believe that he performed these functions in isolation: belonging to the episcopal order, he is in communion with the other bishops, while the priests are his collaborators, according to an order well established by God. As in the *AT*, the bishop and the presbyters collaborate closely in the exercise of the pastoral ministry, but the day is gone when the bishop was the only priest. The presbyters are redefined as priests of secondary rank *(sacerdotes secundi meriti)*.[189]

Conclusions. 1) The relationship between the episcopal order and the presbyteral order remains close, as in the *AT*. The change of social context, however, makes it necessary for the bishops to provide themselves with subordinate assistants in the ministry of direction. The relationship between the two ministries is modified.

2) We are witness here to the birth of the "hierarchy" at the summit of which is found the bishop. On the second level we find the presbyter, and he is defined as an attentive collaborator.

3) Lastly, the presbyters must perform almost the same tasks as the bishop as his collaborators and his assistants, but they always act in a subordinate relationship to him. According to the prayers, they support the episcopal order in its mission, and they thus obtain an office of secondary degree. Nowhere is it said that the presbyters participate in the priesthood of the bishop, but rather, they exercise the same ministry as he, under his authority.

---

[189]For the evolution of priestly vocabulary, see P.-M. GY, "Remarques sur le vocabulaire . . . ," 138–140.

6. LATER INFLUENCE OF THE
SACRAMENTARIUM VERONENSE

The two Leonine ordination prayers form the nucleus of the ordination prayers of the Roman Pontifical in use until the Second Vatican Council. The current prayer for the ordination of priests is still that of the Leonine Sacramentary. A list of the sources of this prayer is given by P. Jounel.[190]

The prayer of episcopal ordination can be reconstituted down through the centuries starting from the *Sacramentarium Veronense*; we find it in many of the liturgical sources: Santantoni has reproduced the principal variations of them.[191] We can thus measure the vast influence of these Roman prayers, especially in the Latin Church.

7. CONCLUSION: STRUCTURING OF THE CHURCH AND THE SUBSTANCE OF ORDAINED MINIISTRY

The importance for the history and the theology of ordination of the documents studied here can hardly be exaggerated, because they have remained the basis of ordination ritual down to our time. It is appropriate, therefore, to describe clearly the structure of the Church which is revealed therein, as well as the substance of the ministry of the bishop and of the presbyter.

a. *Structure of the Church*

What sort of structuring of the Church do these texts reveal? They offer several points of contact with the structuring of the Church described in the *Apostolic Tradition*, but at the same time they indicate a development.

1) The Eucharistic setting of the ordination liturgy is maintained, but the liturgical roles are much more explicit and detailed. The eschatological dimension of ministry is still emphasized, for Sunday celebration (beginning with sunset on Saturday evening) is henceforth the rule for every ordination. The paschal/pentecostal aspect is accentuated by the preparatory fasts required of the whole community. Except for the meeting on Saturday evening (for episcopal election), the principal stages of the ordination ritual remain within the Eucharistic celebration. The newly ordained, whether bishop or presbyter, celebrates the Eucharist according to his rank. At the moment

---

[190]P. JOUNEL, "L'ordination sacerdotale . . . ," 54f.
[191]A. SANTANTONI, *L'ordinazione episcopale* . . . , 233f., nn. 2–16.

of Communion, the newly ordained receives some of the Eucharistic bread *(fermentum)* in order that he may receive Communion for a certain time after his ordination, a sign of the communion which exists between the celebrant and the ordinand.

2) The choice of ministers still remains in the province of the people and the clergy of the local Church, a fact which shows that the entire Church is responsible for the apostolic faith and that the distinction between clerics and laity does not undermine a true collaboration for the good of the Church. In the case of the election of a bishop, a preliminary examination before the ordination is added. This rite reveals the meaning of the participation of the other Churches in the acceptance of the elect, while the delegation of the Church which has elected him gives testimony as to his moral qualities, and especially to his faith. This is also the purpose of the scrutinies. As in the *AT*, the election of the ministers should not be separated from the process of ordination, because the Church considers itself by this act the instrument of the will of God. This is why the ordination prayers always have God for the subject: it is God who raises up the ministries in the community. The collaboration and the participation of several wills during this entire process shows that the local Church conceives of itself as a true communion (within itself, and in communion with other local Churches). The text of the *brevis advocationis* (OR 36, 9), and the election and its preliminaries (OR 34, 14ff.), emphasize particularly this fraternal communion.

3) The principle of one bishop per locality is maintained. The prayers of the Leonine Sacramentary reveal that in Rome there was a decision not to multiply the number of bishops; it was preferred to give the presbyters greater participation in episcopal duties, as, for example, the celebration of the Eucharist, rather than create new dioceses.[192]

4) Lastly, we note a concentration of attention on the functions of the bishop, his authority, his status and his role as the center of unity. The presbyters participate in certain tasks of the bishop, but that of conferring ordination is always reserved to him (this was already the case in the *AT*). The bishop alone has the responsibility for the entire Church and he ensures its unity. The symbol of the *cathedra* grows in

---

[192]Cf. LEO THE GREAT, *Ep. XII, Ad episcopos africanos provinciae mauritaniae caesariensis*, 10 (PL 54, 654) on the sufficiency of presbyteral ministers in the smaller cities.

importance: the rite of installation is focused on the seat in the *Ordines Romani*.

b. *Substance of Episcopal and Presbyteral Ministries*

Ordination, which is a complex process, continues to be seen as a gift of the Spirit as well as a human choice. Whatever the function conferred, it is the gift of the Spirit. The prayers confirm this, in very figurative and mystical language.

The ministry of the bishop is seen as threefold: *prophetic*, in the announcement of the Word of God; *priestly*, in the celebration of the Eucharist and the sacraments; and *royal*, in the exercise of governing the Church which is entrusted to him.

In the Leonine ordination prayers, the tension bishop–priests is evident, especially in the prayer of presbyteral ordination, where the author emphasizes the secondary nature of the office of presbyter. The *munus triplex*, however, is described in this prayer rather than in that of episcopal ordination. This shows that the substance of the presbyteral ministry is still strongly linked to that of the episcopacy.

The collective role of the presbyterium is less evident here. We see this clearly in the use of the term "priest" *(sacerdos)* for presbyters, while this term was reserved to the bishop alone until the time of the Leonine Sacramentary.

C. GALLICAN USAGE

Unfortunately, no liturgical book affords us direct access to the Gallican ordination ritual: the Gallican prayers have only survived interwoven with those of the Roman ritual. It is from the Roman ritual that it is possible to attempt a reconstruction of the Gallican ordinations (rite and prayers).[193]

---

[193]Cf. B. KLEINHEYER, *Die Priesterweihe* . . . , 99 and his three articles on the non-Roman elements in the liturgy of ordinations: id., "Studien zur nichtrömisch-westlichen Ordinationsliturgie. Folge 1: Die Ordinationsliturgie gemäss dem Leofric-Missale," *ALW* 22, 1 (1980) 93–107; "Folge 2: Ein spätantik-altgallisches Ordinationsformular," *ALW* 23, 3 (1981) 313–366; "Folge 3: Handauflegung zur Ordination im Frühmittelalter," *ALW* 32, 2 (1990) 145–160. According to his plausible hypothesis, the author affords us access to an early state of the Gallican rite of diaconal, presbyteral and episcopal ordinations. He has identified nine texts of Gallican provenance: an allocution (concerning the choice of the elect), an invitatory, and a prayer for the ordinand. See *ALW* 23, 3 (1981) 314f. That this might be the nucleus of the Gallican liturgy is confirmed by J. PINELL, "Le

1. PRINCIPAL WITNESSES

The earliest source of Gallican usage is found in a ritual of Gallic origin of the seventh century which served as the source for the ordination rituals of the Old Gelasian Sacramentary (Ge) and of the *Missale Francorum (MF)*.[194] The *Statuta Ecclesiae antiqua (SEA)*, a document of liturgical-canonical nature, originating in the south of Gaul, represents another source: as early as the seventh century it was drawn on by the Gallican and Frankish sacramentaries.

a. *The* Missale Francorum *(first half of the eighth century) and the Old Gelasian Sacramentary* (Vat. Reg. 316, *of the mid-eighth century*)

These two liturgical books allow us to discern the Gallican traditions. The first, composed in Gaul, dates (according to the manuscript tradition) to the first half of the eighth century. Both have used Gallican materials which were combined with Roman elements.

The *Missale Francorum* presents the ordinations in an ascending order (from the minor orders to the episcopacy), the reverse order from that of the *AT*. This fact points to a change in the conception of the ministries: the Church is no longer founded strictly on the *episkopē* of the bishop, but rather on a clerical body organized around the ascending ranks of an ecclesiastical *cursus*.

As for the Old Gelasian Sacramentary, it is classified as a Roman liturgical book because it is of Roman provenance. The area represented by the Gelasian includes, besides the city of Rome, the regions of Gaul where it was "widely used at least until around 750, the date of *Vat. Reg. 316.*"[195]

The distribution of ordinations is somewhat strange in the Old Gelasian: we find, in first place, presbyteral ordination, followed by

'famiglie liturgiche' —la liturgia gallicana," in S. MARSILI, J. PINELL, A. M. TRIACCA, et al., *Anàmnesis, introduzione storico-teologica alla liturgia*, vol. 2, *La liturgia, panorama storico general* (Turin: Marietti, 1978) 66. As for the prayer of episcopal ordination, see P. DE CLERCK, "La prière gallicane 'Pater sancte' de l'ordination épiscopale," in G. FARNEDI (ed.), *Traditio et progressio. Studi liturgici in onore del Prof. Adrien Nocent, OSB* (Rome: Pontificio Ateneo S. Anselmo, 1988) 163–176.

[194]For the description of the filiation of the ordination rituals, see A. CHAVASSE, *Le sacramentaire gélasien (Vaticanus Reginensis 316). Sacramentaire presbytéral en usage dans les titres romains au VIIᵉ siècle* (Tournai: Desclée, 1958) 5–27.

[195]C. VOGEL, *Medieval Liturgy . . .* , 69f. and also E. PALAZZO, *Le moyen âge . . .* , 66–72.

diaconal ordination (chapters XX–XXIV), then that of minor orders (chapters XCV–XCVI); at the end, in chapter XCVIIII, we find the ordination of the bishop. Here again we see the ascending order: it will henceforth be found in all liturgical books. This fact will influence later theological thought.

b. *The* Statuta Ecclesiae antiqua *(ca. fifth century)*

This document is a collection of canons composed in Marseilles towards the end of the fifth century, probably by the monk Gennadius; his intentions were to reform, and sometimes he was polemical.[196] The ritual of the *SEA* does not represent a true liturgy; rather, the author seems to have wanted to correct current usage by invoking an earlier tradition represented by some canons of his own fabrication. For this reason, we find several similarities between this ritual and that of the *AT*, with possibly some contact with the *Apostolic Constitutions*, particularly regarding an element such as the imposition of the Gospel book.[197]

This document is important, because the ritual which it presents is found again in the sacramentaries of Gaul from the eighth century onwards, in the *Ordines Romani* in the B collection, and, lastly, in the Roman Pontifical.[198]

The order of sequence in the ordinations is the usual descending order, as in the *AT*, maintained in Roman usage.

2. ECCLESIAL CONTEXT

Early Christianity was an urban phenomenon, each city having only one community with only one bishop. Each community was autonomous and was given the structure necessary for its functioning. But with time, the Church organized itself into greater geographical areas, as, for example, the liturgical regions in which the Church of Rome exercised its influence.[199] This is still the period of the urban

[196]Ch. MUNIER, *Les Statuta ecclesiae Antiqua* (Paris: Presses Universitaires de France, 1960) 195–197 and 208–227 and P. F. BRADSHAW, *Ordination Rites . . . ,* 14f.

[197]Ibid., 179f. B. BOTTE, "Le rituel d'ordination des *Statuta ecclesiae Antiqua,*" *RTAM* 11 (1939) 232f.

[198]Cf. A. SANTANTONI, *L'ordinazione episcopale . . . ,* 74f. Bradshaw, however, seems to think that the *SEA* is "an imagined ideal" rather "than a faithful reflection of actual Gallican practice," P. F. BRADSHAW, *Ordination Rites . . . ,* 101f.

[199]For a description of these liturgical regions in the Church of Rome, see A. CHAVASSE, *Le sacramentaire . . . ,* 75–86, with the references in note 127; and

Church, but new structures were already developing, with the multiplication of places of worship. Roman ordination prayers speak clearly of the situation of this Church in which the authority of the bishop over the collegial body of presbyters was increased, even though the presbyters participated in the *munus triplex* of the bishop. In this context, it seems that, except in Rome, the presbyters, the deacons and the other ministers lived near the bishop.

Another evolution occurred: the appearance of rural parishes with their own ministers.[200] Canons 68 and 87 of the *SEA* witness to this situation, where we find a presbyter at the head of the minor clergy. This context brought about a change in the relationship between the bishop and the presbyters, without threatening the authority of the bishop: even if the presbyter was to celebrate the Eucharist and preside over the building up of the local community, the bishop retained overall supervision of the parishes in the diocese. Also, the symbol of the *cathedra* continued to play an important role in the definition of episcopal function. It is in this new ecclesial context that we must study Gallican usage.

3. RITUAL ELEMENTS

We will examine the following three documents: the *Missale Francorum*, the *SEA*, and the Gelasian Sacramentary, regarding the ministry of the bishop and that of the presbyter. In order to respect the new sequence of ordinations according to Gallican usage, we will follow the ascending order in the presentation of these documents.

a. *Presbyter*

The three new elements of Gallican usage that we will study here are the allocution *Quoniam*,[*71] dealing with the choice of the presbyter, the invitatory *Sit nobis*,[*72] which introduces the Gallican prayer of ordination, and the anointing of the hands of the newly ordained.[*74–*75]

The purpose of this allocution, spoken by the bishop, was to obtain the approval of the people in the choice of the future presbyter. In

---

J. F. BALDOVIN, *The Urban Character of Christian Worship: The Origin, Development and Meaning of Stational Liturgy* (Rome: Edizioni Orientalia Christiana, 1987).

[200]For example, see the history of the evolution of this system for Gaul in the book by P. IMBART de la TOUR, *Les paroisses rurales du 4ᵉ au 11ᵉ siècle*, reprinted [1st ed., 1900] (Paris: Picard, 1979).

Rome, and in the early Church in general, the right of a community to choose its ministers was very important. In this text we can see, possibly, a trace of the Roman system in force for the choice of presbyter. Roman practice (OR 36, 9,[*24] OR 39, 5[*46] and Ge 141[*70]) was to offer the people the opportunity of bringing to the attention of all any possible objection to one of the elect ("that the people also be consulted concerning the choice of those who are to be appointed to the regulation of the altar, since concerning his activity and present conduct what is sometimes unknown to most people is known to a few, and it is inevitable that someone will more readily yield obedience to the ordained man to whom he has given consent when he was being ordained"[*71]). Two reasons are given to justify the consultation: 1) the fear that, even if the bishop and his brother priests judge that the elect is worthy and suitable to God, ". . . either favor [may] lead astray or feelings [may] deceive one or perhaps a few persons, [so] the opinion of many must be sought"; 2) it is the "common interest" *(causa communis)* which links the captain of the ship to the passengers; if their opinions converge, obedience will be more easily assured, because "it is inevitable that someone will more readily yield obedience to the ordained man to whom he has given consent when he was being ordained."[201] In any case, the system of election in use is not very clear: was it a matter of encouraging unfavorable objections concerning the elect to surface, or of making known the choice already made by the bishop (and possibly by his presbyters)?

Perhaps we see here traces of a type of election in use in Gaul: election by acclamation. The text seems to invite the assembly to acclaim the elect, as in the case of the election of the bishop[*76] by the acclamation *dignus est*. Just before the last phrase of the allocution, we find an affirmation which is in conformity with the ancient meaning of election: "We know, however, that what is most acceptable to God, the single consent of the minds of all, will come through the Holy Spirit *(scimus tamen, quod est acceptabilius deo, aderit per spiritum sanctum consensus unus omnium animorum)*."

---

[201]Cf. LEO THE GREAT, *Ep. X, Ad episcopos* . . . , 4 (PL 54, 632f.). Here the text speaks of a bishop rather than a presbyter. D. N. POWER, *Ministers of Christ* . . . , 74, has suggested that the fact that the presbyter in the context of the Gallican Church occupied a position of authority and of presidency in the parish justified the transposition from the rite normally used for the selection of the bishop.

The second element to examine is the invitatory, called in the *MF* *consummatio presbyterii*, which follows the Roman prayer of ordination. It is worthwhile to reproduce this interesting text for more than one reason:

"May it be our common prayer, brethren, that this man, who is chosen for the aid and furtherance of your salvation *[in adiutorium et utilitatem vestrae salutis]*, may by the mercy of divine assistance secure the blessing of the presbyterate, in order that he may obtain by the privilege of virture the sacerdotal gifts of the Holy Spirit, so that he be not found wanting in his office."*72

This invitation to pray for the elect reveals that the ordination is seen as a blessing, that is to say, a gift for which the community must implore the Lord. The one who is chosen is therefore ordained for a concrete community, "for the aid and furtherance of [its] salvation." Nothing is said of the collegial organ of the presbyterium, but the connection to a community is made: the ordinand appears as its servant (his efforts *[virtutum]* are expended for it). Lastly, the power through which the newly ordained may accomplish all this comes to him through the priestly gifts received from the Holy Spirit. We see that a sacerdotal qualification is clearly expressed here.

The consecration of the hands of the new presbyter constitutes the third element of the rite. The *MF* gives two prayers for the anointing of the hands,*74–*75 while the Gelasian apparently gives none.[202] But this last sacramentary contains a prayer of anointing (Ge 756) after the ordination prayer of the sub-deacon which seemingly belongs to presbyteral ordination (the text is the same as the *MF* 8, 33*74). The *MF* contains the oldest testimony to the anointing of the hands of the presbyter, unknown in Rome.[203]

The examination of the two prayers reveals that they are somewhat vague. The first asks that the hands of the presbyter be sanctified to bless and to consecrate. The second, also very general, makes an allu-

[202]Cf. B. KLEINHEYER, *Die Priesterweihe . . .* , 116; A. CHAVASSE, "Le rituel d'ordination du Sacramentaire gélasien," *BCE* 36 (1962) 19–37, here p. 31.

[203]The anointing of the hands was a particularity of the Gallican liturgy; in Rome, Nicholas I, in 864, knew "no document which sanctioned such a usage": quoted by M. ANDRIEU OR IV, 15. For the complete history of ordination anointings, see G. ELLARD, *Ordination Anointings in the Western Church Before 1000 A.D.*, reprinted [1st ed., 1933] (N.Y.: Kraus Reprint, 1970).

sion to David, king and prophet. The sanctifying power of chrism is expressed in the anointing of the hands of the new presbyter. A. Santantoni emphasizes that this is clear also in the anointing of catechumens, and, later, in the anointing of the head of the bishop.[204] With this anointing, the idea of "being set apart" begins to emerge. We have already noted that the tendency to emphasize the "personal holiness" of the minister is present in the Roman ordination prayers; henceforth, the rite of anointing will symbolize this fact visually. This second prayer is used for the anointing of the hands of bishops in the sacramentaries of the Gelasian type of the eighth century.

Conclusions. 1) The allocution *Quoniam* shows that the bishop has a certain initiative in the ordination of presbyters, because it is probably he who makes the choice of a person worthy "of a superior rank in the Church" and, according to Gallican usage, it was he who presented the future presbyter for the acclamation of the people.

2) Since the presbyter was to occupy a position of authority in the parish, it was necessary to safeguard his selection by the entire Church (people and clergy); for this reason the bishop explicitly mentions that he has consulted his co-presbyters regarding the person presented for ordination.

3) A new concept makes its appearance: the presbyter "presides *[regimen]* at the altar." This ministry of the altar is the only function mentioned in the entire allocution. It refers surely to the celebration of the Eucharist. If this is the case, we will need to explore the meaning of the expression *"ad regimen altaris."*

4) This Church still takes it for granted that the selection of presbyters should be the result of the consent of all, the work of the Holy Spirit.

5) The invitatory specifies the theological basis of the presbyteral office: the elect is chosen for a concrete community, for a specific ministry in a parish (he is ordained "for the furtherance of your salvation"). Here the purpose of ordination is much clearer than in the allocution.

6) The invitatory relates the means by which the new presbyter will fulfill his duty: the priestly gifts given by the Holy Spirit. Here we have a specific sacerdotal qualification of the presbyterate.

[204]A. SANTANTONI, *L'ordinazione episcopale* . . . , 171, nn. 15 and 16.

7) The anointing is ambiguous at this stage of development: it illustrates most probably the progression of the idea that the presbyter is "set apart," in the sense of the sanctification of his person. We pray that the holy hands of the presbyter may carry out the benedictions and blessings required of the ministry of the priest.

8) Lastly, we should note that all sense of the collegiality of the presbyterate is lost. The priest appears only as a person responsible for a local community.

b. *Bishop*

Three elements of Gallican usage are worthy of attention: the examination required by the *SEA;*[*66–*68] the allocution *Servanda est;*[*76] the imposition of the evangelistary according to the *SEA;*[*69] and the long invitatory *Deum, totius sanctificationis,*[*79] followed by the Roman ordination prayer with the interpolation *Sint speciosi.*

Before the ordination of a person to the episcopate, it was necessary to evaluate his moral qualities, his life, and his faith. In one form or another, such a scrutiny was always in use in the Church since the Pastoral Epistles. The canonico-liturgical document of the *SEA* does not contain a standard examination, but rather a schema of an examination which is moral,[*66] dogmatic[*67] and disciplinary.[*68] The rubrics for each order follow, and they will be found also in the *MF* and the Gelasian.

Only the qualities of the bishop are presented by the author, which shows the importance of this office. We should also note that the *SEA* maintain the descending order, starting with the episcopacy. Even while attaching special importance to the person of the bishop, the author is aware of the abuses of episcopal authority when it is isolated, and when the bishop allows the deacons to give free rein to their ambitions, as the presbyters (his collaborators) are sent out to the parishes at the request of the bishops. In canons 2, 57, and 61, the author tries to restore the concept of the collegial council of presbyters who help the bishop in the selection of ordinands, in the judgment of ecclesiastical cases, and in the administration of ecclesiastical properties (cf. canons 10, 14, 50). Here again we find the original nature of the presbyterate as it was described in the *AT* and in the early Church.[205]

[205]For a discussion of the sources of these disciplinary canons, see Ch. MUNIER, *Les Statuta . . .* , 125–169.

The moral qualities required include humility, prudence, mercy, diligence in the study of the faith, chastity, etc.*[66] These are the qualities traditionally prescribed. After assuring these moral virtues, it was necessary to ascertain that the elect adhered to the truths of the Christian faith.*[67] Certain truths mentioned particularly are the mysteries of the Trinity, the incarnation, the two natures of Christ, creation, redemption, and the canon of the Scriptures; basically, it is an explanation of the brief lines of OR 34, 27 (cf. vol. IV, comparative table, III.1). Lastly, we find disciplinary prescriptions relative to the election and ordination to the episcopacy contained in the *AT* and the canons of the early Church*[68] (the person ordained bishop must be elected by the entire people; the participation of all the bishops of the province is necessary, as well as the approval of the metropolitan).

Under the heading "recapitulation of the ordinations of the Church," the *SEA* give a series of canons*[69] which became, in fact, the rubrics of ordinations in the liturgical books. For the two ministries studied here, we again find the tradition of the early Church: the bishop is ordained with the imposition of hands by all the bishops present, while two among them impose the evangelistary on the head of the elect, and another bishop pronounces the blessing (canon 90). A presbyter is ordained with the imposition of hands and the prayer said by the bishop, while all the presbyters join the bishop in the act of imposing hands (canon 91). Close reliance on the document of the *Apostolic Tradition* is evident in the rubrics concerning deacons, which reads as follows: A deacon is ordained by the bishop alone, who blesses him while imposing hands on his head; he is not ordained *(consecratur)* for the priesthood, but for service *(non ad sacerdotium sed ad ministerium)* (canon 92).

This document displays, however, one innovation: the imposition of the evangelistary must be performed by *two bishops*. At the ordination of a pope (cf. pp. 96ff.), we saw that it was two deacons who hold the evangelistary over the head of the elect. This innovation witnesses to the anti-deacon tendency of the *SEA*, but it does not change the meaning of the rite. It is the practice of the *SEA* which will be retained by the Roman Pontifical (for the ordination of all bishops) until the revision after the Second Vatican Council, which will restore the early usage reserving this gesture for the two deacons.

The second innovation is the bishop's allocution,[206] *Servanda est*,[*76]
in which the bishop is called a "priest" *(sacerdos)*, and the presbyters
appear as a collective entity with the rest of the clergy. The author
wanted to emphasize the agreement with the tradition *([lex] antiqua
ecclesiae)* of what was being done: after the death of a bishop, his successor should be chosen according to the testimony of the presbyters
and all the clergy, and on the advice of the citizens and the assembly.
This procedure differs from the election of a presbyter; it is much
more precise in its prescriptions. The favorable testimony of all is required here, because what is at stake is the choice of the shepherd of
the flock. This allocution also gives a description of the functions of
the bishop: he teaches the faith, he gives an example of patience, he
instructs through religious doctrine *(doctrinam religionis instituat)*, he
gives an example of charity through his efforts, and he exercises constant care and solicitude *(pervigili cura et instanti sollicitudine)*. The
moral qualities required are almost the same as those we find in the
SEA.

The third element is the long invitatory, *Deum, totius sanctificationis*,[*79]
a wordy and difficult text. The main idea seems to be that God, the
source of all holiness and of the rites, has himself chosen the elect,
has made him sit among the elders, and has placed him among the
princes, that is, among the bishops of God's people.[207] All this is done
in agreement with the procedure found in the Gallican allocution,
namely, through the participation of several wills *(concordibus sua in-
spiratione)*. The rest of the invitatory concerns the blessing of the elect
for his pastoral task: the prayer asks that he may have the necessary
qualities (humility, fear of the Lord, zeal for the flock, piety, holiness
and all the gifts of the high priesthood) to fulfill his pastoral responsibilities as the head or the guide *(rector)* of the people who are entrusted to him. Lastly, it says that the elect is chosen by all *(ex
omnibus elictus)* and expresses the hope that all will pray for the one
upon whom lies the charge of praying for all. A. Santantoni sees here
the figure of the mediator applied to the person of the bishop.[208] This
invitatory ends with the acclamation of the people: *Dignus est*.

[206]Does the metropolitan pronounce this allocution? B. KLEINHEYER, "Folge
2 . . . ," 325, answers in the affirmative.
[207]Cf. D. N. POWER, *Ministers of Christ* . . . , 77f.
[208]A. SANTANTONI, *L'ordinazione episcopale* . . . , 80.

Conclusions. 1) Ordination to the episcopacy is important enough to require certain moral qualities, which are largely the same as those mentioned in the tradition of the Roman ritual.

2) The greater the responsibility, the more precise and detailed are the prescriptions. The *SEA* are a good example of this truth in their schema for the moral, doctrinal and disciplinary examination.

3) Episcopal ministry is seen in its pastoral aspect. The images repeatedly invoked are those of shepherd and flock (allocution); the pastoral concern which the elect must exhibit (invitatory) is referred to several times. His ministry is qualified as priestly, and he himself is seen as an intercessor.

4) In the allocution, as well as in the invitatory, God is seen as the source of all: of the ministerial gifts, of the sanctification of the person of the minister, and of the people who are entrusted to him. In this context, the minister labors for the good order of the Church and the growth of the faith (allocution). Indeed, one of the tasks of the bishop is the teaching of the faith and Christian life.

5) Lastly, the entire Church is engaged in the selection of the bishop. We do not see clearly the way in which he is elected, but several times the documents speak of the necessary testimony of the clergy, the people, the civil authorities, and the other bishops for this election.

4. ORDINATION PRAYERS

Three prayers will be examined here, one for presbyteral ordination, and two for that of a bishop: 1) *Sanctificationum omnium,* which was definitively transferred to the moment of the anointing of the hands of the presbyters in the Roman Pontifical, where it remained until it was suppressed at the time of the revision of Paul VI in 1968; 2) for episcopal ordination: *Sint speciosi,* the Gallican interpolation which is found in the Roman prayer; 3) the prayer *Pater sancte,* which Kleinheyer's thesis considers a part of the Gallican ritual of ordinations, while others attribute it to the Hispanic liturgy.[209]

[209]Cf. the three articles of B. KLEINHEYER, "Studien zur . . . ," especially "Folge 2 . . . ," 313–366; CHANOINES REGULIERS DE MONDAYE, "L'évêque d'après . . . ," 779f. have also suggested a Gallican origin. A. SANTANTONI believes that the origin is Hispanic: see *L'ordinazione episcopale . . .* , 89–106; P.-M. GY asks if it "is necessary to mark a frontier between the two [Gallican and

a. *Presbyter*[*73]

As we will see, this prayer emphasizes the example of the presbyter seen in a role independent from that of the bishop, and having as its principal function the presidency of the Eucharistic celebration. P. Jounel says that "this prayer is much closer to the oriental texts than to the Roman ones."[210] Here is the text:

"Author of all sanctification, of whom is true consecration, full benediction: you, Lord, spread forth the hand of your blessing on this [your] servant N., whom we set apart [dedicamus] with the honor of the presbyterate, so that he may show himself to be an elder [seniorem] by the dignity of his acts and the righteousness of his life, taught by these instructions which Paul presented to Titus and Timothy; that meditating on your law day and night, O almighty one, what he reads he may believe, what he believes he may teach, what he teaches he may practice. May he show in himself justice, loyalty, mercy, bravery; may he provide the example, may he demonstrate the exhortation, in order that he may keep the gift of your ministry pure and untainted; and with the consent of your people may he transform the body and blood of your Son by an untainted benediction [inmaculata benedictione transformet]; and in unbroken love may he reach to a perfect man, to the measure of the stature of the fullness of Christ, in the day of the justice of eternal judgment with a pure conscience, with full faith, full of the Holy Spirit; through . . ." (MF 8, 32[*73])

Before moving on to a more detailed analysis of this prayer, a few general remarks are in order. Curiously, we find neither an epiclesis nor an anamnesis in this prayer. In their place, we find the request for a blessing upon the elect from the hand of God, which sets the ordinand apart (dedicare). At the end of the prayer, however, we find a prayer that the heart of the ordinand may be filled with the Holy Spirit.

This Gallican formulary is comprised of a certain number of biblical references (for example, Ps 1:2 and Eph 4:13). It is through an ex-

---

Hispanic liturgies] during this time": see "Les anciennes prières d'ordination," *LMD* 138 (1979) 96. Lastly, the article of P. DE CLERCK, "La prière gallicane . . . ," 163–176, dispels all doubts about the Gallican origins of this text.

[210]P. JOUNEL, "L'ordination sacerdotale . . . ," 60f.

emplary life and just conduct that this presbyter will show that he is one of the true elders, because his life corresponds to the examples and the virtues cited in the letters of Paul to Titus and Timothy, two models of presbyters. In the persons of Titus and Timothy we see individual persons, not a collegial entity: in the Gallican prayer, the ordinand is an elder *(senior)* through the worthiness of his life, and not through his membership in the council of presbyters gathered around the bishop. The presbyter himself presides over the community while celebrating the Eucharist *(per obsequium . . . benedictione transformet)*.[211] This is one of the presbyteral functions we find expressed here, the other being the duty to teach *(quod legerit . . . docuerit imitetur)*.

α) *Biblical Images Employed.* We find only two direct references to the Scriptures: ". . . night and day, meditating on your law," which comes from Psalm 1:2 ("but their delight is in the law of the Lord, and on his law they meditate day and night"); and ". . . may he come to the stature of the perfect man, "which comes from Ephesians 4:13 (". . . until all of us come to the unity of the faith and of the knowledge of the Son of God, to maturity, to the measure of the full stature of Christ"). Both of these references apply to the person of the minister.

The first image of the presbyter is in keeping with his title, because his life is an example of someone who is centered upon the Word of God, who believes in what he meditates upon, who in turn teaches by his actions. His authority, like that of true presbyters as Paul

---

[211]The verb "transformare" has been the object of several studies, cf., for example, P. BATIFFOL, "Transformare," *Bulletin d'ancienne littérature et d'archéologie chrétiennes* 1, 1 (1911) 54–55; R. FALSINI, "La 'trasformazione del corpo e del sangue di Cristo,'" *Studi francescani* (Florence) 52, 3–4 (1955) 307–359; J. A. FRENDO, *The "Post secreta" of the "Missale Gothicum" and the Eucharistic Theology of the Gallican Anaphora* (Malta: St. Joseph's Home, 1977) 71–85; M. RULE, "'Transformare' and 'Transformatio,'" *JTS* 12, 1 (1911) 413–427. The ancient Eucharistic expression ("may he, in the faith of your people, transform the Body and the Blood of your Son through the immaculate blessing" should be read *"panem et vinum in corpus et sanguinem . . . transformet"* in the Romano-Germanic Pontifical of the tenth century (=PRG XVI, 34). As for the different debates concerning the notion of *transubstantiatio,* see the concise studies of P.-M. GY, "L'eucharistie dans la tradition de la prière et de la doctrine," *LMD* 137 (1979) 81–102, esp. 92–102; B. NEUNHEUSER, *L'eucharistie. I. Au moyen âge et à l'époque moderne* (Paris: Cerf, 1966) 57–130.

taught, comes from his just conduct. Indeed, in the prayer for the ordinand it is asked that he may prove just, constant, merciful, courageous *(iustitia, constantia, misericordia, fortitudo)* so that he may keep the ministry pure and without blemish. The last prayer for the ordinand uses the quotation from Ephesians, which, in its context, applies to the Body of Christ, that is, to the entire Church and not only to the minister. Here this quotation becomes a prayer for the ordinand, that he may "come to maturity, to the measure of the full stature of Christ." The prayer therefore is centered upon the ordinand. But in the Letter to the Ephesians, the text is not focused on the ministers themselves, but on their task and their responsibility to their neighbor. In commenting upon this passage of the ordination prayer, D. N. Power rightly asks whether this last petition always had the same purpose, namely, to pray for the elect; perhaps it originally referred to the people entrusted to the minister.[212] The proximity of this request to the celebration of the Eucharist may indicate the intention of the author of this prayer: whoever presides at the edification of the Church (which is one of the gifts bestowed to build up the Body of Christ—cf. Eph 4:12) should also serve his people by transforming with a holy blessing the bread and wine into the Body and Blood of Christ.

One last point: the biblical image used here is borrowed from the New Testament. In the Roman prayer, we noted that the prayer was composed of images from the Old Testament, and more specifically, the image of the Old Testament priesthood. In the Gallican prayer, what is emphasized is the ministry of the sacraments and of the Word. In the invitatory, the presbyteral ministry is qualified as priestly.

β) *Qualities Requested for the Ordinand.* A blameless life is prayed for, as well as conduct worthy of the ordinand's office: the presbyter must be formed in the discipline of the school of Paul and exemplify the list of qualities of the presbyters of Crete mentioned in Titus 1:5-9, especially justice, constancy, mercy and fortitude.

γ) *Gifts Received by the Ordinand.* The Gallican prayer has little to say concerning the gifts received: we find only one wish—that the ordinand may arrive at the final judgment with a pure conscience, a true faith and a heart filled with the Holy Spirit. If we associate this

---

[212]D. N. POWER, *Ministers of Christ . . .* , 77.

phrase with that of the invitatory which asks that the elect obtain the sacerdotal gifts of the Holy Spirit, can we conclude that these are the only gifts received? The text of this prayer alone does not allow such an affirmation.

Conclusions. 1) The Gallican prayer appears to be a prayer exhorting the presbyter to lead an exemplary life, following the model given by the letters of Paul. No gift of the Spirit is sought for the elect, and the qualities requested for the ordinand are all of a moral order: just conduct, worthy morals.

2) The ministerial tasks are those of presiding at the Eucharist (and the sacraments), and teaching the baptized. Probably the edification of the Body of Christ is also included as one of these tasks, but the connection to the bishop is not made explicit.

3) The collegial entity of the presbyterium gathered around the bishop is not mentioned. This reveals the structure of the rural Gallican Church, which required that the residence of the presbyter be in the parish, far from the bishop.

4) This prayer puts the emphasis on the person of the minister, rather than on the task. Nevertheless, the quotation from Ephesians, right after the mention of the Eucharist, testifies to a close relationship with the task.

5) The presbyteral ministry is not explicitly qualified as priestly in this prayer, and the images used make no reference to the Old Testament as the Roman prayers do. There is also missing a true epiclesis and a true anamnesis of the history of salvation, as we find in the preceding rituals.

b. *Bishop*[*80–*81]

In the Gallican documents, the prayer for the ordination of the bishop has not been preserved, but we find it inserted in the Roman prayer in the form of an interpolation between the words *sinceritas pacis* and *tribuas eis*. In reality, it is rather a cento of biblical texts that deal with the episcopal ministry. Secondly, according to the theory of Kleinheyer, the ordination prayer *Pater sancte*[*81] is a part of the collection of Gallican texts. This prayer ceased to be used when the Roman texts arrived in Gaul, but it is preserved in the *Leofric Missal*[213] and in

---

[213]F. E. WARREN (ed.), *The Leofric Missal as Used in the Cathedral of Exeter during the Episcopate of Its First Bishop A.D. 1050–1072 Together with Some Account of*

the English Pontificals.[214] We note the influence of the *Apostolic Tradition*; because of certain elements in the text, P.-M. Gy believes that this prayer should be dated before the end of the struggles against Arianism around the sixth century.[215] We will first study the Gallican addition, followed by a prayer probably of Gallican origin.

The following is the text of the interpolation, *Sint speciosi*:

"May their feet, by your aid, be beautiful for bringing good tidings of peace, for bringing your good tidings of good [Rom 10:15, cf. Isa 52:7].[216] Give them, Lord, a ministry of reconciliation [2 Cor 5:18] in word and in deeds and in power of signs and of wonders [Rom 15:18f.]. Grant to them, O Lord, that they may use the keys of the kingdom of heaven [Mt 16:19] for upbuilding, not for destruction [2 Cor 13:10], and may not glory in the power which you bestow. Whatsoever they bind on earth, may it be bound also in heaven, and whatsoever they loose on earth, may it be loosed also in heaven [Mt 16:19; cf. Mt 18:18].

"Whose sins they retain, may they be retained; and whose sins they forgive, do you forgive [Jn 20:23]. Whoever blesses them, may he be blessed; and whoever curses them, may he be filled with curses [Gen 27:29]. May they be faithful and wise servants, whom you, Lord, set over your household that they may give them food in due season [Mt 24:45], in order that they may show forth an entire perfect man [Col 1:28]. May they be unwearied in watchfulness; may they be fervent in spirit [Rom 12:11]. May they hate pride, love truth, and never be so overcome by faintness or fear as to abondon it. May they

---

the Red Book of Derby, the Missal of Robert of Jumièges and a Few Other Early Manuscript Service Books of the English Church, offset reprint [1st ed. 1883] (Westmead, Farnborough-Hants, Great Britain: Gregg International Publishers, Ltd., 1968) 217. Cf. also H. B. PORTER, *The Ordination Prayers . . . ,* 72f. on the origin of this prayer included in the Gallican family.

[214]Cf. A. SANTANTONI, *L'ordinazione episcopale . . . ,* 98f., who gives the following books: the Pontificals of Magdalen College, of Robert, of Winchester, of Lanalet, of Sherborne or of St. Dunstan, and the Sacramentary of Saint-Vaast/ Corbie.

[215]P.-M. GY, "Ancient Ordination . . . ," 72. Concerning its relationship to the prayer of the *AT*, see, id., "La théologie des prières . . . ," 602; B. KLEINHEYER, "Folge 2 . . . ," 361; A. SANTANTONI, *L'ordinazione episcopale . . . ,* 99f.; H. B. PORTER, *The Ordination Prayers . . . ,* 73.

[216]The biblical references are not found in the original text.

not put light for darkness nor darkness for light; may they not say evil is good nor good evil [Isa 5:20]. May they be debtors to the wise and to the unwise [Rom 1:14], and may they have fruit of the benefit of all [Rom 1:13]." (*MF* 9, 40*[80])

The departures from the Roman prayer are clear. The bishop is not presented here as the heir of Moses and Aaron. He is not spoken of as the head of a local Church on whom the other minor ministries depend. This Gallican addition presents another type of bishop, which the biblical images will reveal.

α) *Biblical Images Employed.* The urban bishop has been transformed into a missionary bishop who takes to the road to announce the Good News. He is a missionary of peace and of reconciliation "in word and in deeds, and in power of signs and of wonders." Episcopal ministry is seen in the lineage of the apostles (sent to evangelize the whole world) and of the prophets (sent to proclaim the reign of God through signs and wonders). He is also clearly the minister of the Word, an aspect missing in the Roman prayer. In the Gallican prayer, the bishop is associated with New Testament personages and their ministry of the Word (preaching and evangelizing), while in the other texts, which we have already studied, the bishop is associated with Old Testament personages and their ministry as leaders or ministers of the cult. Nevertheless, even though the presidency of a local Church is not mentioned here, we understand that the Gallican bishop had all the power necessary to govern his Church, because he has received, like St. Peter, the keys of the kingdom to build, to bind or to loose, and to reconcile sinners (to retain and to forgive sins). Lastly, we can say that he is also a shepherd or, better yet, in the terms of this interpolation, a good steward/servant of the house of the Lord, who knows how to feed the flock.

These biblical images give a beautiful description of the episcopal tasks which include preaching the Gospel, presiding over the community, building it up with the food of the Word (preaching), the Eucharist, and the reconciliation of sinners.

β) *Qualities Requested for the Ordinand.* This interpolation asks for those moral qualities necessary for the fulfillment of this office. Strangely, these qualities are often expressed in the negative. For example, the prayer asks that the new bishop may be strong enough not to have recourse to human means in his preaching ("enticing words of human wisdom") or not to mistake the bad for the good or the darkness for the light. But certain positive qualities such as humility, truthfulness, constancy, and piety are also included in this list. Here we have a description (more precise than in the other prayers heretofore studied) of a man which corresponds to that of the good bishop of the Pastoral Epistles

γ) *Gifts Received by the Ordinand.* There is no epiclesis in this Gallican interpolation. Two passages suggest the gifts received when the text speaks of preaching. Reference is made to a manifestation of the Spirit and of power: the ordinand has received the gifts of the Spirit which should be manifest in his preaching, because persuasion is not effected through human wisdom, but, according to the promises of the Lord, the Spirit will prompt with what must be said. Elsewhere, reference to the power received (the keys of the Kingdom) to build and not to destroy recalls the power to preside at the building up of the Church. We see that here the term used is "power" *(potestas):* the Roman prayer attributes it to God (cf. *59), but here it is held by the ordinand in order to build up the Church. Besides these references, we have no other example of the gifts received by the ordinand as a result of the prayer.

Conclusions. 1) The most noteworthy innovation is the break with the image of the bishop who is permanently settled in a city. The Gallican interpolation assigns the greater importance to the ministry of the Word (the Roman texts, by comparison, put the accent on a cultic image) and shows clearly that the Gallican bishop must be a true missionary, sent to announce the Good News, like the apostles and the prophets. This evangelization is carried out not only through preaching (the bishop is a preacher—1 Cor 2:4), but also through the life of the ordinand, because he must be an example for his people, which was true also of his Roman confrere. It has been suggested that a great bishop such as St. Martin or St. Amand may have served as a model for the life which a bishop should lead.[217]

2) Connected with evangelization we find reconciliation in word and in deed. According to the biblical quotations, this reconciliation is effected through the forgiveness of sins (Jn 20:23) and through the

[217]P. JOUNEL, "Ordinations," in A.-G. MARTIMORT and collaborators, *The Church at Prayer . . . ,* III, 166f.

exercise of the power to bind and to loose (Mt 16:19). The Gallican bishop appears as a priest and a judge.

3) The bishop of Gaul appears as a figure who has all the moral qualities necessary to fulfill the difficult charge of the episcopacy. Besides his positive qualities, he also has a power which he should not abuse, because it is the Spirit and divine power which should make themselves manifest in his preaching for the building up of the Church.

4) Finally, we should not forget that this cento is inserted in the middle of the Roman prayer, so that we should recall all the traits that have already been mentioned above. The idea of a priestly ministry is seen, therefore, in conjunction with the images used in this prayer.

Pater sancte

After having studied the Gallican interpolation, we can move on to the prayer *Pater sancte*, the text of which follows:

"Holy Father, almighty God, who through our Lord Jesus Christ have from the beginning formed all things and afterwards at the end of time, according to the promise which our patriarch Abraham had received, have also founded the Church with a congregation of holy people, having made decrees through which religion might be orderly ruled with laws given by you; grant that this your servant may be worthy in the services and all the functions faithfully performed, that he may be able to celebrate the mysteries of the sacraments instituted of old. By you may he be consecrated to the high priesthood to which he is elevated. May your blessing be upon him, though the hand be ours. Command, Lord, this man to feed your sheep and grant that as a diligent shepherd he may be watchful in the care of the flock entrusted to him. May your Holy Spirit be with this man as a bestower of heavenly gifts, so that, as that chosen teacher of the Gentiles taught, he may be in justice not wanting, in kindness strong, in hospitality rich; in exhortation may he give heed to readiness, in persecutions to faith, in love to patience, in truth to steadfastness; in heresies and all vices may he know hatred, in strifes may he know nothing; in judgments may he not show favor, and yet grant that he may be favorable. Finally, may he learn from you in abundance all the things which he should teach your people to their health. May he reckon priesthood itself to be a task, not a privilege. May increase of honor come to him, to the encouragement of his merits also, so that through these, just as with us now he is admitted to the priesthood, so with you hereafter he may be admitted to the kingdom; through . . ."[218] (*ML*, p. 217, *81)

This prayer is found in the *ML* under the title of *Consecratio* instead of the Roman prayer which follows with the title *Item alia consecratio*, a fact which shows that the prayer *Pater sancte* had been considered as a prayer proper to this liturgical book. The construction of this prayer is also most interesting. It begins with an anamnesis of the history of salvation in which God, the Father, is the creator of the universe. Briefly, he is the origin of everything for his Church and for his new minister. Beginning with creation, continuing through Jesus Christ, and up to the foundation of the Church, according to the promise made to Abraham, God has foreseen the rules and the laws according to which religion will evolve.

At this point we find a prayer for the ordinand, asking that he may be worthy of celebrating the sacramental mysteries and exercising the pastoral duties which are entrusted to him because of his elevation to the high priesthood, in order that he might carry on the new worship desired by God. Apparently, the prayer does not contain a true epiclesis; however, it does recognize the need for the gifts of the Holy Spirit (described as "the dispenser of heavenly gifts") who helps the minister with the full panoply of the virtues. The remainder of the prayer enumerates the qualities necessary for the fulfillment of his office.

α) *Biblical Images Employed.* Three biblical images are recorded: one is pastoral, one Pauline, and the last, priestly. The pastoral image is already presented in the *AT* and in the Roman prayer: the bishop appears as a guardian, a shepherd who must watch over and pasture his flock with the help of the gifts of the Holy Spirit. The Pauline image is that of the person qualified to be bishop, that is, someone who is just, gentle, hospitable, judicious, patient, etc. Thirdly, we find the priestly image, but with different connotations from those that we saw in the *AT* and in the Roman prayer. Here we find no figure from the Old Testament. Rather, we are given a description of the ministry to which the elect is ordained, for we find either the term "high

---

[218]English translation from P. F. Bradshaw, *Ordination Rites . . . ,* 236.

priesthood" or the term "priesthood" alone, used without elaboration of its substance. The ministry to which the elect is elevated through consecration by God is qualified as priestly, but apparently this phrase should be linked to the preceding one: ". . . to be worthy of the power to celebrate the mysteries of your sacraments . . ." In this context we can say that the ministry described is sacramental. At the end of the prayer where the term priesthood makes its appearance, it is identified twice with the ministry itself: the prayer affirms that the ministry is not an honor, but a charge *(opus)*. Lastly, the term signifies the concrete and certainly collegial reality to which the ordaining bishops belong, who pray that, through the merits obtained by the worthy exercise of the ministry, the ordinand may, at the end of his service, be received close to God.

β) *Qualities Requested for the Ordinand.* These qualities include faithfulness, justice, gentleness, a sense of hospitality; joyfulness, faith, patience, and perseverence. The new bishop should also have the qualities necessary to defend the faith in times of persecution, and against heresies, vices and jealousies which can exist in the community (cf. 1 Tm 3:1-7). The classic picture of the bishop appears again as we have seen it in all the documents studied up till now.

γ) *Gifts Received by the Ordinand.* In order that the ordinand may fulfill all the important duties entrusted to him, he must, of course receive all that he needs. Nevertheless, the text does not say clearly what these gifts are. We have seen that the prayer asks that "the Holy Spirit . . . may help him." He is ordained to dispense the heavenly gifts; will all of these gifts be placed at his disposal? The text is silent on this question.

Conclusions. 1) This prayer presents a somewhat pastoral image of the bishop. One senses the influence of the *AT* here, an influence which makes more explicit the office of bishop in this Church. The bishop demonstrates all the qualities of a good pastor, vigilance and concern for the flock of which he is the head and the guide, presiding over the "gathering of the saints."

2) These functions are made explicit: as guide and head of the Church, the bishop is also the celebrant of the sacraments, teaching the truth for the benefit of the people, and encouraging the faithful in

the face of heresy and persecution. The source of his strength is the Lord who gives the Spirit, the dispenser of heavenly charisms. The bishop is also a judge, because he must judge according to the wisdom of God.

3) The episcopal ministry is described as priestly; it is a charge, and not an honor. Here we see some departure from the Roman prayer, which speaks clearly of the ministry as an honor or a rank.

4) Lastly, the prayer says that the office comes from God, because it is God alone who confers the high priesthood. Ordination is seen as sacramental: through the hand of the ordaining bishop it is the blessing of God which descends upon the ordinand and raises him to the priesthood.

5. RELATIONSHIP BETWEEN EPISCOPACY AND PRESBYTERATE

One of the great changes which took place during this period has to do with the concept of the collegiality of the presbyterium. Circumstances required the presbyter to assume more and more the care of an urban or rural parish, because their multiplication toward the end of the fourth century made it impossible for the bishop to be present as the head of all communal celebrations. The role of the bishop as head of the community, presiding at the liturgical assembly, and teacher of his Church, in short, the pastor, was maintained in principle, but with great difficulty. It is the presbyters, placed at the head of these rural and urban communities, who will help the bishop in fulfilling all his duties. In Rome we saw that the bishop and his presbyters were linked in a very close way: the *fermentum*[219] symbolized this unity between the bishop (as the sole head of the Church) and his presbyters, who represent him in the *tituli*. The Gallican rituals which we have studied here attest to a different stage of develop-

---

[219]Cf. the letter of INNOCENT I, *Ep. XXV, Ad Decentium* . . . , 5, (ed. R. Cabié) 26f. Cf. G. H. LUTTENBERGER, "The Decline . . . ," 24–26. On the problem of the multiplication of Eucharistic celebrations and the disappearance of the rite of the *fermentum*, see N. MITCHELL, *Cult and Controversy: The Worship of the Eucharist Outside of Mass* (N.Y.: Pueblo Publ. Co., 1982) 34–38; J. A. JUNGMANN, *Pastoral Liturgy* (New York: Herder and Herder, 1962) [trans. from the German *Liturgisches Erbe und pastorale Gegenwart. Studien und Vorträge* (Innsbruck: Tyrolia-Verlag, 1960)] 2nd part, ch. 7: "'Fermentum.' A Symbol of the Unity in the Church."

ment. The Gallican prayers do not concern themselves with a presbyteral movement claiming that the presbyters are equal to the bishops[220] or attempting once more to diminish the stature of the Roman deacons;[221] the Roman prayers alone reflect these difficulties, while the *SEA* witness to the tensions which existed by trying to limit the power of the bishop (canons 2, 10) or the prestige of the deacons who were replaced by the bishops in the imposition of the Gospel book during the ordination of the bishop.

To gain a better idea of the relationship between the episcopacy and the presbyterate, we must consider two realities which are connected and which should be examined together: the use of Old Testament allegories (to such a degree that the Verona Sacramentary no longer mentions Christ), and the increasing use of priestly vocabulary for bishops and then for presbyters. We can explain the recourse to the Old Testament typologies in the rituals of ordination by the progressively sacrificial interpretation of the Eucharist. Since the priesthood is linked to the sacrifice in the typology of the Old Testament, the tendency was to see Christian realities already prefigured in the images and even in the vocabulary of the Old Testament.

The same process is attested in the priestly vocabulary progressively applied to presbyters. In Rome, the liturgical texts maintain more or less closely the ancient identification of the terms "priest" (*sacerdos*) and "bishop." Nevertheless, during the Carolingian period, the Gallican texts which we have examined identify the presbyters as priests, and they make the distinction between *episcopi* and *sacerdotes*.[222] The *MF* (*74–*75) uses prayers of anointing which emphasize that the hands of the priests are consecrated; the implication is that they can, like the bishop, give that which is holy: the Eucharist, baptism, etc. In the Gallican prayer for the ordination of priests, a phrase has been added to accentuate their role as celebrants of the Eucharist in the service of their people. Because the presbyter had, in fact, become the local minister presiding over a small commu-

[220]D. N. POWER, *Ministers of Christ* . . . , 78–85.

[221]F. PRAT, "Les prétentions . . . ," 471–472. The *SEA* reflect also the tensions between deacons and presbyters: see the remarks of J. GIBAUT, "Amalarius of Metz and the Laying on of Hands in the Ordination of a Deacon," *Harvard Theological Review*, 82, 2 (1989) 233–240, esp. 234–237.

[222]Cf. P.-M. GY, "Remarques sur le vocabulaire . . . ," 133–135.

nity (he can normally celebrate the Eucharist and perform the other pastoral duties), he was also called "priest" *(sacerdos)*, even though he remained subordinate *(secundi meriti)* to episcopal authority. We see here a process of moving away from the typical division of the early Church (bishop/assembly) to a new division manifested in the prayers of ordination (bishop, priests/assembly).[223] The council of the presbyterium gathered around the bishop is no longer taken into consideration, while the idea of a priest as one set apart with manifestly superior moral qualities has gained ground.

The loss of the sense of the bishop's presidency over the presbyterium, even the sense of the collegiality of the presbyterate itself, in conjunction with a more hierarchical conception of the ministry, will lead to a situation where the episcopal office is diminished, while the presbyteral office grows in importance; all the more that the presbyters are assuming responsibility for the parishes, and the person of the bishop becomes less visible. Increasingly, the presbyter participates in the *munus triplex* (word, sacrament, and government). Even if the bishop is described as the "captain of the ship," the presbyter is selected "for assistance and the advancement of the salvation" of the community, and for "the regulation of the altar," since he changes "the bread and wine into the Body and Blood of [your] Son." In short, a greater similarity between his ministry and that of the bishops can be clearly seen.

The prayer of episcopal ordination (the Gallican interpolation) presents the person of the bishop much more as an evangelist than as a sedentary person, residing in a city. The imagery of the Roman prayers is reversed here, because it is rather the presbyter who appears sedentary in a parish, while the bishop is on the road announcing the blessings and the signs of the Kingdom of God.

Briefly, the key word to describe the relationship bishop/presbyter seems to be "responsible autonomy." The local communities are henceforth under the authority and the presidency of the presbyters. The bishops exercise their function of pastoral episcopacy in a less direct way; the texts say that they have the responsibility to see that only men highly qualified are chosen (with the approval of the people) for the presbyteral ministry (as well as the other ministries in

[223]This is the perception of G. DIX, *The Shape of the Liturgy* (London: Adam & Charles Black, 1945) 34.

the Church). The Gallic bishop probably gave his presbyters autonomy in ministerial matters, while he considered it a part of his normal episcopal functions to periodically visit their parishes.

6. CONCLUSION: STRUCTURING OF THE CHURCH AND THE SUBSTANCE OF ORDAINED MINISTRY

With the expansion of Christendom and the implantation of the Gospel, the Church encountered new forces in its life. Its structure was modified according to the new needs, and certain changes affected the substance of the ordained ministry (presbyteral and episcopal) which in turn influenced the perception of the Church across space and time. This having been said, certain conclusions can be proposed:

a. *Structure of the Church*

1) Firstly, the sequence of orders in the sacramentaries becomes ascending. This change demonstrates that a division between the faithful and the ministers has made its appearance. This tendency is characterized by a clericalization of all the ministries now conceived of as a *cursus honorum*. This profound change in ecclesial consciousness will gradually become more rigid yet, as the ministries are no longer conceived of as roles of service in the Church, but rather as steps to climb in an ecclesiastical career.

2) A social and demographic change brought about new situations in the Church (as the multiplication of places of worship, the frequency of Eucharistic celebrations, etc.); the creative responses thus demanded affected the relationship between the specific ministry and the community, and between the bishop, presbyters, and faithful. Until that time, the local Church had always been active in all phases of ordination (selection, verification of the elect's qualities and aptitudes, the act of reception of the minister, and even the silent epiclesis). However, in Gallican usage, the role of the faithful is obscured to the point that they preserve only a right of acclamation in episcopal election; as for presbyters, we are heading towards total silence, because it is no longer evident that the people must acclaim them at the moment of their ordination. The fraternal sense of the Church that we see in Cyprian or in the *AT* is becoming lost.

The relationship between the bishop/presbyter and the assembly has changed by the fact that it is now normal for a presbyter to preside in a parish, by the loss of the collegial sense of the presbyterium, and the genesis of a missionary image of the bishop; from all this, the "presbyter" himself becomes "priest" (*sacerdos*), with the result that a new ecclesiological equilibrium is being created. The collegial reality of the preceding period is lost. We can say that the increasing use of priestly vocabulary referring to bishops and then to presbyters helped to produce a situation of autonomy of clerics, to which the prayer language attests when it speaks of "one set apart" (by, for example, the moral quality of his life, the seriousness of his morals, etc.; cf. *73). The mediation of the Church is less central in the entire process, while the ministry has become more autonomous. Even the bishop, with his enthronement and his anointing, is in the process of becoming a regal figure, a lord more than a servant.[224] The two principal elements in the rites of ordination still remain the imposition of hands and the consecratory prayer, but to understand what is now taking place, we must note that this liturgical core is beginning to be covered up by other rites which so gain in importance that these two acts are obscured. We have already noted the importance of the moral exhortations and the comparisons that have been established between the person of the minister and other people in secular life. During the development of the ritual elements, we have witnessed the phenomenon of the increasingly visual aspect of the liturgy, with the multiplication of gestures, of anointings, of vestments. The ecclesiological equilibrium which ensured the responsibility in solidarity of all the members of the Church is now in the process of disappearing.

3) Even though the Eucharistic framework of ordination is maintained, the sense of the Church as a fraternal communion is no longer expressed with the same clarity as before. The Eucharistic phrase of the prayer of presbyteral ordination (*73) witnesses to a shift toward an inversion of the original meaning of the ministry; we no longer perceive that the priest presides at the Eucharist because he presides at the building up of the Church. The ordination prayers focus on the person of the minister, rather than on the substance of his ministry.

4) Even though we have not studied the diaconate explicitly, we can make the following observation regarding the position occupied in the structure of the Church by the deacons, and especially the

---

[224]Cf. the description of HINCMAR OF RHEIMS, *Ep. XXIX* . . . , (PL 126, 188A); M. ANDRIEU, "Le sacre épiscopal . . . ," 40–54.

archdeacon, the closest collaborator of the bishop. In Rome, we noted that he exercised authority over the other ministers (even the presbyters), that he watched over the administration, that he presided at the distribution of alms, and that he controlled the ordinations—that is to say, one could not be ordained presbyter without the consent of the deacons, and without being presented by the archdeacon. Moreover, he had the task of educating the young clergy, whence, at the beginning of diaconal or presbyteral ordination, the request made to the archdeacon to testify "whether the ordinands are worthy." In the structure of the Church, the figure of the archdeacon was in fact a sort of "vicar general."[225]

5) Lastly, we must note a shift in the meaning of the *"episkopē."* The Roman ordination prayers reflect a tighter organization, linked more closely to the episcopal ministry, in which the other ministries are subordinated to the bishop. At that time a theological conflict concerning the nature of the distinction between the presbyterate and the episcopacy was not yet resolved. In Gaul, however, the organization of the Church is more flexible due to the growth of the number of believers, the result of the evangelization of the countryside. Another type of pastoral supervision springs up according to which the bishop exercises less constant and immediate control over all the elements of ecclesial life: the bishop must move around very often.

b. *Substance of Episcopal and Presbyteral Ministries*

The ordination rites have shown that the two ministries studied have three elements in common: presiding over a Church, presiding at the Eucharist, and exercising the ministry of the Word. Here the presbyters exercise a much broader and more individual ministry: they share with the bishop the task of building up the Church through mission work, preaching, the pastorate and the governance of a community, and the celebration of the sacraments, especially the Eucharist.

---

[225]The role played by the (arch)deacon in the ordination rite is attested for Rome by AMBROSIASTER (*Quaestiones Veteris et Novi Testamenti*, CI, 9–10 [CSEL 50, 1908]) and by St. JEROME (*Ep. CXLVI, Ad Evangelium*, 2 [PL 22, 1194]). For the other roles of the archdeacon, see A. AMANIEU, "Archidiacre," in R. NAZ (ed.), *Dictionnaire de droit canonique*, vol.1 (Paris: Letouzey et Ané, 1935) cols. 948–1004.

Episcopal ministry takes on a missionary form rather than a sedentary form (as seen in the Pastoral Epistles). The bishop's responsibilities include evangelization, presiding at worship, and governing his Church. Since the local Church could no longer constitute a single assembly, the bishop had to find another way to exercise his presidency. Through certain individuals such as Isidore of Seville,[226] some specific functions were reserved to the bishop: the power to confirm, to ordain clerics, and to reconcile penitents. An effort was thus made to maintain the Church as a communion of persons even when the oneness of the liturgical assembly was lost. However, the enumeration of the functions proper to each order permits an interpretation of the pastoral ministry in terms of functions rather than in terms of responsibility and of service. It is important to identify the presbyteral ministry as sharing in episcopal responsibility in the *munus triplex*, which derives from the nature of the presbyterate rather than from a delegation of the bishop. The rites that we have examined tend certainly in this direction.

D. ADDITIONS AND CHANGES TO THE OLD RITUAL

A history of the evolution of the ritual elements will not be given here. This work has been done by B. Kleinheyer and A. Santantoni (who have already been quoted).[227] Rather, we will look for the ecclesiological meaning of these elements. We will have the opportunity to discuss these in the third part when we compare the Roman Pontifical of Clement VIII (PR 1596) (which is modeled roughly on the Pontifical of Durandus of Mende) with that of Paul VI (PR 1968) and that of John Paul II (PR 1990).

The Carolingian period is characterized by the accumulation of texts and rituals in the same liturgical book. Sometimes these texts explain the theological meaning of ministry in very different ways. One example of the accumulation of texts is the insertion of certain Gallican texts among Roman texts; even the prayer of episcopal ordination has been interrupted by a Gallican interpolation. The auxiliary rites multiply, like a theatrical production, to explain the meaning of

---

[226]ISIDORE OF SEVILLE, *De ecclesiasticis officiis*, lib. II, cap. VII, 2 (PL 83, 787) and *Etymologiarum*, lib. VIII, cap. XII, 21 (PL 82, 292).

[227]B. KLEINHEYER, *Die Priesterweihe* . . . ; id., "Studien zur . . ."; A. SANTANTONI, *L'ordinazione episcopale* . . . .

the prayers which had become inaccessible to the faithful due to the language problem. The unity of the nucleus of the Roman rite (imposition of hands and consecratory epiclesis) begins to be broken down when the nucleus is surrounded by explanations which receive greater importance.[228] However, some of these elements were already present in the old Roman ritual, but in a more discreet form, without emphasis. What are these elements? There are five: anointing, investiture, *traditio instrumentorum*, concelebration, and certain elements unique to each order.

1. ANOINTING

The act of anointing is already found in the biblical tradition in the case of kings (1 Sam 10:1; 16:13; 1 Kings 1:39; 2 Kings 9:6) and of priests (Lev 4:5; 8:12; 16:32; Ex 28:41 [sons of Aaron]; 29:7; 40:15 [sons of Aaron]; Num 3:3 [sons of Aaron]). In the case of the prophets, the anointing is mostly spiritual (1 Kings 19:16-19; 2 Kings 2:9-15; Isa 61:1). According to these texts, the Spirit of the Lord is perceived as a gift which God communicates to someone so that a task may be accomplished on behalf of all the people. The effect of anointing is the communication of the Spirit of God.[229]

In the New Testament, the anointing par excellence is that of Christ, anointed in the Holy Spirit and in power (Acts 10:38). But Christians also receive an anointing which allows them to participate in the anointing of Christ (2 Cor 1:21; 1 Jn 2:20, 27). For the New Testament, the Holy Spirit is God himself; the connection between anointing and the communication of God is closer, because all who believe in the Word of God must be baptized (cf. Mt 28:19)[230] in the name of the Holy Spirit, as in the name of the Father and the Son.

The prayer of the *Veronense* speaks of a heavenly anointing descending unto the extremities of the body of the new bishop.[*58] With the passage of time this metaphorical anointing materialized in an anointing with oil. We have already explained how the ancients interpreted it (for example, Leo the Great) from a viewpoint which maintained a proper balance between the unique priesthood of Christ, the

[228]Cf. P. JOUNEL, "Ordinations . . . ," 164f.

[229]Cf. J. R. VILLALÓN, *Sacrements dans l'Esprit. Existence humaine et théologie existentielle* (Paris: Beauchesne, 1977) 213–233.

[230]Ibid., 103–106, 252–275.

priestly, royal and prophetic role of the entire people, and the gift from God to certain members of the body to enable them to organize or structure the people so that the mission might be fulfilled. It remains for us to see whether this balance has been maintained.

a. *Priest*

We have already spoken briefly of the anointing of the hands, but its ecclesiological context has bearing on the meaning of the presbyterate. The text of PR 1596*[106]–*[107] mentions the power to bless, to consecrate and to sanctify (". . . may all that is blessed be blessed, and all that is consecrated be consecrated and sanctified . . ."). According to the information given by Kleinheyer, this gesture has been interpreted either as the consecratory power of the priest, or as a purification carried out that the life of the minister may be pure and holy because he must be an example for those over whom he is to preside.[231] The idea according to which the priest has the obligation to build up the Church still survives, but it is outweighed by the concept of "power over" the Church, connected to the power of sanctification, that is to say, making something holy *(sacrum dans).*[232] This is not consistent with the meaning of ministry that we have seen in the early rites, where the pastoral ministry was a part of the charismatic structure of the Church (the multiplicity of gifts, of services, of ministries given to the Church). Sacerdotal ministry was bestowed on the presbyterate (and the episcopacy) with ordination, but this does not mean that the minister would have personally received a sacerdotal character; it is due to his duty to preside in the Church that the minister has a priestly, prophetic and royal function. The act and the

[231]For example, AMALARIUS OF METZ, *Liber officialis*, II, 13, 1, ed. Hanssens, II, p. 227; THEODULPH OF ORLEANS, *Capitula ad presbyteros parochiae suae*, I (PL 105, 193); cf. B. KLEINHEYER, *Die Priesterweihe* . . . , 114–142, 154–161. As for the origins of anointing, the thesis of G. ELLARD, *Ordination Anointings* . . . , holds that this gesture came to Rome by way of Ravenna (towards 925); this thesis is questioned by J. H. CREHAN, "Medieval Ordinations," 325, n. 4. For a theological interpretation of this gesture, see L. OTT, *Le sacrement* . . . , 130–134 and B. KLEINHEYER, *Die Priesterweihe* . . . , 140.

[232]Cf. D. N. POWER, *Ministers of Christ* . . . , 101–104. Moreover, Y. CONGAR, *L'Eglise de saint Augustin* . . . , 169–176, explained the reason for this change of mentality rooted in the shift from an ecclesiology of communion to an ecclesiology of power. See also the observations of E. SCHILLEBEECKX in *The Church with a Human Face* . . . , 203–208.

text of the anointing of the hands of the priest indicates a shift in the concept of the ministry of the priest away from what we saw in the early Church. We will take into consideration this difficulty later when we examine the theological meaning of the ordained ministry of bishops and priests.

b. *Bishop*

The bishop receives two anointings: one on the hands, the other on the head. The ʳ ɾayer for the anointing of the hands of the bishop of PR 1596*162–*16 is drawn from that of the anointing of hands of priests.[233] Yet its meaning has changed, because no reference is made to the sacrifice which the bishop offers, but rather to the acts and rites which he performs. The hands have become a means of attracting the blessing of God*165 over his Church (". . . may all that you bless be blessed; may all that you sanctify be sanctified, and may the imposition of your consecrated hands contribute to the salvation of all").

We must place this image in conjunction with the second anointing of the elect, upon his head. We have already spoken of this anointing, but it behooves us to remember that the great prayer of ordination which speaks of a heavenly anointing is interrupted with a physical anointing with oil. The prayer found in PR 1596*157 adds nothing to the gesture. The interpretation given by Amalarius which sees the bishop as mysteriously inserted into Christ, the head of the Church, is no longer clearly seen in this rite.[234] The ordination of the bishop and the consecration of the king are in symbiosis and are modeled one on the other. Unfortunately, the meaning of the bishop's duty to preside is overshadowed by the sense of the power of the king, the royal privileges, which assume a predominant place in the interpretation of the rite. The rite of presbyteral anointing takes on a more priestly sense, whereas the rites of episcopal anointing are interpreted in the perspective of the power received by the bishop.[235]

2. INVESTITURE

We have seen that in Rome, in the the early rites, the elect is presented for ordination already vested (OR 34, 11 and 37). Yet, with the

---

[233]Cf. A. SANTANTONI, *L'ordinazione episcopale* . . . , 170f.

[234]Cf. AMALARIUS OF METZ, *Liber officialis*, II, 14, 6, ed. Hanssens, II, p. 235. The bishop is seen as the vicar of Christ ("*Vicarius Christi efficitur pontifex*").

[235]Cf. L. OTT, *Le sacrement* . . . , 132f.

passage of time and the increasing tendency to make the meanings visualized which accompanied the evolution of the rites, the original understanding of the principal elements of the imposition of hands is lost, as well as the prayer of epiclesis. We will attempt, therefore, to understand the meaning of the investitures.[236]

a. *Priest*

The liturgical investiture is a rite more explanatory than essential. In fact, the texts which accompany the gestures of crossing the stole on the chest of the ordinand,[*101] of vesting with the chasuble[*102] and unfolding it,[*116] make reference to the virtues required of the new priest, namely, charity, perfection, and innocence. We see here the development of rites which are given spiritual explanations derived from medieval allegories of the priestly vestments.[237] We are to see in them signs of the virtues which the wearer must practice. A reading drawn from the Epistle to the Colossians describes in this context the behavior worthy of every new person, resurrected with Christ: "As God's chosen ones, holy and beloved, clothe yourselves with compassion, kindness, humility, meekness, and patience. Bear with one another and, if anyone has a complaint against another, forgive each other; just as the Lord has forgiven you, so you also must forgive. *Above all, clothe yourselves with love, which binds everything together in perfect harmony* [italics ours]. And let the peace of Christ rule in your hearts, to which indeed you were called in the one body. And be thankful" (Col 3:12-15). The new priest is exhorted to live in greater conformity with the gift which he has received through his ordination. In the same way, in the prayer which accompanies the bestowal of the stole, an allusion is made to the Gospel of St. Matthew (Mt 11:30). Once again we hear of the complete dependence that a minister should have in relation to the Lord: "Take my yoke upon your

[236]On the meaning of the liturgical vestments, there are some references in L. OTT, *Le sacrement* . . . , 135ff. On the use of liturgical vestments, see J. BRAUN, *Die liturgische Gewandung im Occident und Orient nach Ursprung und Entwicklung, Verwendung und Symbolik* (Freiburg im Breisgau: Herder, 1907) 149ff., 562ff. and 701; and ANDRIEU OR IV, 129–184; B. KLEINHEYER, *Die Priesterweihe* . . . , 123–134, 154–159.

[237]As, for example, *De Vestimentis Sacerdotalibus,* ed. M. GERBERT, *Monumenta veteris liturgiae Alemannicae,* vol. 2, reprint [1st ed., 1779] (Hildesheim: Olms, 1967) 290. For the evolution of the formulary of this rite, see B. KLEINHEYER, *Die Priesterweihe* . . . , 104f., 128–132 and 154–157.

shoulders and learn from me *(mathete ap' emou)* . . . my yoke is easy and my burden is light." The ordinand must learn that he is a disciple of the Lord and that the form of his ministry derives from that of his Master, Christ, the unique Priest of the Church. All these texts should be understood in a spiritual sense.

b. *Bishop*

OR 34, 37 explains very simply that the elect is presented, after the psalm, already vested.[*16] PR 1596 does the same.[*124] But due to the tendency in the Carolingian period to explain and to show visibly, an entire series of rites (coming from the medieval pontificals) is found which are joined to the end of the imposition of hands and the prayer. We will study these rites below (in number 5) in the framework of the elements unique to each order.

3. *TRADITIO INSTRUMENTORUM*

We have seen that the Roman liturgy of ordinations was striking for the simplicity of the two acts: the imposition of hands, and the prayer. The rite of the handing over of the instruments, and the other explanatory rites, are of non-Roman origin; more specifically, they are Gallican and Frankish. The purpose of these supplementary rites was to illustrate the reality of the grace and the sacramental power received in the ordination. We are speaking of the bestowal of the chalice, the bread and wine for the priest[*108–*109] and of the bestowal of the crozier,[*166–*167] the ring,[*168–*169] and the book of the Gospels[*170–*171] for the bishop.

a. *Priest*

The bishop presents each ordinand with a chalice containing some wine mixed with water, and a paten with some bread, saying, "Receive the power to offer to God the sacrifice, and to celebrate Mass for the living and the dead. In the name of the Lord." It is clear that this prayer describes the office of priest in terms of Eucharistic power. Ordination confers, then, the power "to offer to God the sacrifice and to celebrate . . ." This wording reveals one of the main ideas relative to presbyteral ministry at the time, the definition of priesthood as the power to consecrate the Eucharist.[238] We have passed

---

[238]The prayer for the bestowal of the paten and the chalice (*"Accipe potestatem . . ."*[*109]) is very typical of the theology of the time because the priesthood is

from a concept of the ordained ministry as service of the Church, exercised in the heart of the community for its edification, to a concept of the ordained ministry as something personally possessed for oneself. This shift is very important, and it will be necessary to return to it when we essay some theological reflections on the overall development. It will suffice here to note that, ecclesiologically speaking, the ordained ministry is separating from the process of the building up of the Church, and is placing itself above it.

b. *Bishop*

In the case of the ordination of a bishop, we find the bestowal of the pastoral staff (or the crozier), the ring, and the book of the Gospels. From the moment that the episcopal staff appears as a liturgical artifact in the seventh century (probably in Spain), it signified the governance

---

understood as a power and defined by the functions of worship, if not by the Eucharistic celebration. One thinks of PETER DAMIAN, *Opusculum Sextum. Liber qui appellatur gratissimus,* cap. 15 (PL 145, 118D); ALBERT THE GREAT, *De sacramentis,* tract. 8, q. 2 (". . . *Consecrare enim est principalis actus ad quem sunt actus omnium ordinum,. . ."*) *Opera Omnia,* ed. Aschendorff, 26, 139; THOMAS AQUINAS, *In IV Sent.,* d. 24, q. 2, a. 2, ad. 2 (". . . *sic solus sacerdos habet actus immediate ad Deum ordinatos, quia ipse solus potest gerere actus totius Ecclesiae qui consecrat eucharistiam, quae est sacramentum universalis Ecclesiae"*) (Only the priest is capable of carrying out actions directed immediately towards God, because only the one who alone consecrates the Eucharist, the sacrament of the entire Church, is capable of carrying out an action for the entire Church), *Opera Omnia,* Parma ed., vol. 7^2, 897; id., *Summa Theologiae,* III, q. 74, a. 2, sed contra et 2um (here a priest can consecrate all the bread sold in the market and all the wine in the wine cellar), *Opera Omnia,* Leonine ed., vol. 12, 146f.); id., *Summa Theologiae,* III, q. 65, a. 3 (". . . *sacramentum ordinis ordinatur ad eucharistiae consecrationem . . ."*), *Opera Omnia,* Leonine ed., vol. 12, 60); BONAVENTURE, *In Librum IV Sententiarum,* d. 18, p. 1, a. 3, q. 2 (given powers: ". . . *Una principalis, et prima, quae est ipse ordo, vel potestas conficiendi . . ."*), *Opera Omnia,* ed. Vivès, vol. 6, 17f. Also, see the commentaries of the following authors on this subject: L. OTT, *Le sacrement . . . ,* 134–138; Y. CONGAR, *L'Eglise de saint Augustin . . . ,* 169–176, 235–241; E. SCHILLEBEECKX, *Ministry . . . ,* 54–58 and id., *The Church with a Human Face . . . ,* 203–208. In the "Ordinals of Christ," medieval books which foster clerical spirituality, we find examples of the interpretation given to each order in the ecclesiastical hierarchy. These books associate one phase of the life of Christ to each order. Recently these books have been studied for their content and their spirituality; the derived comparative tables are most interesting: see R. E. REYNOLDS, *The Ordinals of Christ from Their Origins to the Twelfth Century* (Berlin/N.Y.: Walter De Gruyter, 1978) passim, esp. 160–191.

of a particular Church and the pastoral ministry entrusted to the bishop, while the episcopal ring signified authority and jurisdiction.[239] At the time of the Investiture Struggle these two insignia played an important role because of their symbolism. It is here that we see two traditions emerge in the meaning of the pastoral staff and the ring: their usual religious meaning, and the meaning that secular powers wanted to give them. The feudal system had introduced the awarding of a bishopric as a benefice linked to feudal subjection. In a symbolic manner, the prince consigned the staff and later the ring, too, as symbols of his authority and his office. Towards the end of the eleventh century and the beginning of the twelfth, the authorities realized the dangers inherent in this symbolic language; a struggle, therefore, broke out between the Church and the secular princes for investiture. Eventually a double tradition of symbols evolved: one lay, and the other liturgical. In this double tradition we see the consummation of the long development of the distinction between power founded on ordination and power of jurisdiction.[240] According to this distinction, the bestowal of the book of the Gospels expressed the essential role which the bishop played in the transmission of the apostolic faith.

The prayers for the *traditio* of each insignia do not reveal much. In the bestowal of the crozier,[*167] episcopal ministry is seen from the angle of pastoral government. The bishop is pastor of the people en-

[239]For the historical evolution of these rites, see A. SANTANTONI, *L'ordinazione episcopale . . .* , 150–156; P. SALMON, *Etude sur les insignes du pontife dans le rit romain: histoire et liturgie* (Rome: Officium libri catholici, 1955); id., "Aux origines de la crosse des évêques," in *Mélanges en l'honneur de Monseigneur Michel Andrieu* (Strasbourg: Palais Universitaire, 1956) 373–383. The pope had another insignia: the ferule or rod, which was given to him the day of his enthronement and taking possession of the *episcopium Lateranense*. The use of these disappeared in the sixteenth century: id., "La 'ferula,' bâton pastoral de l'évêque de Rome," *RevSR* 30, 4 (1956) 313–327; concerning the episcopal ring, V. LABHART, *Zur Rechtssymbolik des Bischofsrings* (Cologne/Graz: Böhlau Verlag, 1963) 110–115.

[240]Cf. A. DUMAS, "La féodalité . . . ," 192–241; Y. CONGAR, *L'Eglise de saint Augustin . . .* , 118–122; and E. SCHILLEBEECKX, *The Church with a Human Face . . .* , 203–208, but especially pp. 192f. where he shows that the notion of "potestas" is at the heart of the entire Investiture Struggle, and that this distinction between the power of ordination and the power of jurisdiction prepared the way for the "absolute ordinations." See also, M. STROLL, *Symbols as Power. The Papacy following the Investiture Contest*, Brill's Studies in Intellectual History, 24 (Leiden/N.Y./Copenhagen: E. J. Brill, 1991) 45–56.

trusted to him, and he must watch over them so that they do not stray from the path of salvation. At the same time, the bishop possesses the authority and the powers necessary to correct his own flock, to be face to face with his people so as to judge the bad and to reprove those who have wandered astray, but also to encourage those who remain on the right path. The biblical images evoked are those of Psalm 23:4 (God is the true shepherd of his people: "Even though I walk through the darkest valley, I fear no evil, for you are with me; *your rod and your staff*, they comfort me"); cf. 1 Peter 5:4, where Christ is the sovereign Pastor and guide of his people; and 1 Corinthians 4:21, where Paul recognizes that sometimes it is necessary to choose between coercion or kindness in his mission as apostle. The pastoral staff is therefore a symbol either of the episcopal office or of the help which God gives to him,[241] and its meaning has been fairly constant in the liturgical texts.

In a different way, the ring has known successive and sometimes divergent interpretations. Long ago, Isidore of Seville saw in it the dignity and the authority of the bishop; the earliest prayers for its bestowal spoke of the episcopal ring as a seal, a symbol of the major-domo, the key of the stewardship over the treasury of the Lord entrusted to him.[242] But the problem, even with the bestowal of the crozier, of the *traditio* of these episcopal insignia was compounded by the questions of the temporal and spiritual powers of the bishop, in the Investiture Struggle.[243] Yet the symbolism of nuptial fidelity will supplant these interpretations towards the tenth century, and the ring will henceforth be interpreted as a sign of the fidelity of the bishop to his Church (the spouse of God).[*169]

Lastly, the bestowal of the book of the Gospels is a very eloquent gesture, explained further by the prayer of *traditio*: "Receive the Gospel, and go announce it to the people who is entrusted to you *(populo tibi commisso)*; since God has the power to increase his grace in you . . . ."[*171] The bishop is thus seen as the minister who will

---

[241]For example, INNOCENT III, *De sacro altaris mysterio*, I, 45 (PL 217, 790).

[242]Cf. A. SANTANTONI, *L'ordinazione episcopale* . . . , 160 (text of ISIDORE OF SEVILLE, *De ecclesiasticis officiis*, lib. II, cap. V, 12 [PL 83, 784]). For the texts of the bestowal and the blessing of the ring, see pp. 276ff., and M. ANDRIEU, "Le sacre épiscopal . . . ," 59–62.

[243]Cf. A. FLICHE and V. MARTIN (eds.), *Histoire de l'Eglise* . . . , vol. 7 *L'Eglise au pouvoir* . . . , 235f.; P. BATIFFOL, "La liturgie . . . ," 753.

build up the people which is entrusted to him, by means of the true food of the Word of God, which is itself grace and strength for the minister.

From these three rites a clear image emerges of the bishop as a gift from God to the Church, for he is guide, pastor, and *paterfamilias*. According to these texts, the bishop does not appear as "a lord" of the Church, but rather as its servant, who acts on the part of God, the only Guide, Pastor and Father of his Church. This image is in agreement with those that we find in the first prayers of episcopal ordination (from the *Apostolic Tradition*), and they help us to understand better the meaning of the later ordination prayers.

4. CONCELEBRATION

It is necessary to distinguish between the old conception of concelebration and the modern one. In the ancient documents (for example, the *Apostolic Tradition*, and also OR 34), Eucharistic concelebration was seen as unique, with the participation of all according to the schema: one community, one altar, one Eucharist. It was celebrated by all, each according to his rank and role. By contrast, in the modern period concelebration (very often, among only priests, but sometimes with bishops) is a single collective liturgical act in which each of the concelebrants, in liturgical vestments, pronounces the words of Eucharistic consecration. The only concelebration (besides that of Holy Thursday) was the concelebration of new priests at their ordination.[244] Let us analyze the meaning of concelebration in the ordination rites found in PR 1596.

[244]Besides R. TAFT, "*Ex oriente lux*? Some Reflections on Eucharistic Concelebrations," *Worship* 54, 4 (1980) 308–325 reprinted in id., *Beyond East and West: Problems in Liturgical Understanding* (Washington, D.C.: The Pastoral Press, 1984) 81–99, one can read with interest the work of R. SCHULTE, *Die Messe als Opfer der Kirche. Die Lehre frühmittelalterlicher Autoren über das eucharistische Opfer* (Münster: Aschendorff, 1959) where the author rightly shows that the Eucharist is the offering of the Church. It seems that the Church until the early Middle Ages saw the liturgical assembly as an organic unity in which each member had the qualification and the capacity to offer the sacrifice because each was a member of the Body of Christ. Each individual member offers, because the priestly body of Christ *(corpus Christi sacerdotis)* offers (cf., for example, pp. 37–45, 50–52, 188f.). Examples of this underlying ecclesiology in the rites of concelebration are found in the following articles: B. BOTTE, "Note historique sur la concélébration dans l'Eglise ancienne," *LMD* 35 (1953) 9–23; A. RAES, "La

a. *Priest*

The Pontifical of the Roman Curia (PR XIII, X, 34) is the first to treat of concelebration in the modern sense.[245] PR 1596 indicates that the priests say all the prayers, from the offertory to the last Gospel; likewise, they make all the gestures at the same time as the bishop (that is to say, they sign themselves and they beat their breasts with him). The underlying theology emphasizes the necessity for each priest of pronouncing all the words. With this theology we have another sense of the value of the participation of each celebrant (cleric or lay). We saw briefly above that the explanatory rites emphasize the role of the priest more in the sense of "power over" (as *confectio sacramenti*), bringing out the sacerdotal action and leaving in the shadows the unique role of the rest of the assembly, who have an irreplaceable role for a correct understanding of the Eucharistic mystery.[246] The concelebration that is found here (PR 1596) purposes to express the unity of the priesthood, not without the danger of clericalization.

b. *Bishop*

We recall that in the *AT,* after the ordination of a new bishop, he himself presides at the Eucharistic celebration. In the tradition of the medieval pontificals, it is rather the consecrator who has the privilege of presiding at the Eucharist which follows, which raises some difficult questions for the theology of the episcopacy as found in these liturgical books. The question turns on the sacramental reality of the episcopacy, a question which will not find a definitive response before the Second Vatican Council.[247] The "sacramentality of the episcopacy" was expressed concretely by the presiding of the bishop at this first Eucharist as bishop, namely, as leader and person primarily responsible for the building up of the Church of Christ in that particu-

---

concélébration eucharistique dans les rites orientaux," *LMD* 35 (1953) 24–47; R. TAFT, *"Ex oriente. . . ."*

[245]ANDRIEU PR II, 349; B. KLEINHEYER, *Die Priesterweihe . . . ,* 182–187 for the evolution of the rubrics.

[246]Concerning this role, read Y. CONGAR, "L''ecclesia' ou communauté chrétienne sujet intégral de l'action liturgique," in J.-P. JOSSUA and Y. CONGAR (eds.), *La liturgie après Vatican II. Bilans, études, prospective* (Paris: Cerf, 1967) 241–282; H.-M. LEGRAND, "The Presidency . . . ," 432–435.

[247]*Lumen gentium* 21 expresses the specific meaning of the "sacramentality" of the episcopacy.

lar place. The practice of concelebration at an episcopal ordination where the newly ordained (a resident bishop) does not preside at the Eucharist at the head of his people bears witness to the loss of the sense of the sacramentality of the episcopacy, as well as the obfuscation of the connection between the Church and the Eucharist.

5. ELEMENTS UNIQUE TO EACH ORDINATION

This last section studies the concluding rites. For the priest, there is the recitation of the *Credo*, a second imposition of hands and its prayer, the promise of obedience, and the final admonition. In the case of the bishop, we find the blessing of the miter and gloves, the enthronement, and the chanting of the *Te Deum*.

a. *Priest*

α) *Recitation of the* Credo. This practice is ascribed by William Durandus to the tradition of the Gallican Church; B. Kleinheyer thinks that it expresses the desire to see the ordinands exercise one of the functions of their office, that of preaching,[248] just as the deacons, after receiving the book of the Gospels, were then to read from it. Is this another way to illustrate the functions of presbyteral ministry? It would seem so. One could also see here the confessional dimension of the ministry; since this takes place before the assembly, the congregation is seen as conjointly responsible for the faith proclaimed. In fact, there was, until the reform of the Pontifical (in 1967), a second *Credo* in its usual place.*113

β) *Second Imposition of Hands and* Accipe spiritum sanctum. Each ordinand presents himself to the bishop, who imposes both his hands on his head, pronouncing the prayer: "Receive the Holy Spirit; those whose sins you forgive, they shall be forgiven; whose sins you retain, they shall be retained"*115 (cf. Jn 20:23). This phrase, in conjunction with the bestowal of the paten and chalice, expresses the two principal functions of the priest at that time: the power to consecrate the Eucharist, and the power to remit sins.[249] This second imposition of hands is to be viewed rather as part of the bestowal of the instruments, the investiture, and the anointing of the hands, and it bears

---

[248]Cf. B. KLEINHEYER, *Die Priesterweihe* . . . , 206f.

[249]D. N. POWER, *Ministers of Christ* . . . , 98–107, 115–126, has followed the development of the presbyteral functions in scholastic theology.

witness to the loss of the clarity of the ancient gesture of ordination consisting of a simple imposition of hands and the prayer,[250] in favor of the explanatory rites. This second imposition of hands is followed by the unfolding of the chasuble, which represents the climax of the "staging" of the ordination rite. These rites do not act as substitutes for the very simple and eloquent gesture of the imposition of hands accompanied by the prayer; their purpose is to explain and to make explicit (sometimes in an overly detailed and literal way) the powers and the graces of the order conferred.

γ) *Promise of Obedience.*[*117–*118] According to B. Kleinheyer, the promise of obedience was introduced into the initial questioning found in PRG XVI, 23 at the moment when the ordinand was presented to the bishop; it is founded on the feudal idea of obedience: that of a vassal or a subject.[251] It may also have had a more precise origin at the time of the Investiture Struggle, when clerics were subject to lay authorities, the pastors of churches situated on the property of feudal landlords being selected by them and ordained only for worship. These priests were considered as serfs of the feudal landlord.[252] The purpose of the promise in the ordination rite is therefore to oppose this feudal practice: it emphasizes that the priest is the subject of the bishop and his alone. We are far here from the collegial exercise of one of the ministries of the Church: presiding over the building up of the Church, and the proclamation of the Gospel. What we have here is an effect produced in the heart of the Church by an evolution that was external to it; the relationship between the bishop and his priests reveals the subjection of the priests to the bishop: their collaboration has lost its earlier visibility. This fact also implies a new way of conceiving of the theological relationship between the episcopacy and the presbyterate.[253]

[250]Cf. B. KLEINHEYER, *Die Priesterweihe . . .* , 210.

[251]Ibid., 148–150; M. RIGHETTI, *Manuale di storia liturgica*, vol. 4, *I sacramenti— i sacramentali* (Milan: Ancora, 1959) 307f.

[252]V. FUCHS, *Der Ordinationstitel von seiner Entstehung bis auf Innozenz III. Eine Untersuchung zur kirchlichen Rechtsgeschichte mit besonderer Berücksichtigung der Anschauungen Rudolph Sohms*, reprint [1st ed., 1930] (Amsterdam: Verlag P. Schippers, 1963) 151–195.

[253]The debate between theologians and canonists centers on the question whether the episcopacy is a sacrament or an honor and a dignity, and on the

b. *Bishop*

α) *Benediction and Bestowal of Miter and Gloves.*[*172–*175] Several sources[254] afford an explanation of the liturgical headdress of the bishop: the meaning of these insignia will help us in our understanding of the episcopal office. Since these rites are found at the end of the ordination ceremony, it seems that they did not have great importance. In the case of the miter, we hear that God himself places it on the head of the new bishop. As in the case of the other complementary elements of the ordination rite, the interpretation of this gesture is allegorical. The images used recall the figures of Moses and Aaron mentioned in the ordination prayer. The bishop resembles Moses "already glowing with luminous rays," but transformed into a fearsome athlete "of the truth by the dual power of two Testaments . . . with the help of your grace." Here we see the bishop's role as guardian of the truth or even protector of the weak, which is properly his.

Besides the miter, PR 1596 provides also for the imposition of gloves with two rather curious prayers. Both speak of the dignity of the hands of the bishop; in the blessing, we hear that because his hands touch the divine mysteries, they should be kept pure and clean. In the prayer accompanying their bestowal, the gloves are compared to the skin of the kid which covered the hands of Jacob, thanks to which he received the blessing of his father. These hands will offer the salutary host; they are therefore worthy of the blessing and the grace of the Lord. Once again this interpretation is typical of the period, and allows us to see how the office of the bishop was understood. Through the person of the bishop the graces and blessings of the Lord will come to his people through the new bishop's principal actions such as the Eucharistic celebration and the anointings with chrism in the sacraments of confirmation and ordination, the consecration of kings and abbots, or sometimes altars, churches, etc. The concept of the bishop as head of the Church is absent: principally he is seen in his cultic role.

---

power which is his. L. OTT, *Le sacrement* . . . , 201–214, presents the principal elements of this debate.

[254]For example, ANDRIEU OR IV, 169–184; P. SALMON, *Etude sur les insignes* . . . , 27–28, 39–46; A. SANTANTONI, *L'ordinazione episcopale* . . . , 177–179.

β) *Enthronement and the Chant* Te Deum.*[176] Even if the new bishop is ordained outside of his cathedral, the enthronement takes place according to the (extra-Roman) manner already established towards the middle of the ninth century.[255] The principal consecrator takes the new bishop by the right hand, at the same time that one of the two other bishops takes his left hand, and they seat him on the *cathedra*. After his enthronement, all sing the *Te Deum* (during which the newly consecrated bishop moves around the church, blessing the people) followed by the collect: "O God, shepherd and ruler of all the faithful, look down favorably on this your servant whom you have chosen to lead your Church; grant him, we beseech you, to be of help, both in word and in example, to those of whom he is the leader, so that, together with the flock entrusted to him, he may reach eternal life. Through Jesus Christ our Lord."[256]

The central idea is that of the presidency of the government of the Church, expressed in pastoral terms. The bishop is the head and pastor of the flock which is entrusted to him; as such, he must be a model for the faithful, not only to reach eternal life with them, but to be able to guide them on the path as a true "pastor and guide" of all. We note, lastly, that the new bishop is established by God, for the prayer sees the action of God operating through human actions. We have already encountered this conception in the early Church; although the medieval Church tended toward allegorization, the vision of the early Church is found here, seeing the act of ordination as an act of God.

The enthronement completed, the consecrated bishop thanks the consecrator and the assistants by singing to them *"Ad multos annos"* three times.

6. CONCLUSIONS

Our brief survey of the changes brought about in the ordination rites during the centuries preceding the Roman Pontifical PR 1596

[255]Cf. M. ANDRIEU, "Le sacre épiscopal . . . ," 62f., A. SANTANTONI, *L'ordinazione episcopale . . .* , 184f.

[256]Deus, omnium fidelium pastor et rector, hunc famulum tuum, quem Ecclesiae tuae praeesse voluisti, propitius respice: da ei, quaesumus, verbo et exemplo, quibus praeest proficere, ut ad vitam, una cum grege sibi credito, perveniat sempiternam. Per Christum Dominum nostrum.

shows clearly that the nucleus of the imposition of hands and the spoken prayer of epiclesis remained intact, even though it was somewhat obscured by the addition of complementary descriptive rites. The accretion of these new rites (coming principally from north of the Alps) enriched the ordinations from a visual and dramatic perspective. The compilers of the new rites respected the ancient received tradition; they simply added their new creations to the old. As a result, there was a loss of intelligibility and coherence. This is seen in the absence of a vision proper to each ministry, or a clear picture of the respective functions of the priest and the bishop. Several conceptions of the priest and the bishop are juxtaposed in the same ceremony of ordination.

Moreover, a new underlying ecclesiology emerges which will no longer be based on the concept of fraternity and communion: it is founded henceforth on a theology of inalienable powers possessed by an individual (in this case, the hierarchical ministers). The relationship between the Church and its ministers weakens, especially when the ministry is defined in terms of power received in the ordination rite. The idea that the ministry is a service, a gift of God for his community, is no longer emphasized. This evolution is apparent especially in the texts which we have examined (for example, the *traditio* of the paten and the chalice, or the gloves for the bishop). The debates concerning the sacramentality of the episcopacy also witness to this fact. All of this obscures the meaning of ministry seen henceforth in a framework more juridical than ecclesiological.

We have noted the new need to explain all the symbols used. The symbol is no longer self-evident, and the passion to allegorize everything was given free rein. Certain elements were already found in the earlier rites, such as the investiture in the *Ordines Romani* in Rome, but without giving them such emphasis. The new attention paid to this gesture bears witness to the progress of the process of sacerdotalization already noted for the beginning of the Carolingian period. This same process is attested in the way in which concelebration was understood within the framework of ordinations; here also, attention is given to the ordinand as a person receiving sacred powers, rather than to the celebration of the Church in communion.

This leads us to a further observation relative to another shift of emphasis in the underlying theology of ordinations. In antiquity, the different orders had a more organic function in the Church; presbyteral ministry had a collegial character, and the episcopacy itself was seen as a collegial body and as an essential reality of the Church. Scholastic theology is unaware of this dimension; the "hierarchical"[257] priesthood, that is to say, the ministers of the Church, acting in the name of the faithful, end up by taking the place of the *ecclesia*. The *ordo* is no longer seen in a collegial and ecclesial context; it is henceforth understood essentially in terms of powers transmitted by the act of ordination and possessed personally by the ordinand. For example, the episcopacy is no longer considered as an *ordo* in the Church, but rather as an honor *(dignitas in ordine)*.[258]

When the liturgy became incomprehensible to the faithful because Latin was no longer spoken, the liturgy of ordinations of PR 1596 became problematic: some additions were made to help the faithful understand, but they also had the effect of introducing some different theological emphases, evolved over more recent centuries. The original nucleus of the liturgy of ordinations had not been changed: the Church wanted to conserve the tradition, and did safeguard it, but it became difficult to reconcile the underlying ecclesiology of communion in this tradition with the new ecclesiology which made the

---

[257]The expression "ministerial or hierarchical priesthood" is found two times in the documents of Vatican II: *Lumen gentium* 10 *("sacerdotium ministeriale seu hierarchicum")* and *Optatam totius* 2 *("ad Christi sacerdotium hierarchicum")*. The expression can also be found in the writings of Pope Pius XII: Encyclical *Mediator Dei* of 20 November 1947, *AAS* 39, 14 (1947) 553 *(hierarchicum consecutum esse sacerdotium)* used again in his allocution to the cardinals on Feb. 11, 1954 *(Magnificate Dominum, AAS* 46, 14–15 [1954] 668). Nonetheless, we read in the document of the International Theological Commission, "Select Themes of Ecclesiology on the Occasion of the Eighth [sic!] Anniversary of the Closing of the Second Vatican Council," trans. from Latin *(Documenta 13: Themata selecta de ecclesiologia occasione XX anniversarii conclusionis concilii oecumenici Vaticani II)* in INTERNATIONAL THEOLOGICAL COMMISSION, *Texts and Documents 1969–1985,* ed. M. Sharkey (San Francisco: Ignatius Press, 1989) 290: ". . . Although this phrase does not appear directly or explicitly in the New Testament, it has been used constantly in Tradition since the third century. The Second Vatican Council went back to it regularly, while Synod of Bishops of 1971 devoted to it a document all its own." Nonetheless, no proof is cited to demonstrate this "constant use in the Tradition." We may wonder whether the commission did not mean that the term "sacerdos" is applied to the "ministry" of bishops and priests.

[258]Cf. P.-M. GY, "Remarques sur le vocabulaire . . . ," esp. 130–131; and Y. CONGAR, "L' 'Ecclesia' . . . ," 261–268.

liturgy of ordinations as incomprehensible as the Latin. In the third part of this study we will return to this point in order to clarify the differences between the ordination liturgies of PR 1596 and those of PR 1968 and PR 1990.

E. INSTITUTIONAL DISSOCIATION BETWEEN MINISTRY AND *ECCLESIA*

Before moving on to our theological reflection, we must look at a whole series of facts in the history of the theology of the ordained ministry which provoked a split between the pastoral ministry and the *ecclesia*. Our later rites reproduce this split in all the accretions of an explanatory nature to the rite. This division grew very gradually from changes in the practice of ministry itself, which were determined by factors less theological than social and economic.[259] This progressive disassociation can be seen in three stages in the history of the Church: with the ordination "*ad missam*" of the Carolingian era;[260] in the change from the "ecclesiological title" of ordination to the "economic title;"[261] lastly, in the ordination of mendicant religious

---

[259]Cf. E. SCHILLEBEECKX, *Ministry* . . . , 52–58; id., *The Church with a Human Face* . . . , 154–208; J. RATZINGER, *Principles of Catholic Theology: Building Stones for a Fundamental Theology*, trans. from German [*Theologische Prinzipienlehre: Bausteine zur Fundamentaltheologie* (Munich: Erick Wewel, 1982)] (San Francisco: Ignatius Press, 1987) 250–258.

[260]O. NUSSBAUM, *Kloster, Priestermönch, und Privatmesse. Ihr Verhältnis im Westen von den Anfängen bis zum hohen Mittelalter* (Bonn: Peter Hanstein Verlag, 1961) 250–258; A. HÄUSSLING, *Mönchskonvent und Eucharistiefeier: Ein Studie über die Messe in der abendländischen Klosterliturgie des frühen Mittelalters und zur Geschichte der Messhäufigkeit* (Münster: Aschendorff, 1973); C. VOGEL, "La multiplication des messes solitaires au Moyen Age. Essai de statistique," *RevSR* 55, 3 (1981) 206–213; id., "La vie quotidienne du moine en Occident à l'époque de la floraison des messes privées," in A.-M. TRIACCA and A. PISTOIA (eds.), *Liturgie, spiritualité, culture* (Rome: Ed. liturgiche, 1983) 341–360; id., "Une mutation cultuelle inexpliquée: le passage de l'eucharistie communautaire à la messe privée," *RevSR* 54, 3 (1980) 231–250, to be read with the more precise details furnished by J. H. CREHAN, "Priesthood, Kingship, and Prophecy," *TS* 42, 2 (1981) 216–231; N. K. RASMUSSEN, "Célébration épiscopale et célébration presbytérale: un essai de typologie," in *Segni e riti nella chiesa altomedievale occidentale* (Spoleto: Centro Italiano di Studi sull'Alto Medioevo, 1987) 2, 581–603; and, for a general history of the Carolingian world, R. RICHE, *La vie quotidienne dans l'Empire carolingien* (Paris: Hachette, 1975).

[261]V. FUCHS, *Der Ordinationstitel* . . .; C. VOGEL, "Titre d'ordination . . .";

exempt in relationship to the bishops[262] and, very closely related, the relationship between preaching and the "canonical mission."[263]

1. ORDINATION *"AD MISSAM"*

Even if there is no agreement between Häussling, Nussbaum and Vogel on the interpretation of certain aspects of the evolution of the *"missa privata,"* there is consensus on the historical effects produced by the multiplication of Masses celebrated for different reasons (for example, the multiplication of sanctuaries and monasteries, the "votive Masses" in honor of the saints and especially the Virgin, the development of the system of fines levied as penance, etc.).[264] This multiplication will necessitate a corresponding number of priests.

---

id., *"Vacua manus impositio.* L'inconsistance de la chirotonie absolue en Occident," in *Mélanges liturgiques offerts au R.P. Dom Bernard Botte* (Louvain: Abbaye du Mont César, 1972) reprinted in id., *Ordinations . . .*, 149–162; INNO-CENT III, *Ep. ad Zamorensem episcopum* (1198), in Ae. FRIEDBERG (ed.), *Corpus Iuris Canonici, Pars secunda Decretalium collectiones*, reprint [1st ed. 1881] (Graz: Akademische Druck u. Verlagsanstalt, 1959) col. 469 (= Decretales Gregorii IX, Lib. III, Tit. V, De Praebendis et dignitatibus, cap. 16).

[262]This topic has been studied by Y. CONGAR, "Aspects ecclésiologiques de la querelle entre mendiants et séculiers dans la seconde moitié du XIIIe siècle et le début du XIVe," *Archives d'histoire doctrinale et littéraire du Moyen Age* 28 (1961), 35–151; and J. RATZINGER, "Der Einfluss des Bettelordensstreites auf die Entwicklung der Lehre vom päpst-lichen Universalprimat, unter besonderer Berücksichtigung des heiligen Bonaventura," in J. AUER and H. VOLK (eds.), *Theologie in Geschichte und Gegenwart* (Munich: Karl Zing Verlag, 1957) 697–724.

[263]This topic has been studied by M. PEUCHMAURD, "Le prêtre ministre de la parole dans la théologie du XIIe siècle (Canonistes, moines et chanoines)," *RTAM* 29, 1 (1962) 52–76; id., "Mission canonique et prédication. Le prêtre ministre de la parole dans la querelle entre Mendiants et Séculiers au XIIIe siècle," *RTAM* 30, 1 (1963) 122–144 and *RTAM* 30, 2 (1963) 251–276.

[264]C. VOGEL, "Une mutation . . .," 234f. and 240–246 (read with the corrections furnished by J. H. CREHAN, "Priesthood, . . .," 224–227); A. HÄUSSLING, *Mönchskonvent . . .*, 238–251, 323–327; O. NUSSBAUM, *Kloster, . . .*, 124–132. The disagreement is explained by Häussling who does not accept the way in which Nussbaum uses the term "private Mass," because the idea of a "solitary Mass" hardly existed at the beginning of the Middle Ages. It is later that we encounter this meaning given to the *"missa privata"* (which was, moreover, a Mass deprived of the presence of the other ministries): cf. A. HÄUSSLING, *Mönchskonvent . . .*, 246, 285. What is important for our purpose is the *multiplication* of Masses and the frequency of the celebration. Everyone is in agreement on this point. Read also K. RAHNER and A. HÄUSSLING, *The Celebration of the Eucharist,*

From that moment onward, the priest was seen independently from his role presiding over the building up of the community (by preaching the Word and celebrating the sacraments), and assuming a role almost exclusively cultic. Thus the priest is seen as having been given a Eucharistic power in a personal way; in other words, the conception of the priest also changed with the gradual passage from a conception of the Eucharist as the praise of God for his saving action in history, and as the building up of the united community, to a conception of the Eucharist seen more specifically as intercession.[265] From all these developments, a gradual division ensued between the pastoral ministry and the *ecclesia,* which was seen in the growing autonomy of the priests in relationship to the faithful.

2. FROM "ECCLESIOLOGICAL TITLE" TO "ECONOMIC TITLE"

The disassociation of the ordained ministry from its ecclesial context can be seen also in the progressive practice of absolute ordination, that is to say, an ordination of a priest or a deacon without a concrete ministry. In canon 6 of the Council of Chalcedon (451) we find an insistence upon the necessity for an ordination to be "relative" (to a specific community) in order to produce its effects:

"No one, whether presbyter or deacon or anyone at all who belongs to the ecclesiastical order, is to be ordained without title *[apolelumenōs],* unless the one ordained is specifically assigned to a city or village church or to a martyr's shrine or a monastery. The sacred synod has decreed that the ordination of those ordained without title *[apolutōs]* is null *[akuron cheirothesian],* and that they cannot operate anywhere *[mēdamou],* because of the presumption of the one who ordained them."[266]

---

trans. from German [*Die vielen Messen und das eine Opfer: Eine Untersuchung über die rechte Norm der Messhaufigkeit* (Freiburg: Herder, 1951)] (New York: Herder and Herder, 1968), not only for the multiplication of Masses, but also for the economic structure which came in as part of this phenomenon.

[265]Cf. A. HÄUSSLING, *Mönchskonvent* . . . , 251–255 (change in the perception of the meaning of the Eucharist) and 268–271 (for the self-perception of the clerics). Cf. also in this sense, J. RATZINGER, *Principles of Catholic Theology,* 254–257.

[266]Cf. J. ALBERIGO et al., *Conciliorum Oecumenicorum Decreta,* 3rd ed. [1st ed. 1962] (Bologna: Istituto per le scienze religiose, 1973) 90 (hereafter COD); translation from N. P. TANNER (ed.), *Decrees of the Ecumenical Councils* . . . , I, 90; see also VOGEL, "Titre d'ordination . . . ," 72, reprinted in *Ordination,* [135], who demonstrates the acceptance of this canon in the Church as much in the East as in the West.

This canon and its acceptance in the early Church expresses a profound sense of the rootedness of the ordained ministry in a concrete Church. A minister without an ecclesial function was a contradiction in terms for the Church. But as we have seen, this function was interpreted more and more in a cultic sense in the Carolingian period.

This understanding of "title" will little by little be replaced by another conception. The change in the meaning of absolute ordination is seen in Lateran III (1179). There we see that the interdiction only held for the cleric for whom revenue sufficient for his subsistence could not be assured. "If a bishop ordains someone as deacon or priest without a definite title from which he may draw the necessities of life [necessaria vitae], let the bishop provide him with what he needs until he shall assign him the suitable wages of clerical service in some church, unless it happens that the person ordained is in such a position that he can find the support of life from his own or family inheritance [de sua vel paterna hereditate subsidium]."[267]

E. Schillebeeckx in his commentary on the shift of meaning of canon 6 of Chalcedon notes that the financial aspect escaped his view in his first book, Ministry, and he adds: "Here absolute consecrations are ipso facto regarded as null and void, though the bishop who makes such consecrations must bear the financial consequences. This rule, although it is disciplinary, still expresses the old essentially ecclesial significance of the ministry. . . absolute consecrations are rejected. The bishop who performs them must himself provide for expenses in the maintenance of those who have been consecrated, at his own cost."[268]

---

[267]Lateran Council, canon 5: Episcopus si aliquem sine certo titulo, de quo necessaria vitae percipiat, in diaconum vel presbyterum ordinaverit, tamdiu necessaria ei subministret, donec in aliqua ei ecclesia convenientia stipendia militiae clericalis assignet; nisi forte talis qui ordinatur existerit, qui de sua vel paterna hereditate subsidium vitae possit habere. (COD, p. 214 and J. D. MANSI, Sacrorum conciliorum nova et amplissima collectio, new ed. L. PETIT and J. B. MARTIN, reprint [1st ed. 1759–1798] (Graz, 1960–1961) XXII: 220. Translation from N. P. TANNER (ed.), Decrees of the Ecumenical Councils . . . , I, 214. For the history of the Council, see R. FOREVILLE, Latran I, II, III et Latran IV (Paris: Editions de l'Orante, 1965); for the question of absolute ordinations, V. FUCHS, Der Ordinationstitel . . . , 268–274.

[268]E. SCHILLEBEECKX, The Church with a Human Face . . . , 154–156, here 154.

But a letter of Innocent III to the bishop of Zamora (1198) recalls one last time the inconsistency of absolute ordination: "Although our predecessors have declared null and void *[irritae et inanes]* the ordinations of those who have been promoted without precise assignment, we ourselves desiring to act with kindness order only that the bishop consecrators, or their successors, assure the ordained their subsistence until they may obtain an ecclesiastical benefice *[ecclesiasticum beneficium]*; this, in order that we may not give the impression of being deaf to the recriminations of poor clerics."[269]

Here, "the *titulus* torn from its ecclesial and ministerial reality is reduced to a benefice and a material guarantee of existence."[270] This new economic interpretation of the *titulus* differs greatly from the meaning of this same concept in the early Church, where the title connected the ministry to a concrete community. The deeper meaning of this shift is that the act of ordination was sufficient in itself to create a minister, outside of any ecclesial context. Moreover, certain non-theological considerations (namely financial) can from now on have priority over the theological in matters of ecclesiology. This fact, and that of the ordination *"ad missam,"* prepared the way for a deeper division in the relationship ministry/*ecclesia*. This is seen in the ordinations of religious mendicants.

3. MINISTRY OF RELIGIOUS MENDICANTS, EXEMPT FROM A RELATIONSHIP WITH BISHOPS

At the center of the conflicts between the secular powers and the mendicants in the thirteenth century, we find the question of the connection between the ordained ministry and a specific Church. In fact,

---

[269]INNOCENT III, *Ep. ad Zamorensem . . .*: "Licet autem praedecessores nostri ordinationes eorum, qui sine certo titulo promoverentur, in iniuriam ordinantium irritas esse voluerint et inanes, nos tamen, benignius agere cupientes, tam diu per ordinatores vel successores eorum provideri volumus ordinatis, donec per eos ecclesiastica beneficia consequantur, ne forte clamores clericorum pauperum quos in aures Domini Sabaoth credimus introire, indurata facie negligere videamur."

Quoted and translated by C. VOGEL, "Titre d'ordination . . .," 140, reprinted in id., *Ordinations . . .* , [140]. See the brief commentary of V. FUCHS, *Der Ordinationstitel . . .* , 274–279.

[270]C. VOGEL, "Titre d'ordination . . .," 78, reprinted in id., *Ordinations . . .* , [141].

the secular clergy had risen up against a new phenomenon in the Church of the period (the mendicant orders, of apostolic life, came under neither the organization of monastic orders nor that of canons). They were released by papal mandate from the authority of the local bishops for the service of the entire Church.

According to the secular clergy, invoking divine law, the organization of the Church gravitates around communities assembled into parishes, dioceses, and provinces, as well as into the universal Church.[271] The legitimacy of the pastoral ministry as well is linked to this order of things. The only pastoral jurisdictions recognized are those of the bishops and of the pastors, successors of the apostles and of the seventy-two disciples, to whom are entrusted respectively the mission of preaching and that of the pastoral ministry of the Lord. This somewhat rigid view was marked by the Dionysian concept of the hierarchy.[272] For the secular Masters it was unthinkable that someone might assume a ministry without having the *cura animarum*: the regular service of a concrete community. Here we hear once more the echo of canon 6 of the Council of Chalcedon.

To respond to their objections, the mendicants had recourse to a canonical mission received from the pope, exempting them from the bishops of the locality. These delegations conceded to the mendicant orders (customarily, through "papal bulls") the authorization to preach throughout the entire Church. This fact demonstrates the effect of the dissociation of pastoral ministry from its ecclesial context. It is the canonical mission which replaces ordination as the qualification for preaching. Certainly, these men very generally had been ordained, but since they had not received a pastoral office in a particular community, and since they did not have the means of subsistence, they followed their particular vocation only through the permission of the pope. Moreover, the question of power arose, because it was a supreme and universal power that these mendicants had received for this mission, namely, the power of the "universal episcopacy" of the pope.[273] The final result of the privileged exemption

[271]Y. CONGAR, "Aspects ecclésiologiques . . . ," 63–80 for the theses of secular Masters.

[272]Y. CONGAR, ibid., 114ff. + bibliography; and M. PEUCHMAURD, "Mission canonique . . . ," 139–144, 251, esp. 142ff.

[273]For a discussion of this aspect of the conflict, consult the works of Congar

granted to the mendicants is that the pastoral ministry can exist independently from a particular community; ministerial competency is no longer the fruit of a process which is *ecclesial, liturgical, confessional* and *juridical,* necessarily linked to the structuring of the local Church—henceforth it arises from a juridical decision resting upon a "power over" the universal Church.[274]

---

and of Ratzinger already quoted (n. 262) as well as: Y. CONGAR, "De la communion des Eglises à une ecclésiologie de l'Eglise universelle," in Y. CONGAR and B.–D. DUPUY (eds.), *L'épiscopat . . .* , 227–260, esp. 240–248.

[274]Cf. E. SCHILLEBEECKX, *The Church with a Human Face . . .* , 189–194.

Chapter 2

Theological Reflection

A. IMAGES EMPHASIZED BY THE RITUALS

For the Carolingian period, it is appropriate to examine theologically the episcopacy and the presbyterate together, since the presbyterate was always seen as deriving from the exercise of the *episkopē*. This can be seen in the images emphasized all throughout the rites of ordination. These images describe admission to pastoral ministry as the work of the Spirit of God, with its purpose being the building up or the construction of the Church. The pastoral ministry is seen as the service *(diakonia)* of representing Christ, and the minister is defined by his role in the Church, that is to say, by the service which he renders to the entire community. This is a very important point, because it relates directly to the New Testament conception of ministry: the solidarity of the members of the body in service *(diakonia)*, for the building up of the Body of Christ (Eph 4:11-16; cf. 1 Cor 12:20-31). In this context the role of the ministers is to represent and to actualize the relationship between Christ and his Church; this role is carried out in communion with Christ as deacon, pastor and overseer *(episkopos)* (cf. Jn 13:14; Lk 22:26f.; Jn 10:11; 1 Pet 2:25; 5:1-4).

The pastoral charge is therefore clearly emphasized in the images of the ordination rites. In the *Apostolic Tradition*, the fact that the entire Church (Christians [baptized and ministers] of the local Church, the heads of the neighboring Churches) is active in the ordination process demonstrates the solidarity of the different services in the Church; so ordination itself is seen from the viewpoint of the Church as essentially an epiclesis. This fact is revealed also in the Eucharist when the Church's deepest reality is made manifest as the Body of Christ, whose members are linked in the Holy Spirit.

The minister, bishop or presbyter, is seen as taking part in the movement of the history of salvation under the power *(dynamis)* of the Spirit poured out upon him, as in the case of Christ, the apostles, and the elders chosen by Moses (*AT* 3 and 8). The bishop receives the pastoral grace of the one who is chosen by God to serve his brothers and sisters as Christ does when he pastures the holy flock (cf. 1 Pet 5:2-4). Several images present this idea: the pastoral/prophetic image made explicit by the the gift of the *spiritus principalis* (in the case of the bishop), and that of the Spirit "of governing and of counsel" (in the case of presbyters); also, that of the Spirit of direction of the Church requested for the bishop, who is its head, and for the presbyters, members of the college who help the bishop in this essential and fundamental function. At the head of a priestly people, the minister is a servant of the Spirit of Christ, who dwells in the ecclesial body.

In this context the function of the bishop is to ensure the heart of God's plan, the communion of the multitude of the faithful in the one Body of the Lord. The image of the newly ordained, surrounded by the neighboring bishops, his presbyterium and deacons, and facing the people who are entrusted to him, is very expressive of the ecclesiological reality of his office: to see that the other ministries are exercised only in respect of the *koinōnia,* which assumes the harmony of all the services in unity. Briefly, the pastoral office of the bishop is exercised within the communion of the ministries and the charisms of the one Spirit.

After the pastoral image, that of (high) priest is the second to be evoked. Elsewhere we have seen that the minister receives a priestly office because he has a pastoral charge. The priestly image is present in almost all the prayers studied, Roman and other, and it is applied as much to the episcopal ministry as to the presbyteral ministry.

Nevertheless, when we begin to take the difference between bishop and presbyter into consideration, we note that, with the addition of non-Roman prayers and rites (especially in the framework of presbyteral ordination), the simple vision of the ancient rite which describes the presbyter as entering into his own *ordo presbyterorum* to act as collaborator of the bishop has been obscured. The later rites emphasize his cultic role, as in the Gallican ordination prayer with its explicit reference to the Eucharistic celebration, and again later the *porrectio instrumentorum* and the second imposition of hands related to the power to forgive sins. Moreover, the later rites have a tendency to see the presbyter independently from the presbyterium, and they thus envisage the exercise of the pastoral ministry in some isolation.

The images of the episcopacy have remained for the most part close to the Roman prayers. The later additions clarified the episcopal office by adding the ministry of the Word (the bishop as evangelist and prophet) to the ministry of presiding over the community for the celebration of the Eucharist and the sacrament of reconciliation (cf. the Gallican prayer *Sint speciosi*). Even with the prayer *Pater Sancte* we remain close to the Roman images: the pastoral image (the bishop as guardian/pastor), and the priestly image (the bishop as minister of the sacraments). To these two images we add that of the bishop as a just, gentle, hospitable, judicious and patient person: New Testament virtues.

In summary, we have seen that the most important images relating to the ministry of bishops and priests express their function and their responsibility within the Church and in regard to the Church: within the Church, because the pastoral ministry is an office which can be exercised only in the communion of the ministries and charisms of the entire ecclesial body. Moreover, this ministry cannot be understood otherwise than in the communion of a single Church which is the bearer of the variety of charisms of the Spirit, some of which structure this Church. In this Church the ordained ministry is the *diakonia* that represents Christ, and the minister is responsible for the *koinōnia* of all. The ordained ministry is not seen as the source, but as a symbol of this reference to the Spirit.

Those who are ordained exercise their ministry vis-à-vis the Church, because they preside at the different services in obedience to Christ, and they are guided by the Spirit so that the Church may fulfill its responsibility of sharing the gift received, announcing to the world the Word of God and salvation in Jesus Christ. The pastoral duty is qualified as priestly because the ministry of direction must, as priestly, watch over the Church by presiding at the community's liturgical life as the ministry of Christ. The bishops and priests, therefore, must preach the Word, celebrate the sacraments (especially the Eucharist), and forgive sins. When the pastoral metaphors (pastor—flock) are emphasized, we note that they are not the only ones to be used, because the ordination liturgies see the ecclesial community as a living organism in which each must fulfill the active role which is entrusted to him or her. The history of the Church shows us what happens when this dynamic loses its vitality: the disassociation of the ministry of the local Church, and the problem of absolute ordinations,[1] the autonomy of clerics, and the clericalization of the concept of ministry (which brings about a religious disqualification of Christians and a split between baptized and ministers), the conflicts between priests and deacons (and other groups in the heart of the Church), the loss of the collegiality of ministry in the Church and between the Churches, the diminished perception of the sacramentality of the episcopacy and, lastly, an opposition between ministry and charism.[2]

PR 1596 came at the end of a long history of liturgies and theologies of the ordained ministry: we can see in it the imbalances of earlier periods. The next section will show a shift even more pronounced in the concept of the ordained ministry as it was understood at the time of the *AT*, tending to reshape itself according to a hierarchical and clerical model. The ordination rituals bear witness to this shift by emphasizing the "historical" approach rather than an "eschatological" approach, almost overlooking the latter, as Zizioulas has shown in his study on the apostolicity of the Church.[3] This shift results in a theological imbalance where Christology occupies the whole field to the point of effacing the pneumatological. The structure of the Church is expressed in a linear hierarchy, and no longer according to a Trinitarian concept.

---

[1]Cf. the dossier established by C. VOGEL, *Ordinations . . .* ; read with J. LECUYER, *Le sacrement de l'ordination . . . .*

[2]H.-M. LEGRAND, "La réalisation de l'Eglise . . . ," 181–209. As for the opposition between ministry and charism, it has its roots in the interpretation of the lists of charisms in the Pauline literature. One reads with great interest the historical and exegetical work by U. BROCKHAUS, *Charisma und Amt. Die paulinische Charismenlehre auf dem Hintergrund der frühchristlichen Gemeindefunktionen*, 2nd. ed. (Wuppertal: Theologischer Verlag Rolf Brockhaus, 1972). In his work B. COOKE, *Ministry . . .* , has discerned certain vagaries in the history of the conception of ministry. E. J. KILMARTIN, "Office and Charism: Reflections on a New Study of Ministry," *Theological Studies* 38, 3 (1977) 547–554 contributes some important nuances to the hermeneutic of Cooke.

[3]Cf. supra, pp. 18ff.

B. THE PERSON OF THE ORDAINED MINISTER AND THE QUALITIES REQUIRED

Roman soberness in the ordination rites (imposition of hands and epicletic prayer) gives way to prolixity in the explanatory rites, which were veritable "productions" (anointing, investing, *traditio* of objects associated with the office, moral exhortations). These changes accumulated very slowly over the centuries, and they ended by masking the meaning of the original core of the ordinations. With the addition of these rites, the meaning of the ministries is displaced from that of the service of the Church, accomplishing its task in the world, to that of the powers and graces received by the person of the ordained minister. We see this displacement even in the organization of the liturgical books. In the ancient Roman liturgical book, the sequence of ordinations was in descending order (bishop–presbyter–deacon or bishop–deacon–presbyter), while in the books of Gallican or Frankish origin the sequence was ascending: it begins with a rite of initiation (tonsure) and continues in a *cursus honorum* which develops later into a hierarchy of ecclesiastical functions. Attention is centered on clerics as a group of men "set apart."

This juxtaposition of prayers and rites is organized and harmonized in the pontificals (particularly in the PRG and the PGD). One could say that in them the tendencies already noted reach their apogee, and that they lead to a very different ecclesiology from that of the early Church. The subject of the sacramental actions of the Church is no longer the *ecclesia* itself; due to the increased sacralization of ecclesial functions and the creation of a group of clerics within the Church, the true subject (the *ecclesia*) tends to be reduced to the clerics as persons set apart, having the power to dispense the sacraments.

Among the structural elements of ordinations which suggest these conclusions are found in the following: the transformation of the election carried out by the local Church in Christian antiquity into a simple approval by acclamation of the choice made by the clerics,[*24, *34] later by a silent approbation;[*84, *86, *125] the organization of the liturgical books, especially the pontificals: they begin henceforth with entrance into the clerical state followed by the ascending sequence of ordinations; the prayers accompanying the new rites which accentuate henceforth either the powers received or the grace of the office received.[*88, *107, *109, *121, *147, *174, *175] Even if the texts (especially the ordination prayers) have retained vestiges of an ecclesiology where ordination had for its ritual subject the totality of the *ecclesia*,[4] the new emphasis we have seen above isolates the minister and attributes to him a certain autonomy in regard to the body of the faithful. The distinction between clerics and laity begins to make its appearance in the liturgical texts.[5]

The multiplication of absolute ordinations demonstrates the extreme weakness of the reference of the priesthood to the service of a concrete community: the minister possesses the power personally. The liturgical texts, however, do not in themselves express this concept, because the liturgies are juxtaposed in the same ritual texts[6] which are very different in theological content. Nevertheless, other facts show the disastrous results stemming from the disassociation of the ministry from its ecclesial context: the person of the minister is isolated, and certain powers and qualifications are attributed to him personally and ontologically. To understand this situation better, we must examine the qualities required of the minister.

According to the ordination prayers, the qualities most often prayed for stem from the New Testament tradition of the Pastoral Epistles (1 Tim 3:1-7 *[episkopoi]*; 1 Tim 3:8-13 [deacons]; 2 Tim 2:22-26 [all the ministers]; and Titus 1:6-9 [presbyters]), a tradition of integrity of life and conduct, of certainty in the faith, and holiness. However, all these elements are deliberately oriented towards the service of others in the Church. This fact is important, because it brings out the intimate relationship between the person of the minister

[4]L. C. MOHLBERG, L. EIZENHÖFER and P. SIFFRIN (eds)., *Missale Francorum (Cod. Vat. Reg. lat. 257)* (Rome: Herder, 1957) nos.. 25, 31, 39 (hereafter MF).

[5]A good sampling of types of argumentation and interpretation from the Scholastic period in L. OTT, *Le sacrement . . .* , especially in chapter 5. The history of the doctrines and the development of ecclesiology in the Scholastic period is analyzed by Y. CONGAR, *L'Eglise de saint Augustin . . .* , 157–176, esp. 169ff.

[6]References to the theological texts in D. N. POWER, *Ministers of Christ . . .* , 115–126; J. GALOT, *La nature du caractère sacramentel. Etude de théologie médiévale* (Paris/Bruges: Desclée de Brouwer, 1957), to read with H.-M. LEGRAND, "The 'Indelible' Character and the Theology of Ministry," *Concilium*, 4, 8 (1972) 54–62; Y. CONGAR, "Ordinations *invitus, coactus*, de l'Eglise antique au canon 214," *RSPT* 50, 2 (1966) 169–197 and E. SCHILLEBEECKX, *A Church with a Human Face . . .* , 161–194.

and the object of his ministry. This relationship is rooted in the gift of the Spirit, because the charism of the Spirit establishes the person in his function and gives him at the same time the power to fulfill his ministry. Ever since the struggle of St. Augustine and others against Donatism, the question of the dependence of sacramental grace on the *personal* holiness of the minister has been resolved in favor of the objectivity of the gift of grace offered by God to the Church, precisely because it is not the holiness of the minister which is communicated, but that of Christ.[7] In this context, the references in the rites to the holiness of life or the conduct of the ministers must be understood, first of all, as stemming from Christian reality, and, secondarily, as the fruit of the worthy exercise of their ministry. Christian reality is the new state received in baptism, the God-centered and priestly life proper to all the baptized. The community the minister is charged to pasture is "a chosen race, a royal priesthood *[basileion hierateuma],* a holy nation, God's own people" (1 Pet 2:9; cf. 1 Pet 5:1-4). It is within this reality and for its service that the ministries are established, and they are considered by the New Testament as gifts of the Holy Spirit to the Church for its edification and common good (Eph 4:11ff.; cf. Rom 12:4-11; 1 Cor 12:4-11, 28 where Paul ranks the ministries among the charisms of the Spirit). From this viewpoint, the true subject of ministry remains the *ecclesia* and the service of the Gospel, the sacraments, and the edification of an eschatological community where Christ is the only Pastor, maintaining primacy over the person of the minister. In this way the ministry remains within the concrete context of the communion of a local Church, and the ministry is not isolated in a group of holy clerics, set apart from the rest of the baptized.[8]

C. FUNCTIONS OF THE ORDAINED MINISTRIES

There is no need to repeat here the observations already made above: rather, we must make explicit the uniqueness of the functions attributed to each ministry and the collaboration among them.

---

[7] Cf. Y. CONGAR, *L'Eglise de saint Augustin* . . . , 13–21.

[8] We note that for THOMAS AQUINAS ministerial order is "for the building up of the Church" (. . . *data est enim eis "ad Ecclesiae aedificationem," secundum Apostoli dictum* . . .)—the quotation is from 2 Cor 13:10—*Summa Contra Gentiles,* IV, 74 (*Opera Omnia,* Leonine edition, 15, 237), where we see that for the author ministerial order is a grace given for the sake of others.

The link between the episcopacy and the presbyterate in the exercise of the *episkopē* remains strong, but it is exercised differently by each. In an ordination, only the bishop can fulfill the function of link with the Church, in a way the presbyter cannot. Only the bishop witnesses to the apostolic faith[9] of his Church before another Church during the ordination of another bishop. Because they bear witness in solidarity to the one faith of the Church, the bishops present receive the faith of the Church where the ordination takes place. This is one of the meanings of the participation of the bishops at episcopal ordinations in the reception of the election, the imposition of hands, the kiss of peace, and the Eucharistic celebration.

In the same perspective, we have seen that only the bishop is installed in the episcopal chair, a symbol of his presidency of the local Church; from this seat he nourishes and watches over the flock entrusted to him. The role of gathering into unity all the diversity of charisms of the Spirit poured out in the Church is certainly made manifest when the bishop presides at the Eucharistic celebration with all the clergy and faithful of his Church.

Even if in the New Testament period there existed some vagueness in the distinction between the two ministries, in certain situations the needs of the local communities led to a differentiation between the exercise of the presbyterate and of the episcopacy both in the ecclesial communion and for its sake, to safeguard the fundamental responsibility of the *episkopē*. B.-D. Dupuy has shown that the distinction between the function of the presbyters and that of the bishops is more historical than dogmatic, and he suggests that it would always be wise to analyze them from their points in common and not from the differences between the two ministries. This perspective is important: it allows the Church to structure differently the ordained ministries if historical circumstances require it.[10] The ordi-

[9]Cf. the article by E. J. KILMARTIN, "Apostolic Office: Sacrament of Christ," *Theological Studies* 36, 2 (1975) 243–264, esp. 254–260; and J.-M.-R. TILLARD, *Church of Churches. The Ecclesiology of Communion,* trans. of the French [*Église d'églises: l'ecclésiologie de communion*] by R. C. De Peaux (Collegeville: The Liturgical Press/Michael Glazier Book, 1992) 175–211.

[10]B.-D. DUPUY, "Is there a Dogmatic Distinction between the Function of Priests and the Function of Bishops" *Concilium* 4, 4 (1968) 38–44. See the article by J. MOUDRY, "Bishop and Priest in the Sacrament of Holy Orders," *The Jurist* 31, 1 (1971) 163–186.

nation prayers attest that the bishop represents the Church more fully (than other clergy).[11]

The greatest change came in the functions exercised by the presbyters. The sacramental or cultic functions remain related to the principal axis of the episcopal or presbyteral ministry: leading the community through the proclamation of the Gospel, presiding at worship (especially the Eucharist), and ruling the Church, always in the name of Christ. This responsibility is first of all collegial, even though cultural needs may have constrained the Church to modify, here and there, the form of its ministry. For example, the presbyter in the Gallican prayer of presbyteral ordination is no longer seen in the collegial context usual until then. The tendency of the later rites toward visual externalization and "productions" led to greater emphasis on the sacerdotal function: the bestowal of the instruments, anointing, and even investiture would occupy center stage, so much so that the other dimensions of the ministry (prophecy, governing, collegiality) would remain in the shadows. In the twelfth century, as P.-M. Gy has shown, the term *sacerdos* was most often, in fact almost exclusively, used to identify the *presbyteros*, while the application of the same word to the bishop became less and less frequent. This fact can be marshalled for the thesis according to which the episcopacy was no longer one of the orders (*ordo* = sacramental), but only a *dignitas in ordine*.[12] The roots of such a tendency are found in the presbyterianism of Ambrosiaster and of St. Jerome for whom the distinction between the presbyterate and the episcopacy was a matter simply of Church discipline. One of the results of this entire process will be the specialization of the vocabulary: the bishops, when the episcopacy ceased to constitute an *ordo*, will no longer be "ordained," but "consecrated" in their new dignity. These distinctions effected at the level of theological reflection towards the end of the eleventh and the beginning of the twelfth centuries were introduced into the Pontifical of the Roman Curia in the thirteenth century, almost at the same time as

[11]Cf. J. MOUDRY, "Bishop and Priest . . . ," 181 and the article by J.-M.-R. TILLARD, "'Ministère' ordonné . . . ," 145–166, esp. 162–166.

[12]Cf. P.-M. GY, "Remarques sur le vocabulaire . . . ," 125–145, esp. 130–135. The author quotes Hugh of St. Victor and Peter Lombard for the introduction of this distinction: see p. 130, n. 1.

the birth of the distinction between the power of orders and the power of jurisdiction.[13]

The definition of a priest at this time lay mostly in terms of powers received during the ordination (cf. supra, pp. 166f.), the principal one being the power to consecrate the Body of Christ (in principle shared by the presbyters and the bishops). But the bishop was very often associated with confirmation and ordination, and the priests with baptism, penance, and the Eucharistic celebration, that is to say, with the functions of worship. This identification of the presbyteral ministry with the functions of the cult almost to the exclusion of the episcopal ministry contributed to the situation where the episcopal ministry was no longer recognized as sacramental by a large number of theologians. This situation lasted until the Second Vatican Council.

A word must be said about the functions of the deacons, even though the diaconate is not strictly speaking the object of this study. We have seen that, since the *AT*, the diaconate was a part of the one ordained ministry, but that this ministry was not conceived of as sacerdotal. Even if it was bestowed by a sacramental act (the imposition of hands and the epiclesis) and the deacon received a ministry of the Word and a pastoral task (like the episcopacy and the presbyterate), the deacon did not share the responsibility of presiding over the entire life of a Church.[*7] As the prayer of diaconal ordination mentions,[*8]

[13]From the twelfth century on, the multiplication of absolute ordinations, seen in their economic context, and the theological understanding of the episcopacy as a non-sacramental dignity (in the thirteenth century) contributed to the creation of a split between ministerial order and jurisdiction which lay at the heart of the quarrel between the Seculars and the Mendicants in which the collegial consciousness of the early Church is no longer found. Here we see the pope vested with the fullness of jurisdiction, while the bishops represent only a certain level without a sacramental basis. Besides the references quoted in note 262, for the distinction between order and jurisdiction, see Y. CONGAR, "Ordre et juridiction dans l'Eglise," *Irénikon* 10 (1933) 22–31, 97–110, 243–252, 401–408 reprinted in id., *Sainte Eglise. Etudes et approches ecclésiologiques* (Paris: Cerf, 1963) 203–237; M. VAN DE KERCKHOVE, "La notion de juridiction chez les Décrétistes et les premiers Décrétalistes (1140–1250)," *Etudes franciscaines* 49, 4 (1937) 420–455; D. E. HEINTSCHEL, *The Medieval Concept of an Ecclesiastical Office. An Analytical Study of the Concept of an Ecclesiastical Office in the Major Sources and Printed Commentaries from 1140–1300* (Washington, D.C.: The Catholic University of America, 1956); G. ALBERIGO, "La juridiction. Remarques sur un terme ambigu," *Irénikon* 49, 2 (1976) 167–180.

the appropriate station is that of "service." The ministerial functions exercised by the deacons were the service of the Word, of the liturgy, and lastly, of charity (cf. supra, pp. 66ff.). This service was closely tied to the ministry of the bishop, and since the presbyters were the helpers or the collaborators of the bishop, the ministry of the deacons was also in an indirect relationship with the presbyteral college.[14] We have also seen that the role of the archdeacon in the dioceses was important. With the distinction between order and jurisdiction, we find the first of the deacons (in the sense of the early Church) in the twelfth century, but vested with his own ecclesiastical dignity. Some real powers were attributed to him in the structure of the medieval Church when he acted as the *"oculus episcopi"* and as *"praepositus"* of a diocese. His place was beside the bishop (who was also considered not as belonging to a sacramental order, but as having a *"dignitas"*) in the administration of the diocese. His juridical powers extended to the entire diocese because of the jurisdiction attributed to him, and not through his ordination. This fact again shows the danger which exists when a split between lawful right and sacrament is created.[15]

D. PRIESTLY MINISTRY PROPER TO BISHOPS AND TO PRESBYTERS

The liturgical tradition of the Church bears witness to the fact that the bishops and presbyters were ordained principally in view of a pastoral (royal) charge to rule the Church and to pasture the flock (cf. *3, *6, *59, *63–*64 (*98), *72, *76, *79, *81, *128–*135, *160).[16] P.-M. Gy has demonstrated the complexity of the theological balance of the ordination prayers, showing that ordination in the Churches of the East and the

[14]H.-M. LEGRAND has noted that ". . . the hierarchy bishop–priest–deacon is not a linear, descending hierarchy . . . but a triangular hierarchy in which priests and deacons are in immediate relationship to the bishop; without, however, the triangle being represented as an isosceles triangle, since as the Council of Nicaea declared, deacons "servants of the bishop, are of a lower rank than priests" [canon 18]," "Vocation au diaconat et interpellation: réflexion ecclésiologique à partir de la tradition," *Documents Episcopat* 3 (Feb. 1985) 7.

[15]Cf. A. AMANIEU, "Archidiacre," cols. 948–1004; D. E. HEINTSCHEL, *The Medieval Concept . . .* , for the development of the distinction between powers of order and jurisdiction, and especially in medieval ecclesiastical legislation. As for the archdeacon, see pp. 51–65.

[16]Cf. the article by H.-J. SCHULZ, "Das liturgisch-sakramental . . . ," 208–255. In this article the author demonstrates that from the time of the *Apostolic*

West conferred the *tria munera*, namely, the pastoral ministry, that of the Word, and that of the sacraments.[17] The rites present the priestly ministry in the light of its primary aspect as a pastoral and prophetic charge; the prayer of episcopal ordination in the *AT* qualifies the pastoral and prophetic ministry as priestly for the first time (cf. supra, pp. 54–60).

There was a progressive sacerdotalization of the vocabulary, to such a degree that the priestly aspect of the ministry became the greater. The list of presbyteral and episcopal tasks attests to this: *Sacerdotem etenim oportet offerre, benedicere, praeesse, praedicare, et baptizare,*[*88] and *Episcopum oportet judicare, interpretari, consecrare, ordinare, offerre, baptizare et confirmare* ("For the priest is to offer [sacrifice], bless, preside, preach, and baptize" and "the bishop is to judge, interpret, consecrate, ordain, offer [sacrifice], baptize, and confirm"—tr. of editor.[*147] These lists are clear: the first task of the priest is to *offer*, and that of the bishop is to *judge*.[18] The concern of this period was to list what each ministry could or could not do, while the notion of ecclesiastical order (*ordo* = *"Church order"*) was no longer present in their minds, from the twelfth century on, as it had been earlier; the concept no longer describes an organic and collegial reality, but rather a hierarchical priesthood understood in terms of powers transmitted through ordination, powers possessed personally.[19] The unique Eucharistic celebration was no longer the place where the entire *ecclesia* offers the Eucharist while the bishop presides, assisted by his presbyterium, his deacons and other ministers. On the contrary, in the multiplicity of Eucharists celebrated, the priestly role of all the faithful was weakened, while "the celebration . . . became the act of *the priest*, at which the faithful were present."[20] The organic nature of

---

Tradition the first category to describe ministry is that of responsibility for the Church, the pastoral charge or office. With the conceptual separation of the presbyterate from the episcopacy, in the ordination rituals during the eighth and thirteenth centuries, the cultic functions of priests are given more emphasis than their function of presiding over the community: see pp. 237–242.

[17]P.-M. GY, "La théologie des prières . . . ," 599–617, esp. 608f.

[18]Cf. D. N. POWER, *Ministers of Christ . . .* , 103.

[19]Cf. P.-M. GY, "Remarques sur le vocabulaire . . . ," 129–133; L. OTT, *Le sacrement . . .* , 191–195; A. CHAPELLE, *Pour la vie du monde. Le sacrement de l'Ordre* (Brussels: Institut d'Etudes Théologiques, 1978) 137–161; B. COOKE, *Ministry . . .* , ch. 30.

[20]Y. CONGAR, "L' 'Ecclesia' . . . ," 241–282, esp. 265.

the Church as a communion, a place where all the charisms of the Spirit were found, was lost sight of. The meaning of ordination is better expressed when one understands admission to the pastoral ministry as the work of the Spirit of God, whose purpose is the building up of the Church. The Eucharistic context of ordination makes this reality quite clear. This truth was obfuscated by the theological imbalance we have discussed, revealed by facts such as the multiplication of absolute ordinations, the distinction between powers of order and powers of jurisdiction, the "*missio canonica,*" etc.

The ordination prayers, however, have remained almost identical since the *Sacramentarium Veronense.* The changes made in these prayers have not altered the sense of the priestly ministry, not even the Gallican prayer (*Deus sanctificationum omnium auctor*[*73, *103]) which made direct reference to the Eucharistic task of the minister. This priestly duty remained understood according to the original perspective of the early Church as the *service of the people (in obsequium plebis tuae):* the liturgical dimension of the pastoral ministry is to build up the family of God (cf. *87–*91). In this way the oneness of the priesthood of Christ is safeguarded, because the priestly ministry of a priest or a bishop is seen as an instrumentality: it is Christ who is the author of salvation, and it is Christ who offers through the ministry of the bishop or the priest. Here the priesthood is not a "thing" given to someone without reference to a real community, but it is an attribute which describes certain aspects of pastoral ministry (liturgical dimension/sacramental relationship).[21]

---

[21]This is a very important point, because it rightly places the ordained ministry in its correct ecclesiological context. In the first chapter we have shown that the early Church understood its identity within the perspective of "communion" and "fraternity." The process of election and of ordination expressed this truth through the different roles assumed by the actors during the entire process. From this viewpoint, the ministries are seen as service of the *koinōnia,* and more particularly in its function of building up the Church. J.-M.-R. TILLARD traces the development of this consciousness in the Church (cf. *Church of Churches . . . ,* esp. 2–45, 169–230). The important biblical passages in this regard, Eph 4: 10-13 and 1 Cor 12:4-11, affirm that it is Christ who builds the Church through the Holy Spirit, inspiring and instituting the ministries. The operant word is *"diakonia."* Describing the place of the ordained ministry in relationship to the gift of justice and holiness imparted by Christ to his Body, the Church, B. Sesboüé says

E. ESCHATOLOGICAL MEANING OF THE ORDAINED MINISTRY

On the subject of the apostolicity of the Church we have already seen that two types of pneumatology must be maintained in proper

---

the following: "Whoever says 'ministry' also says 'stewardship' or 'management' in the name of another. The minister is never the author or the master of what he manages . . . This affirmation holds true for the entire Church which is 'minister' of all the sacraments, celebrated *in virtute Christi*. Such is, in fact, the dynamic between the *Ecclesia convocata*, the 'community of the called,' and the *Ecclesia convocans*, the 'divine call' [de Lubac]. The Church, justified by faith and the sacraments becomes in her turn minister of justification (Paul says "of reconciliation": 2 Cor 5:18), that is, *minister of the gift that she receives and of which she is constituted*": B. SESBOÜE, "Les sacrements de la foi. L'économie sacramentelle, célébration ecclésiale de la justification par la foi," *LMD* 116 (1973) 108f. reprinted in id., *Pour une théologie œcuménique* (Paris: Cerf, 1990) 112. Here we see that the uniqueness and the sovereignty of the priesthood of Christ are preserved, because it is not in his own name that the minister acts, but in the name of Christ *(in persona Christi)* and in an ecclesial context *(in persona Ecclesiae)*.

The work of B.-D. MARLIANGEAS, *Clés pour une théologie du ministère: In persona Christi, In persona Ecclesiae* (Paris: Beauchesne, 1978) still remains fundamental for the correct interpretation of these two expressions (and their equivalents) in sacramental theology. Without repeating his entire work, the basic meaning of the expression "in persona Christi" bears citing: ". . . what we see here is a conferring upon a given person words (most often) which are proper to a 'representative.' When this representative effaces himself, so to speak, before the one whom he represents, it is no longer he, but the one he represents, who speaks or acts" (p. 97). In summary, the minister (bishop or priest) represents Christ by his ordination. This is not all—for he only represents Christ by representing the Church, the mystical body of Christ. This is where the communal dimension of ordained ministry comes into play. We have seen the close relationship of the ordained ministry to the body of the priestly, baptized people. Now, Christ has expressed his will that there be unity between himself and the members, and between these services (Jn 17: 22f.) so that the world may know his mission and the redemptive love of the Father who sent Him. The purpose of ordained ministry is therefore to serve this salvific will of Christ by equipping the Church for her mission. The unique priesthood of Christ is preserved intact, because it is this priesthood which is the efficacious cause of ministerial action in the Church. In sum, it is always Christ who acts in the Church through his envoys. The bond of unity between Christ and his ministers is the Holy Spirit who is the source of all ministerial action. We have seen that it is the Spirit who is the principal agent throughout the entire process of the election and ordination of ministers in the Church.

balance: the anamnetic or historical approach, and the epicletic or eschatological approach (cf. supra, pp. 18ff.). This typology is borne out also in regard to the ministry and to ordination (cf. infra, I). The New Testament sees the ministry of the Church as the actualization of the presence of Christ in the world (Lk 10:16) and it places the birth of the Church on Pentecost as well as its mission to spread into the whole world to bring the Good News (Acts 2). The Church is thus understood as the place of the irruption of the *eschaton* into history by the inversion of Babel,[22] the site of the gathering of the people and of their dispersion for the evangelization and service of the world. The Good News which brings people into *koinōnia* with God is the proclamation of salvation: "What no eye has seen, nor ear heard, nor the human heart conceived, what God has prepared for those who love him" (1 Cor 2:9). This communion translates into a new and personal relationship with God, and as a communion of brothers and sisters. These new and enduring relations with God are rooted in the decisive passage which takes place in baptism (incorporation into the mystery of Christ and of the Church), sealed by the fire of the anointing and nourished with the Eucharist (the eschatological feast of the community of saints—cf. 1 Cor 5 and 6), the climax of the entire process. It is here that the unique mystery of the total Christ is made visible; it is here that the ministry of Christ is at work "gathering up all things" (Eph 1:10); it is here that our "communion in the life and the communion even of the Trinity"[23] is realized. The establishment of the Church is thus seen as taking place in and through the Spirit. Through this process, we see that the Spirit actualizes the event of the building up of the Body of Christ in history, with the community expressing the communion of the Spirit inseparable from the presence of Christ (cf. Acts 2;17-21 [= Joel 3:1-5]; 1 Thess 4:15-18).

The universal dimension of the Church and its fundamental connection with the cosmic design of salvation are concentrated in its extension and its apostolicity. This dynamic aspect of the structure of the Church is obvious in the early Church, in the presbyteral colleges (of the Palestinian Churches), and in the mono-episcopacies (of which Ignatius of Antioch was an example) where apostolic continu-

[22]H.-M. LEGRAND, "Inverser Babel, mission de l'Eglise," *Spiritus* 11, 43 (1970) 323–346.
[23]J. D. ZIZIOULAS, *Being as Communion . . .* , 114f.

ity and the catholicity of the Church[24] are clearly expressed. In both, the succession and the continuity of the Church are understood in the convocation of the Church into one single place, through the Eucharistic gathering, as the eschatological act in which the Church is the community of saints gathered around the Lord who will judge the world.[25]

The eschatological meaning of the ordained ministry is therefore discerned particularly clearly in the structure of ordinations, which are always celebrated during the Eucharist, where the dispersed people of God gather together as the Body of Christ, the temple of the Holy Spirit. It is here that all the elements of the Church are found which were spoken of by St. Paul (1 Cor 14), by the *Didachē* (ch. 15), and by the *AT* (chs. 2 and 4). Zizioulas has shown the reasons why the ordination must take place in a Eucharistic context (cf. supra, p. 31), and why the bishop is the sole minister of ordination:

"Because of his place in the structure of the community, especially in its eucharistic form, the bishop is the one through whom all charismatic manifestations of the Church must pass, so that they may be manifestations not of individualism but of the *koinōnia* of the Spirit and of the community created by it."[26] [And further:]

". . . The bishop is the one who maintains the unity of the body in the multiplicity of ministries and charisms, because he is the head of the concrete community, especially when this community exhibits its communal character in the Eucharistic assembly at which he presides. This role of the bishop can in itself justify the exclusive right he has to confer ordination, a right furthermore justified by the fact that he does not confer it except in the context of the community, so long as we consider ordination in its communal aspect."[27]

[24]Cf. supra, pp. 22ff.; B.-D. DUPUY, "Teologia dei ministeri . . . , 618ff.; the two important chapters of J. D. ZIZIOULAS, *Being as Communion* . . . , ch. 4 "Eucharist and Catholicity," and ch. 5 "Apostolic Continuity and Succession." The author does not forget that there is another approach ("historical") rooted in biblical and patristic sources, but he believes that a synthesis of the two perspectives is necessary to do justice to the truth.

[25]Cf. *Didachē*, 9–10; 1 Cor 5-6, as well as the study of J. D. ZIZIOULAS, *Being as Communion* . . . , and, recently, J.-M.-R. TILLARD, *Church of Churches* . . . , 84–105.

[26]J. D. ZIZIOULAS, *Being as Communion* . . . , 198.

[27]J. D. ZIZIOULAS, *L'être ecclésial*, Perspective orthodoxe, 3 (Geneva: Labor et Fides, 1981) 178.

Here we sense the necessity of seeing ordination essentially as an epiclesis, a concept to which all the ordination rituals attest. Moreover, this epiclesis can only be understood in reference to the deepest manifestation of the reality of the local Church (the Eucharist), in which the communion is realized in its eschatological fullness. This is why in the early Church every absolute ordination (without a concrete office) was forbidden, because the ministry must be understood as a constitutive part of the structure of the community, and, as such, it requires the reception of the Church.[28]

Other elements of the ordination rituals in which the eschatological aspect of the ministry is apparent (in the sense already described) are the prescription of Sunday as the day of ordination in its Eucharistic framework (in which normally all the orders of the Church are present), the election, and the scrutiny before the people.

F. THE PNEUMATOLOGICAL MEANING OF THE ORDAINED MINISTRY: CHARISM AND FUNCTION

The essence of the charism/function dynamic of the ordained ministry can be grasped by examining the structure of the entire process and the content of the prayer of epiclesis. An overall view shows that a balanced Trinitarian theology can surely not oppose these two aspects of ordained ministry.

From the beginning, the entire structure of election–ordination was conceived of as a single act which was liturgical, ecclesial and juridical.[29] Nevertheless, over time, this process was elaborated into several steps to which the descriptive rites were added to explain more clearly, by going into detail, the overall meaning of the ordination. We have seen throughout the entire evolution of this institution that this process was never understood as a contract, but as a matter of grace (charism). The fact that in the early Church *electio, ordinatio* and *jurisdictio* were inextricably linked is attested by the perception of the role of the Holy Spirit during the whole process. The Church was aware that it is invested with the power of the Spirit in order to fulfill the mission entrusted to it: to proclaim the Good News of salvation

[28]Cf. canon 6 of the Council of Chalcedon (451); cf. J. ALBERIGO et al., COD, p. 90, and the historical dossier established by C. VOGEL in *Ordinations . . .*, [1]–[181].

[29]Cf. above, I, A, 2, α (pp. 28–50).

in Jesus Christ and to manifest the coming of the Kingdom of God which was begun by Christ and which, through the same Spirit, is in the process of being fulfilled. We have seen more than once that this consciousness was apparent in the act of choosing the ministers, then most obviously in the epiclesis and the imposition of hands, and, lastly, in the assembly itself (in the role of the clergy and the faithful of the local Church and in the high points of communal life, such as the Eucharist and the celebration of Christian initiation).[30]

At this point we should note two important theological categories: bearing witness, and the dual concept of tradition–reception.[31] One of the functions of the neighboring bishops present at the ordination of a bishop is that of bearing witness to the identity (in time and in space) of the Church in which the ordination takes place with the Churches they represent. They are witnesses to and guarantors of the apostolic faith (see above, C). This fundamental structure of the apostolicity and the communion of the Churches is manifest from the first to the last rite which we have studied. Even though the local Church

---

[30]Cf. above, I, 2, a–b (α) (pp. 28–31, 39, 47) and I, B, a, α (pp. 89f.).

[31]Y. CONGAR notes: "If there is one truth universally affirmed since antiquity up to and including Vatican II, it is that the entire Church bears responsibility for both faith and Tradition; that the universal Church alone can be an adequate repository for them, under the sovreignty of the Spirit which was promised to the Church and which is indwelling in her. This is the reason the witness of several neighboring bishops was required for an election and an ordination, and even the witness of the community of the faithful. This is why the broadest possible unanimity, concord, and consensus have always been seen as a sign of the action of the Holy Spirit, and therefore a guarantee of truth . . . ," ". . . the acceptance [of the elect] as an ecclesiological reality" *RSPT* 56, 3 (1972) 369–403 (+ bibliography), here p. 380. This dynamic is at the evangelical basis of Christian life, because the elect receives from his Church, remaining faithful to this tradition, this word of truth which he passes on. H.-M. LEGRAND speaks of witnessing as one of the fundamental structures of the Gospel, and he notes several times that apostolicity is transmitted according to the dynamic of the *traditio-receptio*: the elect and the Church mutually receive each other: "La réalisation de l'Eglise . . . ," 162f. and 194–202. Several other authors have also shown the importance of these two categories: to the bibliography cited by Congar, the following works can be added: J. D. ZIZIOULAS, "The Theological Problem of "Reception"," *Bulletin—Centro Pro Unione* 26 (1984) 3–6; E. J. KILMARTIN, "Reception in History: An Ecclesiological Phenomenon and Its Significance," *Journal of Ecumenical Studies* 21, 1 (1984) 34–54; J.-M.-R. TILLARD, *Church of Churches* . . . , 108–140 and 223–230.

has chosen its minister, it could not induct him into the ministry by itself. This fact is clear from the solidarity of the Churches witnessing to the apostolic faith of the Church, a fact which also plays in the dual notion tradition–reception. But the category of witness is not limited to that of bishops, because all the members of the local Church bear witness to the personal qualities of the elect (the examination done before the people) and to his faith (this is the meaning of the scrutiny and, later, of the profession of faith made before the assembly). Virtually the same ecclesiological structures govern the election and the ordination of presbyters.

As for the category of tradition–reception, its importance is perceived at two levels: within the local Church, and between the Churches. Principally, the ordained ministry was understood as a gift of God to the Church, made in response to the prayer (epiclesis) of the assembly. Through the imposition of hands, the judgment of God is manifested; the local Church receives what it asks for, and the Spirit equips the Church to fulfill its task in the world.

Through the imposition of hands in episcopal ordination, the other local Churches (represented by their leaders in the persons of the bishops) acknowlege and affirm their communion in the apostolic faith with the Church which has just received its new pastor. In this sense, it is the bishops who give the apostolic ministry. We note that this act of reception deals not only with the person of the new bishop, but also with the Church in which he will preside over the communion of charisms of the Spirit. At the same time, the new bishop is received into the episcopal communion of the apostolic Churches.[32] The bishop who watches over the apostolic faith in his Church will represent it in turn at the synods, and during episcopal ordinations he will serve as a link assuring communion.

Through the epiclesis of ordination, as we saw above in the liturgical texts, the Church has always understood that ordination bestows on the elect a gift of the Holy Spirit. It is always within the prayer of

[32]The succession in ministry on a given episcopal seat in the Church is seen as a sign of unity and of unaltered transmission (especially in the defense against heresy), as one can see in the writings of Irenaeus. This is the meaning that is given to episcopal lists: cf. L. KOEP, "Bischofsliste," *Reallexikon für Antike und Christentum*, vol. 2, cols. 410–415, and above, I, A, 1, a). See also J.-M.-R. TILLARD, *Church of Churches . . .* , 175–184, esp. 182ff.

the community that the imposition of hands and the invocation of the Spirit are carried out, that is to say, at the heart of the gathering of all the charisms of the community, the Eucharistic synaxis. The subject of the epiclesis is the entire assembly, and it is God himself who gives the Holy Spirit to the elect, who then becomes the minister of the gifts of the Spirit.

Since the Spirit is active at each step in the celebration, we perceive the pneumatological meaning of ministry and of the entire structure of the Church, which is revealed by the ordination process. This is possible when the Church is seen as a communion of services in which each person lives out of the gift of the Spirit, in view of the common good (cf. 1 Cor 12:5-7). Through this process, the community, bearer of the Spirit, calls one of its brethren, acknowledging his apostolic faith and personal qualities necessary[33] for the service of the communion. Through the imposition of hands and the invocation of the Holy Spirit, he is established in his ministry and enters into a new state in relationship to his brothers and sisters. But, this gift implies certain obligations: towards his Church (and, in the case of the bishop, towards the communion of Churches as well), because the community is always in need of being built up (the eschatological dimension of ministry), and it always needs those who are sent. The grace of the Spirit is therefore the very foundation of the institution itself of ordained ministry, as it is also of all charisms and service in the Church. This institution ushers certain individuals into new relationships, which are personal and enduring, with God and with the brothers and sisters. Herein lies the essence of this institution founded on the grace of God. Moreover, this is the reason why we should not disassociate either the office from the act of ordination, or *electio*, *ordinatio*, and *jurisdictio*.

G. THE QUESTION OF THE GOVERNANCE OF THE CHURCH

The pneumatological aspect of the ministry needs to be grasped in order to understand the factor of the governance of the Church

---

[33]In the early Church the elect often was ordained against his will, in fact sometimes forced and constrained. This fact is a good illustration of the obedience of Christians to the judgment of God. Cf. Y. CONGAR, "Ordinations *invitus*, . . ."

(which can be seen on several levels: within the Church in which the bishop and the presbyterium preside, and among the Churches), because this aspect will make possible a relational conception of ordained ministry (and of the Church as well). Even though the expression of this relational dimension has not always been clearly maintained in the process of election–ordination, a theological balance may be restored through our study of the early rites of ordination and the ways of understanding them in the early Church.[34] Lastly, from the structure itself of the process and of the prayer of epiclesis we will see that the direction of the Church is exercised in a collegial and personal manner, but always rooted in the local Church. Deplorable results occur when the ordained ministry is detached from its ecclesial context.[35]

"Pro vobis episcopus, vobiscum christianus." This beautiful expression of St. Augustine (*Sermo* 340, 1) indicates that he conceived of the pastoral ministry as rooted *in* the community of the baptized and dependent on the Spirit; he goes on to explain how he understood this relationship: "The first noun (i.e., *episcopus*) is a received office *(officium)*, the second *(christianus)*, a grace." He did not see his ministry as a gift for himself, but, rather, a gift to put at the service of the "common good." It is precisely that which we see expressed in the ordination prayers when the tasks of each ordained ministry were described.[36] Moreover, we saw that the concept emphatically put forth by Cyprian was found present in the process of election–ordination, namely, the necessary participation of the people in the choice of ministers, but also during the exercise of authority on the part of the bishop (and of his presbyterium)[37] in the life of the community.

Thus the responsibility for Christian life is assumed by all in the brotherhood, and the ministry of direction is placed in the framework

[34]See above I, A, 1–6 (pp. 10–85).

[35]This is what we have seen above with the multiplication of absolute ordinations, the proliferation of private Masses, and the development of the separation between order and jurisdiction (I, E).

[36]Cf. *3, *6, *8, *59, *64, *73, *81.

[37]*Ep.* 66, 8: "The bishop is in the Church and the Church is in the bishop": the expression demonstrates the necessity of reception for the bishop to enter into his office. Elsewhere Cyprian confirms the association of the people, the presbyters and deacons in any decision made by those who have the ministry of direction in the Church: cf. *Ep.* 14, 4; 34, 4.

of *diakonia*. Nevertheless, this fact does not keep the ministry from being exercised in a personal way. For this liberty is also part of the specific nature of the grace of the Holy Spirit received through the imposition of hands and the prayer of all: the minister is established in a new relationship with his brethren. Here we find the correct expression of the relationship between the person of the minister and the object of the ministry. The ordination prayers are clearly explicit: a bishop, just as a presbyter or a deacon, receives a specific grace which entails certain responsibilities but also gives the authority to fulfill them.

Lastly, the function of the bishop in the direction of the Church is collegial, in two ways: with his brothers in the presbyterium over which he presides, and also with his confreres the bishops, who represent other apostolic Churches. At the level of the local Church, with "his collaborators," the priests, and in immediate relationship with the deacons, the bishop preaches the Gospel, administers the sacraments, and governs the Church. The roles played by the different ministers at the time of choosing new ministers show the essential nature of the process of election–ordination. Nevertheless, this right of election by the clergy and the people was reduced to a gesture of consent during the ceremony of the imposition of hands; this is attested, for example, by the first monition of the bishop in the ordination of a priest (*84–*86, cf. *24, *46, *71). By presiding over an apostolic Church, the bishop is considered as installed in a relationship with other apostolic Churches, for the shared responsibility for the legacy of the apostolic faith (its proclamation and its correct teaching), and for the visible unity of the Churches.[38]

[38]In the Church, there are different means and institutions which express the communion and the visible unity between the Churches (such as the exchange of letters, synods, ecumenical councils, and certainly the celebration of the Eucharist and the ordination of bishops). Some important bibliographies regarding these institutions are found in the following works: Y. CONGAR, *L'Eglise de saint Augustin* . . . ; H.-M. LEGRAND, "La réalisation de l'Eglise . . . ," especially ch. III and pp. 342–345; id., "Communion ecclésiale . . . , 125–148; L. BOUYER, *L'Eglise de Dieu, Corps du Christ et Temple de l'Esprit* (Paris: Cerf, 1970) esp. 531–567; J.-M.-R. TILLARD, *Church of Churches* . . . , esp. 144–168 and ch. IV.

H. THE STRUCTURING OF THE CHURCH AND ORDINATION

The study of ordination procedures for the episcopacy and the presbyterate help us to lay bare the ecclesiological underpinnings. Without repeating all the preceding research, we will refer to the conclusions already drawn[39] and to the tables of the structure of ordinations and some prayers of epiclesis in order to obtain an overview of the totality of the rituals.[40] This section sums up with the remark that two models result from this research: that of the rituals of the *Apostolic Tradition,* and, later, those of PR 1596. By examining the interaction between the different actors and the inter-relationship of the constitutive elements all throughout the process of admission to ordained ministry we may identify two ecclesiological models, corresponding to very different theological tensions or balances.

1. FIRST MODEL

In the model which we can call that of the early Church,[41] all the elements of the process of admission to ordained ministry (*electio–ordinatio–jurisdictio*) form an indissoluble unity, particularly apparent in the case of the episcopacy. This fact reflects the communal reality of the Church, which is revealed in what the actors in the ordination actually do. If we can permit ourselves an anachronism, ordination can be described as an "in-depth dialogue" between them, which has as its purpose the discernment of the judgment of God and of his Christ for the Church. The local Church, conscious of being created in the very image of the triune God, is revealed in the ordination ceremony as a communion of persons interdependently responsible in all their diversity. The prayer of epiclesis pronounced at the moment of episcopal ordination (*AT* 3) recalls the origin and the apostolic reality of this community, "the place of the unceasing praise of God" founded upon the apostles by the gift of the Holy Spirit through Jesus Christ, through whom everything returns to the

---

[39]Cf. I, A, 6, a (pp. 78–83); I, B, 7, a (pp. 125–127) and I, D, 6 (pp. 168–171).

[40]Cf. I.1; I.2 for the structures of the rituals, and II.1; II.2 for the prayers contained in these rituals.

[41]The idea of applying heuristic models to the study of the theological balance of the structure of the Church is borrowed from H.-M. LEGRAND, who has developed this type of model for the analysis of ordination in the early Church: cf. "La réalisation de l'Eglise . . . ," 209ff.

origin, God the Father. The relationships thus inaugurated are seen from their pneumatico-Christological aspect. These relationships are also revealed in the structure itself of election, in which the elect is not seen as simply chosen on the horizontal level (according to purely human actions), but as chosen by the Spirit; the community receives this decision, this judgment from God. The same reality is expressed in the shared responsibility which is found in the necessary cooperation of the leaders of the neighboring Churches, a fact which also reveals the universality of the Church of God, as well as its apostolic dimension. For the bishops present are witnesses to the apostolic identity of the Church which is receiving its new head with the other apostolic Churches they represent. This shared responsibility is evident at several levels in the category of "witness": the people and the clergy of the locality are witnesses to the good conduct and the faith of the elect; the other apostolic Churches are in solidarity with the Church in which the ordination takes place by the collaboration that their leaders bring to it: they are ministers of the gift of the Spirit, witnesses and guarantors of the apostolic faith.[42]

The communion which exists between the Churches is also expressed in the act of reception by the bishops present of the newly ordained as a colleague in the same ministry. Grasping the dynamic of the *"traditio–receptio"* is essential for an understanding of this double action, which is both horizontal and vertical. What is being enacted at the heart of this local Church is acknowledged in the totality of the Church: the elect, on the horizontal plane, becomes at the same time the leader of a local community and a member of a college of bishops, while on the vertical plane the ordination is conferred as a judgment of God and a gift of the Holy Spirit.

We note the importance of this dynamic of the reception exercised by the community especially in the relativity of the gesture of the imposition of hands (the *cheirotonia*): the imposition of hands is not always necessary, and it is insufficient in itself for the elect to accede to ministry in the early Church. In other words, the imposition of hands was not considered as sufficient when other juridical or ecclesial conditions were lacking. That is to say, the rite cannot exist separate

---

[42]This is the meaning of the scrutiny of the elect: cf. *AT* 2*1, *SAE* 1*66–*68; cf. also the example of CYPRIAN, *Ep.* 38, 1 where he does not refer to the person of the bishop but to clerics in general *("in ordinationibus clericis").*

from its ecclesial meaning: it has no existence in an absolute autonomy that would derive from its material performance. Nor is it the
putting into practice of a pre-existent theory: it is an ecclesial *process*.
Behind the rite always stands the reception by the Church. This fact
allows us to better grasp the insertion of the ministry *into* the Church
and the role which the imposition of hands plays as a symbol of
transmission within the framework of an act of reception exercised
by the community.

It is the epiclesis of the entire assembly (the vertical action of God)
which preserves the ritual gesture of the *cheirotonia* (the horizontal
human action) from its autonomy. The Holy Spirit bestows a specific
charism for presiding over the edification of the Church upon the one
who becomes a minister of Christ. This person, therefore, takes his
place at the head of and in the presence of the Christian people, who
are also endowed with the grace of God (cf. 1 Pet 4:10), received from
the Spirit for the good of all (cf. 1 Cor 12:7). In this context we remember the beautiful expression of St. Augustine: "With you I am
Christian, for you I am bishop." Again we note the presence of the
Holy Spirit, enabling the newly ordained to exercise his pastoral and
priestly office in collaboration with other charisms and services, all
fruits of the one Holy Spirit. The Spirit is thus the principle both of
diversity and of identity for the Church. Thanks to the charism received, the ordained minister guides this Church and has primary responsibility for the proclamation of the Gospel, whence his role in
the liturgy of the community.

Two other facts again confirm the reality of the communal and
Trinitarian structure of the Church, a structure discerned from the
unfolding of the process of ordination: the Eucharistic framework
which surrounds the entire process and the eschatological dimension
signified by the choice of Sunday as the day of ordination.

The Eucharistic celebration is the locus where all the baptized,
bearers of the gifts of the Spirit, are united in their diversity by
Communion in one bread and one cup (cf. 1 Cor 12:12-15, 27; and 1
Cor 10:16ff.). It is the newly ordained who will preside at this
Communion as the first act of his ministry, because he presides also
at the communion of the Church. At the precise moment when the
local Churches are gathered together in the persons of their bishops
around the Eucharistic table, we also see the responsibility that the

ordained ministry assumes with regard to the communion among the Churches, in a structure of tradition and of reception. Here we find the highest expression of the truth of the Church of God, gathered by the Spirit into one single body to celebrate the memorial of the Lord, in continuity and in communion with the first apostolic community. This truth is linked to the eschatological meaning of this celebration, the day of the memorial of the resurrection and of Pentecost. This fact expresses the pneumatological and Christological foundation of ordained ministry. The category of "witness" is still pertinent here, because it is through the ministry of the bishop that the link is made between the testimony formerly given by the apostles and that of the Church today, from the moment that the Church proclaims the Gospel, celebrates the Eucharistic feast, and is gathered together to await the return of Christ.

2. SECOND MODEL

As mentioned above (cf. I, E), there were some regrettable consequences of the institutional disassociation between ministry and *ecclesia*, which became part of the practice of the Church. The rituals of PR 1596 are heirs to these consequences. The elements of the process of admission to ordained ministry which were indissolubly connected in the preceding model are henceforth separated and emptied of their pneumatological content. In the early Church, the *vocatio* of the minister was mediated by the other Christians and ministers, according to the needs of the service of the Gospel, in a particular time and a specific place; in later times this *vocatio* no longer is seen as the business of the people as bearers of the Spirit, but rather a very personal reality (the priests, even if the ritual called them "elect," were more properly "candidates"). The "election" of bishops is less and less an election or consultation *"a clero et populo"* and tends to become in many cases a simple nomination.[43] The ecclesial process of *electio*, which includes three elements (the Christian, God, and the Church [clergy and faithful] of a place) and which is also the place of reception, is short-circuited: the role of the faithful, and even to a certain degree that of the ministers, is reduced to a simple attestation of a *fait*

---

[43]Regarding the history of this change, see J. GAUDEMET, "Bishops: From Election to Nomination," *Concilium* 137 (1980) 10–15; J. BERNHARD, "The Election of Bishops at the Council of Trent," *Concilium* 137 (1980) 24–30.

accompli. This is what H.-M. Legrand calls "the religious disqualification of the laity and the process of rendering the pastors autonomous," a fact which, according to him, is the "product of a faulty pneumatology, because the Holy Spirit is the one who enables and demands of Christians to say 'we' together, while the absence of the Spirit leads to a division between clergy and laity."[44] The result is a weakening of the communion of the local Church, in the sense that a division enters into the heart of the community between Christians who are fully active and others who are passive. From this point on, ordination is seen principally as a transmission of powers.[45]

Furthermore, the distinction between order and jurisdiction is seen to creep in, from an insufficiency in the dynamics of "ordained ministry/local Church" and "gift of the Spirit/function." It is the epiclesis which preserves the ritual gestures from becoming automatic. As soon as the epiclesis is obscured by other gestures of oftentimes ambiguous meaning, imbalances that we have just described can be discerned. In all the prayers of the early tradition of the Church, contrary to a conception of the ministry elaborated at the end of the twelfth century (which defined the ordained ministry, or rather the priesthood, by its "power to consecrate"), the ministry of the bishop or of the priest is linked to the function of building up and presiding over the *ecclesia.* But with the distinctions and juxtapositions in place, a somewhat linear and descending schema results, in which what is happening is seen as the transmission of powers from Christ through the apostles, Christ choosing the bishops and the presbyters, who have the ultimate power over the Church. This model corresponds to that which Zizioulas describes as historical, ignorant of the pneumatological and eschatological dimensions, and considering only one (historical) aspect of the mission of the Church.[46] In this structure, ordinations without titles or assignments are possible because it is a

---

[44]These terms have been used several times in his articles; see examples in H.-M. LEGRAND, "La réalisation de l'Eglise . . . ," 184–187; the quotation is on p. 185.

[45]This is the significance of most of the explanatory rites: thus, for the priest, the anointing of the hands,[*106–*107] the *porrectio instrumentorum,*[*108–*109] the second imposition of hands;[*114–*115] for the bishop, the anointing of the hands,[*161–*165] the bestowal of the crozier,[*167] and the giving of the gloves.[*175]

[46]Cf. the analysis above (pp. 18ff.).

personal power (over the Body of Christ, to consecrate, to absolve, etc.) which is bestowed, and not a ministerial office of presiding at the building up of the Church.

Placing these two models side by side, we see that in the first the Church is structured after a dynamic which respects the Trinitarian life received in the sacraments of initiation, and the communal dimension of salvation. The second model takes into account only the Christological dimension. But, when God encounters us, it is as Father, Son, and Holy Spirit. This is the importance of the balance represented by the ecclesial structure of the Church as evinced by the entire process of admission to ordained ministry in the early Church.

I. THE FRAMEWORK OF ORDINATION

An ordination, therefore, is always celebrated in the context of the Eucharistic liturgy. It is the moment when all the orders of the Church are gathered together in one place: the bishop, who alone confers ordination because he presides at the Eucharistic community, surrounded by the presbyteral college (of which he is also a member, as its head), the deacons, and all the people who are present. Even though the Eucharistic context is retained in PR 1596, we see nevertheless a change in the relationships between the actors. Two important shifts in the equilibrium of the whole of the ordination explain these changes: a shift from an ecclesiological conception of ordained ministry to an eclipse of pneumatology, and towards the supremacy of Christology in the understanding of ordained ministry.

1. FROM AN ECCLESIOLOGICAL CONCEPT OF THE ORDAINED MINISTRY TOWARDS ITS INCREASING ISOLATION

Throughout this study we have seen that the process of ordination includes a complex of actions and roles which inaugurate new, personal, and enduring relationships between the new minister, his Christian brethren, and God. Moreover, in the early Church the ordained ministry was seen in the context of a sacramental and Trinitarian ecclesiology in which ordination is presented as one of the communal, liturgical, and juridical actions through which the Church is built up. When it was a matter of the ordination of a bishop, we saw that the entire life of the *Catholica* was involved. We saw that, eventually, the meaning of ordained ministry was disjoined from its concrete and communal ecclesial context, finally becoming autonomous: the minister could perform certain actions outside of any ecclesial context, and these actions could be considered valid.

The three institutional elements of the entire process, election *(vocatio)*, the epiclesis of the entire assembly accompanied by the imposition of hands, and the jurisdiction *(missio)*, which are joined in the early Church, are little by little disassociated from each other. In this structure which was coming unraveled, several elements and prayers were later inserted which rarely shed light on or explained the central act of the institution of a Christian brother in his new relationships with his brethren and in the service of the Gospel.

This shift is marked by several facts, such as ordination (more and more frequent) without a see or a pastoral office, without ecclesiastical assignment (leading consequently to the multiplication of private Masses), the distinction between "power of order" and "power of jurisdiction" (which made several other shifts possible: the supplanting of the category of ministry by that of priesthood, the attribution of "powers" to a minister independent from his office), the ordination *"ad missam,"* the conflict between secular priests, monks and mendicants, etc. In our view, the growing unintelligibility of the accretions to the auxiliary rites in the liturgical books attests to this evolution. Even though the nucleus of ordination (that is, the epiclesis and the imposition of hands) is found in every rite, these explanatory rites speak of powers bestowed upon the ordinand or the virtues required of the ordinand, or they ask God for these things for him. In the very organization of some liturgical books we move from a descending enumeration to an ascending order of all the ranks of the hierarchy. The great debates during the scholastic era on the sacramentality of the episcopacy also witnesses to the difficulty of thinking of the episcopal ministry as priestly. Henceforth, one acted as if the priest was the pinnacle, and the bishop a sort of supplement, the episcopacy a dignity added to the priesthood. Very quickly the priesthood became the antecedent necessary for the episcopacy. Only Rome preserved for a long time the ancient custom of the permanence of each order.[47] All these changes tended towards the separation of the subject and

---

[47]M. ANDRIEU, "La carrière . . . ," 90–120, esp. 106f.

the object, towards the progressive autonomy of the person of the minister in relationship to his ministry rooted in its ecclesial context, a disastrous direction which will result in the disarticulation of the Church as a concrete structure of communion.

In fact, with the disintegration of the ecclesiological processes of admission to ordained ministry (election, epiclesis, mission) in three distinct steps, their essence was lost; ordination as a process which was communal, liturgical and juridical was lost sight of. The liturgical aspect was emphasized to the point of eclipsing the two other aspects; the communal dimension which was concerned with the entire Church assumed a reduced or nominal form, with the accent now put on the person, and vocation becoming the business of the individual, God, and the bishop. Lastly, it was necessary to add jurisdiction, because ordination was no longer conceived of as the entrance into an office which concerned both the local Church and the entire Church.[48] These shifts eventually reveal the underlying imbalance in the theological basis.

2. FROM A BALANCED TRINITARIAN THEOLOGY TOWARDS THE ECLIPSE OF PNEUMATOLOGY, AND TOWARDS THE SUPREMACY OF CHRISTOLOGY IN THE UNDERSTANDING OF ORDAINED MINISTRY

On the basis of scriptural and patristic studies, Zizioulas affirms the necessity of several conditions for a proper articulation of ordained ministry: Christology, pneumatology, and eschatology. We saw above the importance of these elements for our understanding of the ecclesial context (communal and relational) of ministry, especially for Irenaeus, Cyprian and the *Apostolic Tradition*. This understanding will again be necessary to articulate the theological foundations of all ordained ministry. As a preliminary reflection to his examination of the relationship between ordination and communion, Zizioulas writes:

"Christ . . . is only present to the world in and through the presence and the action of the Holy Spirit. In the New Testament this affirmation is so essential that the incarnation itself of Christ is inconceivable without the work of the Spirit (Lk 1:35). We can Christologically conceive of ministry only in the context of pneumatology, and this

[48]Cf. H.-M. LEGRAND, "Grâce et institution . . . ," 139–172, esp. 160–162.

finally leads to the involvement of the whole Trinity. The ministry of the Church cannot be reduced to anything less than the action and the involvement of God in history since the beginning.

"Wherever the Holy Spirit breathes it immediately follows that the *eschaton* makes an irruption into history and that people are led to enter into *communion* among themselves and with God in the form of a *community*. We see this happen particularly on Pentecost when, as Acts 2 tells us, the descent of the Spirit on the disciples and their companions . . . is seen both as a purely eschatological event ushering in the 'last days' into history, and as the creation of the community of the Church (Acts 2, 41ff.) . . . The ministry of the Church has precisely for its purpose to be the charismatic presence, in the world, of the *eschaton* by which the world is called to repentance and to its incorporation into Israel, the people of God, through baptism in Christ and participation in the royal banquet already existentially actualized from now on in the Eucharistic community."[49]

This is the theological foundation of all ordained ministry in the early Church, as we have ascertained in our study of the process of admission to ordained ministry. The Trinitarian perspective allows the relational and non-individual articulation of the theology of ordained ministry, because the Church is seen in the same relational and communal context, as a communion of the baptized and as a continuation of the community and of the eschatological mission of the apostles. Thus, ordination was conceived of as an act of inauguration or of distribution of the charisms of the Church. Therefore, the insistence upon the communal context is to be maintained at all costs, because the Church has understood that there could be no ministry without this ecclesial context (interdiction of all absolute ordinations)!

The intuition of Zizioulas again points the way to an understanding of what has happened. In referring to chapters 12 and 13 of the First Letter to the Corinthians, he has illuminated the communal and therefore the Trinitarian meaning of ordination.

". . . All the charisms (and therefore all the ministries) in the Church are defined not in themselves, but as *entirely relational concepts*. We can even say that the explicit intention of these two chapters . . . was

[49]J. D. ZIZIOULAS, "Ordination et communion," *Istina* 16, 1 (1971) 5f.

to combat at the root any notion of a charism considered by itself. An authentic charism of the Holy Spirit is one which is in itself related to the other charisms and to the Body of Christ. This appears obvious not only from the insistence of Paul on the idea of the interdependence of the members of Christ (and it must be noted that here in the argument of Paul there is a correspondence between the charisms and the 'members of the body'), but especially, and in a striking way, by reason of what is presented in chapter 13 on the notion of charity. It is only thanks to this notion that we can have some idea of the mystery which is involved necessarily in every act of ordination.

". . . In the light of charity and in the context of communion, ordination *so deeply and existentially binds* the ordained minister to the community that in his new state after ordination we can in no way see him as a separate individual: he has become a *relational entity*.

". . . In a context of communion an ordination necessarily means *an involvement with a community* . . . It is precisely by reason of this existential perception of the Church that during the first centuries people could not conceive of the "catholicity" as outside of the local Church, and ordination was reserved to the Eucharistic synaxis, where the communion with all its divine and human dimensions was fully actualized.

". . . Through ordination, the Church becomes the community which *binds the world to God,* and that is the essential meaning of mission. Mission is not a method of action (that is to say, a sending forth, a going outside of oneself, etc.), but an attribute stemming from the very nature of the Church . . . Through ordination the Church turns its gaze outside, not however to remain behind, but to be involved. This is the *ek-stasis* of our communion, which must also be the going forth on mission. Any *ek-stasis* that leaves us behind is not the *ek-stasis* of a communion. It is precisely in this last sense that ordination seen in the light of the communion makes the Church a missionary Church."[50]

We see clearly that this description corresponds to the relational structure of the communion of Persons in the Trinity, where unity and diversity are not in opposition, but the very dynamic of the reality of God. Zizioulas has, we think, profoundly grasped and explained

[50]Ibid., 8–10.

the meaning of the structure of ordination which shows a Trinitarian balance. By studying the evolution of the institution, we have seen the ecclesiological disequilibrium which appears when one of these elements in the balance is suppressed.

Moreover, we have noticed that the eclipse of the pneumatological dimension produced an ecclesial structuring which poorly expresses the communion among all the members of the Church. The relationships among them are profoundly changed: responsibility for the life of the Church is no longer shared by all the members (the role of the laity changes in the selection of ministers, especially in the election of the bishop; they are no longer witnesses either to his ability or to the quality of his faith); ordained ministers appear *above* the community (absolute ordinations are the rule, the minister can perform functions outside of the community); the powers of the ordained ministry are conceived of in terms of powers personally possessed ("power over the Body of Christ"), etc. All this is the result of the absorption of the pneumatological function by the Christological function. Theological reflection gives a central place to the priesthood of the priest (from the time of the practice of absolute ordination).

Another consequence can be identified: the minister is more and more closely identified with Christ in his role of mediation and of sacrifice. The powers of the priest are most often reduced to a power individually possessed, without intrinsic reference to the community of the baptized, to such a degree that attention is concentrated upon the transmission of the power to offer the Eucharistic sacrifice, and upon the priestly character[51] (see the importance of the anointing of the hands and the *porrectio instrumentorum*). We risk losing from view the aim of the ministry, which is the pastoral service of the people entrusted to the charge of the minister, and not just the service of worship.[52]

[51]The most concise presentation of the facts relative to the character of orders still remains that of J. GALOT, *La nature du caractère* . . . Concerning the interpretation of the pronouncements of Trent on the character of orders and the related epistemological problems, see the studies of H.-M. LEGRAND, "The 'Indelible' Character . . . ," and id., "La réalisation de l'Eglise . . . ," 241–243 + bibliography.

[52]The study of the ordination process in the *AT* shows the prime importance of the category of "pastoral office" in its conception, which prohibits the isolation of the priestly function as a special sacrificial and consecratory power. See the study of H.-J. SCHULZ, "Das liturgisch-sakramental . . . ," 208–255, especially

Lastly, the legitimation of the authority of ordained ministers will be focused on the sacramental power expressed in later prayers such as *"Sacerdotem oportet offerre . . ."*[88] and *"Accipe potestatem offerre sacrificium . . . ,"*[109] where the essence of the ordained ministry is thought of in terms of the priesthood and centered, therefore, upon the cult, and linked to the figure of Christ as mediator. As for the bishops, since their ordination was not generally considered as sacramental, their powers were expressed in juridical terms. Often the figure of the bishop was associated with that of the feudal lord, and his authority was considered more administrative than sacramental.[53] We see also that in episcopal ordination, often celebrated outside of the Church in which the new bishop will preside, it is the minister of the ordination who presides at the Eucharistic celebration which follows, and no longer the newly ordained,[54] a fact which, supplementing the analyses which we have just completed, again shows that episcopal ordination was no longer conceived of as admission to a pastoral ministry, intended to preside at the building up of the Church. Here the connection between pneumatology and Christology is lost.

216, and also our discussion of the biblical images used in the prayers of episcopal ordination, I, A, 3, α.

[53]By way of example, THOMAS AQUINAS did not consider the episcopacy a sacramental order: *In IV Sent.*, d. 24, q. 3, a. 2, sol. 2 (*Opera Omnia*, Parma ed., vol. 7², 901) and he affirmed that "no one can receive the episcopal power if he did not first have the priestly power" (. . . *Sed episcopalis potestas dependet a sacerdotali: quia nullus potest recipere episcopalem, nisi prius habeat sacerdotalem. Ergo episcopatus non est ordo*) (*In IV Sent.*, d. 24, q. 3, a. 2, q^a. 2, sed contra [*Opera Omnia*, 901]).

[54]For example, towards the middle of the thirteenth century we read in PR XIII that ". . . *consecratus qui celebranti consecratori concelebrare debet, accedat ad dextrum cornu altaris . . .*" (". . . the consecrated one who must concelebrate with the celebrant-consecrator approaches the right corner of the altar . . .") (XI, 34 [ANDRIEU PR II, 365]). It is clear that it is not the newly ordained who presides at the celebration. The same facts are presented in the article by A.-G. MARTIMORT, "Le rituel de la concélébration eucharistique," *EL* 77, 3 (1963) 147–168, reprinted in *Mens Concordet Voci*, pour Mgr A. G. Martimort à l'occasion de ses quarante années d'enseignement et des vingt ans de la Constitution "Sacrosanctum Concilium" (Paris: Desclée, 1983) 279–298; for the concelebration of episcopal ordination, see 286–288 [=*EL*, 158–160], for the concelebration of presbyteral ordination, pp. 288–292 [=*EL*, pp. 160–165].

It is only in a balanced Trinitarian context that we find the solidarity of all those who make up the Church. In such a context authority is conferred through ordination, while at the same time it is confirmed and sustained by a continual process of ecclesial receptivity, because everyone feels responsible for the service of the Gospel and the building up of the Church, each in different ways according to the charism given to each person for the well-being of all (1 Cor 12:7). This life is truly lived in a communal way in such structures and concrete relations as the synodality of the Church, the fraternal exchange of visits and letters of communion, Eucharistic hospitality, participation at episcopal ordinations, etc. The institution of ordination, seen from this Trinitarian viewpoint, attests to the capital importance of preserving a proper balance between Christology and pneumatology.

In conclusion, as we proceed to the second part of our study, we will observe the first attempts at reform in the rituals of ordination composed between the sixteenth and the seventeenth centuries. For all the changes we have seen are important to explain the reactions of the Reformation, even though the ministry was not the principal interest of the theologians, such as, for example, Martin Luther or John Calvin. There were other, deeper, burning issues such as the question of justification, the relationship between grace and works, the place of the Word in theology and in life, etc. Nevertheless, to understand the revisions in the rituals of ordination of the reformers, some of which were radical, it was first necessary to clarify certain shifts in the theology and the practice of the Latin Catholic Church towards the end of the Middle Ages. We also needed to analyze the theological and ecclesiological balance, and its roots in the early and patristic tradition.

EXCURSUS: ORDO–ORDINATIO–CONSECRATIO–BENEDICTIO–CHEIROTONIA

Without referring again to our previous study of these terms, we can benefit from a quick survey of their technical meanings, because they have all undergone an evolution of meaning in their passage through time and space.

ORDO[55]

Although it is not a biblical term, *ordo* has been frequently used by Christian authors. In Tertullian, who is the first to use it (to describe Christian realities), the *ordo episcoporum* seems to mean a succession or list of bishops.[56] His other uses of the word *ordo* imply rather a particular social body within the people of God. The evolution of the vocabulary ended in the twelfth century with the systematization of sacramental theology by theologians who distinguished *ordo* (the sacramental aspect of the priesthood) and *dignitas* (the non-sacramental aspect of the episcopacy);[57] this led to the medieval distinction between "power of order" and "power of jurisdiction," a concrete sign of the underlying split between charism and institution.

ORDINATIO/CONSECRATIO/BENEDICTIO

In Tertullian, *ordinare/ordinator/ordinandus* "are terms reserved exclusively to the priestly function . . . *Ordinare* sometimes seems to contain the idea of sanctification and of (divine) ratification." In Cyprian, they mean "installation properly accomplished with the participation of the people" in an ecclesiastical office.[58] P.-M. Gy has shown that, in a manner parallel with the distinction *ordo/dignitas* (sacramental/non-sacramental), a distinction was made between *ordinare* (sacramental) and *consecrare* (non-sacramental) on the theological level: this

---

[55]Besides the dictionary articles, see the studies of P.-M. GY, "Remarques sur le vocabulaire . . . ," and id., "Ancient Ordination . . . ," 79–81, where the author accepts the corrections made by P. VAN BENEDEN, *Aux origines d'une terminologie sacramentelle: Ordo, ordinare, ordinatio dans la littérature chrétienne avant 313* (Louvain: Spicilegium sacrum Lovaniense, 1974) (+ bibliography). To be read with the book review of the same work by H.-M. LEGRAND, in which he agrees with the positive results of this research, while putting forward three reservations concerning the "criticizable historical method, rigid theological references, and their replacement by an overly fuzzy conceptuality." Cf. H.-M. LEGRAND, "Recherches sur le presbytérat et l'épiscopat," *RSPT* 59, 4 (1975) 676–680, here 678.

[56]P. VAN BENEDEN, *Aux origines . . .* , 19ff.

[57]Cf. P.-M. GY, "Ancient Ordination . . . ," 79. By way of example, Gy cites HUGH OF ST. VICTOR, *De sacramentis*, II, 3, 5 (PL 176, 423B) and PETER LOMBARD, *Sententiae IV*, 24, 14 (Quaracchis, 2nd ed., 902). See also id., "Remarques sur le vocabulaire . . . ," 125ff.; D. N. POWER, *Ministers of Christ . . .* , 61–63.

[58]Cf. P. VAN BENEDEN, *Aux origines . . .* , 61ff. and 92.

vocabulary was introduced in PR XIII and almost completely supplanted the early vocabulary found in the PR of Durandus.

"In the ancient vocabulary there was not much difference between *ordinare, consecrare,* and *benedicere.* Nevertheless, at least in the patristic era, *ordinare* has a broader sense than *consecrare* or *benedicere,* and it meant not only the ordination prayer, but the whole process which this prayer terminates . . . In a more specific way, *consecratio* and *benedictio* are, in the Roman sacramentaries, the proper designation of ordination prayers, and there is no apparent distinction of meaning between these two words. *Benedictio* no longer has the meaning of blessing God as in primitive Christianity, neither yet exactly its modern sense, because it appears to have a strong deprecative connotation, exclusive of any indicative use . . . To sum up these various ideas, one could say that in the Roman sacramentaries the ordination prayer is called a consecration or blessing in the sense that it invokes the divine blessing or consecration, especially the blessing of the Holy Spirit."[59]

We note the evolution: the process by which a Christian is chosen and installed in an ecclesiastical office, an aspect implied in the words *ordinare* and *ordinatio,* is little by little lost from sight, so that these terms end up meaning only the liturgical office of the imposition of hands.

CHEIROTONIA

The Greek term *cheirotonia* (with the verb *cheirotonein*) has been studied at length.[60] In his study, P. Van Beneden notes that "the semantic evolution of *ordinare* differs from that of *cheirotonein,* because, while this latter term came to mean the consecratory imposition of hands, *ordinare,* although sometimes meaning substantially the same thing, never meant 'to impose hands.'"[61] We will therefore retain the

[59]P.-M. GY, "Ancient Ordination . . . ," 80. A. Santantoni gives a list of these words used in the liturgical books: see A. SANTANTONI, *L'ordinazione episcopale* . . . , 52f. In fact, *ordinare* and *ordinatio* grew in prestige and became the technical terms for sacramental *ordo.* See, lastly, the article of Y. CONGAR, "Note sur une valeur des termes 'ordinare, ordinatio,'" *RevSR* 58, 1–2–3 (1984) 7–14.

[60]See especially the dossier (+ bibliography) established by C. VOGEL, *Ordinations.*

[61]P. VAN BENEDEN, *Aux origines* . . . , 52.

broader meaning given to *cheirotonia* which includes the entire process (the election and the imposition of hands which bestows an ecclesiastical office).

Bibliography

1. ABBREVIATIONS

A. BIBLICAL REFERENCES

For biblical references we have used *The Holy Bible, The New Revised Standard Version* (NRSV), Thomas Nelson Publishers, Nashville, 1989.

The following abbreviations are used for the books of the Bible:

Old Testament

Gen	Genesis	2 Chr	2 Chronicles	Dan	Daniel
Ex	Exodus	Ezra	Ezra	Hos	Hosea
Lev	Leviticus	Neh	Nehemiah	Joel	Joel
Num	Numbers	Esth	Esther	Am	Amos
Deut	Deuteronomy	Job	Job	Ob	Obadiah
Josh	Joshua	Ps	Psalms	Jon	Jonah
Judg	Judges	Prov	Proverbs	Mic	Micah
Ruth	Ruth	Eccl	Ecclesiastes	Nah	Nahum
1 Sam	1 Samuel	Song	Song of Solomon	Hab	Habakkuk
2 Sam	2 Samuel	Isa	Isaiah	Zeph	Zephaniah
1 Kings	1 Kings	Jer	Jeremiah	Hag	Haggai
2 Kings	2 Kings	Lam	Lamentations	Zech	Zechariah
1 Chr	1 Chronicles	Ezek	Ezekiel	Mal	Malachi

Apocryphal/Deuterocanonical Books

Tob	Tobit	Song of Thr	Prayer of Azariah and the
Jdt	Judith		Song of the Three Jews
Add Esth	Additions to Esther	Sus	Susanna
Wis	Wisdom	Bel	Bel and the Dragon
Sir	Sirach (Ecclesiasticus)	1 Macc	1 Maccabees
Bar	Baruch	2 Macc	2 Maccabees
1 Esd	1 Esdras	3 Macc	3 Maccabees
2 Esd	2 Esdras	4 Macc	4 Maccabees
Let Jer	Letter of Jeremiah	Pr Man	Prayer of Manasseh

New Testament

Mt	Matthew	Eph	Ephesians	Heb	Hebrews
Mk	Mark	Phil	Philippians	Jas	James
Lk	Luke	Col	Colossians	1 Pet	1 Peter
Jn	John	1 Thess	1 Thessalonians	2 Pet	2 Peter
Acts	Acts of the	2 Thess	2 Thessalonians	1 Jn	1 John
	Apostles	1 Tim	1 Timothy	2 Jn	2 John
Rom	Romans	2 Tim	2 Timothy	3 Jn	3 John
1 Cor	1 Corinthians	Titus	Titus	Jude	Jude
2 Cor	2 Corinthians	Philem	Philemon	Rev	Revelation
Gal	Galatians				

B. ABBREVIATIONS

Adv. Haer.   *Adversus Haereses,* A. ROBERTS and J. DONALDSON (eds.), *The Ante-Nicene Fathers,* vol. I., Grand Rapids: Wm. B. Eerdmans, 1981; A. ROUSSEAU, *Contre les hérésies,* Paris: Cerf (coll. "SC," 100, 152/153, 210/211, 263/264, 293/294) 1965–1982.

ANDRIEU OR   M. ANDRIEU, *"Les Ordines Romani" du haut moyen âge,* Louvain: Spicilegium sacrum Lovaniense (coll. "Etudes et documents," 11, 23, 24, 28, 29), 1931–1961.

ANDRIEU PR   M.ANDRIEU, *Le Pontifical romain au moyen âge,* Vatican City: Bibliothèque apostolique vaticane (coll. "Studi e testi," 86, 87, 88, 99), 1938–1941.

AT   *Apostolic Tradition,* in W. A. JURGENS, *The Faith of the Early Fathers,* 3 vols., Collegeville: The Liturgical Press, 1970, vol. I; *La Tradition Apostolique de saint Hippolyte. Essai de reconstitution.* 5th improved ed. by A. Gerhards and S. Felbecker, Münster: Aschendorff (coll. "LQF," 39), 1989.

Ge   Old Gelasian Sacramentary, Manuscript of the Vatican Library, Reginen. Lat. 316, L. C. MOHLBERG, L. EIZEN-HÖFER and P. SIFFRIN (eds.), *Liber sacramentorum Romanae aeclesiae ordinis anni circuli,* 3rd improved ed., Rome: Herder (coll. "Rerum ecclesiasticarum documenta," Series maior, Fontes 4), 1981.

Gr   Gregorian Sacramentary, J. Deshusses (ed.), *Le sacramentaire grégorien. Ses principales formes d'après les plus anciens manuscrits. Edition comparative,* t. 1, *Le sacramentaire, le supplément d'Aniane,* 2nd ed., Fribourg: Editions Universitaires Fribourg (coll. "Spicilegium Friburgense," 16), 1979.

Hist. Eccl.	*Histoire ecclésiastique d'Eusèbe de Césarée*, ed. G. BARDY, Paris: Cerf (coll. "SC," 31, 41, 55, 73), 1952–1960.
MANSI	J. D. MANSI, *Sacrorum conciliorum nova et amplissima collectio*, new ed., L. Petit and J.-B. Martin, reprint [1st ed. 1759–1798], Graz, 1960–1961, 60 vols.
MF	Missale Francorum, Manuscript of the Vatican library, Reginen. Lat. 257, L. C. MOHLBERG, L. EIZENHÖFER, and P. SIFFRIN (eds.), *Missale Francorum*, Rome: Herder (coll. "Rerum ecclesiasticarum documenta," Series maior, Fontes 2), 1957.
ML	Leofric Missal, F. E. WARREN, *The Leofric Missal as used in the Cathedral of Exeter during the Episcopate of its First Bishop A.D. 1050–1072 together with Some Account of the Red Book of Derby, the Missal of Robert of Jumièges and a few other early Manuscript Service Books of the English Church*, anastatic reprint [1st ed. 1883], Westmead, Farnborough-Hants: Gregg International Publishers, Ltd., 1968.
OR	*Ordines Romani*, M. ANDRIEU, *Les "Ordines Romani" du haut moyen âge*, Louvain: Spicilegium sacrum Lovaniense (coll. "Etudes et documents," 11, 23, 24, 28, 29), 1931–1961.
PGD	Pontifical of William Durandus, ANDRIEU PR III, *Le Pontifical de Guillaume Durand*, Vatican City: Bibliothèque apostolique vaticane, 1940.
PR	*Pontificale Romanum*
PR XII	Roman Pontifical of the XIIth century, ANDRIEU PR I, *Le Pontifical romain du XIIe siècle*, Vatican City: Bibliothèque apostolique vaticane, 1938.
PR XIII	Roman Pontifical of the XIIIth century, ANDRIEU PR II, *Le Pontifical de la Curie romaine au XIIIe siècle*, Vatican City: Bibliothèque apostolique vaticane, 1940.
PRG	Romano-Germanic Pontifical of the Xth century, C. VOGEL and R. ELZE, *Le Pontifical romano-germanique du dixième siècle*, Vatican City: Bibliothèque apostolique vaticane (coll. "Studi e testi," 226, 227, 269), 1963–1972.
SEA	*Statuta ecclesiae antiqua*, Ch. MUNIER, *Les Statuta ecclesiae antiqua. Edition, études critiques*, Paris: Presses Universitaires de France (coll. "Bibliothèque de l'Institut de Droit canonique de l'Université de Strasbourg," 5), 1960, reprinted in

218

Concilia Galliae A. 314-A. 506, Turnhout: Brépols, 1978 (= CC 148), pp. 162–188.

Ve   Sacramentary formerly called Leonine, Manuscript of Verona, Bibl. capitolare, LXXXV/[80], L. C. MOHLBERG, L. EIZENHÖFER and P. SIFFRIN (eds.), *Sacramentarium Veronense*, 3rd improved ed., Rome: Herder (coll. "Rerum ecclesiasticarum documenta," Series maior, Fontes 1), 1978.

Manuals, Lexicons, Dictionaries

DACL   *Dictionnaire d'archéologie chrétienne et de liturgie* published under the direction of F. CABROL, H. LECLERCQ and H. MARROU, Paris: Letouzey et Ané, 1907–1953.

RAC   *Reallexikon für Antike und Christentum*, Stuttgart: Hiersemann Verlag, 1950ff.

TDNT   *Theological Dictionary of the New Testament*, begun by G. KITTEL and continued by G. FRIEDRICH. Trans. of the German *[Theologisches Wörterbuch zum Neuen Testament]* by G. W. Bromiley, Grand Rapids: Wm. B. Eerdmans, 1964ff.

Collections

BETL   Bibliotheca ephemeridum theologicarum Lovaniensium, Gembloux: J. Duculot, 1947ff.

CC   *Corpus christianorum collectum a monachis O.S.B. abbatiae S. Petri in Steenbruge, series latina*, Turnhout/Paris: Brépols, 1954ff.

CSEL   *Corpus scriptorum ecclesiasticorum latinorum editum consilio et impensis Academiae litterarum . . . Vindobonensis*, Vienna: Tempsky, 1866ff.

PG   *Patrologiae cursus completus, series graeca*, J.-P. MIGNE (ed.), Petit-Montrouge: Ateliers catholiques, 1857–1866, 161 vols.

PL   *Patrologia cursus completus, series latina*, J.-P. MIGNE (ed.), Petit-Montrouge: Ateliers catholiques, 1844–1864, 221 vols.

SC   *Sources chrétiennes*, collection directed by H. de LUBAC and J. DANIELOU (then C. MONDESERT), Paris: Cerf, 1942ff.

US   *Unam Sanctam*, Paris: Cerf, 1937ff.

Reviews and Periodicals

AAS *Acta apostolicae sedis. Commentarium officiale*, Rome, then Vatican City: Typis Polyglottis Vaticanis, 1909ff.

BLE *Bulletin de littérature ecclésiastique*, Paris: Lecoffre, then Toulouse: Université catholique de Toulouse, 1899ff.

EL *Ephemerides liturgicae*, Rome: Ed. liturgiche, 1887ff.

JTS *Journal of Theological Studies*, London: Macmillan, then Oxford: Clarendon, 1900ff.

LMD *La Maison-Dieu, Revue de pastorale liturgique*, Paris: Cerf, 1945ff.

LQF *Liturgiegeschichtliche* (then *Liturgiewissenschaftliche*) *Quellen und Forschungen*, Münster: Aschendorff, 1919ff.

NRT *Nouvelle revue théologique*, Tournai and then Louvain: Casterman, 1869ff.

QL *Questions liturgiques et paroissiales*, then *Questions liturgiques*, Louvain: Abbaye du Mont César, 1910–1969.

RDC *Revue de droit canonique*, Strasbourg: Université de Strasbourg, 1951ff.

RechSR *Recherches de science religieuse*, Paris: Bureau de la Revue, 1910ff.

RevSR *Revue des sciences religieuses*, Strasbourg: Palais Universitaire, 1921ff.

RHE *Revue d'histoire ecclésiastique*, Louvain: Charles Peeters, later Bureau de la Revue, then Université catholique de Louvain, 1900ff.

RSPT *Revue des sciences philosophiques et théologiques*, Paris: Lecoffre, then Vrin, 1907ff.

RTAM *Recherches de théologie ancienne et médiévale*, Louvain: Abbaye du Mont César, 1929ff.

Collections of Articles

Liturgie W. RORDORF, *Liturgie, foi et vie des premiers chrétiens*, Paris: Beauchesne, 1986.

Ordinations C. VOGEL, *Ordinations inconsistantes et caractère inamissible*, Turin: Bottega d'Erasmo (coll. "Etudes d'histoire du culte et des institutions chrétiennes," 1), 1978.

Documents of Vatican Council II

CD	Decree *Christus Dominus* on the pastoral office of bishops in the Church of Vatican II (October 28, 1965)
DH	Declaration *Dignitatis humanae* on religious liberty of Vatican II (December 7, 1965)
GS	Pastoral Constitution *Gaudium et spes* on the Church in the modern world of Vatican II (December 7, 1965)
LG	Dogmatic Constitution *Lumen gentium* on the Church of Vatican II (November 21, 1964)
PO	Decree *Presbyterorum ordinis* on the ministry and life of priests of Vatican II (December 2, 1965)
SC	Constitution *Sacrosanctum concilium* on the sacred liturgy of Vatican II (December 4, 1963)

Church and Ecclesial Organizations

ICEL	International Commission on English in the Liturgy
SCM	Student Christian Movement Press
SPCK	Society for Promoting Christian Knowledge
USCC	United States Catholic Conference

Varia

col.	column
ET	English translation
fasc.	fascicle
L	Latin version
n. (nn.)	note (notes)
no. (nos.)	number (numbers)
NS	new series
SAE	Sahidic, Arabic and Ethiopian version
n.d.	no date
n.p.	no place
n.p.n.d.	no place, no date
t.	tome
vol.	volume

2. SOURCES

A. HISTORICAL AND LITERARY SOURCES

Patristic Sources

ALBERT THE GREAT. *Opera Omnia*, t. 26, *De Sacramentis*. Münster: Aschendorff, 1958.

AMALARIUS OF METZ. *Amalarii episcopi opera liturgica omnia*, t. 2, *Liber officialis*. Ed. J.-M. Hanssens. Vatican City: Biblioteca apostolica vaticana (coll. "Studi e testi," 139), 1948.

AMBROSIASTER. *Quaestiones Veteris et Novi Testamenti* CI, 9–10 [CSEL 50, p. 196 = PL 35, 2302].

AMBROSE OF MILAN. *Des sacrements; Des mystères*. Rev. and enlarged ed. on the explanation of the Symbol. Text established, French trans. and annotated by B. Botte. Paris: Cerf (coll. "SC," 25bis), 1961.

AUGUSTINE OF HIPPO. *Enarratio in Psalmum CXXXII* (CC 40, pp. 1926–1935).

BONAVENTURE. *Opera Omnia*, t. 6, *In Librum IV Sententiarum*. Paris: Vivès, 1866.

CELESTINE I, *Ep. IV, Ad episcopos provinciae Viennensis et Narbonensis* (PL 50, 429–436).

CLEMENT OF ROME. *Epître aux Corinthiens*. Intro., text, French trans., notes and index by A. Jaubert. Paris: Cerf (coll. "SC," 167), 1971.

CYPRIAN OF CARTHAGE, *Saint Cyprien. Correspondance*. Text established and French trans. by L. Bayard. 2nd ed. Paris: "Les Belles Lettres" (coll. "Universités de France"), 1961–1962. 2 vols. ET: *Saint Cyprian, Letters (1–81)*, trans. by R. B. Donna, in *The Fathers of the Church*, vol. 51. Washington, D.C.: The Catholic University of America Press, 1964.

ID. *Saint Cyprien. L'Oraison dominicale*. Text, French trans., intro. and notes by M. Réveillaud. Paris: Presses Universitaires de France (coll. "Etudes d'histoire et de philosophie religieuses," 58), 1964.

CYRIL OF ALEXANDRIA. *Expositio sive Commentarius in Ioannis Evangelium* (PG 73).

Didachē; *La Doctine des douze Apôtres (Didachē)*. Intro., text, French trans., appendix and index by W. Rordorf and A. Tuilier. Paris: Cerf (coll. "SC," 248), 1978.

EUSEBIUS OF CAESAREA, *Histoire ecclésiastique*. Greek text, French trans. and annotations by G. Bardy. Paris: Cerf (coll. "SC," 31, 41, 55, 73), 1952–1960.

Expositio Missae. [Anonymous.] Ed. M. Gerbert, *Monumenta veteris liturgiae Alemannicae,* t. 2. Reprint [1st ed. 1779]. Hildesheim: Olms, 1967, pp. 282–293.

FRIEDBERG, Ae. (ed.). *Corpus Iuris Canonici.* Editio lipsiensis secunda post Aemilii Ludouici Richteri curas ad librorum manu scriptorum et editionis romanae fidem recognouit et adnotatione critica instruxit Aemilius Friedberg. *Pars prior, Decretum Magistri Gratiani. Pars secunda, Decretalium collectiones.* Reprint [1st ed. 1881]. Graz: Akademische Druck u. Verlagsanstalt, 1959.

GELASIUS I. *Ep. IX, Ad episcopos Lucaniae* (PL 59, 47–57).

HILARY OF POITIERS. *Tractatus in Psalmum CXXXII* (CSEL 22, pp. 684–690).

HINCMAR OF RHEIMS. *Ep. XXIX, Ad Adventium episcopum Metensem* (PL 126, 186–188).

HIPPOLYTUS OF ROME. *La Tradition Apostolique de saint Hippolyte. Essai de reconstitution.* Ed. B. Botte, 5th ed. improved by A. Gerhards and S. Felbecker. Münster: Aschendorff (coll. "LQF," 39), 1989, containing a complete critical apparatus and essential bibliography; a less technical ed., also by B. Botte, *La Tradition Apostolique d'après les anciennes versions.* 2nd ed. Paris: Cerf (coll. "SC," 11bis), 1968. ET: CUMING, G. J., *Hippolytus: A Text for Students.* 2nd ed. reprint. Bramcote, Nottingham: Grove Books (coll. "Grove Liturgical Study," 8), 1991, pp. 8–15; JURGENS, W. A. *The Faith of the Early Fathers,* vol. I. Collegeville: The Liturgical Press, 1970.

IGNATIUS OF ANTIOCH. *Lettres.* Greek text, intro., French trans. and notes of P.-Th. Camelot. 4th rev. and corrected ed. Paris: Cerf (coll "SC," 10), 1969.

INNOCENT I. *Ep. XXV, Ad Decentium episcopum Eugubinum.* Ed. R. Cabié. Louvain: Publications universitaires (coll. "Bibliothèque de la RHE," 58), 1973.

INNOCENT III. *De sacro altaris mysterio* (PL 217, 773–914).

ID. *Ep. ad Zamorensem episcopum,* col. 469, in FRIEDBERG, Ae. (ed.). *Corpus Iuris Canonici,* Pars secunda, *Decretalium collectiones.* Leipzig, 1881.

ID. *Selected Letters of Pope Innocent III Concerning England* (1198–1216). London: Thomas Nelson and Sons, 1953.

IRENAEUS OF LYONS. *Contre les hérésies. Dénonciation et réfutation de la gnose au nom menteur.* French trans. by A. Rousseau. Paris: Cerf, 1984. This work uses the French translation from the edition published in the collection "SC": Book I = "SC," 263/264, 1979; Book II = "SC," 293/294, 1982; Book III = "SC," 210/211, 1974; Book IV = "SC," 100 (2 vols.), 1965; Book V = "SC," 152/153, 1969; ET: *Adversus Haereses.* ROBERTS, A., DONALDSON, J. (eds.). *The*

Ante-Nicene Fathers, vol. I, *The Writings of the Fathers down to A.D. 325*. Grand Rapids: Wm. B. Eerdmans, 1981.

ID. *Démonstration de la prédication apostolique*. French trans. by L.-M. Froidevaux. Paris: Cerf (coll. "SC," 62), 1959; ET: *Proof of the Apostolic Preaching*, in QUASTEN, J., PLUMPE, C. (eds.). *Ancient Christian Writers*, vol. 16, trans. and annotated by J. P. Smith. Westminster, Md./London: Newman Press/Longmans, Green and Co., 1952.

ISIDORE OF SEVILLE. *De ecclesiasticis officiis* (PL 83, 737–828).

ID. *Etymologiarum* (PL 82, 73–728).

JEROME. *Commentariorum in Epistolam ad Titum* (PL 26, 555–600).

ID. *Epistula ad Evangelum* 146, 2 [ed. Labourt VIII, p. 118 = CSEL 56, p. 310 = PL 22, 1192].

LEO THE GREAT (I). *Ep. VI, Ad Anastasium Thessalonicensem episcopum* (PL 54, 616–620).

ID. *Ep. IX, Ad Dioscorum Alexandrinum episcopum* (PL 54, 624–627).

ID. *Ep. X, Ad episcopos per provinciam Viennensem constitutos* (PL 54, 628–636).

ID. *Ep. XII, Ad episcopos africanos provinciae mauritaniae caesariensis* (PL 54, 645–656B).

ID. *Ep. XIV, Ad Anastasium Thessalonicensem episcopum* (PL 54, 666–677).

ID. *Ep. CLXVII, Ad Rusticum Narbonensem episcopum* (PL 54, 1197–1209).

ID. *Tractatus 3 item in natale eiusdem* (of Sept. 29, 443), (CC 138, pp. 10–15).

ID. *Tractatus 4 item in natale eiusdem* (of Sept. 29, 444), (CC 138, pp. 16–21).

ID. *Letters*, trans. E. Hunt. New York: Fathers of the Church, 1957.

MANSI, J. D. *Sacrorum conciliorum nova et amplissima collectio*. New ed., L. Petit and J.-B. Martin. Reprint [1st ed. 1759–1798]. Graz, 1960–1961, 60 vols.

PETER DAMIAN. *Opusculum Sextum. Liber qui appellatur gratissimus. Ad Henricum Archiepiscopum Ravennatem* (PL 145, 99–160).

THEODORE OF MOPSUESTIA. *Theodori episcopi Mopsuesteni [Commentarius] in Epistolas B. Pauli. The Latin Version with the Greek Fragments with an Introduction, Notes and Indices*, t. 2, *I. Thessalonians—Philemon, Appendices, Indices*. Ed. H. B. Swete. Reprint [1st ed. 1882]. Westmead, Farnborough-Hants, Great Britain: Gregg International Publishers, Ltd., 1969.

ID. *Commentary of Theodore of Mopsuestia on the Lord's Prayer and On the Sacraments of Baptism and the Eucharist*. Ed. A. MINGANA, *Woodbrooke Studies. Christian Documents Edited and Translated with a Critical Apparatus*, t. VI. Cambridge: W. Heffer & Sons, 1933.

THEODORET OF CYR. *Quaestiones in Numeros* (PG 80, 349D–400).

THEODULF OF ORLEANS. *Capitula ad presbyteros parochiae* (PL 105, 191–208).

THOMAS AQUINAS. *Sancti Thomae Aquinatis. Opera Omnia*. Parma: Petri Fiaccadori [= ed. of Parma], 1852–1873, t. 25. Re-edition with new intro. of V. J. Bourke. N.Y. : Musurgia Publ., 1948–1949.

ID., *Sancti Thomae Aquinatis. Opera Omnia*. Rome: Typographia Polyglotta, later Leonine Commission [= ed. Leonine], 1882–1948, t. 16.

B. LITURGICAL SOURCES

Edited Sources

1. *Oriental Liturgies*

Apostolic Constitutions; FUNK, F. X. *Didascalia et Constitutiones apostolorum*. Anastatic reprint [1st ed. 1905]. Turin: Bottega d'Erasmo, 1979. Ordinations in Book VIII, t. 1, pp. 470–525. Critical edition with French trans. and notes by METZGER, M. *Les Constitutions apostoliques*, t. 3, *Livres VII et VIII*. Paris: Cerf (coll. "SC," 336), 1987, pp. 138–233. ET: DONALDSON, J. *Constitutions of the Holy Apostles*. Grand Rapids: Wm. B. Eerdmans Publishing (coll. "The Ante-Nicene Fathers," 7), 1977; GRISBROOKE, W. J. *The Liturgical Portions of the Apostolic Constitutions: A Text for Students*. Bramcote, Nottingham: Grove Books (coll. "Alcuin/GROW Liturgical Study," 13–14; "Grove Liturgical Study," 61), 1990, pp. 71–78.

Euchologion of Serapion of Thmuis; FUNK, F. X. *Didascalia et Constitutiones apostolorum . . .* , Ordinations, t. 2, pp. 188–191. ET: BRIGHTMAN, F. E., "The Sacramentary of Serapion of Thmuis," *JTS* 1 (2), 1900, pp. 266–267; BARRETT-LENNARD, R.J.S. *The Sacramentary of Sarapion of Thmuis: A Text for Students, with Introduction, Translation, and Commentary*. Bramcote, Nottingham: Grove Books (coll. "Alcuin/GROW Liturgical Study," 25), 1993, pp. 41–47.

Testamentum Domini; RAHMANI, I. E. *Testamentum Domini nostri Jesu Christi*. Reprint [1st ed. 1899]. Hildesheim: Olms, 1968. ET: COOPER, J., MACLEAN, A. J. *The Testament of Our Lord Translated into English from the Syriac with Introduction and notes*. Edinburgh: T & T Clark (coll. "Ante-Nicene Christian Library Supplement"), 1902; SPERRY-WHITE, G. *The Testamentum Domini: A Text for Students, with Introduction, Translation, and Notes*. Bramcote, Nottingham: Grove Books (coll. "Alcuin/GROW Liturgical Study," 19; "Grove Liturgical Study," 66), 1991, pp. 40–45. Critical edition of the Ethiopic by BEYLOT, R. *Testamentum Domini éthiopien. Edition et traduction*. Louvain: Peeters, 1984.

2. Western Liturgies

a) Roman Liturgy

Apostolic Tradition; BOTTE, B. *La Tradition Apostolique de saint Hippolyte. Essai de reconstitution.* 5th improved ed. by A. Gerhards and S. Felbecker. Münster: Aschendorff (coll "LQF," 39), 1989. ET: CUMING, G. J. *Hippolytus: A Text for Students.* 2nd ed. reprint. Bramcote, Nottingham: Grove Books (coll. "Grove Liturgical Study," 8), 1991, pp. 8–15; JURGENS, W. A. *The Faith of the Early Fathers,* vol 1. Collegeville: The Liturgical Press, 1970.

GERBERT, M. (ed.). *Monumenta veteris liturgiae Alemannicae,* reprint [1st ed. 1779]. Hildesheim: Olms, 1967.

SACRAMENTARIES

"Leonine": MOHLBERG, L. C., EIZENHÖFER, L., SIFFRIN, P. (eds.). *Sacramentarium Veronense (Cod. Bibl. Capit. Veron. LXXXV/[80]).* 3rd improved ed. Rome: Herder (coll. "Rerum ecclesiasticarum documenta," Series maior, Fontes 1), 1978. ET: BRADSHAW, P. F. *Ordination Rites of the Ancient Churches of East and West.* N.Y.: Pueblo Publishing Company, 1990, pp. 215–218.

Old Gelasian: MOHLBERG, L. C., EIZENHÖFER, L., SIFFRIN, P. (eds.). *Liber sacramentorum Romanae aeclesiae ordinis anni circuli (Cod. Vat. Reg. lat. 316/Paris Bibl. Nat. 7193, 41/56) (Sacramentarium Gelasianum).* 3rd improved ed. Rome: Herder (coll. "Rerum ecclesiasticarum documenta," Series maior, Fontes 4), 1981.

Gregorian: DESHUSSES, J. (ed.). *Le sacramentaire grégorien. Ses principales formes d'après les plus anciens manuscrits. Edition comparative,* t. 1, *Le sacramentaire, le supplément d'Aniane.* 2nd ed. Fribourg: Editions Universitaires Fribourg (coll. "Spicilegium Friburgense," 16), 1979.

ORDINES

ANDRIEU, M. *Les "Ordines Romani" du haut moyen âge.* Louvain: Spicilegium sacrum Lovaniense (coll. "Etudes et documents," 11, 23, 24, 28, 29), 1931ff. 5 vols.

PONTIFICALS

ANDRIEU, M. *Le Pontifical romain au moyen âge.* Vatican City: Bibliothèque apostolique vaticane (coll. "Studi e testi," 86, 87, 88, 99), 1938ff. 4 vols.

DE PUNIET, P. *The Roman Pontifical. A History and Commentary.* London/New York/Toronto: Longmans, Green and Co., 1932.
Pontificale romanum. Editio iuxta typicam. Turin/Rome: Marietti, 1962. (Basic text is from PR 1596.)

Pontificale Romanum ex Decreto Sacrosancti Oecumenici Concilii Vaticani II Instauratum Auctoritate Pauli PP. VI Promulgatum, t. 1: *De Ordinatione Diaconi, Presbyteri et Episcopi.* Editio typica. Vatican City: Typis Polyglottis Vaticanis,

1968. ET: *The Roman Pontifical Revised by Decree of the Second Vatican Council and Published by Authority of Pope Paul VI*. English translation prepared by The International Commission on English in the Liturgy. Washington, D.C.: ICEL, 1978.

Pontificale Romanum ex Decreto Sacrosancti Oecumenici Concilii Vaticani II Renovatum Auctoritate Pauli PP. VI Editum Ioannis Pauli PP. II Cura Recognitum. De Ordinatione Episcopi, Presbyterorum et Diaconorum. Editio typica altera. Vatican City: Typis Polyglottis Vaticanis, 1990. ET: *The Roman Pontifical. Revised by Decree of the Second Vatican Ecumenical Council edited under the Authority of Pope Paul VI Approved by Pope John Paul II*. Second Typical Edition. *Rites of Ordination of Bishops, Presbyters, and Deacons. For Study and Comment by the Bishops of the Member and Associate-member Conferences of the International Commission on English in the Liturgy*. Washington, D.C.: ICEL, 1993.

"Variationes in rubricis Pontificalis Romani," AAS 42 (8), 1950, pp. 448–455.

VOGEL, C., ELZE, R. *Le Pontifical romano-germanique du dixième siècle*. Vatican City: Bibliothèque apostolique vaticane (coll. "Studi e testi," 226, 227, 269), 1963ff. 3 vols.

LECTIONARIES

Lectionary of Alcuin (IXth century, Cambrai); WILMART, A. "Le lectionnaire d'Alcuin," *Ephemerides liturgicae* 51 (2–3), 1937, pp. 136–197. This lectionary represents Roman usage towards the year 626/627, cf. W. G. STOREY and N. K. RASMUSSEN, *Medieval . . .*, p. 351.

'Comes' of Murbach (VIIth century, Romano-Frankish); WILMART, A. "Le *Comes* de Murbach," *Revue bénédictine* 30 (1), 1913, pp. 25–69. This is the system of readings which became mandatory with the *Missale Romanum* of 1570, cf. W. G. STOREY and N. K. RASMUSSEN, *Medieval . . .*, p. 347.

Carolingian 'Comes' (VIIIth–IXth century, North Italy); AMIET, R. "Un 'comes' carolingien inédit de la Haute-Italie (Paris, BN 9451)," *Ephemerides liturgicae* 73 (4–5), 1959, pp. 335–367.

'Comes' of Corbie (ca. 772/780, Romano-Frankish); FRERE, W. H. *Studies in Early Roman Liturgy: II. The Roman Gospel-Lectionary*. London: Oxford University Press (coll. "Alcuin Club Collection," 30), 1934, pp. 29–58 and *III. The Roman Epistle-Lectionary*. London: Oxford University Press (coll. "Alcuin Club Collection," 32), 1935, pp. 1–24.

Capitulare evangeliorum; KLAUSER, T. *Das römische Capitulare evangeliorum, Texte und Untersuchungen zu seiner ältesten Geschicte*. 2nd ed. Münster: Aschendorff (coll. "LQF," 28), 1972.

CHAVASSE, A. "Les plus anciens types du lectionnaire et de l'antiphonaire romain de la messe. Rapports et date," *Revue bénédictine* 62 (1), 1952, pp. 3–94.

Lectionary for Mass. Collegeville: The Liturgical Press, 1970.

b) Gallican Liturgy

SACRAMENTARIES

Francorum: MOHLBERG, L. C., EIZENHÖFER, L., SIFFRIN, P. (eds.). *Missale Francorum (Cod. Vat. Reg. lat. 257).* Rome: Herder (coll. "Rerum ecclesiasticarum documenta," Series maior, Fontes 2), 1957.

c) Later Sources

COQUIN, R.-G. *Les Canons d'Hippolyte.* Ed. critique de la version arabe avec intr. et trad. Paris: Firmin-Didiot (coll. "Patrologia Orientalis," 31^2), 1966. ET: BRADSHAW, P. F. (ed.). *The Canons of Hippolytus.* English translation by C. Bebawi. Bramcote, Nottingham: Grove Books (coll. "Alcuin/GROW Liturgical Study," 2; "Grove Liturgical Study," 50), 1987, pp. 11–16.

FOERSTER, H. *Liber Diurnus Romanorum Pontificum.* Bern: Francke Verlag, 1958.

MUNIER, Ch. *Les Statuta ecclesiae antiqua. Edition, études critiques.* Paris: Presses Universitaires de France (coll. "Bibliothèque de l'Institut de Droit canonique de l'Université de Strasbourg," 5), 1960; MUNIER, Ch. (ed.). *Concilia Galliae A. 314–A. 506* (= CC 148), pp. 162–188.

WARREN, F. E. (ed.). *The Leofric Missal as used in the Cathedral of Exeter during the Episcopate of its First Bishop A.D. 1050–1072 together with Some Account of the Red Book of Derby, the Missal of Robert of Jumièges and a few other early Manuscript Service Books of the English Church.* Anastatic reprint [1st ed. 1883]. Westmead, Farnborough-Hants, Great Britain: Gregg International Publishers, Ltd., 1968.

3. STUDIES

BIBLICAL STUDIES

BONY, P., COTHENET, E., DELORME, J. et al. *Le ministère et les ministères selon le Nouveau Testament. Dossier exégétique et réflexion théologique.* Paris: Seuil (coll. "Parole de Dieu," 10), 1974.

BRENT, A. *Hippolytus and the Roman Church in the Third Century. Communities in Tension before the Emergence of a Monarch-Bishop.* Leiden/N.Y./Cologne: E. J. Brill (coll. "Supplements to Vigiliae Christianae," 31), 1995.

BROCKHAUS, U. *Charisma und Amt. Die paulinische Charismenlehre auf dem Hintergrund der frühchristlichen Gemeindefunktionen.* 2nd ed. Wuppertal: Theologischer Verlag Rolf Brockhaus, 1975.

BROWN, R. E. *The Churches the Apostles Left Behind*. London: G. Chapman, 1984.

ID. *The Community of the Beloved Disciple: The Life, Loves, and Hates of an Individual Church in New Testament Times*. Mahwah: Paulist, 1979.

ID. "*Episkopē* and *Episkopos*: The New Testament Evidence," *Theological Studies* 41 (2), 1980, pp. 322–338, reprinted in WORLD COUNCIL OF CHURCHES. Section on Faith and Order. *Episkopē and Episcopate in Ecumenical Perspective*. Geneva: WCC (coll. "Faith and Order Paper," 102), 1980, pp. 15–29.

ID. *Priest and Bishop. Biblical Reflections*. Paramus/N.Y./Toronto: Paulist Press, 1970.

CAZELLES, H. "Bible et temps liturgique: eschatologie et anamnèse," *LMD* (147), 1981, pp. 11–28.

COLSON, J. *L'évêque dans les communautés primitives. Tradition paulinienne et Tradition johannique de l'épiscopat des origines à saint Irénée*. Paris: Cerf (coll. "US," 21), 1951.

COPPENS, J. *L'imposition des mains et les rites connexes dans le Nouveau Testament et dans l'Eglise ancienne. Etude de théologie positive*. Paris: Gabalda, 1925.

ID. "L'imposition des mains dans les Actes des Apôtres," pp. 405–438, in KREMER, J. (ed.). *Les Actes des Apôtres: traditions, rédaction, théologie*. Actes du 28ᵉ Colloquium Biblicum Lovaniense—août 1977. Gembloux: J. Duculot (coll. "BETL," 48), 1979.

COTHENET, E. "Prophétisme et ministère d'après le Nouveau Testament," *LMD* (107), 1971, pp. 29–50.

DELLING, G. "Osmē," pp. 493–495, in *TDNT*. Grand Rapids: Wm. B. Eerdmans, 1967, t. 5.

DELORME, J. "Diversité et unité des ministères d'après le Nouveau Testament," pp. 283–346, in BONY, P., COTHENET, E., DELORME, J., et al. *Le ministère et les ministères selon le Nouveau testament. Dossier exégétique et réflexion théologique*. Paris: Seuil, 1974.

ELLIOTT, J. H. *The Elect and the Holy. An Exegetical Examination of 1 Peter 2:4-10*. Leiden: E. J. Brill (coll. "Supplements to Novum Testamentum," 12), 1966.

ID. "Ministry and Church Order in the NT: A Traditio-Historical Analysis (1 Pt 5, 1-5 & plls.)," *Catholic Biblical Quarterly* 32 (3), 1970, pp. 367–391.

HOFFMAN, L. A. "Jewish Ordination on the Eve of Christianity," *Studia Liturgica* 13 (2–4), 1979, pp. 11–41. (= VOS, W. & WAINWRIGHT, G. [eds.]. *Ordination Rites*. Papers Read at the 1979 Congress of *Societas Liturgica*. Rotterdam: Liturgical Ecumenical Center Trust, 1980.)

LECUYER, J. "Mystère de la Pentecôte et apostolicité de la mission de l'Eglise," pp. 167–208, in *Etudes sur le sacrement de l'Ordre*. Paris: Cerf, 1957.

LEGRAND, H.-M. "Inverser Babel, mission de l'Eglise," *Spiritus* 11 (43), 1970, pp. 323–346.

LEMAIRE, A. "The Ministries in the New Testament: Recent Research," *Biblical Theology Bulletin* 3 (2), 1973, pp. 133–166.

LOHSE, E. *Die Ordination im Spätjudentum und im Neuen Testament*. Göttingen: Vandenhoeck & Ruprecht, 1951.

MIGUENS, M. *Church Ministries in New Testament Times*. Arlington: Christian Culture Press, 1976.

PATRISTIC PERIOD

BÂRLEA. O. *Die Weihe der Bischofe, Presbyter und Diakone in vornicänischer Zeit*. Munich: Rumänische akademische Gesellschaft (coll. "Societas Academica Dacoromana—Acta Philosophica et Theologica," 3), 1969.

BATTIFOL, P. *Cathedra Petri*. Paris: Cerf (coll. "US," 4), 1938.

BERAUDY, R. "Le sacrement de l'Ordre d'après la Tradition apostolique d'Hippolyte," *BCE* (38–39), 1962, pp. 338–356.

BEVENOT, M. "'Sacerdos' as Understood by Cyprian," *JTS* NS 30 (2), 1979, pp. 413–429.

BOTTE, B. "L'Esprit Saint et l'Eglise dans la 'Tradition apostolique' de saint Hippolyte," *Didaskalia* 2 (2), 1972, pp. 221–233.

BRADSHAW, P. F. "Medieval Ordinations," pp. 369–379, in JONES, C., WAINWRIGHT, G., YARNOLD, E. & BRADSHAW, P. F. (eds.). *The Study of Liturgy*. Rev. ed. London/N.Y.: SPCK/Oxford University Press, 1992.

ID. "The Participation of Other Bishops in the Ordination of a Bishop in the *Apostolic Tradition* of Hippolytus," pp. 335–338, in LIVINGSTONE, E. A. (ed.). *Studia Patristica*, t. XVIII/2. Papers of the 1983 Oxford Patristics Conference. Critica, Classica, Ascetica, Liturgica. Kalamazoo/Louvain: Cistercian Publications/Peeters Press, 1989.

CAMPENHAUSEN, H. von. *Ecclesiastical Authority and Spiritual Power in the Church of the First Three Centuries*. Trans. of the German [*Kirchliches Amt und geistliche Vollmacht*] by J. A. Baker. London: Adam & Charles Black, 1969.

COLSON, J. *L'évêque, lien d'unité et de charité chez saint Cyprien de Carthage*. Paris: S.O.S., 1961.

ID. *Ministre de Jésus-Christ ou le sacerdoce de l'Evangile. Etude sur la condition sacerdotale des ministres chrétiens dans l'Eglise primitive*. Paris: Beauchesne (coll. "Théologie historique," 4), 1966.

ID. "L'organisation ecclésiastique aux deux premiers siècles de l'Eglise," pp. 55–83, in MEERSSEMAN, G. G., POLVERINI, L., SORDI, M. et al. *Problemi di storia della Chiesa: La Chiesa antica—secolo II–IV*. Milan: Vita e Pensiero, 1970.

CONGAR, Y. "Note sur une valeur des termes 'ordinare, ordinatio,'" *RevSR* 58 (1–2–3), 1984, pp. 7–14.

COWDREY, H.E.J. "The Dissemination of St. Augustine's Doctrine of Holy Orders during the Later Patristic Age," *JTS* NS 20 (2), 1969, pp. 448–481.

COYLE, J. K. "The Laying on of Hands as Conferral of the Spirit: Some Problems and a Possible Solution," pp. 339–353, in LIVINGSTONE, E. A. (ed.). *Studia Patristica*, t. XVIII/2. Papers of the 1983 Oxford Patristics Conference. Critica, Classica, Ascetica, Liturgica. Kalamazoo/Louvain: Cistercian Publications/Peeters Press, 1989.

DE CLERCK, P. "'Lex orandi, lex credendi': The Original Sense and Historical Avatars of an Equivocal Adage," *Studia Liturgica* 24 (2), 1994, pp. 178–200.

DIX, G. *Apostolikē Paradosis. The Treatise on the Apostolic Tradition of St. Hippolytus of Rome, Bishop and Martyr*. 2nd revised ed. Pref. and bibliogr. by H. Chadwick. London: SPCK, 1968.

ID. "The Ministry in the Early Church c. A.D. 90–410," pp. 183–303, in KIRK, K. E. (ed.). *The Apostolic Ministry. Essays in the History and the Doctrine of Episcopacy*. London: Hodder & Stoughton, 1946.

EHRHARDT. A. *The Apostolic Succession in the First Two Centuries of the Church*. London: Lutterworth, 1953.

ELERT, W. *Eucharist and Church Fellowship in the First Four Centuries*. Trans. of the German *[Abendmahl und Kirchengemeinschaft in der alten Kirche hauptsäch-lich des Ostens]* by N. E. Nagel. St. Louis: Concordia Publishing House, 1966.

FAIVRE, A. *Naissance d'une hiérarchie. Les premières étapes du cursus clérical*. Paris: Beauchesne (coll. "Théologie historique," 40), 1977.

ID. *Ordonner la fraternité. Pouvoir d'innover et retour à l'ordre dans l'Eglise anci-enne*. Paris: Cerf (coll. "Histoire"), 1992.

FERGUSON, E. "Jewish and Christian Ordination: Some Observations," *Harvard Theological Review* 56 (1), 1963, pp. 13–19.

ID. "Laying on of Hands: Its Significance in Ordination," *JTS* NS 26 (1), 1975, pp. 1–12.

FUELLENBACH, J. *Ecclesiastical Office and the Primacy of Rome. An Evaluation of Recent Theological Discussion of First Clement*. Washington, D.C.: Catholic University of America Press (coll. "The Catholic University of America Studies in Christian Antiquity," 20), 1980.

GAUDEMET, J. *L'Eglise dans l'Empire romain (IVe–Ve siècles)*. 1st ed. [1958] updated in 1989. Paris: Sirey (coll. "Histoire du droit et des institutions de l'Eglise en Occident," 3), 1989.

GRANFIELD, P. "Episcopal Elections in Cyprian: Clerical and Lay Participation," *Theological Studies* 37 (1), 1976, pp. 41–52.

ID. "The *Sensus Fidelium* in Episcopal Selection," *Concilium* (137), 1980, pp. 33–38.

GRYSON, R. "Les élections ecclésiastiques au IIIe siècle," *RHE* 68 (2), 1973, pp. 353–404.

ID. *Les origines du célibat ecclésiastique du Ier au VIIe siècle*. Gembloux: Duculot (coll. "Recherches et synthèses; section d'histoire," 2), 1970.

GY, P.-M. "Remarques sur le vocabulaire antique du sacerdoce chrétien," pp. 125–145, in *Etudes sur le sacrement de l'Ordre*. Paris: Cerf, 1957.

HANSSENS, J.-M. *La liturgie d'Hippolyte.——Ses documents—Son titulaire—Ses origines et son caractère*. 2nd ed. corrected and enlarged [1st ed. 1959]. Rome: Pont. Institutum Orientalium Studiorum (coll. "Orientalia Christiana Analecta," 155), 1965.

JILEK, A. "Bischof und Presbyterium. Zur Beziehung zwischen Episkopat und Presbyterat im Lichte des Traditio Apostolica Hippolyts," *ZKT* 106 (4), 1984, pp. 376–401.

ID. *Initiationsfeier und Amt. Ein Beitrag zur Struktur und Theologie der Ämter und des Taufgottesdienstes in der frühen Kirche (Traditio Apostolica, Tertullian, Cyprian)*. Frankfurt am Main/Bern/Cirencester: P. Lang (coll. "Europäische Hochschulschriften": Série 23, Théologie, 130), 1979.

JURGENS, W. A. (ed.). *The Faith of the Early Fathers*. 3 vols. Collegeville: The Liturgical Press, 1970.

KILMARTIN, E. J. "Ministry and Ordination in Early Christianity against a Jewish Background," *Studia Liturgica* 13 (2–4), 1979, pp. 42–69. (= VOS, W. & WAINWRIGHT, G. [eds.], *Ordination Rites*. Papers Read at the 1979 Congress of *Societas Liturgica*. Rotterdam: Liturgical Ecumenical Center Trust, 1980.)

KING, P. *An Inquiry into the Constitution, Discipline, Unity and Worship of the Primitive Church, that Flourished within the First Three Hundred Years after Christ*. Reprint [1st ed. 1691]. N.Y.: G. Lane & P. P. Sandford, 1841.

KOEP, L. "Bischofsliste," cols. 407–415, in *RAC*, t. 2.

KRETSCHMAR, G. "Die Ordination im frühen Christentum," *Freiburger Zeitschrift für Philosophie und Theologie* 22 (1–2), 1975, pp. 35–69.

LAFONTAINE, P.-H. *Les conditions positives de l'accession aux Ordres dans la première législation ecclésiastique (300–492).* Ottawa: Ed. de l'Université d'Ottawa (coll. "Publications sériées," 71), 1963.

LANNE, E. "Les ordinations dans le rite copte; leurs relations avec les *Constitutions apostoliques* et la *Tradition* de saint Hippolyte," *L'Orient syrien* 5 (1), 1960, pp. 81–106.

LAURANCE, J. D. *'Priest' as Type of Christ. The Leader of the Eucharist in Salvation History according to Cyprian of Carthage.* N.Y./Bern/Frankfurt am Main/Nancy: P. Lang (coll. "American University Studies": Series 7, Theology and Religion, 5), 1984.

LECUYER, J. "Episcopat et presbytérat dans les écrits d'Hippolyte de Rome," *RechSR* 41 (1), 1953, pp. 30–50.

ID. "La succession des évêques d'Alexandrie aux premiers siècles," *BLE* 70 (2), 1969, pp. 81–99.

ID. "Le problème des consécrations épiscopales dans l'Eglise d'Alexandrie," *BLE* 65 (4), 1964, pp. 241–257.

ID. "Le sens des rites d'ordination d'après les Pères," *L'Orient syrien* 5 (4), 1960, pp. 463–475.

LEGRAND, H.-M. "Communion ecclésiale et Eucharistie aux premiers siècles," *L'Année canonique* 25, 1981, pp. 125–148.

ID. "The Presidency of the Eucharist According to the Ancient Tradition," *Worship* 53 (5), 1979, pp. 413–438.

ID. "Theology and the Election of Bishop in the Early Church," *Concilium* 7 (8), 1972, pp. 31–42.

LEMAIRE, A. *Les ministères aux origines de l'Eglise. Naissance de la triple hiérarchie: évêques, presbytres, diacres.* Paris: Cerf (coll. "Lectio Divina," 68), 1971.

ID. *Les ministères dans l'Eglise.* Paris: Centurion (coll. "Croire et comprendre"), 1974.

LIGIER, L. "Le *Charisma veritatis certum* des évêques: ses attaches liturgiques, patristiques et bibliques," pp. 247–268, in *L'homme devant Dieu. Mélanges offerts au Père Henri de Lubac,* t. 1, *Exégèse et patristique.* Paris: Aubier (coll. "Théologie," 56), 1963.

LODS, M. *Confesseurs et martyrs, successeurs des prophètes dans l'Eglise des trois premiers siècles.* Neuchâtel/Paris: Delachaux et Niestlé (coll. "Cahiers théologiques," 41), 1958.

LUIKS, A. G. *Cathedra en mensa. De plaats van preekstoel en avondmaalstafel in het oudchristelijk kerkgebouw volgens de opgravingen in Noord-Afrika.* Franeker: T. Wever, 1955.

LUTTENBERGER, G. H. "The Decline of Presbyteral Collegiality and the Growth of Individualization of the Priesthood (4th–5th centuries)," *RTAM* (48), 1981, pp. 14–58.

ID. "The Priest as a Member of a Ministerial College. The Development of the Church's Ministerial Structure from 96 to c. 300 A.D.," *RTAM* (43), 1976, pp. 5–63.

MACCARONE, M. "Lo sviluppo dell'idea dell'episcopato nel II secolo e la formazione del simbolo della cattedra episcopale," pp. 85–206, in MEERSSE-MAN, G. G., POLVERINI, L., SORDI, M. et al. *Problemi di storia della Chiesa: La Chiesa antica—secoli II–IV*. Milan: Vita e Pensiero, 1970.

MAGNE, J. "En finir avec la 'Tradition' d'Hippolyte," *BLE* 89 (1), 1988, pp. 5–22.

MARROU, H.-I. "'Doctrina' et 'Disciplina' dans la langue des Pères de l'Eglise," *Bulletin du Cange, Archivum latinitatis medii aevi* (ALMA) 9, 1934, pp. 5–25.

MARTIMORT, A.-G. "Nouvel examen de la 'Tradition Apostolique' d'Hippolyte," *BLE* 88 (1), 1987, pp. 5–25.

ID. "Tradition apostolique," cols. 1133–1146, in *Dictionnaire de spiritualité, ascétique et mystique. Doctrine et histoire*. Paris: Beauchesne, 1991, t. 15.

ID. "La Tradition apostolique d'Hippolyte," *L'Année canonique* 23, 1979, pp. 159–173.

MC CUE, J. F. "Apostles and Apostolic Succession in the Patristic Era," pp. 138–177, in EMPIE, P. C., MURPHY, T. A. (eds.). *Lutherans and Catholics in Dialogue*, t. 4, *Eucharist and Ministry*. Washington, D.C: USCC, 1970.

MESLIN, M. "Ecclesiastical Institutions and Clericalization from A.D. 100 to 500," *Concilium* 7 (5), 1969, pp. 14–21.

METZGER, M. "Nouvelles perspectives pour la prétendue *Tradition apostolique*," *Ecclesia orans* 5 (3), 1988, pp. 241–259.

MOLLAND, E. "Le développement de l'idée de succession apostolique," *RHPR* 34 (1), 1954, pp. 1–29.

MONCEAUX, P. *Histoire littéraire de l'Afrique chrétienne depuis les origines jusqu'à l'invasion arabe*, t. 2, *Saint Cyprien et son temps*. Anastatic reprint [1st ed. 1902]. Brussels: Culture et Civilisation, 1966.

MORTARI, L. *Consacrazione episcopale e collegialità. La testimonianza della Chiesa antica*. Florence: Vallecchi (coll. "Testi e ricerche de scienze religiose," 4), 1969.

OSAWA, T. *Das Bischofseinsetzungsverfahren bei Cyprian. Historische Untersuchungen zu den Begriffen iudicium, suffragium, testimonium, consensus.*

Frankfurt am Main/Bern: P. Lang (coll. "Europäische Hochschulschriften": Série 23, Théologie, 178), 1983.

PATERNOSTER, M. *L'imposizione delle mani nella Chiesa primitiva*. Rassegna delle testimonianze bibliche, patristiche, e liturgiche fino al secolo quinto. Tentativo de ricerche dell'antica tradizione liturgica in ordine al conferimento del ministero in connessione con il gesto dell'imposizione delle mani. Rome: Ed. liturgiche, 1977.

PIETRI, Ch. *Roma christiana. Recherches sur l'Eglise de Rome, son organisation, sa politique, son idéologie de Miltiade à Sixte III (311–440)*. Paris: Bocard (coll. "Bibliothèque des Ecoles Françaises d'Athènes et de Rome," 1ère série, 224–225), 1976. 2 vols.

PINTO DE OLIVEIRA, C.-J. "Signification sacerdotale du ministère de l'évêque dans la Tradition Apostolique d'Hippolyte de Rome," *Freiburger Zeitschrift für Philosophie und Theologie* 25 (3), 1978, pp. 398–427.

PRAT, F. "Les prétentions des diacres romains au quatrième siècle," *RechSR* 3 (5), 1912, pp. 463–475.

QUASTEN. J., PLUMPE, J. C. (eds.). *The Ancient Christian Writers*. Westminster, Md./London: Newman Press/Longmans, Green and Co., 1952.

QUINN, J. D. "'Charisma veritatis certum': Irenaeus, *Adversus Haereses* 4, 26, 2," *Theological Studies* 39 (3), 1978, pp. 520–525.

RAFFA, V. "Partecipazione collettiva dei vescovi alla consacrazione episcopale," *EL* 78 (2), 1964, pp. 105–140.

RICHTER, K. "Zum Ritus des Bischofsordination in der 'Apostolischen Überlieferung' Hippolyts von Rom und davon abhängigen Schriften," *ALW* (17/18), 1975/1976, pp. 7–51.

ROBERTS, A., DONALDSON, J. (eds.). *The Ante-Nicene Fathers*, vol. I, *The Apostolic Fathers with Justin Martyr and Irenaeus*. Grand Rapids: Wm. B. Eerdmans, 1981.

RORDORF, W. *Liturgie, foi et vie des premiers chrétiens*. Paris: Beauchesne (coll. "Théologie historique," 75), 1986.

ID. "L'ordination de l'évêque selon la Tradition Apostolique d'Hippolyte de Rome," *QL* 55 (2–3), 1974, pp. 137–150, reprinted in id., *Liturgie*, pp. 123–136.

ID. "Origine et signification de la célébration du dimanche dans le christianisme primitif," *LMD* (148), 1981, pp. 103–122, reprinted in id., *Liturgie*, pp. 29–48.

ID. *Sabbat et dimanche dans l'Eglise ancienne*. French version of the German *[Sabbat und Sonntag in der Alten Kirche]* by E. Visinand and W. Nussbaum. Neuchâtel: Delachaux et Niestlé (coll. "Traditio christiana," 2), 1972.

ID. *Sunday—The History of the Day of Rest and Worship in the Earliest Centuries of the Christian Church.* Trans. of the German [*Der Sonntag*: *Geschichte des Ruhe- und Gottesdiensttages im ältesten Christentum*] by A.A.K. Graham. Philadelphia/London: Westminster Press/SCM, 1968.

SCHLINK, E. "La succession apostolique," *Verbum Caro* 18 (69), 1964, pp. 52–86.

SCHULTZ, H.-J. "Das liturgisch-sakramental übertragene Hirtenamt in seiner eucharistischen Selbstverwirklichung nach dem Zeugnis der liturgischen Überlieferung," pp. 208–255, in BLÄSER, P., FRANK, S., MANNS, P. et al. *Amt und Eucharistie.* Paderborn: Verlag Bonifatius-Drückerei (coll. "Konfessions-kundliche Schriften des Johann-Adam-Möhler-Instituts," 10), 1973.

STAM, J. E. *Episcopacy in the Apostolic Tradition of Hippolytus.* Basel: Friedrich Reinhardt (coll. "Theologische Dissertationen," 3), 1969.

STILLINGFLEET, E. *Irenicum [Irenicon]: A Weapon-Salve for the Churches' Wounds or the Divine Right of Particular Forms of Church Government.* Reprint [1st ed. 1661]. Philadelphia: M. Sorin, 1842.

STOCKMEIER, P. "The Election of Bishops by Clergy and People in the Early Church," *Concilium* (137), 1980, pp. 3–9.

STOMMEL, E. "Die bischöfliche Kathedra im christlichen Altertum," *Münchener theologische Zeitschrift* 3 (1), 1952, pp. 17–32.

TILLARD, J.-M.-R. "L'Evêque et les autres ministères," *Irénikon* 48 (2), 1975, pp. 195–200.

ID. "'Ministère' ordonné et 'Sacerdoce' du Christ," *Irénikon* 49 (2), 1976, pp. 145–166.

TURNER, C. H. "Cheirotonia, cheirothesia, 'epithesis cheirōn (and the Accompanying Verbs)," *JTS* 24 (96), 1923, pp. 496–504.

VAN BENEDEN, P. *Aux origines d'une terminologie sacramentelle: Ordo, or-dinare, ordinatio dans la littérature chrétienne avant 313.* Louvain: Spicilegium sacrum Lovaniense (coll. "Etudes et documents," 38), 1974.

VANDENBROUCKE, F. "La concélébration, acte liturgique communautaire," *LMD* (35), 1953, pp. 48–55.

VAN UNNIK, W. C. "The Authority of the Presbyters in Irenaeus' Works," pp. 248–260, in JERVELL, J., MEEKS, W. A. (eds.). *God's Christ and His People: Studies in Honour of Nils Alstrup Dahl.* Oslo: Universitetsforlaget, 1977.

ID. "*Dominus vobiscum*: The Background of a Liturgical Formula," pp. 270–305, in HIGGINS, A.J.B. (ed.). *New Testament Essays. Studies in Memory of Thomas Walter Manson 1893–1958.* Manchester: Manchester University Press, 1959.

VILELA, A. *La condition collégiale des prêtres au IIIe siècle*. Paris: Beauchesne (coll. "Théologie historique," 14), 1971.

VOGEL, C. "Le ministre charismatique de l'eucharistie. Approche rituelle," pp. 181–209, in GRELOT, P., DUPONT, J., TRAGAN, P.-R. et al. *Ministères et célébration de l'eucharistie*. Rome: Ed. Anselmiana (coll. "Studia Anselmiana," 61; "Sacramentum," 1), 1973, reprinted in id., *Ordinations*, pp. [197]–[209].

ID. "Titre d'ordination et lien du presbytre à la communauté locale dans l'Eglise ancienne," *LMD* (115), 1973, pp. 70–85, reprinted in id., *Ordinations*, pp. [135]–[148].

ID. "Unité de l'Eglise et pluralité des formes historiques d'organisation ecclésiastique du IIIe au Ve siècle," pp. 591–636, in CONGAR, Y., DUPUY, B.-D. (eds.). *L'épiscopat et l'Eglise universelle*. Paris: Cerf: 1962.

ID. "*Vacua manus impositio*. L'inconsistance de la chirotonie absolue en Occident," pp. 511–524, in *Mélanges liturgiques offerts au R.P. Dom Bernard Botte*. Louvain: Abbaye du Mont César, 1972, reprinted in id., *Ordinations*, pp. [149]–[162].

WILLIAMS, G. "The Ministry of the Ante-Nicene Church (c. 125–325)," pp. 27–59, in NIEBUHR, H. R., WILLIAMS, D. D. (eds.). *The Ministry in Historical Perspectives*. N.Y.: Harpers & Brothers, 1956.

ZIZIOULAS, J. D. "The Eucharistic Community and the Catholicity of the Church," *One in Christ* 6 (3), 1970, pp. 314–337, reprinted in id., *Being as Communion*. Crestwood, N.Y.: St. Vladimir's Seminary Press, 1985, pp. 143–169.

ID. "Episkopē and Episkopos in the Early Church. A Brief Survey of the Evidence," pp. 30–42, in WORLD COUNCIL OF CHURCHES. Section on Faith and Order. *Episkopē and Episcopate in Ecumenical Perspective*. Geneva: WCC (coll. "Faith and Order Paper," 102), 1980.

ID. *L'Eucharistie, l'Evêque et l'Eglise durant les trois premiers siècles*. Trans. from the Greek by J.-L. Palierne. Paris: Desclée de Brouwer (coll. "Théophanie"), 1994.

ZOLLITSCH, R. *Amt und Funktion des Priesters. Eine Untersuchung zum Ursprung und zur Gestalt des Presbyterats in den ersten zwei Jahrhunderten*. Freiburg/Basel/Vienna: Herder (coll. "Freiburger theologische Studien," 96), 1974.

HIGH MIDDLE AGES AND MIDDLE AGES

ANDRIEU, M. "La carrière ecclésiastique des papes et les documents liturgiques du moyen âge," *RevSR* 21 (3–4), 1947, pp. 90–120.

ID. "L'onction des mains dans le sacre épiscopal," *RHE* 26 (2), 1930, pp. 343–347.

ID. "Le sacre épiscopal d'après Hincmar de Reims," *RHE* 48 (1–2), 1953, pp. 22–73.

BALDOVIN, J. F. *The Urban Character of Christian Worship: The Origin, Development and Meaning of Stational Liturgy.* Rome: Edizioni Orientalia Christiana (coll. "Orientalia Christiana Analecta," 228), 1987.

BATTIFOL, P. "La liturgie du sacre des évêques dans son évolution historique," *RHE* 23 (4), 1927, pp. 733–763.

ID. "Transformare," *Bulletin d'ancienne littérature et d'archéologie chrétiennes* 1 (1), 1911, pp. 54–55.

BERAUDY, R. "Les effets de l'Ordre dans les préfaces d'ordination du Sacramentaire léonien," pp. 81–107, in FOURREY, R., LALLIER, M., BERAUDY, R., et al. *La tradition sacerdotale: études sur le sacerdoce.* Le Puy: Xavier Mappus (coll. "Bibliothèque de la Faculté catholique de théologie de Lyon," 7), 1959.

BOTTE, B. "Caractère collégial du presbytérat et de l'épiscopat," pp. 97–124, in *Etudes sur le sacrement de l'Ordre.* Paris: Cerf (coll. "Lex orandi," 22), 1957.

ID. "Note historique sur la concélébration dans l'Eglise ancienne," *LMD* (35), 1953, pp. 9–23.

ID. "L'Ordre d'après les prières d'ordination," pp. 13–35, in *Etudes sur le sacrement de l'Ordre.* Paris: Cerf (coll. "Lex orandi," 22), 1957.

ID. "Le rituel d'ordination des *Statuta Ecclesiae Antiqua*," *RTAM* (11), 1939, pp. 223–241.

ID. "*Secundi meriti munus*," *QL* 21 (2), 1936, 84–88.

BRAUN, J. *Die liturgische Gewandung im Occident und Orient nach Ursprung und Entwicklung, Verwendung und Symbolik.* Freiburg-im-Breisgau: Herder, 1907.

BUTLER, S., FERRARA, D. M. "Quaestio Disputata 'In Persona Christi.' A Response to Dennis M. Ferrara," *Theological Studies* 56 (1), 1995, pp. 61–80 (followed by "A Reply to Sara Butler," pp. 81–91.

CHANOINES REGULIERS DE MONDAYE. "L'évêque, d'après les prières d'ordination," pp. 739–780, in CONGAR, Y., DUPUY, B.-D. (eds.) *L'épiscopat et l'Eglise universelle.* Paris: Cerf, 1962.

CHAVASSE, A. "Le rituel d'ordination du sacramentaire gélasien," *BCE* (36), 1962, pp. 19–37.

ID. *Le sacramentaire gélasien (Vaticanus Reginensis 316). Sacramentaire presbytéral en usage dans les titres romains au VIIe siècle.* Tournai: Desclée (coll. "Bibliothèque de théologie," Série 4: "Histoire de la théologie," 1), 1958.

CONGAR, Y. "Aspects ecclésiologiques de la querelle entre mendiants et séculiers dans la seconde moitié du XIIIᵉ siècle et le début du XIVᵉ," *Archives d'histoire doctrinale et littéraire du Moyen Age* 28, 1961, pp. 35–151.

ID. "La collégialité de l'épiscopat et la primauté de l'évêque de Rome dans l'histoire," pp. 95–122, in id., *Ministères et communion ecclésiale*. Paris: Cerf, 1971.

ID. "La consécration épiscopale et la succession apostolique constituent-elles chef d'une Eglise locale ou membre du collège?," pp. 123–140, in id., *Ministères et communion ecclésiale*. Paris: Cerf, 1971.

ID. "De la communion des Eglises à une ecclésiologie de l'Eglise universelle," pp. 227–260, in CONGAR, Y., DUPUY, B.-D. (eds.) *L'épiscopat et l'Eglise universelle*. Paris: Cerf, 1962.

ID. "Two Factors in the Sacralization of Western Society during the Middle Ages," *Concilium* 7 (5), 1969, pp. 28–35.

ID. "L'Ecclésia' ou communauté chrétienne, sujet intégral de l'action liturgique," pp. 241–282, in JOSSUA, J.-P., CONGAR, Y. (eds.) *La liturgie après Vatican II. Bilans, études, prospective*. Paris: Cerf (coll. "US," 66), 1967.

ID. "Ministères et structuration de l'Eglise," pp. 31–49, in id., *Ministères et communion ecclésiale*. Paris: Cerf, 1971.

ID. "Ordinations *invitus, coactus*, de l'Eglise antique au canon 214," *RSPT* 50 (2), 1966, pp. 169–197, reprinted in id., *Droit ancien et structures ecclésiales*. London: Variorum Reprints (coll. "Collected studies series," 159), 1982.

ID. "Ordre et juridiction dans l'Eglise," *Irénikon* 10, 1933, pp. 22–31, 97–110, 243–252, 401–408, reprinted in id., *Sainte Eglise. Etudes et approches ecclésiologiques*. Paris: Cerf (coll. "US," 41), 1963, pp. 203–237.

ID. "La 'réception' comme réalité ecclésiologique," *RSPT* 56 (3), 1972, pp. 369–403.

CREHAN, J. H. "Medieval Ordinations," pp. 320–331, in JONES, C., WAINWRIGHT, G., YARNOLD, E. (eds.). *The Study of Liturgy*. London: SPCK, 1978.

ID. "Priesthood, Kingship, and Prophecy," *Theological Studies* 42 (2), 1981, pp. 216–231.

CROUZEL, H. "La doctrine du caractère sacerdotal est-elle en contradiction avec la tradition occidentale d'avant le XIIᵉ siècle et avec la tradition orientale?," *BLE* 74 (4), 1973, pp. 241–262, reprinted in id., *Mariage et divorce, célibat et caractère sacerdotaux dans l'Eglise ancienne*. Turin: Bottega d'Erasmo (coll. "Etudes d'histoire du culte et des institutions chrétiennes," 2), 1982, pp. 285–306.

DE CLERCK, P. "La prière gallicane 'Pater sancte' de l'ordination épisco-pale," pp. 163–176, in FARNEDI, G. (ed.). *Traditio et progressio. Studi liturgici in onore del Prof. Adrien Nocent, OSB*. Rome: Pontificio Ateneo S. Anselmo (coll. "Studia Anselmiana," 95; "Analecta liturgica," 12), 1988.

DENIS-BOULET, N.-M. "Titres urbains et communauté dans la Rome chré-tienne," *LMD* (36), 1953, pp. 14–32.

DETSCHER, A. F. "The Ancient English Ordination Rites for Presbyters," *Ecclesia orans* 2 (2–3), 1985, pp. 139–162, 241–264.

DOMAGALSKI, B. "Römische Diakone im 4. Jahrhundert—Zum Verhältnis von Bischof, Diakon und Presbyter," pp. 44–56, in PLÖGER, J. G., WEBER, H. J. (eds.). *Der Diakon, Wiederentdeckung und Erneuerung seines Dienstes*. Freiburg/Basel/Vienna: Herder, 1981.

EISSING, D. "Ordination und Amt des Presbyters. Zur Interpretation des römischen Priesterweihegebetes," *ZKT* 98 (1), 1976, pp. 35–51.

ELLARD, G. *Ordination Anointings in the Western Church Before 1000 A.D.* Reprint [1st ed. 1933]. New York: Kraus Reprint (coll. "Monographs of the Mediaeval Academy of America," 8), 1970.

FALSINI, R. "La 'trasformazione del corpo e sangue di Cristo,'" *Studi frances-cani* (Florence) 52 (3–4), 1955, pp. 307–359.

FERRARA, D. M. "Representation or Self-Effacement: The Axiom *In Persona Christi* in St. Thomas and the Magisterium," *Theological Studies* 55 (2), 1994, pp. 195–224.

FLICHE, A., MARTIN, V. (eds.). *Histoire de l'Eglise depuis les origines jusqu'à nos jours*, t. 7, *L'Eglise au pouvoir des laïques* (888–1057). Paris: Bloud & Gay, 1948.

FOREVILLE, R. *Latran I, II, III et Latran IV*. Paris: Editions de l'Orante (coll. "Histoire des conciles œcuméniques," 6), 1965.

FRENDO, J. A. *The "Post secreta" of the "Missale Gothicum" and the Eucharistic Theology of the Gallican Anaphora*. Malta: St. Joseph's Home, 1977.

FRERE, W. H. "Early Forms of Ordination," pp. 263–312, in SWETE, H. B. (ed.). *Essays on the Early History of the Church and the Ministry*. London: Macmillan, 1918.

ID. "Early Ordination Services," *JTS* 16 (63), 1914/1915, pp. 323–371.

ID. *Pontifical Services*. London: Longmans, Green & Co., 1901.

FUCHS, V. *Der Ordinationstitel von seiner Entstehung bis auf Innozenz III. Eine Untersuchung zur kirchlichen Rechtsgeschichte mit besonderer Berücksichtigung der Anschauungen Rudolph Sohms*. Anastatic reprint [1st ed. 1930]. Amsterdam: Verlag P. Schippers (coll. "Kanonistische Studien und Texte," 4), 1963.

GALOT, J. *La nature du caractère sacramentel. Etude de théologie médiévale.* 2nd ed. Paris/Louvain: Desclée de Brouwer (coll. "Museum Lessianum," section théologique, 52), 1958.

GAUDEMET, J. "Bishops: From Election to Nomination," *Concilium* (137), 1980, pp. 10–15.

ID. *Les élections dans l'Eglise latine des origines au XVIe siècle.* Paris: Fernand Lanore (coll. "Institutions–société–histoire," 2), 1979.

GIBAUT, J. "Amalarius of Metz and the Laying on of Hands in the Ordination of a Deacon," *Harvard Theological Review* 82 (2), 1989, pp. 233–240.

GROSSI, P. "Unanimitas. Alle origini del concetto di persona giuridica nel diritto canonico," *Annali di storia del diritto* (2), 1958, pp. 228–331.

GY, P.-M. "Les anciennes prières d'ordination," *LMD* (138), 1979, pp. 93–122.

ID. "Ancient Ordination Prayers," *Studia Liturgica* 13 (2–4), 1979, pp. 70–93. (= VOS, W. & WAINWRIGHT, G. [eds.]. *Ordination Rites.* Papers Read at the 1979 Congress of *Societas Liturgica.* Rotterdam: Liturgical Ecumenical Center Trust, 1980.)

ID. "Les bases de la pénitence moderne," *LMD* (117), 1974, pp. 63–85.

ID. "L'eucharistie dans la tradition de la prière et de la doctrine," *LMD* (137), 1979, pp. 81–102.

ID. "La notion de validité sacramentelle avant le Concile de Trent," *Revue du droit canonique* 28 (1), 1978, pp. 193–202, reprinted in id., *La liturgie dans l'histoire.* Paris: Cerf/Editions Saint-Paul (coll. "Liturgie"), 1990, pp. 165–175.

ID. "La théologie des prières anciennes pour l'ordination des évêques et des prêtres," *RSPT* 58 (4), 1974, pp. 599–617.

HAUSSLING, A. *Mönchskonvent und Eucharistiefeier: Ein Studie über die Messe in der abendländischen Klosterliturgie des frühen Mittelalters und zur Geschichte des Messhäufigkeit.* Münster: Aschendorff (coll. "LQF," 58), 1973.

HEINTSCHEL, D. E. *The Medieval Concept of an Ecclesiastical Office. An Analytical Study of the Concept of an Ecclesiastical Office in the Major Sources and Printed Commentaries from 1140–1300.* Washington, D.C.: The Catholic University of America Press (coll. "Canon Law Studies," 363), 1956.

HOPE, D. M. *The Leonine Sacramentary: A Reassessment of Its Nature and Purpose.* London: Oxford University Press (coll. "Oxford Theological Monographs"), 1971.

HOUSSIAU, A. "La formation de la liturgie romaine du sacre épiscopal," *Collectanea Mechliniensia* NS 18 (3), 1948, pp. 276–284.

ID. "Le sacerdoce ministériel dans l'Eglise ancienne," pp. 1–47, in HOUSSIAU,

A., MONDET, J.-P. *Le sacerdoce du Christ et de ses serviteurs selon les Pères de l'Eglise*. Louvain-la-Neuve: Centre d'histoire des religions (coll. "Cerfaux-Lefort," 8), 1990.

IMBART de la TOUR, P. *Les paroisses rurales du 4ᵉ au 11ᵉ siècle*. Reprint [1st ed. 1900]. Paris: Picard (coll. "Les origines religieuses de la France"), [1979].

JANINI, J. *S. Siricio y las cuarto Témporas. Una investigación sobre las fuentes de la espiritualidad seglar y del Sacramentario Leoniano*. Valencia: Seminario metropolitano de Valencia, 1958.

JOUNEL, P. "L'ordination sacerdotale dans le rite romain," *BCE* (36), 1962, pp. 46–81.

KILMARTIN, E. J. "Apostolic Office: Sacrament of Christ," *Theological Studies* 36 (2), 1975, pp. 243–264.

ID. "Episcopal Election: The Right of the Laity," *Concilium* (137), 1980, pp. 39–43.

ID. "Reception in History: An Ecclesiological Phenomenon and Its Significance," *Journal of Ecumenical Studies* 21 (1), 1984, pp. 34–54.

KLEINHEYER, B. *Die Priesterweihe im römischen Ritus: eine liturgiehistorische Studie*. Trier: Paulinus-Verlag (coll. "Trierer theologische Studien," 12), 1962.

ID. "Studien zur nichtrömisch-westlichen Ordinationsliturgie," Folge 1: "Die Ordinationsliturgie gemäss dem Leofric-Missale," *ALW* 22 (1), 1980, pp. 93–107. Folge 2: "Ein spätantik-altgallisches Ordinationsformular," *ALW* 23 (3), 1981, pp. 313–366. Folge 3: "Handauflegung zur Ordination im Frühmittelalter," *ALW* 32 (2), 1990, pp. 145–160.

ID. "Supplicatio litanica," pp. 463–478, in JOUNEL, P., KACZYNSKI, R., PASQUALETTI, G. (eds.). *Liturgia opera divina e umana. Studi sulla riforma liturgica offerti a S.E. Mons. Annibale Bugnini in occasione del suo 70⁰ compleanno*. Rome: Ed. Liturgiche (coll. "Bibliotheca Ephemerides liturgicae," Subsidia, 26), [1982].

LABHART, V. *Zur Rechtssymbolik des Bischofsrings*. Cologne/Graz: Böhlau Verlag (coll. "Rechtshistorische Arbeiten," 2), 1963.

LECUYER, V. "Note sur la liturgie du sacre des évêques," *EL* 66 (4), 1952, pp. 369–372.

ID. "Orientations présentes de la théologie de l'épiscopat," pp. 781–811, in CONGAR, Y., DUPUY, B.-D. (eds.). *L'épiscopat et l'Eglise universelle*. Paris: Cerf, 1962.

LUBAC, H. de. *Exégèse médiévale. Les quatre sens de l'Ecriture*. Paris: Aubier (coll. "Théologie," 41), 1959, t. 1.

MARLIANGEAS, B.-D. *Clés pour une théologie du ministère: In persona Christi, In persona Ecclesiae*. Paris: Beauchesne (coll. "Théologie historique," 51), 1978.

MARTIMORT, A.-G. *Les "ordines", les ordinaires et les cérémoniaux*. Turnhout: Brépols (coll. "Typologie des sources du moyen âge occidental," 56), 1991.

ID. "Le rituel de la concélébration eucharistique," *EL* 77 (3), 1963, pp. 147–168, reprinted in *Mens Concordet Voci, pour Mgr. A.G. Martimort à l'occasion de ses quarante années d'enseignement et des vingt ans de la Constitution "Sacrosanctum Concilium."* Paris: Desclée, 1983, pp. 279–298.

MC DEVITT, A. "The Episcopate as an Order and Sacrament on the Eve of the High Scholastic Period," *Franciscan Studies* 20 (1–2), 1960, pp. 96–148.

MICHELS, T. *Beiträge zur Geschichte des Bischofsweihetages im christlichen Altertum und im Mittelalter*. Münster: Aschendorff (coll. "LQF," 10), 1927.

MITCHELL, J. "An Inquiry into Concelebration," *Clergy Review* 48 (3), 1963, pp. 154–157.

MORETON, B. *The Eighth-Century Gelasian Sacramentary*. London: Oxford University Press, 1976.

NUSSBAUM, O. *Kloster, Priestermönch und Privatmesse. Ihr Verhältnis im Westen von den Anfängen bis zum hohen Mittelalter*. Bonn: Peter Hanstein Verlag (coll. "Theophaneia. Beiträge zur Religions- und Kirchengeschichte des Altertums," 14), 1961.

PALAZZO, E. *Le moyen âge. Des origines au XIIIe siècle*. Paris: Beauchesne (coll. "Histoire des livres liturgiques"), 1993.

PEUCHMAURD, M. "Mission canonique et prédication. Le prêtre ministre de la parole dans la querelle entre Mendiants et Séculiers au XIIIe siècle," *RTAM* 30 (1), 1963, pp. 122–144; ibid., 30 (2), 1963, pp. 251–276.

ID. "Le prêtre ministre de la parole dans la théologie du XIIe siècle (Canonistes, moines et chanoines)," *RTAM* 29 (1), 1962, pp. 52–76.

RASMUSSEN, N. K. "Célébration épiscopale et célébration presbytérale: un essai de typologie," pp. 581–603, in *Segni e riti nella chiesa altomedievale occidentale*. Settimane di studio del Centro Italiano di Studi sull'Alto Medioevo XXXIII (11–17 aprile 1985). Spoleto: Centro Italiano di Studi sull'Alto Medioevo, 1987, t. 2.

RATZINGER, J. "Der Einfluss des Bettelordensstreites auf die Entwicklung der Lehre vom päpstlichen Universalprimat, unter besonderer Berücksichtigung des heiligen Bonaventura," pp. 697–724, in AUER, J., VOLK, H. (eds.). *Theologie in Geschichte und Gegenwart*. Munich: Karl Zink Verlag, 1957.

REYNOLDS, R. E. *The Ordinals of Christ from Their Origins to the Twelfth Century*. Berlin/N.Y.: Walter De Gruyter (coll. "Beiträge zur Geschichte und Quellenkunde des Mittelalters," 7), 1978.

RICHE, P. *La vie quotidienne dans l'Empire carolingien.* Paris: Hachette, 1975.

RICHTER, K. *Die Ordination des Bischofs von Rom. Eine Untersuchung zur Weiheliturgie.* Münster: Aschendorff (coll. "LQF," 60), 1976.

RULE, M. "'Transformare' and 'Transformatio,'" *JTS* 12 (1), 1911, pp. 413–427.

SALMON, P. *Etude sur les insignes du pontife dans le rit romain: histoire et liturgie.* Rome: Officium libri catholici, 1955.

ID. "La 'ferula,' bâton pastoral de l'évêque de Rome," *RevSR* 30 (4), 1956, pp. 313–327.

ID. "Aux origines de la crosse des évêques," pp. 373–383, in ANFRAY, M. et al. *Mélanges en l'honneur de Monseigneur Michel Andrieu.* Strasbourg: Palais Universitaire (= *RevSR*, hors série), 1956.

SANTANTONI, A. *L'ordinazione episcopale. Storia e teologia dei riti dell'ordinazione nelle antiche liturgie dell'Occidente.* Rome: Ed. Anselmiana (coll. "Studia Anselmiana," 69; "Analecta Liturgica," 2), 1976.

SCHULTE, R. *Die Messe als Opfer der Kirche. Die Lehre frühmittelalterlicher Autoren über das eucharistische Opfer.* Münster: Aschendorff (coll. "LQF," 35), 1959.

STROLL, M. *Symbols as Power. The Papacy following the Investiture Contest.* Leiden/N.Y./Copenhagen: E. J. Brill (coll. "Brill's Studies in Intellectual History," 24), 1991.

VAN DE KERCKHOVE, M. "La notion de juridiction chez les Décrétistes et les premiers Décrétalistes (1140–1250)," *Etudes franciscaines* 49 (4), 1937, pp. 420–455.

VOGEL, C. "Chirotonie et chirothésie. Importance et relativité du geste de l'imposition des mains dans la collation des ordres," *Irénikon* 45 (1), 1972, pp. 7–21; ibid., 45 (2), 1972, pp. 207–238, reprinted in id., *Ordinations,* pp. [69]–[116].

ID. "La multiplication des messes solitaires au moyen âge. Essai de statistique," *RevSR* 55 (3), 1981, pp. 206–213.

ID. "La vie quotidienne du moine en Occident à l'époque de la floraison des messes privées," pp. 341–360, in TRIACCA, A.-M., PISTOIA, A. (eds.). *Liturgie, spiritualité, cultures.* Conférences Saint-Serge, XXIXᵉ semaine d'études liturgiques, Paris, 29 juin–2 juillet 1982. Rome: Ed. Liturgiche (coll. "Bibliotheca Ephemerides liturgicae," Subsidia, 29), 1983.

ID. "L'imposition des mains dans les rites d'ordination en Orient et en Occident," *LMD* (102), 1970, pp. 57–72, reprinted in id., *Ordinations,* pp. [117]–[132].

ID. "Une mutation cultuelle inexpliquée: le passage de l'eucharistie communautaire à la messe privée," *RevSR* 54 (3), 1980, pp. 231–250.

ZIZIOULAS, J. D. "The Theological Problem of 'Reception,'" *Bulletin—Centro Pro Unione* (26), 1984, pp. 3–6, reprinted in *One in Christ* 21 (3), 1985, pp. 187–193.

METHODOLOGICAL STUDIES AND HUMAN SCIENCES

BRADSHAW, P. F. *The Search for the Origins of Christian Worship. Sources and Methods for the Study of Early Liturgy.* London: SPCK, 1992.

CAZENEUVE, J. *Sociologie du rite. (Tabou, magie, sacré).* Paris: Presses universitaires de France (coll. "SUP," section "Le sociologue," 23), 1971.

CHAUVET, L.-M. *Du symbolique au symbole. Essai sur les sacrements.* Paris: Cerf (coll. "Rites et symboles," 9), 1979.

ID. *Symbol and Sacrament. A Sacramental Representation of Christian Existence.* Trans. of the French *[Symbole et sacrement. Une relecture sacramentelle de l'existence chrétienne]* by P. Madigan and M. Beaumont. Collegeville: The Liturgical Press/Pueblo Book, 1995.

DOMBOIS, H. *Das Recht der Gnade. Ökumenisches Kirchenrecht, I.* 2nd ed. Witten: Luther Verlag (coll. "Forschungen und Berichte der evangelischen Studiengemeinschaft," 20), 1969.

DOUGLAS, M. *Natural Symbols. Explorations in Cosmology.* N.Y./London: Pantheon Books/Barrie & Jenkins, 1970.

ELIADE, M. *Aspects du mythe.* Paris: Gallimard (coll. "Idées," 32), 1969.

ID. *Patterns in Comparative Religion.* Trans. of the French *[Traité de l'histoire des religions]* by R. Sheed. Reprinted [1st ed. 1958]. N.Y./Cleveland: World Publishing Co., 1971.

FINK, P. F. "The Sacrament of Orders: Some Liturgical Reflections," *Worship* 56 (6), 1982, pp. 482–502.

GADAMER, H. G. *Truth and Method.* Trans. of the German *[Wahrheit und Methode]* by J. Weinsheimer and D. G. Marshall. 2nd rev. ed. N.Y.: Crossroad, 1992.

GEFFRE, C. *Le Christianisme au risque de l'interprétation.* 2nd ed. [1st ed. 1983]. Paris: Cerf (coll. "Cogitatio fidei," 120), 1988.

GISEL, P. "Du symbolique au symbole ou du symbole au symbolique? Remarques intempestives," *RechSR* 75 (3), 1987, pp. 197–210, reprinted in MOINGT, J. (ed.). *Les sacrements de Dieu.* Paris: Recherches de science religieuse, 1987, pp. 197–210.

HOFFMANN, J. "Grâce et institution selon Hans Dombois: une nouvelle approche du mystère de l'Eglise," *RSPT* 52 (4), 1968, pp. 645–676; ibid., 53 (1), 1969, pp. 41–69.

IRWIN, K. W. *Context and Text. Method in Liturgical Theology.* Collegeville: The Liturgical Press/Pueblo Book, 1994.

KOMONCHAK, J. A. "History and Social Theory in Ecclesiology," pp. 1–53, in LAWRENCE, F. (ed.). *Lonergan Workshop II.* Chico, Calif.: Scholars Press, 1981.

LONERGAN, B.J.F. *Method in Theology.* Reprint of 2nd ed. [1st ed. 1971]. Toronto: University of Toronto Press, 1994.

MAERTENS, J.-T. "Un rite de pouvoir: l'imposition des mains," *Sciences religieuses/Studies in Religion* 6 (6), 1976–1977, pp. 637–649; ibid., 7 (1), 1978, pp. 25–39.

MARTY, F. "Signe, symbole, sacrement," *RechSR* 75 (2), 1987, pp. 59–76, reprinted in MOINGT, J. (ed.). *Les sacrements de Dieu.* Paris: Recherches de science religieuse, 1987, pp. 59–76.

MESLIN, M. *L'expérience humaine du divin. Fondements d'une anthropologie religieuse.* Paris: Cerf (coll. "Cogitatio fidei," 150), 1988.

ID. *Pour une science des religions.* Paris: Seuil, 1973.

MOINGT, J. (ed.) *Enjeux du rite dans la modernité.* Paris: Recherches de science religieuse, 1991. [= Extracts of *RechSR* 78 (3 and 4), 1990. See also the following: OLIVIERO, P., OREL, T. "L'expérience rituelle" + bibliography, pp. 17–60 (= *RechSR* 78 (3), 1990, pp. 329–372); HAMELINE, J.-Y. "Eléments d'anthropologie, de sociologie historique et de musicologie du culte chrétien" + bibliography, pp. 85–112 (= *RechSR* 78 (3), 1990, pp. 397–424); CHAUVET, L.-M. "Ritualité et théologie," pp. 197–226 (= *RechSR* 78 (4), 1990, pp. 535–564); and GAGNEBIN, L. "Rite et contre-rite?," pp. 227–241 (= *RechSR* 78 (4), 1990, pp. 565–579).]

RICŒUR, P. "Herméneutique et critique des idéologies," pp. 25–61, in CASTELLI, E. (ed.). *Démythisation et idéologie.* Actes du colloque organisé par le Centre international d'études humanistes et par l'Institut d'études philosophiques de Rome, 4–9 janvier 1973. Paris: Aubier/Montaigne, 1973.

TURNER, V. *The Ritual Process. Structure and Anti-Structure.* Chicago: Aldine Publishing, 1969.

VAN DER LEEUW, G. *La religion dans son essence et ses manifestations. Phénoménologie de la religion.* French edition revised and updated by the author with the collaboration of the translator J. Marty. Paris: Payot (coll. "Bibliothèque scientifique"), 1970.

VERGOTE, A. *Interprétation du langage religieux*. Paris: Seuil, 1974.

ID. *Religion, foi, incroyance. Etude psychologique*. Brussels: P. Mardaga (coll. "Psychologie et sciences humaines," 126), 1983.

GENERAL WORKS

ALBERIGO, G. "La juridiction. Remarques sur un terme ambigu," *Irénikon* 49 (2), 1976, pp. 167–180.

ID., (ed.). *Les églises après Vatican II: dynamisme et prospective*. Paris: Beauchesne, 1981.

ALLMEN, J.-J. von. "L'Eglise locale parmi les autres Eglises locales," *Irénikon* 43 (4), 1970, pp. 512–837.

AMANIEU, A. "Archidiacre," cols. 948–1004, in NAZ, R. (ed.). *Dictionnaire de droit canonique*, t. 1. Paris: Letouzey et Ané, 1935.

BARNETT, J. M. *The Diaconate: A Full and Equal Order. A Comprehensive and Critical Study of the Origin, Development, and Decline of the Diaconate in the Context of the Church's Total Ministry and a Proposal for Renewal*. N.Y.: Seabury Press, 1975.

BELTRANDO, P. *Diaconi per la Chiesa. Itinerario ecclesiologico del ripristino del ministero diaconale*. Milan: Istituto Propaganda Libraria (coll. "Fede e Cultura"), 1977.

BERNHARD, J. "The Election of Bishops at the Council of Trent," *Concilium* 137, 1980, pp. 24–30.

BIRMELE, A. *Le salut en Jésus-Christ dans les dialogues œcuméniques*. Paris/ Geneva: Cerf/Labor et Fides, 1986.

BOTTE, B. "Les ordinations dans les rites orientaux," *BCE* 36, 1962, pp. 13–18.

BOTTE, B., GELIN, A., SCHMITT, J. et al. *Etudes sur le sacrement de l'Ordre*. Paris: Cerf (coll. "Lex orandi," 22), 1957.

BOUYER, L. *The Church of God*. English trans. of the French *[L'Eglise de Dieu, Corps du Christ et Temple de l'Esprit]*. Cincinnati: Franciscan Herald Press, 1983.

BRADSHAW, P. F. *Ordination Rites of the Ancient Churches of East and West*. N.Y.: Pueblo Publishing Company, 1990.

ID. "Patterns of Ministry," *Studia Liturgica* 15 (1), 1982/1983, pp. 49–64.

BRENT, A. *Cultural Episcopacy and Ecumenism. Representative Ministry in Church History from the Age of Ignatius of Antioch to the Reformation with Special Reference to Contemporary Ecumenism*. Leiden/N.Y./Cologne: E. J. Brill (coll. "Studies in Christian Mission," 6), 1992.

CABIE, R. "Christian Initiation," pp. 11–100, in MARTIMORT, A. G. and collaborators. *The Church at Prayer. An Introduction to the Liturgy*, t. 3. CABIE, R. et al. *The Sacraments*. New edition. Trans. of the French [*Les sacrements*] by M. J. O'Connell. Collegeville: The Liturgical Press, 1987.

CABROL, F. "Impositions des mains," cols. 391–413, in *DACL*, 1926, t. 7, 1st part.

CHAPELLE, A. *Pour la vie du monde. Le sacrement de l'Ordre*. Brussels: Institut d'Etudes Théologiques, 1978.

CONGAR, Y. *I Believe in the Holy Spirit*, vol. 1, *The Holy Spirit in the 'Economy,' Revelation and Experience of the Spirit*. Trans. of the French [*Je crois en l'Esprit Saint*, t.1, *L'Esprit Saint dans l'"Economie,' révélation et expérience de l'Esprit*] by D. Smith. N.Y./London: Seabury Press/Geoffrey Chapman, 1983.

ID. *I Believe in the Holy Spirit*, vol. 2, *Lord and Giver of Life*. Trans. of the French [*Je crois en l'Esprit Saint*, t. 2, "*Il est Seigneur et Il donne la vie*"] by B. Smith. N.Y./London: Seabury Press/Geoffrey Chapman, 1983.

ID. *I Believe in the Holy Spirit*, vol. 3, *The River of the Water of Life (Rev. 22:1) Flows in the East and in the West*. Trans. of the French [*Je crois en l'Esprit Saint*, t. 3, *Le fleuve de Vie (Ap 22, 1) coule en Orient et en Occident*] by D. Smith. N.Y./London: Seabury Press/Geoffrey Chapman, 1983.

ID. *L'Eglise de saint Augustin à l'époque moderne*. Paris: Cerf (coll. "Histoire des dogmes," III: Christologie–sotériologie–mariologie, 3), 1970.

ID. *Ministères et communion ecclésiale*. Paris: Cerf (coll. "Théologie sans frontières," 23), 1971.

ID. "Romanité et catholicité. Histoire de la conjonction changeante de deux dimensions de l'Eglise," *RSPT* 71 (2), 1987, pp. 161–190.

CONGAR, Y., DUPUY, B.-D., (eds.). *L'épiscopat et l'Eglise universelle*. Préf. de A.-M. Charue. Paris: Cerf (coll. "US," 39), 1962.

COOKE, B. *Ministry to Word and Sacraments. History and Theology*. Philadelphia: Fortress Press, 1976.

DE CLERCK, P. "Ordination, ordre," cols. 162–206, in MATHON, G., BAUDRY, G.-H., GUILLUY, P. (eds.). *Catholicisme hier aujourd'hui demain*. Paris: Letouzey et Ané, [1984], t. 10, fasc. 44.

DESCAMPS, A.-L. "L'origine de l'institution ecclésiale selon le Nouveau Testament," pp. 91–138, in MONNERON, J.-L., SAUDREAU, M., DEFOIS, G., et al. *L'Eglise: institution et foi*. Brussels: Facultés universitaires Saint-Louis (coll. "Publications des Facultés universitaires Saint-Louis," 14), 1979.

DIX, G. *The Shape of the Liturgy*. London: Adam & Charles Black, 1945.

DUPUY, B.-D. "Teologia dei ministeri ecclesiastici," pp. 605–649, in FEINER, J., LÖHRER, M. (eds.). *Mysterium Salutis. Nuovo corso di dogmatica come teologia della storia della salvezza*, t. 8, *L'evento salvifico nella comunità di Gesù Cristo.* Italian trans. of the German *[Das Heilsgeschehen in der Gemeinde: Gottes Gnadenhandeln* (Mysterium Salutis. Grundriss heilsgeschichtlicher Dogmatik, 4, 2)] by D. Pezzeta. 2nd ed. Brescia: Queriniana, 1977.

ID. "Is there a Dogmatic Distinction between the Function of Priests and the Function of Bishops," *Concilium* 4 (4), 1968, pp. 38–44.

EVANS, G. R. *The Church and the Churches. Toward an Ecumenical Ecclesiology.* N.Y.: Cambridge University Press, 1994.

FERRARO, G. *Le preghiere di ordinazione al diaconato, al presbiterato et all'episcopato.* Naples: Dehoniane, 1977.

GALOT, J. *Theology of the Priesthood.* Trans. of the Italian *[Teologia del sacerdozio]* by R. Balducelli. San Francisco: Ignatius Press, 1984.

GALTIER, P. "Imposition des mains," cols. 1302–1425, in *Dictionnaire de théologie catholique.* Paris: Letouzey et Ané, 1927, t. 7, 2nd part.

GRELOT, P. *Eglise et ministères: pour un dialogue critique avec Edward Schillebeeckx.* Paris: Cerf (coll. "Théologies"), 1983.

GROSSI, V., DI BERARDINO, A. *La Chiesa antica: ecclesiologia e istituzioni.* Rome: Borla (coll. "Cultura cristiana antica-studi"), [1984].

HALLEUX, A. de. "Ministère et sacerdoce," *Revue théologique de Louvain* 18 (3), 1987, pp. 289–316; ibid., 18 (4), 1987, pp. 425–453, reprinted in id., *Patrologie et œcuménisme: recueil d'études.* Louvain: Leuven University Press/Presses Universitaires de Louvain (coll. "BETL," 93), 1991, pp. 710–765.

HANSSENS, J.-M. "Les oraisons sacramentelles des ordinations orientales," *Orientalia Christiana Periodica* 18 (3–4), 1952, 297–318.

JOUNEL, P. "Ordinations," pp. 139–179, in MARTIMORT, A. G. and collaborators. *The Church at Prayer. An Introduction to the Liturgy*, t. 3, CABIE, R. et al. *The Sacraments.* New edition. Trans. of the French *[Les sacrements]* by M. J. O'Connell. Collegeville: The Liturgical Press, 1987.

JUNGMANN, J. A. *La liturgie de l'Eglise romaine.* French trans. of the German *[Der Gottesdienst der Kirche]* by M. Grandclaudon. Mulhouse/Paris-Tournai: Salvator/Casterman, 1957.

ID. *Tradition liturgique et problèmes actuels de pastorale.* French trans. of the German *[Liturgisches Erbe und pastorale Gegenwart. Studien und Vorträge]* by P. Kirchenhoffer. Le Puy/Lyon: Xavier Mappus, 1962. (2nd part, ch. 7: "'Fermentum.' Un symbole d'unité dans l'Eglise. Survivance au Moyen Age.")

KASPER, W. *Theology and Church*. Trans. of the German *[Theologie und Kirche]* by M. Kohl. London: SCM, 1989.

KILMARTIN, E. J. "Office and Charism: Reflections on a New Study of Ministry," *Theological Studies*, 38 (3), 1977, pp. 547–554.

KIRK, K. (ed.). *The Apostolic Ministry. Essays on the History and the Doctrine of Episcopacy*. London: Hodder & Stoughton, 1946.

KLEINHEYER, B. "Handauflegung zur Geistmitteilung oder: Der Geist weht, wo die Kirche feiert," *Liturgisches Jahrbuch* 30 (3), 1980, pp. 154–173.

ID. "Ordinationen und Beauftragungen," pp. 7–65, in KLEINHEYER, B., SEVERUS, E. v., KACZYNSKI, R. *Sakramentliche Feiern II: Ordinationen und Beauftragungen—Riten um Ehe und Familie—Feiern geistlicher Gemeinschaften—Die Sterbe—und Begräbnisliturgie—Die Benediktionen—Der Exorzismus.* Regensburg: Verlag Friedrich Pustet, 1984. (= vol. 8 of *Gottesdienst der Kirche. Handbuch der Liturgiewissenschaft.*)

LECUYER, J. "La prière d'ordination de l'évêque," *NRT* 89 (6), 1967, pp. 602–603.

ID. *Le sacrement de l'ordination: recherche historique et théologique*. Paris: Beauchesne (coll. "Théologie historique," 65), 1983.

ID. "L'oasis d'Elim et les ministères dans l'Eglise," in BÉKÉS, G. J. and FARNEDI, G. (eds.) *Lex orandi, lex credendi. Miscellanea in onore di P. Cipriano Vagaggini*. Rome: Anselmiana, 1980, pp. 295–329.

LEGRAND, H.-M. "The 'Indelible' Character and the Theology of Ministry," *Concilium* 4, (8), 1972, pp. 54–62.

ID. "Insertion des ministères de direction dans la communauté ecclésiale," *RDC* 23 (1–4), 1973, pp. 225–254.

ID. "La réalisation de l'Eglise en un lieu," pp. 143–345, in LAURET, B., REFOULE, F. (eds.). *Initiation à la pratique de la théologie*, t. 3, *Dogmatique*, 2. 2nd corrected ed. Paris: Cerf, 1986.

ID. "Le développement d'églises-sujets: une requête de Vatican II—fondements théologiques et réflexions institutionnelles," pp. 159–169, in G. ALBERIGO (ed.). *Les églises après Vatican II: dynamisme et prospective*. Paris: Beauchesne, 1981.

ID. "Recherches sur le presbytérat et l'épiscopat," *RSPT* 59 (4), 1975, pp. 676–680.

ID. "Vocation au diaconat et interpellation: réflexion ecclésiologique à partir de la tradition," *Documents Episcopat* 3, Feb. 1985, p. 7.

LIGIER, L. "La prière et l'imposition des mains: autour du nouveau Rituel romain de la Confirmation," *Gregorianum* 53 (3), 1972, pp. 407–484.

MC DONNELL, K. "Ways of Validating Ministry," *Journal of Ecumenical Studies* 7 (2), 1970, pp. 209–265.

MC KENZIE, J. L. "The Gospel According to Matthew," pp. 62–114, in BROWN, R. E., FITZMYER, J. A., MURPHY, R. E. (eds.). *The Jerome Biblical Commentary*, t. 2, *The New Testament and Topical Articles*. Englewood Cliffs, N.J.: Prentice-Hall, Inc., 1968.

MEERSSEMAN, G. G., POLVERINI, L., SORDI, M. et al. *Problemi di storia della Chiesa: La Chiesa antica—secoli II–IV*. Milan: Vita e Pensiero, 1970.

MITCHELL, N. *Cult and Controversy: The Worship of the Eucharist Outside Mass*. N.Y.: Pueblo Publishing Company (coll. "Studies in the Reformed Rites of the Catholic Church," 4), 1982.

MOHLER, J. A. *The Origin and Evolution of the Priesthood*. Staten Island, N.Y.: Alba House, 1970.

MOUDRY, J. "Bishop and Priest in the Sacrament of Holy Orders," *The Jurist* 31 (1), 1971, pp. 163–186.

NEUNHEUSER, B. *L'eucharistie. 1. Au Moyen âge et à l'époque moderne*. French trans. of the German *[Eucharistie im Mittelalter und Neuzeit]* by A. Liefooghe. Paris: Cerf (coll. "Histoire des dogmes," 25; IV: Sacrements, 4b), 1966.

OSBORNE, K. B. *Priesthood. A History of Ordained Ministry in the Roman Catholic Church*. N.Y./Mahwah, N.J.: Paulist Press, 1988.

OTT, L. *Le sacrement de l'Ordre*. French trans. of the German *[Das Weihesakrament]* by M. Deleporte. Paris: Cerf (coll. "Histoire des dogmes," 26; IV: Sacrements, 5), 1971.

PINELL, J. "Le 'famiglie liturgiche'—la liturgia gallicana," pp. 62–67, in MARSILI, S., PINELL, J., TRIACCA, A. M. et al. *Anamnesis, introduzione storico-teologica alla liturgia*, t. 2, *La liturgia, panorama storico generale*. Turin: Marietti, 1978.

PORTER, H. B. *The Ordination Prayers of the Ancient Western Churches*. London: SPCK (coll. "Alcuin Club Collections," 49), 1967.

POWER, D. N. *Ministers of Christ and His Church. The Theology of the Priesthood*. London: Geoffrey Chapman, 1969.

PUNIET, P. de. "Consécration épiscopale," cols. 2579–2604, in *DACL*, 1914, t. 3, 2nd part.

RAES, A. "La concélébration eucharistique dans les rites orientaux," *LMD* 35, 1953, pp. 24–47.

RAHNER, K. "Dogmatique de la concélébration," *QL* 36 (3), 1955, pp. 119–135.

RAHNER, K., HÄUSSLING, A. *The Celebration of the Eucharist*. Trans. of the German [*Die vielen Messen und das eine Opfer*]. N.Y./London: Herder & Herder/Burns & Oates, 1968.

RATZINGER, J. *Frères dans le Christ. L'Esprit de la fraternité*. French trans. of the German [*Die christliche Brüderlichkeit*] by H.-M. Rochais and J. Evrard. Paris: Cerf, 1962.

ID. *Principles of Catholic Theology. Building Stones for a Fundamental Theology*. Trans. of the German [*Theologische Prinzipienlehre*] by M. F. McCarthy. San Francisco: Ignatius Press, 1987.

RIGHETTI, M. *Manuale di storia liturgica*, t. 4, *I sacramenti–i sacramentali*. 2nd ed. Milan: Ancora, 1959.

SALMON, P. "Aux origines de la crosse des évêques," pp. 373–383, in *Mélanges en l'honneur de Monseigneur Michel Andrieu*. Strasbourg: Palais Universitaire, 1956.

SCHILLEBEECKX, E. *Ministry. Leadership in the Community of Jesus Christ*. Trans. of the Dutch [*Kerkelijk ambt: Voorgangers in de gemeente van Jezus Christus*] by J. Bowden. N.Y.: Crossroad, 1981.

ID. *The Church with a Human Face. A New and Expanded Theology of Ministry*. Trans. of the Dutch [*Pleidooi voor Mensen in de Kerk. Christelijke Identiteit en Ambten en de Kerk*] by J. Bowden. N.Y.: Crossroad, 1985.

SCHMAUS, M. "Ämter Christi," pp. 457–459, in HÖFER, H., RAHNER, K. (eds.). *Lexikon für Theologie und Kirche*. 3rd ed. [1st ed. 1936]. Freiburg-im-Breisgau: Herder, 1957, t. 1.

SWETE, H. B. (ed.). *Essays on the Early History of the Church and the Ministry*. London: Macmillan, 1918.

TAFT, R. "Ex oriente lux? Some Reflections on Eucharistic Concelebration," *Worship* 54 (4), pp. 1980, pp. 308–325, reprinted in id., *Beyond East and West: Problems in Liturgical Understanding*. Washington, D.C.: The Pastoral Press, 1984.

TAVARD, G. H. *A Theology for Ministry*. Wilmington: Michael Glazier (coll. "Theology and Life Series," 6), 1983.

TILLARD, J.-M.-R. *Church of Churches. The Ecclesiology of Communion*. Trans. of the French [*Eglise d'églises: l'ecclésiologie de communion*] by R. C. De Peaux. Collegeville: The Liturgical Press/Michael Glazier Book, 1992.

ID. *L'Eglise locale. Ecclésiologie de communion et catholicité*. Paris: Cerf (coll. "Cogitatio fidei," 191), 1995.

VILLALÓN, J. R. *Sacrements dans l'Esprit. Existence humaine et théologie sacramentelle*. Paris: Beauchesne (coll. "Théologie historique," 43), 1977.

VOGEL, C. *Medieval Liturgy. An Introduction to the Sources*. English trans. and revision of the French *[Introduction aux sources de l'histoire du culte chrétien au moyen âge]* by W. G. Storey and N.-K. Rasmussen. Washington, D.C.: The Pastoral Press (coll. "NPM Studies in Church Music and Liturgy"), 1986.

ID. *Ordinations inconsistantes et caractère inamissible*. Turin: Bottega d'Erasmo (coll. "Etudes d'histoire du culte et des institutions chrétiennes," 1), 1978.

WAINWRIGHT, G. *Doxology. The Praise of God in Worship, Doctrine, and Life. A Systematic Theology*. London/N.Y.: Epworth Press/Oxford University Press, 1980.

ID. "The Understanding of Liturgy in Light of Its History," pp. 495–509, in JONES, C., WAINWRIGHT, G., YARNOLD, E. (eds.). *The Study of Liturgy*. London: SPCK, 1978.

ZIZIOULAS, J. D. *Being as Communion. Studies in Personhood and the Church*. Crestwood, N.Y.: St. Vladimir's Seminary Press (coll. "Contemporary Greek Theologians," 4), 1985.

ID. *L'être ecclésial*. Geneva: Labor et Fides (coll. "Perspective orthodoxe," 3), 1981.

ID. "Ordination et communion," *Istina* 16 (1), 1971, pp. 5ff.

ID. "The Bishop in the Theological Doctrine of the Orthodox Church," *Kanon* 7, 1985, pp. 23–35.

Index

3 5282 00408 9341